Beyond Policy Analysis

Public Issue Management in Turbulent Times

FIFTH EDITION

Beyond Policy Analysis

Public Issue Management in Turbulent Times

FIFTH EDITION

by Leslie A. Pal

NELSON EDUCATION

NELSON / EDUCATION

Beyond Policy Analysis: Public Issue Management in Turbulent Times, Fifth Edition

by Leslie A. Pal

Vice President, Editorial Higher Education:
Anne Williams

Acquisitions Editor:
Anne-Marie Taylor

Marketing Manager:
Ann Byford

Developmental Editor:
Jessica Freedman

Photo Researcher and Permissions Coordinator:
Natalie Russell

Senior Content Production Manager:
Natalia Denesiuk Harris

Production Service:
Cenveo Publisher Services

Copy Editor:
Kate Revington

Proofreader:
Lina Suresh

Indexer:
BIM Indexing Services

Senior Production Coordinator:
Ferial Suleman

Design Director:
Ken Phipps

Managing Designer:
Jennifer Leung

Interior Design:
Nelson Gonzalez

Cover Design:
Carianne Sherriff

Cover Image:
Frans Lanting/Corbis

Compositor:
Cenveo Publisher Services

COPYRIGHT © 2014, 2010
by Nelson Education Ltd.

Printed and bound in the United States of America
3 4 5 16 15 14 13

For more information contact Nelson Education Ltd.,
1120 Birchmount Road, Toronto, Ontario, M1K 5G4. Or you can visit our Internet site at http://www.nelson.com

Statistics Canada information is used with the permission of Statistics Canada. Users are forbidden to copy this material and/or redisseminate the data, in an original or modified form, for commercial purposes, without the expressed permissions of Statistics Canada. Information on the availability of the wide range of data from Statistics Canada can be obtained from Statistics Canada's Regional Offices, its World Wide Web site at <http://www.statcan.gc.ca>, and its toll-free access number 1-800-263-1136.

Library and Archives Canada Cataloguing in Publication

Pal, Leslie A. (Leslie Alexander), [date]–

    Beyond policy analysis : public issue management in turbulent times / by Leslie A. Pal. — 5th ed.

Includes bibliographical references and index.
ISBN 978-0-17-650787-9

    1. Policy sciences—Textbooks.
2. Political planning—Canada—Textbooks. I. Title.

H97.P343 2013   320.6
C2012-907065-3

ISBN-13: 978-0-17-650787-9
ISBN-10: 0-17-650787-6

Table of Contents

CHAPTER 10: CONCLUSIONS 391

Preface

This book is entitled *Beyond Policy Analysis* not because I consider policy analysis to be unimportant, but because I consider it so important that we need to think carefully about the craft of policy analysis in the modern world.

The first edition of the book (1997) argued that our world had changed so dramatically that it was important to go beyond conventional categories and tools of analysis. I identified three broad factors that were affecting both the theory and the practice of policy analysis. The first was the changing nature of governance under the pressures of globalization, information technology, demands for more efficient and leaner government, and more deeply diverse societies and cultures. The second was the emerging demand for better and more effective government in the face of these challenges and forces. This demand was not simply about making government more business-like, though in the late 1990s and early 2000s that was the high note in complaints about how modern governments organized themselves and worked; it was also about a renewed appreciation concerning the importance of government and good policy in dealing with a host of new challenges, from terrorism and security to climate change and the global financial crisis. The third factor was a fresh debate within the discipline of policy analysis about its intellectual foundations and practical accomplishments. Then, as now, it seemed to me that these factors force a reconsideration of what we do when we engage in policy analysis.

None of these fundamentals has changed in any significant way—indeed, they have intensified since the fourth edition. It remains impossible to discuss public policy in Canada, or elsewhere for that matter, without considering globalization, information technology, changing public values and cultural assumptions, citizen distrust, new public management techniques and practices, policy networks, consultation, or engagement. But there have been some changes in tone and emphasis since the publication of the last edition, and these are reflected and discussed in this new edition. The most obvious and painful challenge has been the global financial crisis that erupted in 2008. Not every country has been affected in the same way—China and some Southeast Asian states, as well as Canada, have managed reasonably well, certainly in comparison with Greece, Spain, and the tottering European Union. The United States also had to go through a painful adjustment and now is facing an Everest of debt. The crisis was not merely financial, though that aspect sharpened the debate about the best way forward: whether to increase deficits to stimulate moribund economies or impose austerity to reduce debts and deficits. The crisis also raised fundamental questions about public management reform and governance. In Canada, for example, after years of stimulus spending that raised the national deficit, the 2012 budget laid out a path to deficit reduction and eradication by mid-decade that, in turn, depended on a program review across all departments, as well as cuts in personnel and in services. The last edition touched on the financial crisis, but it was just emerging when the book went to press. This edition addresses it in more detail and reflects on its implications for policymaking.

The financial crisis is the economic downside of the global integration of banking systems and economies. Some have argued that it is a grim harbinger of the end of globalization. We review this debate in Chapter 2 and make the point that while the "happy face" globalization of the boom years a decade ago might be turning dour, too many other forces and factors continue to bind countries and economies and even cultures more tightly together. The sense of interdependency around issues such as climate change and security, for example, has increased. As a significant immigrant-receiving country, Canada has also experienced globalization through flows of human populations and the integration of newcomers to our society and economy. Those newcomers are essential for economic growth and a vibrant labour force, but they also pose challenges of social cohesion and accommodation. Europe has continued to face challenges around the integration of immigrant communities, particularly Muslim ones, and this has been reflected in a shift in some segments of European public opinion to support right-wing, anti-immigrant parties (witness the 2012 elections in France and Greece, and earlier in 2010, in the Netherlands). Canada has mercifully been spared these extremes, but ethnic tensions in Quebec led to a 2008 commission on "reasonable accommodation" that raised fundamental questions about citizenship and social cohesion. These conflicts and tensions over ethnic groups and immigration have become entangled with frustrations over economics, particularly over austerity measures. Governments face more volatile and dissatisfied citizens.

On questions of governance, the previous edition spent some time considering the impact of a broad movement called "new public management" (NPM), which started in the 1990s. There were several variants of new public management (e.g., in Scandinavian countries versus Anglo-Saxon democracies), but all boiled down to attempts to make government more business-like, smaller and more efficient, and more focused on policy than on delivery of services (which could be either outsourced or devolved onto different types of agencies). Canada was not immune to the allure of new public management and, indeed, echoed many of its main tenets in various government reform projects between 1985 and 2005. As I noted in previous editions, however, a post-9/11 and post–financial crisis world meant that, at a minimum, government could not abandon its security or economic responsibilities, and, indeed, in many ways, these responsibilities called for larger and more robust government machinery. It was also clear by 2008, whatever one's political inclinations, that government was a necessary and vital tool in addressing some key challenges facing the country, such as healthcare, epidemics, competitiveness in the new, global knowledge economy, and job creation, as various business sectors sagged.

This edition argues that new public management continues to have a strong effect in many areas of governance, but has been overtaken by several new perspectives, some unique to Canada and some more general. One of the more general perspectives, seen reflected in Organisation for Economic Co-operation and Development (OECD) documents and reports, is an even more intense appreciation of the importance of governance for a well-functioning society and economy. In little over a decade, leading international institutions such as the OECD, the World Bank, and the donor community (including international financial institutions) have collectively come to the conclusion that good governance is a key foundation for economic and social development. This notion is not merely rhetoric—there has been an explosion in governance measures and indicators, all based on core assumptions about what constitutes good governance, whether it is the quality of the bureaucracy or financial management systems.

Two other factors are specific to Canada, the first being a renewed emphasis on fiscal probity. The last edition was somewhat agnostic on whether the phobia over deficit spending would continue past the late-2000s, given the constant temptation for governments to spend their way to political popularity. Governments at all levels increased their expenditures substantially in the early 2000s because they had tax revenues and spending was popular. When the financial crisis hit in 2008, they began spending even more, in some cases to prop up their economies (the federal government's version was *Canada's Economic Action Plan*). Now, the emphasis is on returning to balance. Whether that can really happen, given the challenges of balancing tax increases against an economic downturn, is an open question, but even governments like Alberta's, that should be financially stable are grappling with deficits. On the other side of the policy divide are those who see the crisis as the result of greed and many of the solutions as sops to those (e.g., bankers and bond dealers) who caused the crisis in the first place—the 1 percent versus the 99 percent.

The second factor peculiar to Canada (though not exclusively) has been the emphasis on values, ethics, and accountability. The federal Conservatives won the 2006 election in large part due to the sponsorship scandal and the Gomery Inquiry that afflicted their Liberal predecessors. Once in office, they passed the Federal Accountability Act, which introduced sweeping changes across the federal system in terms of oversight and reporting. Indeed, those changes were so extensive that within a year of passing the legislation, there was serious discussion about the federal public sector being tied down and paralyzed by a "web of rules." This concern formed the backdrop to yet another effort at public service renewal—an effort that this time would not be guided by an NPM emphasis on downsizing government, but rather by a sense that the public sector was crucial to Canada's success as a country and that a reinvigorated public service would somehow have to combine service, efficiency, ethics, and accountability. The focus of governments on the economy has driven accountability and ethics issues off the agenda, but not entirely. The public is more severe than ever in its judgments of irresponsible governance, overspending, and profligacy. People want good government, but they also want their governments to be good.

This fifth edition has been thoroughly revised and updated to take account of these shifts, as well as numerous other developments in Canada and internationally since 2010. As with previous editions, each chapter is roughly divided in two: the first half reviews the current literature in the field on the chapter's subject, and the second half goes beyond and looks at contemporary changes and challenges. This edition has a new Chapter 9, which focuses on policy communication. Adding this chapter is based on the conviction that "selling" policy is a key, if underappreciated, phase in the policy process. The forces we briefly outlined above have put an even greater premium on effective and persuasive communication of policy options, precisely because the context is so much more difficult. Each chapter closes with a list of key concepts, which are printed in bold in the text, along with suggestions for further readings. Weblinks relevant to each chapter may be found at the book's website, www.nelson.com/policyanalysis5.

I am grateful for the advice and comments of several colleagues: Graeme Auld, Alexandra Mallett, and Glen Toner, from the School of Public Policy and Administration at Carleton University. Jennifer Robson, also from Carleton University, provided expert and rigorous comments on Chapter 9. Evert Lindquist also provided helpful advice on Chapter 9. Students in my M.A. and Ph.D. policy courses at Carleton contributed many valuable ideas and insights, and I benefited, as well, from seminars and workshops outside of Canada. My thanks, too, to Mohammad Zebian, who provided efficient and comprehensive research support for updates and revisions that went into this edition.

The team at Nelson Education Ltd. was, as always, both professional and supportive: Anne-Marie Taylor, Ann Byford, Jessica Freedman, Natalia Denesiuk Harris, Kate Revington, and P. Sangeetha.

Deepest thanks go to family: Mary, Matthew, Michael, and Meredith. They provided support and love, but also often probing questions and challenges as we discussed the policy issues of the day.

Policy Analysis:
Concepts and Practice

P ublic policies are an essential element in modern democracies in that they provide both guidance for government officials and accountability links to citizens. Governments may do things for a wide variety of reasons—patronage, political competition, reflex, tradition— but when their actions are grounded in policy, they presumably are taking a course of action that has been thought through in terms of the nature of the problem they are addressing and the circumstances they face. Insofar as these policies are visible and measurable to the public, they become key tests of the government's record at election time. Thus, organizing policy work in government and developing a public conversation about policy is central to healthy democratic politics. Despite some misgivings about the specific analytical techniques used by policymakers to achieve their objectives, the importance of policy to democratic governance has enjoyed a resurgence in recent years. Indeed, there has been growing domestic and international interest in developing policy capacity— especially since 2008, under the extreme pressures of the global financial crisis. This chapter introduces the key concepts of public policy and **policy analysis** and explores some of their characteristics. It then reviews some prominent Canadian and international examples of the global policy "movement" that has developed recently in the face of new governance challenges. These challenges are taken up in detail in Chapter 2.

What Is Public Policy?

Citizens expect many things from their governments, but at the very least, they expect intelligent decisionmaking. Perhaps even more important, however, they expect those decisions to flow from some general position or vision. Unfortunately, governments can be very decisive without being terribly intelligent. Intelligent decisions come from operating within some consistent framework, however general. We will return to this issue of consistency below, but for the moment it should be clear that the very nature of intelligent and accountable governance in a democracy demands more than mere decisions—it demands decisionmaking guided by a framework. In short, we expect that our governments have policies. As Hilary Mantel wrote in her best-selling novel *Wolf Hall*, "Princes are not obliged to consistency" (Mantel, 2010).

For the purpose of this book, **public policy** will be defined as a course of action or inaction chosen by public authorities to address a given problem or interrelated set of problems. Several aspects of this definition bear emphasis. First, note that it refers to a course of action. This picks up on the idea of frameworks or patterns—policies are guides to a range of related actions in a given field (Anderson, 2006). A "policymaker" is someone who develops these guides, a "policy-taker" is someone who operates within that **policy framework**, applying it to new situations. Immigration policy, for example, is a broad framework that structures the actions of a host of different organizations, from our foreign embassies to refugee boards at home. When political parties differ over their immigration policies, we know that they differ over first principles (e.g., open versus closed immigration, admission based on family considerations or economic contributions). When a policy is changed, the actions that take place within its framework are reconfigured to yield different results.

Another aspect of the definition is that it refers to action as well as inaction, as long as it has been chosen by public authorities (Kraft & Furlong, 2007, p. 5). As Howlett, Ramesh, and Perl put it, public policy is, "at its simplest, a choice made by government to undertake some course of action" (2009, p. 5). Consider the issue of recognizing same-sex marriages. Until a few years ago, it never would have entered the minds of most policymakers that this was a policy issue to be addressed, and so the absence of action on this front cannot be seen as a policy decision. On the other hand, once courts in Canada, the United States, and elsewhere declared these unions to be legal, government inaction could properly be defined as a policy choice. Another example is the collapse of the financial firm Lehman Brothers in 2008, which was the harbinger of the global financial crisis. The U.S. government deliberately did nothing—it let the company fail. It made a policy decision not to act. Not everything that governments do is policy driven, of course. Indeed, in a "crisis situation," governments have little option but to react. As deLeon (1988) points out, a crisis is a surprise: it is "unpredictable and unavoidable" (p. 116). Rochefort and Cobb (1994) noted that decisionmaking in crisis situations is synonymous with an emergency mentality that enables "quick responses but also tended to produce temporary Band-Aid solutions" to major public problems (p. 21). As well, some actions taken by government agencies are so far down the chain of implementation that they are properly seen as reflections of organizational routine rather than policy per se. The municipal bus driver's route is a function of policy; changes in routes due to road construction or seasonal weather are just administrative decisions.

Finally, note that the definition refers to problems and interrelated sets of problems. Public policy, whatever its symbolic dimensions, is seen by policymakers and citizens as a means of dealing with problems or sometimes with opportunities. In this sense, policies are largely "instrumental"—that is, they are not ends in themselves, or even good in themselves, but are instruments or tools to tackle issues of concern to the political community. But the instrumental character of public policy does not remove it from the realm of values (Stewart, 2009). For one thing, problems and opportunities are defined as such only in relation to goals or things we value. For another, means and ends are not so easily separated—in public policymaking, to use the "right tool" means both using the tool best suited (in an instrumental sense) to the task as well as the tool that is consistent with a morally acceptable range of government behaviour. The appropriate balance of technical or instrumental analysis and values in policy work is a perennial debate in the field. The rationalist roots of policy analysis in the 1960s held out the hope that with enough data and analysis, policy problems could be solved largely in technical terms, without too much contamination by values. A more recent trend in the literature has argued that almost everything in policy analysis is affected by values, and that consequently, the challenge is to develop techniques and processes of tackling public problems that encourage exchanges and ultimately consensus-building among citizens, politicians, and experts (Fischer, 1993, 2009; Fischer & Forester, 1993; Stone, 2001). As we will note below, the contemporary practice among policy analysts seems to have settled on working conscientiously within policy "visions" articulated by democratically elected governments but being sensitive to the way in which the values of both analysts and citizens will affect each phase of the analytical process as well as **policy development**, implementation, and evaluation.

The most important overarching value in public policy is the public interest. It is the touchstone or benchmark for all that democratic governments do. The 2003 Values and Ethics Code for the Public Service, for example, noted that the "democratic mission of the Public Service is to assist Ministers, under law, to serve the public interest" (Treasury Board of Canada Secretariat, 2003; the 2012 version has a similar definition see the detailed discussion in Chapter 10). The 2003 Code stated that "public servants, in fulfilling their official duties and responsibilities, shall make decisions in the public interest." In *A Strong Foundation*, known as the "Tait Report," the Task Force on Public Service Values and Ethics (2000) noted that a "fundamental value of public service is loyalty to the public interest or the public good." The task force argued that devotion to the public interest was the defining characteristic of the public service as a profession. Moreover, the concept is more than purely philosophical—it is commonly referred to in regulatory decisions, and in one estimate, is mentioned 224 times in 84 federal statutes (MacNair, 2006). There is no single definition of the public interest, but there are some basic orientations that stress some balance of the majority's views, common interests within the political community (e.g., clean water and safe streets), and binding values (e.g., respect for minorities) (Pal & Maxwell, 2004). Different political actors will define the public interest in different ways, but will typically justify their policy recommendations by that standard.

This mix of values and technical analysis can be illustrated with reference to a policy field that, at first blush, seems almost completely technical: taxation. At its most basic level, tax policy is about generating revenue for government. Taxes can also be used, however, as instruments that encourage or discourage certain kinds of behaviour: lower business taxes, for example, might encourage investment, while higher "sin" taxes on alcohol and cigarettes might discourage drinking and smoking (Bird & Stoney, 2006). Both of these dimensions entail technical considerations: what is the ideal or best level and incidence of taxation to both produce revenues and have the desired policy outcomes? Overly high levels of taxation will encourage tax evasion, thus lowering yields. Then there are questions of the progressivity of tax rates, the number of income brackets, and so on. But the actual policy debate around taxes in Canada and in other countries is also strongly affected by values. The Conservatives promised to lower the GST (Goods and Services Tax) from 7 percent to 5 percent, and did so through two consecutive budgets in 2006 and 2007. Virtually every economist in the country disagreed with the move, arguing that technically, it made more sense to keep consumption taxes high and lower income taxes, thus lowering disincentives to work. The Tories ignored the advice, partly for political reasons, but also because they believed in the value of lower taxes overall—they reduced both the GST and income taxes in those two budgets. The same value debate can be seen over flat taxes (Alberta has had a flat income tax for years). While there are important technical issues over the efficacy of flat versus progressive taxes, a good part of the debate is between alternative visions of the public interest. Ultimately, the issue of taxes is connected to the values we hold about "fairness." By 2012, most rich countries were struggling with trying to raise tax revenues and lower expenditures, and neither of these was a "technical" issue since it clearly involved winners and losers.

Policies rarely tackle single problems; rather, they deal with clusters of entangled problems that may have contradictory solutions. Many policy problems are complex, which means that they are more than just difficult or complicated. Bourgon (2010, p. 208) argues that complex policy problems are of a different order: they have dynamic complexity (causes and effects are interdependent), social complexity (facts and the nature of the problem are contested), and generative complexity (unforeseen issues come up and combine and recombine with other issues in unpredictable ways). Policy design therefore becomes a process of balancing different solutions that address different aspects of a cluster of problems. Moreover, complex problems of the sort identified by Bourgon require systemic approaches—they simply cannot be broken down into discrete pieces. In 2002, for example, the Liberal government of the time ratified the Kyoto Protocol on climate change and promised substantial cuts in carbon dioxide emissions. The subsequent federal Conservative government openly attacked the Protocol, claiming repeatedly that Canada could not meet its 2012 targets without inflicting severe economic damage. Indeed, at the UN Climate Change Conference in Bali in December 2007, the government initially resisted the targets recommended by the Intergovernmental Panel on Climate Change, proposing its own emissions plan with significantly lower targets. The 2009 Copenhagen Accord on climate change, the successor to Kyoto, is not legally binding on states.

There are severe complications in dealing with this policy problem. First, in the face of global recession, countries are reluctant to throttle emissions through instruments like a carbon tax, and possibly throttle growth as well. Second, in the Canadian case, there is the regional character of the economy—Western provinces, in particular Alberta with its tar sands, are most exposed if the federal government moves seriously to curtail emissions. But the effects could be quite different in the Ontario industrial heartland. Finally, this is not a policy issue that can be resolved within one country's borders. Unsurprisingly, given the technical, regional, and international dimensions of the issue, Ottawa has grappled for consistency and coherence with little success.

The general character of a public policy, therefore, is that it is a guide to action, a plan, a framework, a course of action or inaction designed to deal with problems. This characterization fits with the classic definitions of public policy in the field. Thomas Dye simply defined policy as "whatever governments choose to do or not to do" (2010, p. 1), and Harold Lasswell, the originator of the modern policy sciences, defined it as "the most important choices" (1951, p. 5). Colebatch uses the term "coherence" to describe the same thing: "the assumption that all the bits of the action fit together, that they form part of an organized whole, a single system, and policy has to do with how this system is (or should be) steered" (Colebatch, 1998, p. 3). Cochran and Malone (2005, p. 1) say that public policy consists of "government decisions and actions designed to deal with a matter of public concern." Birkland makes essentially the same point: "The study of public policy is the examination of the creation, by the government, of the rules, laws, goals, and standards that determine what government does or does not do to create resources, benefits, costs, and burdens" (2005, p. 5).

All of these definitions are grounded in a **rational model** of what it means to make decisions and respond to problems: "policy or strategy is formulated consciously, preferably analytically, and made explicit and then implemented formally" (Mintzberg & Jørgensen, 1987, p. 216). The intentional aspect, as we noted above, is important in this classic approach to defining policy. Another approach is to de-emphasize intention in favour of action: organizations can engage in consistent patterns of behaviour that emerge or form rather than being planned. Mintzberg and Jørgensen refer to this as **emergent strategies** that bubble up from all corners of an organization. In this perspective, policy is what governments do, not what they say or intend. As they point out, however, this concept is, at most, a corrective, since no organization could survive through the hothouse generation of uncoordinated strategies.

The definitional exercise does not end there, however. Of what does this guide or framework consist? If someone asked you to search out the government's policy on X and summarize it, what would you look for and where? Let's begin with the "where" since it takes us to yet another aspect of the definition that seems so natural that it is easily overlooked. Policies emanate from public authorities, but not every public servant has the power to articulate policy. Since policy is a guide, it has a normative or coercive dimension: if the policy says you must do X, then you must (should) do X. Of course, not everyone is empowered to make these sorts of statements. Policies get made in organizations all the time, and typically they are made by "management." When we speak of public policy, we are referring to policies that deal with public problems, not organizational routines or structure. Policy, to put it simply, comes from those who have the legitimate authority to impose normative guidelines for action. In a democracy, policy is made by elected officials in concert with advisers from the higher levels of the administration. In strongly hierarchical systems of government like Canada's, public servants often ruefully joke that policy is whatever the minister says it is. The hard truth behind the humour is that since the minister is the elected official at the apex of the government department, only he or she has the right to enunciate policy. If the written documents say one thing and the minister says something else, then that "something else" (at least temporarily) is the policy. Of course, once a policy has been authoritatively announced, non-elected officials can—and usually are required to—re-articulate and fine-tune policy. They also have an obligation to implement policy through programs. As well, the judiciary can get into the policy game by rendering judgments as to whether legislation is constitutional.

Not everyone, therefore, is empowered to articulate policy. But for those who are, what is it that they are saying in a **policy statement**? Every policy has three key elements. The first is the definition of the problem, the second is the goals that are to be achieved, and the third is the instruments or means whereby the problem is to be addressed and the goals achieved.

Problem definition will be considered the central element of a policy statement. If there is no perceived problem, or a problem seems insoluble, one would hardly expect a public policy to solve it (though policies are sometimes framed as efforts to capitalize on an opportunity). In Chapter 3, we will consider the nature of problem definition more closely, but several points should be noted here. First, problems have to be recognized and defined. Recognition might be nothing more than a sense that "something is wrong" or that some new situation is looming. This sense often arises as a result of changes in some fairly systematic indicator that suggest a problem: "Such indicators abound in the political world because both governmental and non-governmental agencies routinely monitor various activities and events: highway deaths, disease rates, immunization rates, consumer prices, commuter and inter-city ridership, costs of entitlement programs, infant mortality rates, and many others" (Kingdon, 1995, p. 90). Second, the process of problem definition can either be exhaustive or casual. The more significant the policy problem, the more complex it is, the more necessary an exhaustive (and expensive) policy inquiry is. The United States, for example, had the 9/11 Commission, as well as the Financial Crisis Inquiry Commission (to examine the domestic and global causes of the 2008 financial crisis). In 1997, Canada launched a Royal Commission on Aboriginal Peoples which spent five years and over $50 million studying the relationship between Aboriginal peoples and Canadian society. On the other hand, editorial pages and TV programs overflow with instant experts on every conceivable public problem, and the policy positions of many groups are quite predictable since they are based less on analysis than on ideology. Third, as noted above, problems usually come in complex clusters, and so problem definitions typically operate across a range of dimensions. For example, trying to enhance innovation in the Canadian economy requires tax policy, research and development in both the private and public sectors, and financial institutions and their lending practices. Fourth, problems can sometimes appear in the guise of a substantially changed context or situation, more like new realities or opportunities to which we have to adapt. The most arresting example of this aspect comes from our foreign policy. The impact of 9/11 and the destruction of the World Trade Center on Canada's security posture, our relations with the United States, our immigration and refugee policies, and our defence policy have been profound. Dealing with the global financial crisis is resulting in equally profound changes in economic and social policy. Fifth, all problem definitions have a causal character: they indicate what the problem or issue is, and bundle that with some indication of the factors that led to it. Without this causal connection, it would be difficult to determine what to do about the problem.

The irony of problem definition is that while it is central to understanding public policy, it is rarely articulated in great detail in a policy statement. Interest groups and the media spend a great deal of time debating problem definitions and causal factors, and governments cannot avoid rooting their policy reactions in the often exhaustive analyses undertaken by their departments or other agencies. However, the policy statement in itself will rarely reflect this level of detail. As the definitions of public policy cited earlier suggest, policy is about action or deliberate inaction. It is the framework or guide, and while problem definition is crucial to understanding the rationale for policy, it is not in itself crucial to the statement of what that guide is to be. From a purely practical point of view, the rationale for an action is often considerably more complex than the action (or statement of what that action will be). The importance of this is simply that doing policy analysis—trying to make sense of a policy statement—involves a fair amount of detective work in tracking down both the policy statement and the supporting rationale in terms of problem definition.

Problem definitions are inextricably bound to **policy goals**. A key distinction, however, is between **general goals** and **policy-specific goals**. Healthcare policy, for example, has, as its most general goal, the maintenance and improvement of health among the Canadian population. At this level, almost no one disagrees about goals—the same is true of general goals in foreign policy, education policy, social policy, and so on. As policies get more specific, however, so do their goals. Those goals are still related to the broader ones, but they are contributory rather than final. A provincial healthcare policy to improve services for at-risk youth will have goals that are directly tied or related to those youth (e.g., safer pregnancies, reduced substance abuse). If achieved, those goals will contribute to the larger goals in the healthcare field.

As with problem definitions, intermediate policy goals sometimes have to be inferred since they are not always clearly stated. Occasionally, policymakers do articulate clear objectives and measurable intermediate goals, though they resist. The Kyoto Protocol, for example, would have had Canada reduce its greenhouse gas emissions by 2012 to 6 percent below what they were in 1990. This never happened. In fact, Canada's emissions increased. The 2007 agreement, signed in Bali, established a range of 25 to 40 percent reductions in the next decade. The 2010

Copenhagen Accord committed developed countries to not exceed 2 degrees Celsius by 2020, but had no benchmarks for emissions (United Nations Framework Convention on Climate Change, 2010). Another example was the 2005 federal–provincial agreement, Strengthen Health Care, which included specific targets for wait times for five priority medical procedures (radiation therapy for cancer, hip/knee replacement, cataract surgery, cardiac bypass surgery, and diagnostic imaging). The Canadian Institute for Health Information was mandated to collect information on how well provinces were doing under the plan. By 2011 most seemed in compliance, but the important point is that with explicit targets and an entity to monitor results based on those targets, policy transparency was increased significantly (Canadian Institute for Health Information, 2011). In both of these examples, the goals are clear and numerical, and so make it easier to hold government to account. However, most policy goals are fuzzy: in these cases, the mere fact that the problem is not getting worse is sometimes used as a claim that the policy goals are being met. Another problem, of course, is that the real goals of the policy might be quite different from the stated goals. Politicians may decide that they want to "send a message" rather than solve a specific problem; the promise by the federal Conservative government to scrap the national long-gun registry is a case in point. The gun registry was introduced in 1995, but took until 2003 to be fully implemented. Originally estimated at a net cost of roughly $80 million, it was tagged by the Auditor General of Canada as approaching $1 billion. The registry became a lightning rod for public anger over waste—and a fine symbol to attack. Another example is the omnibus crime bill (the Safe Streets and Communities Act) introduced by the Harper government in September 2011 (combining nine former crime bills, such as the Protecting Children from Sexual Predators Act and the Ending House Arrest for Property and Other Serious Crimes by Serious and Violent Offenders Act). In the face of arguments that crime rates were at historic lows and that building new prisons would cost as much as $2 billion, Justice Minister Rob Nicholson responded, "We're not governing on the basis of the latest statistics; we're governing on the basis of what's right to better protect victims and law-abiding Canadians" (Chase, 2011, p. A4).

The third key component of a public policy statement is some indication of the nature of the **policy instruments** or means whereby the problem is to be addressed and the goals achieved. Defining a policy problem and determining a solution are frequently overshadowed in the policymaking process by the question of "how." The choice of instruments is also entangled with a choice of the means of implementing those instruments. A government might choose, for example, to dissuade substance abuse through advertising. But who will do the advertising, and how? The first is an instrument choice issue; the second is an implementation issue.

Chapter 1 Policy Analysis: Concepts and Practice

In principle, governments have a wide range of instruments from which to choose to tackle a policy problem and achieve their goals. They can rely on information (the advertising example), they can spend or tax, they can regulate, or in some instances, they can set up agencies that combine these instruments under public auspices and address the problem directly. Linder and Peters (1989, p. 56) list as many as 23 types of instruments, whereas Kirschen (1964) came up with 62 (see Chapter 4).

The theoretically wide range of choices over instruments is quite constrained in the real world. For one thing, even as policies change from time to time, governments take for granted the instruments to achieve their goals. Canadian broadcasting policy, for example, has evolved substantially since the 1960s, but the key instruments of achieving its policy goals—the Canadian Radio-television and Telecommunications Commission and the Canadian Broadcasting Corporation—have remained. Health policy has changed marginally from time to time, and yet the key delivery mechanisms of hospitals, healthcare professions, and public expenditures have been quite stable since the 1960s (though information technology is being used in more sophisticated ways to enhance medical services). Sometimes, of course, policy changes so radically in terms of problem definition and goals that instruments get reconfigured quite dramatically as well. The federal government, for example, decided some years ago that innovation and research were keys to a productive, high-tech economy and that universities, in turn, were the keys to fostering research and innovation. Over the last few years, Ottawa has become a major funder of university research through a host of new policy instruments such as Canada Research Chairs and the Canada Student Grant Program, and its 2007 policy outlined in *Mobilizing Science and Technology*, which promised to spend an additional $1.9 billion.

Instrument choice can also be significantly constrained by perceptions of legitimacy. In only rare cases, for example, are Canadians prepared to accept government coercion over matters of sexual behaviour. Therefore, government action to deal with problems like sexually transmitted diseases has had to rely primarily on informational instruments. Legitimacy is elastic and will change with circumstances (e.g., an epidemic of sexually transmitted diseases could lead to acceptance of stronger government action, just as the SARS crisis in 2003 gave public health and border officials legitimacy to impose stringent controls). Legitimacy is also culturally contingent. The Vancouver Health Authority, for example, has, since 2003, been operating a safe injection site for heroin addicts, called Insite, where addicts can come and get clean needles and shoot up under supervision. As a "harm reduction" strategy, this may make sense in the local context, but the practice has been widely criticized both in Canada and by the United States. The federal Conservatives cut funding in 2006, and the issue went to the British Columbia Supreme Court, which gave

Insite an exemption from the Controlled Drugs and Substances Act. In October 2011, the Supreme Court of Canada handed down a unanimous ruling that Insite provided effective harm reduction and saved lives; it ordered the federal government to reinstate the exemption.

Finally, instrument choice can be limited by legal restrictions—a constitutional division of powers or international agreements that prohibit the use of some policy tools—or by practical constraints. Both are important. In the Canadian case, federalism divides sovereignty between two levels of government, so that the provinces, for example, have control over health and education whereas Ottawa has exclusive powers over employment insurance and banking. Governments can still use some instruments to effect policy changes in fields outside their jurisdiction—the classic Canadian case is Ottawa's use of its spending power in the healthcare and postsecondary education fields. World Trade Organization membership means that countries cannot, outside of narrow boundaries, discriminate in favour of national firms. Human rights conventions do much the same thing in fields as diverse as language and the treatment of children. These legal constraints can be joined by more practical ones. Examples include limits on spending programs due to high deficit levels or, indeed, to high spending levels themselves in the face of global investment markets that demand restraint or austerity. Instrument choice is also often constrained by organizational routines and preferences: regulatory departments reach first for regulatory instruments; finance departments reach first for fiscal instruments; and so on.

Figure 1.1 summarizes the preceding discussion of policy content. If one were asked to find out the government's policy on X, one would (1) seek an authoritative source for the policy statement, and (2) search relevant documents for clues on problem definition, goals, and instruments. All of these concepts and some of their nuances will be explored in greater detail in subsequent chapters. Note that Figure 1.1 connects these elements in a loop. While problem definition is central to an understanding of policy in a logical sense, in reality, the three elements are inextricably entwined. Policymakers' goals orient them toward certain problems they think need solving; expertise with a set of policy tools encourages one to seek out problems and goals that are consistent with what is achievable with the tools. Moreover, it is virtually impossible to understand any one of these elements without considering the others. In this sense, policy analysis is usually iterative: it moves through the loop several times, refining an understanding of any one element in light of the others. The two diamonds at the bottom of the figure refer to actors and related policy frameworks. These are not directly "elements of policy content," but they are important contextual factors that enrich one's understanding of a given policy. For example, it would certainly be true that an analysis of Canada's Afghanistan mission would require knowing

Figure 1.1 Elements of Policy Content

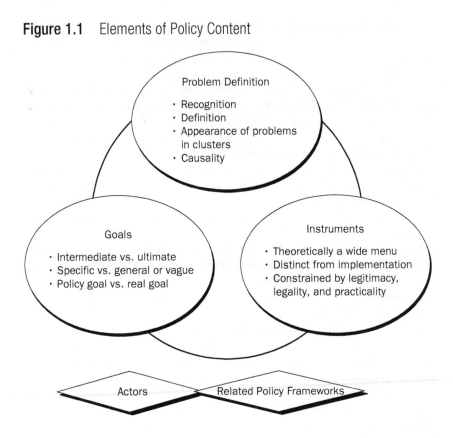

Problem Definition
- Recognition
- Definition
- Appearance of problems in clusters
- Causality

Goals
- Intermediate vs. ultimate
- Specific vs. general or vague
- Policy goal vs. real goal

Instruments
- Theoretically a wide menu
- Distinct from implementation
- Constrained by legitimacy, legality, and practicality

Actors   Related Policy Frameworks

the problem definition (international terrorism, with a strong base in that country), the goals (defeat the Taliban and rebuild the country), and the instruments (military support, aid, and diplomacy). But that understanding would be even deeper if one had a scan of who the key players or actors are with respect to our policy—from military, to key government departments, to the prime minister, opposition parties, and civil society groups. Furthermore, knowing the related policy frameworks—our foreign policy and our international development strategy—situates the Afghanistan mission much more clearly. It sometimes helps to think about a given policy as existing within a wider **policy space** that is populated by other actors/organizations and other policies and programs that tackle different elements of a wider set of problems.

The loop also suggests that there will be consistency between the different elements. A definition of a problem should "fit" somehow with the instruments and goals. **Policy consistency** is an important concept to appreciate, since it underpins both what we do as policy analysts and how we perceive public policies as citizens.

Policies are expected to be consistent in several interrelated ways (see Figure 1.2 below). First, as noted above, we expect policies to have an **internal consistency** among the three elements of problem definition, goals, and instruments. Second, we expect a policy to have **vertical consistency** in the sense that the programs and activities undertaken in its name are logically related to it. This is in part the nub of implementation. Policy statements are normally fairly abstract and general. They must be actualized through an implementation process that elaborates programs and activities to give the policy effect. A municipal policy to maintain the livability of the downtown core assumes programs and initiatives that support business and residential developments in that area. If the municipality simultaneously had programs to disproportionately encourage suburban development, these would, on their face, appear inconsistent with the larger policy framework.

A third type of consistency is **horizontal consistency**, or consistency within the wider policy space and across policy fields, not just within

Figure 1.2 Policy Consistency

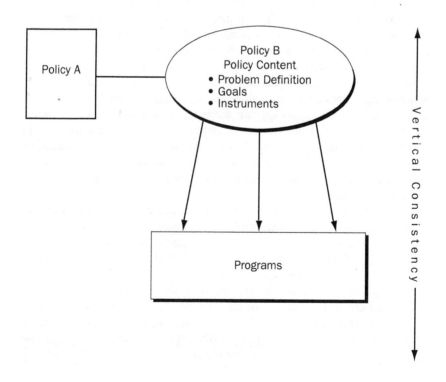

them. This is an expectation that what governments do in one field will not contradict what they do in another. A fiscal policy of restraint coupled with high spending in a wide variety of areas makes no sense—as the struggles of countries like Greece to reduce their deficits in 2011–12 illustrated. This type of consistency is important in democratic politics, since it implies that there is an underlying philosophy of government that cuts across all policy fields. From a policy perspective, when people vote, they often vote less for specific policies than for the "whole package." It is a way of ensuring a degree of accountability, since every part of the government is expected to follow a broadly consistent line of policy. Horizontal consistency varies considerably in the real world, both because of the sheer sprawl of government and the existence of multiple jurisdictions. There are so many actors with some influence over the policy process, and so many agencies with relatively autonomous control of their policy fields, that it is not unusual to have quite widely disparate policy frameworks operating at the same time, even within the same policy space. In systems like Canada's, where the executive has greater control over the policy agenda and is internally more coherent due to the role of the prime minister and the governing party, there is a higher degree of policy consistency. Even here, however, where strong ministers can control their own departments, horizontal consistency is never perfect. Nonetheless, the concept (if not the term) seems to be gaining favour. There have been examples at both the federal and provincial levels of governments or political parties putting coherent and detailed proposals before the electorate (though this varies by election and by party); there has also been growing emphasis in administrative circles on "horizontality." It is tempting to speculate that budgets, primarily because of the pressures of the financial crisis, will continue to be the greatest engines of horizontal policy consistency for many governments. Pre-crisis, when fiscal constraints did not matter as much or were ignored, the budget was little more than a compendium of spending initiatives undertaken by departments. Now that deficits and debt are reaching mountainous proportions, all policy initiatives are measured, trimmed, or cut by their impact on spending levels.

In reflecting on the nature of public policy, we also have to realize what it is not. It is not the implemented program, the behaviours of public servants who put it into effect, or indeed, the reactions of citizens affected by it. If we take the definition developed above, we are forced to realize that public policy—as a course of action—is not the action itself, in the same way that a map is different from the act of travelling. Policies are mental constructs, strings of phrases, and ideas. The text of a policy statement and the programs and actions that follow it are simply evidence for the mental construct. Analyzing policy is akin to trying to figure out which maps people used by studying the paths they took on their journey.

The fact that there was a journey and a destination is not proof that maps were used, as anyone who's taken a pleasant ramble in the woods can attest. But we presume that our governments are doing more than rambling, that they have a plan, that their journeys and their destinations are guided by policy. This presumption will often be proven wrong—government actions may be the result of accident, instinct, or habit, rather than of policy. Once we understand this, we understand the challenge of doing policy analysis—it is nothing less than an attempt to grasp an underlying structure of ideas that supposedly guides action.

What Is Public Policy Analysis?

In this book, **policy analysis** will be defined as the disciplined application of intellect to public problems. This definition is similar to Dunn's: "policy analysis is a process of multidisciplinary inquiry designed to create, critically assess, and communicate information that is useful in understanding and improving policies" (Dunn, 2008, p. 1). Apropos of the last point in the previous section, policy analysis is a cognitive activity—a thinking game, if you will—a large part of which focuses on public policy outputs in terms of their problem definition, goals, and instruments. As Wildavsky (1979) pointed out, it is not exclusively a matter of "cogitation" but of "interaction" as well—of letting problems get solved through experimentation, bargaining, and exchange, rather than exclusively through planning—but the reflective, cognitive aspect is central (p. 11). Hoppe echoes this in his notion of policy problem-structuring as a form of collective "puzzling" (Hoppe, 2010). Ours is a broad definition and is complemented by a thicket of other conceptual terms such as **policy studies**, "policy science," and "policy evaluation." The central distinction to keep in mind is between a style of policy analysis that is more explanatory and descriptive and a style that is more applied or prescriptive, or between what Harold Lasswell (1970) called "knowledge of the policy process" and "knowledge in the policy process" (p. 3). Dobuzinskis, Howlett, and Laycock make a similar point in their definition of policy analysis: it "refers to applied social and scientific research—but also involves more implicit forms of practical knowledge—pursued by government officials and nongovernmental organizations usually directed at designing, implementing and evaluating existing policies, programmes and other courses of action adopted by states" (2007, pp. 3–4). The distinctions among these terms are less important than what they have in common:

> Obviously, the conceptual distinction between these terms is rather indistinct. It would appear that, when the word policy

appears as a prefix to the words science, studies, and analysis, we are talking about activity that investigates some form of government problem or output. This includes studies that examine the policy-making process to determine how it affects the output of that process. (McCool, 1995, p. 10)

Or, as George Graham (1988) argues: "The policy orientation provides a means for dealing with human purposes in the best scientific framework possible to aid those who will make social choices. The instrumental end is better intelligence" (p. 152; quoted in McCool, 1995, p. 10).

All these definitions stress the degree to which this reflection is more than just casual observation—the idea that analysis is disciplined implies that it is both grounded in some method and that it is systematic and multidisciplinary. Dunn (2008, p. 3) stresses the multidisciplinary nature of policy analysis in that it draws on a range of social and behavioural sciences, ethics and other branches of social and political philosophy, normative and behavioural economics, and decision analysis. Indeed, the formal dictionary definition of "analysis" is that it is the process of breaking something complex down to its various simple elements—in our sense, into problem definition, goals, and instruments, but possibly even further with respect to each one of those three key dimensions, and in addition to thinking about actors and related policy frameworks. The methodological basis can vary from a generic (and usually multidisciplinary) approach to one that is solidly grounded in either natural or social sciences. Policy analysis of environmental issues, for example, will be informed by several natural sciences, but this is not to say that only natural scientists can analyze environmental policy. Economics offers an intellectual apparatus that is broadly applicable to a wide range of policy issues, but once again, the central concerns of the policy analyst have less to do with the disciplines that seem to be "naturally" aligned to the policy issue than with the larger issues discussed in the previous section: how well is the problem defined, what are its characteristics, what goals are being pursued, and are the instruments adequate and likely to produce results? As we will see in a moment, there is a host of supplementary issues that also are well within the scope of policy analysis per se, rather than separate disciplines. The other aspect of policy analysis is that it is systematic—it proceeds logically through a series of clearly defined stages to come to its conclusions. It should be possible, in other words, to see how someone arrived at his or her conclusions.

All this may seem self-evident, but it holds three implications of great importance to the way that we view contemporary policy analysis. The first is that, at least insofar as policy analysis seems to be allied with scientific disciplines, not just anyone can do it well. Ordinary citizens have opinions about public policy, but their views may be determined by prejudice or what happened to be on that morning's front page. Sometimes people have extraordinarily strong views about policy that they cannot explain. Once again, this would seem to fall short of policy analysis. The issue this raises, of course, is the division between citizens and experts. Can policy analysis be performed only by those trained to do it? Put another way, do ordinary citizens, when they contemplate public policy issues, engage in "real" policy analysis or merely in fuzzy thinking, and can experts put aside their own personal opinions? These are not merely abstract, philosophical issues; they strike at the heart of the policy process, the engagement of citizens, and the incorporation of expertise in policy advice.

The second implication, given that policy analysis should be disciplined and systematic, is that there will be both good and bad analysis. More disciplined and systematic analysis will be superior to the less disciplined and systematic. This understanding implies some intersubjective standard of judgment that will act as a benchmark for all participants in the analytical process. It points to the need for some training, especially in the use of more technically oriented forms of analysis and data generation (e.g., opinion surveys, cost-benefit analysis). Nonetheless, it has to be acknowledged that policy analysis contains an irreducible element of interpretation and perspective: that it is a form of "practical reason" that relies on a variety of techniques, a good deal of judgment, experience, and exploration (Sanderson, 2009). There is no exact science, for example, of structuring policy problems. As we noted earlier, policy problems are almost always complex and multi-faceted, and so defining or structuring the problem depends very much on which elements the analyst emphasizes and how those elements are imaginatively combined. Yet all analysis should not be viewed as purely subjective. As was mentioned, a substantial part of policy analysis does rely on specific methodological techniques of data gathering, research, and assessment. Moreover, in a democratic policy process, policy problems should be debated and exposed to discussion and criticism, as a means of correcting mistakes as well as generating intersubjective consensus. But policy analysis has, as well, to be self-aware and self-critical in an effort to remove as much unintentional bias as possible. One major example of this type of effort is the treatment of gender in policy analysis. A partial solution has been the development in the last decade of specific techniques of **gender-based analysis (GBA)**, which seek to assess the differential impact of public policies, programs, and legislation on women and men. GBA is designed not to be an add-on in the analytical process, but a perspective that is woven through each step and phase (Aboriginal Affairs and Northern Development Canada, 2010). A recent development has been the extension of GBA to analyzing government budgets and their differential impacts on men and women (Bakker, 2006). A complementary concept is **gender mainstreaming**, an organizational strategy to ensure that a gender perspective is reflected in all types of organizational activities. The United Nations has made a strong commitment to gender mainstreaming, "ensuring that gender perspectives and attention to the goal of gender equality are central to all activities—policy development, research, advocacy/dialogue, legislation, resource allocation, and planning, implementation and monitoring of programmes and projects" (United Nations, 2011).

Policy analysis is also complicated by possible cultural and religious biases—some Aboriginal groups and ethnic minorities argue that prevailing policy reflects the biases and interests of the ruling majority. Most public policy issues will not be as strongly marked by such disputes, but, as we noted earlier, values are at the heart of all policy debates, no matter how apparently technical. And values can be strongly linked to "ways of life" or community sensibilities. Consider for a moment the response authorities face when they decide, for rational reasons, to close schools. Or what municipalities might have to deal with when suggesting name changes to streets.

The third implication is that policy analysis, however much it may draw on other scientific disciplines, is a specific form of inquiry. Policy analysis, for example, has a unique focus when compared to other disciplines: public policies and the several elements that comprise them, along with the processes that produce them and the impacts they ultimately have. Policy analysis has its own traditions of debate, its journals, its schools, and its characteristic intellectual paradigms and issues. It is also different from politics and management: "politics, policy and management draw on three different traditions of enquiry and use three different ways of thinking and operating. Politicians use the world of semantics— they craft meaning with words (usually spoken). Policy advisors use the world of schematics—they design strategies and draw diagrams to represent how reality can be changed. By contrast, managers use the real world of practice—they deliver results through people and organizations" (Quirk, 2011, p. 11).

It is important not to paint too rigid a picture of policy analysis. Taking the two elements of the definition—(1) the disciplined application of intellect and (2) public problems—it is easy to see that if we break each one down into its possible elements, there is a wide variety of possibilities and permutations that might come under the broad rubric of policy analysis. As we will see later in this book, some styles of policy analysis favour advocacy, while others involve managing processes, or even engaging in fundamental philosophical reflection on core ideas that underpin policy debates (Hoppe & Jeliazkova, 2006). While policy analysis has undoubtedly become professionalized (Radin, 2000), and is a recognized occupational category in government, the work done by policy analysts is not narrowly technical. The "disciplined application of intellect" is really

Figure 1.3   Policy Analysis: Types of Reasoning

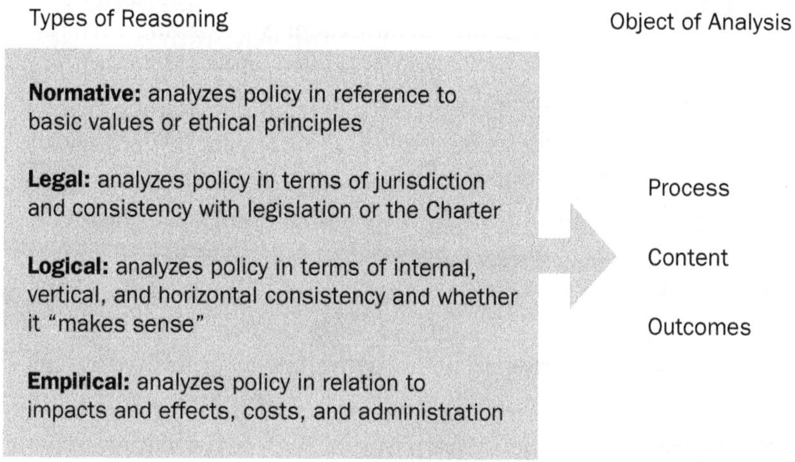

Types of Reasoning

Object of Analysis

Normative: analyzes policy in reference to basic values or ethical principles

Legal: analyzes policy in terms of jurisdiction and consistency with legislation or the Charter

Process

Logical: analyzes policy in terms of internal, vertical, and horizontal consistency and whether it "makes sense"

Content

Outcomes

Empirical: analyzes policy in relation to impacts and effects, costs, and administration

about styles of reasoning, as long as these styles are disciplined and systematic in some recognizable sense. These styles of reasoning are applied to "public problems," but these also have various dimensions: process, content, and outcome, to name only a few. As Figure 1.3 shows, one can reason about (or analyze) policy in several equally legitimate ways: **normative, legal, logical,** and empirical. The figure also highlights some of the dimensions of policy that can be analyzed: process (the various determinants of a policy, the actors and institutions that shaped it), content (problem definition, goals, instruments), and outcomes (legislation, regulations, actual impact or effect).

Defining policy analysis in this way—as the disciplined application of intellect to public problems—deliberately excludes some "other ways of knowing." It does so because it is itself based on a certain epistemology or system of knowledge. That system is **rationalism,** the characteristic form of knowing in the West that is rooted in the Greek and European civilizations. This book is hardly the place to discuss the intellectual history of Western civilization, but it is important to understand what this form of reason implies about how we come to decisions, and what counts as knowledge and what does not. The rational decisionmaking paradigm, a feature of virtually every introductory textbook on policy analysis, is outlined in Box 1.1 (page 20). Note that the procedure is generic: it should apply as well to deciding public policy as it does to choosing a mate or one's wardrobe.

Few of us are this systematic when we make everyday decisions, but the more important a decision, the more likely that we will think about it carefully and perhaps approximate this model. Will approaching a matter

BOX 1.1   THE RATIONAL DECISIONMAKING MODEL

Choose objectives: The first step in making a decision is knowing what one wishes to do or accomplish. Determining this necessarily involves a statement of the problem as well as of goals.

Consider alternatives: Once the problem and goals are identified, the second step is to identify the means by which the objectives may be attained.

Outline impacts: Each alternative will consist of a bundle of costs and benefits, positive and negative impacts on the problem. Measure them.

Determine criteria: A fourth step is to rank all of the alternatives in order of desirability, based on some explicit criterion, such as least cost, for a given objective.

Apply models/scenarios: The final step before implementation is the construction of a model or a scenario to help predict and map out the potential empirical consequences of the chosen alternative.

Implement preferred option: Put the preferred option into effect.

Evaluate consequences: What happened, and how well do the real impacts fit with predicted outcomes?

systematically make for a better decision? Maybe. But making decisions rationally is not the same as making reasonable decisions. A reasonable or good decision is defined less by the process that produced it than by its appropriateness as a solution to the initial problem. While the rational model could, in principle, be used to choose a mate, most people would argue that making this type of decision with the heart or one's emotions is more reasonable.

It is worth taking a moment to consider the implications of the rational model for policy analysis and decisionmaking, if only because "rational" seems synonymous with "reasonable" and the opposition of "rationality" and "intuition" seems to give preference to the former. For one thing, the rational model has embedded within it a strong concern with efficiency, which Herbert Simon (one of the most important decision theorists) defined as choosing alternatives that provide the greatest results for the least cost (Simon, Smithburg, & Thompson, 1958, p. 60).

Simon was convinced throughout his long and distinguished career (he was born in 1916, won the Nobel Prize for Economics in 1978, and died in 2001) that social betterment would come from the application of rational techniques to complex decisions. He acknowledged that pure rationality in decisionmaking was an impossibility, and that, instead, human beings made decisions under various constraints, in a model he described as **bounded rationality** in search of **satisficing** solutions. Mintzberg (1994) has noted how, for Simon, "the fundamental assumption is that continuous knowledge can be broken down into discrete elements, that is, decomposed for the purposes of analysis.... [I]ntuition gets reduced to analysis" (pp. 310–311). The pure rational model presumes certain patterns of thought: it is linear, systematic, self-conscious, purposive, and efficient.

Another way of putting this is that policy analysis, and the rationalism in which it is rooted, is part and parcel of the way "the state sees." James C. Scott (1998) points out the difficulties states had in pre-modern times in fulfilling classic state functions such as raising taxes, conscripting armies, or preventing rebellions. Societies were not "legible" or visible because pre-modern states, confronting patterns of social life that were suited to local conditions, knew little about the identities, location, holdings, wealth, or personal conditions of their subjects. Scott's book traces the way in which the state developed this knowledge through focusing on and analyzing specific bits of information to the exclusion of others. With simplification "an overall, aggregate, synoptic view of a selective reality is achieved, making possible a high degree of schematic knowledge, control, and manipulation" (Scott, 1998, p. 11). Things we take for granted today, such as standard weights and measures, freehold land tenure and cadastral maps (showing plots of individually owned land), grid systems for the layout of cities, official languages, and even permanent patronyms (inherited last names date only from the 20th century in Europe) all had to be invented, and they were invented largely to benefit state administration. As Scott (1998) argues, "the modern state, through its officials, attempts with varying degrees of success to create a terrain and a population with precisely those standardized characteristics that will be easiest to monitor, count, assess, and manage" (pp. 81–82). The statecraft that can be exercised on a "legible" society can be either sinister or benign, organized for oppression or public welfare. The point is that rationalism, as a key part of the modernist project, has deep roots in an impulse to centralize, categorize, and control. It should come as no surprise that the first burst of interest in policy analysis occurred just at the time that the United States was preparing to launch massive new social intervention programs in the 1960s and 1970s; new forms of information and "ways of seeing" had to be organized. That these were driven by a desire to improve public welfare is undeniable, but it is also important to realize that, in practice, rationalism and its offspring, policy analysis, may be closed to more complex social realities grounded in local practice and informal and complex social and economic patterns of behaviour.

This insight should remind us of the limits of policy analysis and rational technique. It may be that better policy will flow from disciplined analysis (methodologically rigorous, systematic, organized, and geared to the breaking down of complex phenomena into their simple components), but it is no guarantee. As we will note in a moment, there is also the possibility that rational technique might blind us to other, equally legitimate, ways of knowing. But at the very least, we should remember that all of the technique and discipline in the world will still run up against uncertainty. We cannot know everything, and hence our policy interventions may go wrong, fall short, or have unintended consequences. This truth was brought home to millions of people all over the world with the global financial crisis that started in 2008. By 2011, policymakers clearly did not know what to do to revive their economies—stimulus (and therefore, deficit) spending, tax cuts, tax increases, deficit reduction, propping up of ailing industries, and bailouts. Even a stimulus tool, such as lowering interest rates to close to 0 percent, had the unintended consequence of encouraging people to borrow more, which had been at the root of the problem in the first place.

The standard definition of policy analysis therefore clearly carries with it some cultural and historical baggage. Even if we substantially relax the definition to include a wider variety of ways of knowing and thinking, it is hard to escape the core assumptions that analysis will demand, at minimum, (1) expertise, (2) reliance on Western science, (3) deductive logic, (4) measurement, and (5) clear and replicable steps or stages. For the last 50 years, this model of rationality has been at the heart of what people do when conducting policy analyses. Indeed, it is far from merely a philosophical framework—it actually forms the foundation for most of the policymaking guides proclaimed by government. The federal government, for example, introduced a *Cabinet Directive on Streamlining Regulation* (Government of Canada, 2007), which came into effect on April 1, 2007. While dealing explicitly with regulatory analysis, the steps in that analysis are clearly informed by the rational model: identify issues, set objectives, plan for implementation, and measure and evaluate.

Despite its ubiquity, the rational model has been challenged and criticized for what it leaves out. So, what's wrong with being rational? It may seem a bit mechanical and plodding but is hardly sinful or dangerous. In summary, the main challenges and criticisms have been these:

The real world is "incremental," not rational. In a famous 1959 article, Charles Lindblom argued that the unforgiving strictures of rational decisionmaking were so unrealistic in terms of the cognitive and political situation faced by most decisionmakers that they made choices by "muddling through." In later work, Lindblom (1979) refined the model, both as a normative and a descriptive framework. In other words, **incrementalism** better described what really went on and, moreover, it had certain advantages over its apparently superior rival. In the real world of politics and administration, of course, there are multiple decisionmakers with conflicting perspectives and priorities, information is in short supply or contradictory, and everything has to be done immediately. In this situation, Lindblom and others argued, decisions get made on the basis of "successive limited comparisons." In this method, goals and values are not neatly separated from each other or from the process of choice. In making decisions, we often clarify what we want and what we believe only through the process of concrete choices in specific situations. As well, we usually make choices against a backdrop of what has been done before—we move in usually small increments from one situation to the next. Incrementalism seems a sorry standard in many respects, slow, halting, without clear vision or conviction, but it probably captures routine, day-to-day public policymaking in most organizations (Allison & Saint-Martin, 2011; Pal, 2011; Weiss & Woodhouse, 1992).

"Facts" lie at the heart of the rational model, but "facts" are constructed through values and theories. The rational model presumes that there are such things as "facts," but critics point out that facts are always constructed through values and perceptions, or more accurately, through deep theories that structure our cognition of reality. These theories are sometimes chosen rationally in the sense of deliberation among a range of alternatives according to multiple criteria, but "however exhaustive the arguments advanced in support of one position, considered judgments concerning the best theory will remain contentious and tentative ..." (Hawkesworth, 1988, p. 87). Frank Fischer and John Forester (1993) have termed this emphasis the "argumentative turn" in policy analysis and planning. For them, policymaking is a "struggle over the criteria of social classification, the boundaries of problem categories, the intersubjective interpretation of common experiences, the conceptual framing of problems, and the definitions of ideas that guide the ways people create the shared meanings which motivate them to act" (Fischer & Forester, 1993, p. 2). The argumentative turn entails, among other things, the critical study of the structure of argument and discourse in policy analysis (Fischer, 1980, 2003); the role of values (Fischer & Forester, 1987); and the deep impact of positivism through its associated logic of technocratic mastery (Fischer, 1990, 2009). This study has been complemented by work such as Dryzek's (1990), exploring the epistemological foundations of policy analysis. This debate is not merely methodological: for deLeon (1997), as for his colleagues in the "post-positivist" school, the issue is developing a "policy sciences of democracy" (especially Chapter 4). Achieving this usually entails greater emphasis on public engagement,

consultation, and deliberation (Hajer & Wagenaar, 2003), something that seems to hold the risk of contaminating "rational" policymaking with the uninformed prejudices of interest groups and the public. Recent research, however, suggests that "if you can assemble a diverse group of people who possess varying degrees of knowledge and insight, you're better off entrusting it with major decisions rather than leaving them in the hands of one or two people, no matter how smart those people are" (Surowiecki, 2005, p. 31). We discuss this question of the "wisdom of crowds" in greater detail in Chapter 6.

Policy analysis has relatively little influence on policymaking. The high point in the fortunes of policy analysis and scientific decision-making was in the 1960s, when the United States decided to adopt the Planning-Programming-Budgeting System (PPBS), later adopted in Canada as well, and then made program evaluation mandatory, thus setting off a boom in the industry in the 1970s (deLeon, 2006). A natural question was whether all this activity was having any effect on the policy process. Carol Weiss and her colleagues began a series of studies through the 1970s to answer this question. Their conclusion was that the "implications of explanatory studies and the recommendations from policy-oriented studies seemed to have little effect on either the day-to-day operations of program management or the long-term directions of public policy" (Weiss, 1983, p. 217). If it was clear that policy analysis did not influence the policy process directly, then what contributions did it make? One early argument was that policy analysis and the rest of the social sciences have a broad "enlightenment" function, providing broad ideas, concepts, insights, and theoretical perspectives (Janowitz, 1972). Another version of this image is the "limestone" metaphor, to capture how science enters politics: "It relies on indirect or cumulative interest and requires no action other than the research itself and the presentation of the findings in a readable way. If circumstances permit (and the research has no control over many of them) the work may, in combination with other work with a similar theme and message, seep into the public consciousness" (Thomas, 1987, p. 57).

There is much to these criticisms, and they have had powerful impacts on the way in which policy analysis is theorized and practised. However, in recent years there has been a resurgence of interest in policy and in developing strong **policy capacity**, a resurgence that has been evident both in Canada (Oliphant & Howlett, 2010) and abroad. There are several broad explanations for this (Pal, 2012). In many countries, after a long focus on management of existing resources through the 1990s to deal with deficits and financial constraint, the realization dawned that just "minding the store" was not enough. Countries faced major challenges and rapidly shifting environments, and without guides, strategy, or vision—in short, public policy—they would be rudderless.

Other countries, such as those in Central and Eastern Europe, lacked a policy tradition—orders had come down from the Communist Party in Moscow—and so they found themselves grappling with similar imperatives, but from a position that forced them to reinvent and reconsider the assumptions both of their state systems and of policy analysis (as understood in the Western state tradition). The continued turbulence of the 2008 financial crisis left the public sector, and hence, intelligent public policy, as the only bulwark against disaster.

Developing, designing, and implementing policy is a key function—an increasingly important one in a turbulent world—of government. The next section provides some examples of the international policy movement that is emerging and some of its characteristics. The deeper forces that underlie the rise of this movement will be explored in the next chapter.

The Policy Movement

To understand the recent resurgence in policy analysis one has to understand its rise and temporary decline. The social sciences, particularly economics, political science, public administration, and planning, developed in the late 19th and early 20th centuries. The idea that these disciplines could be integrated into something distinct—the policy sciences—can be conveniently dated from some key publications by American social scientist Harold Lasswell. As early as 1951, he and colleagues were arguing for a distinct approach they termed the "policy sciences of democracy" and a distinct role for policy analysts (Lasswell, 1951). In Lasswell's view, the policy sciences would integrate the other social sciences in a multidisciplinary enterprise devoted to dealing with public problems and the policy processes of democracy. It was an ambitious vision but clearly gathered momentum through the 1960s.

The terms "public policy" and "policy analysis" began to be used more frequently in the 1960s as the American government began to try to solve problems in a host of areas from racial conflict, urban renewal, transportation, and education (Parsons, 1995, pp. 20–21). Hofferbert (1990) notes that between 1960 and 1975 "national research priorities drew many American social scientists out of the ivory tower and into the political arena, not as politicians or bureaucrats but as experts in the evaluation of public programs" (p. 4). The same was true of Canada. Sutherland (1993) reports that by the mid-1970s "after several years of expansionary budgets and in a climate of general high faith in rationalism, many policy departments and some central agencies had built up good-sized cadres of professional researchers and analysts" (p. 95). Both Hofferbert and Sutherland claim that after this heyday came decline.

This was due, in part, to overweening optimism and the ultimate failure to deliver much except bad news and a preoccupation with deficits and tight spending.

By the late 1990s, the pendulum was swinging back, and "policy capacity" and "policy analysis" were once more key terms in debates over governance and appropriate public management. Why? The reasons will be developed in greater detail in Chapter 2, but generally had to do with several broad but common factors. First, the collapse of the Soviet Union in 1990–91 ended the Cold War and led to the creation of a host of new states in Central and Eastern Europe (including the Russian Federation). These events required a shift in foreign policy in the West, but also gradually created a demand for training in public administration and policy in these countries. Examples will be given below, but the problem for the newly independent countries was that they had had no tradition of distinct public administration or, indeed, of policy development. Second, many Western states in the 1990s experienced an unusual degree of political polarization. The Canadian variant was the rise of the Reform (then Canadian Alliance, and finally newly minted Conservative) party in the early 1990s and the prominence of the Ontario and Alberta Conservative parties as they pursued major program reforms. In the United States, President Bill Clinton had to deal suddenly with a Republican-dominated Congress through the mid-1990s. The rhythms varied, but many European countries saw sharper competition between right and left. The upshot was that, by the end of the decade, debates over policy—and often diametrically opposed policy approaches—were centrally important. Third, there was a growing sense that the solutions and frameworks of the 1980s would no longer suffice for the modern world (Giddens, 1999; Pal, 1999), and this concern too led to more concentrated discussion and debate about public policy issues. Fourth, and partly in response to the previous factor, the early 1990s were a decade of public sector reform in the light of new management theories, but eventually the question arose "reform for what?" Changing administrative structures and processes could not be completely divorced from substance. And finally, after a decade of criticism of the traditional state, it was clear that an effective public sector was an important ingredient in social harmony and economic progress, if not survival. As examples, health and educational services, transportation, communications, security, global epidemics, and biotechnology are all affected by, if not dependent on, state action.

If anything, the emphasis on policy capacity has continued, though for complicated and not always mutually consistent reasons. As mentioned above, a key factor has been the realization of the importance of the state and state policy for a host of social and economic activities. With the exception of American "Tea Party" activists who want a radically smaller state, lower taxes, and almost minimal government intervention, everyone else in the world recognizes that states and their governments deeply affect their lives, for good or ill, and that effect is in part a result of sound policy.

More detail will be developed in Chapter 2, but the following provides some examples from Canada and the rest of the world on the flavour of this policy movement.

CANADA

The first alarm about Canada's policy capacity was sounded by the Clerk of Privy Council, Jocelyne Bourgon, in 1995, in her Third Annual Report to the Prime Minister on the public service, where she noted, "One of the most striking features of western democratic nations in recent years has been that they have all been engaged in rethinking the role of government and the organization of their public sectors. In many nations the essence of governance is being redefined" (Privy Council Office, 1995). She identified the development of policy capacity as a key priority for the public service over the coming years (Bakvis, 2000).

Bourgon's concern about policy capacity helped propel three important initiatives under her tenure. The first was *La Relève*. After years of downsizing (55 000 public servants had left the federal public service), criticism, pay freezes and cuts, it was time to renew the federal public sector. For our purposes, what was most interesting about the initiative was the assumption of the importance of a well-functioning public sector. As Bourgon put it: "In today's global environment, the quality of the public sector will continue to make a significant difference to the performance of nations. A high quality public sector contributes to competitiveness, provides countries with a comparative advantage in their competition for trade and investment, and contributes to the quality of life and the standard of living of citizens" (Privy Council Office, 1996). The second initiative was the creation of the **Policy Research Initiative (PRI)**, which was directed specifically at enhancing policy capacity. A Policy Research Committee, involving more than 30 departments and agencies, was established in 1996. As Lindquist notes, the initiative led to "thematic conferences, workshops with researchers at universities and think tanks, a new journal, the Trends Project with the Social Sciences and Humanities Research Council, and a recruitment program for policy researchers similar to the Accelerated Economist Training Program" (Lindquist, 2006, p. 37). The PRI was embedded in the Privy Council Office, but the emphasis on policy capacity began to wane in the Martin government as it became mired in the sponsorship scandal (fraudulent spending by advertising companies in receipt of government funds). (The PRI was rebranded in 2011 as Policy Horizons Canada.) The third initiative in 1995 was the Deputy Minister Task Force on

Strengthening Our Policy Capacity, which released a report (Fellegi, 1996) with recommendations.

Minority Conservative governments were elected in 2006 and again in 2008, with the Conservatives finally gaining a majority in 2011. The government had ideas and money, but was constrained by its minority position in Parliament. However, it also had an appetite for good policy advice, especially in the face of challenges, and a public service that could provide that advice. In 2007 the new Clerk of the Privy Council (the highest nonelected public official in the federal government) signalled the importance of public sector renewal as a top priority: "[I]f the Public Service, as a core national institution, does not renew itself for future as well as current service to the government and people of Canada, it risks becoming less relevant, less useful and less respected as the years go by. If we do not commit ourselves to a continuing process of renewal, the Public Service will not remain a creative national institution, central to the governance and development of our country" (Privy Council Office, 2007, p. 2). Renewal included strengthening policy capacity to deal with long-term priorities such as "globalization, security, productivity, ageing, competitiveness and climate change" (Privy Council Office, 2008). A Prime Minister's Advisory Committee on the Public Service was created, and in its fifth annual report in 2011, it noted that, despite a spending freeze on operating budgets and an Administrative Services Review that would compel departments and agencies to produce 5 to 10 percent cuts in operating budgets by March 2012, the public service still had to "[m]aintain itself as a stable platform for strategic thinking on medium- and longer-term public policy issues" (Privy Council Office, 2011). While the government has "signature policies" such as being tough on crime and abolishing the long-gun registry, it needs ideas on a host of policy fronts: health, aging, foreign threats, the environment, technology, financial and economic crisis, to name only a few. Policy Horizons Canada highlights the need for more rapid, horizontal, and participatory policy responses in a complex and swiftly evolving world (Policy Horizons Canada, 2011). Most of the OECD and G-20 countries recognize the crucial importance of policy capacity, especially in a world facing the threats it does in 2012. Building policy capacity and supporting public sector reform and renewal have become global concerns.

INTERNATIONAL EXAMPLES

The Organisation for Economic Co-operation and Development (OECD) is an international body of now 34 member states (Chile, Slovenia, Israel, and Estonia joined in 2010) established in 1961. While its core focus is economic growth and wealth creation through trade and markets, it also works on a host of other key policy issues, such as aging, agriculture, biotechnology, education, energy, health, security, sustainable development, trade and transport, and corporate governance.

The OECD also has an interest in governance issues and public sector management (Pal, 2012), principally through its Directorate for Public Governance and Territorial Development (GOV). GOV has published several key international reports on governance. For example, a 1995 report entitled *Governance in Transition: Public Management Reform in OECD Countries* argued that member states were facing unprecedented pressures in terms of global competitiveness and new citizen demands, and would require "radical changes" in traditional governance structures and service delivery (OECD, 1995).

In 2003 and in 2005, the Directorate published policy briefs on public sector modernization that surveyed 20 years of OECD member-country attempts at reform (OECD, 2003, 2005a). As well, in 2005, it published a longer report that was an update and extension of the 1995 document (OECD, 2005b). The animating theme of all three documents was the notion of world "pressures" that have made reform inevitable and unavoidable. For example, the 2003 and 2005 briefs mentioned the word "pressure" 11 and 4 times respectively; and the longer 2005 report cited it 43 times in 205 pages of text. The principal pressures were budgetary (excessive spending) and high citizen demands. In this the OECD proved prescient, since the global financial crisis in 2008, while ignited by failures in financial markets and regulation, led, by 2012, to riots in many European capitals as governments tried to simultaneously impose draconian budget cuts and stimulate their economies.

Through reports like these and perhaps even more so, through a series of meetings each year among thousands of government officials (and not just from member states, but from another 100 countries) as well as nongovernmental organizations, the OECD facilitates a global conversation among governments about public management best practices (e.g., in e-government, integrity, anti-corruption, and budgetary transparency) and public sector reform. And it does so from a position that acknowledges the importance of government and of good governance:

> The crisis has shaken many assumptions and some hard lessons have been learned about the limits of markets. It has also called for revisiting the role of government, redefining the balance between state and market and searching for new ways to boost citizens' trust in both. We have a window of opportunity here to rethink and reform the public sector. Governments loom large in national economies.... The crisis demonstrated, on the one hand, that public policies are the critical anchor of national economies in time of crisis. Decisive and co-ordinated action by governments halted financial market freefall and avoided economic

catastrophe. On the other hand, the ensuing fiscal pressures in many countries have increased the need to cut public expenditures, which in most cases means streamlining the state. This effort to re-structure the state calls for reassessing where and how government should intervene and where it can step back. In short it is not about more or less government, it is about better and more effective governance, about sound institutions and efficient rules and procedures.... (OECD, 2011a)

In addition to these sweeping overviews and broad recommendations on modernizing government, the OECD works on several more specific fronts. One is its SIGMA program (Support for Improvement in Governance and Management in Central and Eastern European Countries), which is a joint effort by the OECD and the European Union (EU) launched in 1992. It works with EU candidate countries (Croatia; the former Yugoslav Republic of Macedonia; Montenegro; and Turkey), potential candidates (Albania, Bosnia and Herzegovina, Serbia, and Kosovo under United Nations Security Council Resolution 1244/99), and countries under the European Neighbourhood Policy (Armenia, Azerbaijan, Egypt, Georgia, Jordan, Lebanon, Moldova, Morocco, Tunisia, and Ukraine). SIGMA's focus is strengthening policymaking capacities and effective public administration that meets EU standards.

Another recent OECD tool is *Government at a Glance*. The second edition appeared in 2011, noting, "In these stormy times, reforming the public sector is a policy priority and should be conducted on the basis of evidence and comparative analysis" (OECD, 2011b). It provides comparative data on public employment, human resource management, transparency, public procurement, and other aspects of public management. This publication is part of an explosion in the last decade of various types of governance indicators (Arndt & Oman, 2006; Buduru & Pal, 2010; Levy, 2007), driven by a conviction among international donors that good governance is crucial to development, and having objective data on governance processes in recipient countries is important for investments in aid.

The World Bank is another influential international organization that has turned its attention to governance and policy capacity in recent years. Founded in 1944, in 2010 the bank channelled $44 billion in loans and other financial instruments to 43 countries (it has a membership of 187 countries). In its 1997 annual report, entitled *The State in a Changing World*, the Bank highlighted the importance of good governance to sustainable economic development:

For human welfare to be advanced, the state's capability— *defined as the ability to undertake and promote collective actions efficiently*—must be increased. This basic message translates into a two-part strategy to make every state a more credible, effective partner in its country's development:

Matching the state's role to its capability is the first element in this strategy. Where state capability is weak, how the state intervenes—and where—should be carefully assessed. Many states try to do too much with few resources and little capability, and often do more harm than good. A sharper focus on the fundamentals would improve effectiveness. But here it is a matter not just of choosing what to do and what not to do—but of how to do it as well.

But capability is not destiny. Therefore the second element of the strategy is to *raise state capability by reinvigorating public institutions*. This means designing effective rules and restraints, to check arbitrary state actions and combat entrenched corruption. (World Bank, 1997) [emphasis in original]

This report was followed in 2000 by a World Bank strategic document entitled *Reforming Public Institutions and Strengthening Governance* (World Bank, 2000). In its most recent reports, the Bank has emphasized empowerment and participation of the poor in the development process, and this has led it to highlight well-functioning public institutions as a key crucible of that participation. By one estimate, World Bank lending for economic reforms fell by 14 percent annually in 2000–2004, but lending on improved governance rose to the point that in 2004, 25 percent of World Bank lending was targeted on law and public administration (Arndt & Oman, 2006, p. 17).

Not only intergovernmental organizations participate in this worldwide movement to develop policy capacity and good governance. There are numerous foundations supporting a host of initiatives to develop democracy and policy capacity, the Eurasia Foundation and the Open Society Foundations among them. The latter, which was established and continues to be funded by billionaire George Soros, has a wide variety of initiatives and institutions around human rights, social justice, local government, media, human migration, education, and governance. Among the governance initiatives are the Local Government and Public Service Reform Initiative (http://lgi.osi.hu/) that focuses on policy capacity development in Central and Eastern Europe, but is now active in Asia and Latin America (the Initiative was ended in 2011). Another initiative is the Central Eurasia Project (http://www.soros.org/about/programs/central-eurasia-project) that "aims to promote social progress and human rights in the South Caucasus, Central Asia, and Mongolia by developing programs and international campaigns that use policy research and advocacy to shape debates on significant economic, political, social and security challenges facing the region." In addition to foundations dedicated to policy development and governance, there is a panoply of nongovernmental organizations, such as Transparency International, Freedom House, and Global Integrity, as well as professional associations, such as the Commonwealth Association for Public Administration and Management.

Canadian and international organizations such as these demonstrate the enormous energy that has gone into public sector reform in the last decades and the prime importance of developing policy capacity as part of the reform agenda. The pace has varied in different countries, as have the circumstances (particularly in Central and Eastern Europe), and even the concepts—sometimes policy is used, sometimes strategy, sometimes horizontal coordination. At the heart of all this international activity, however, is the simple insight that a society's quality of life depends in large measure on the quality of its government, and that the quality of governmental responses to problems depends in large measure on its capacity to think through those problems and develop appropriate and effective solutions. Public policymaking is no more, and no less, than that.

Conclusion

This chapter defined public policy and policy analysis, along with some key associated concepts, and showed how the discipline and practice of policy analysis in its modern guise goes back to the immediate post–World War II era. At the same time, in the second section of the chapter, we showed how after a period of decline, policy and the development of policy capacity through good governance have been enjoying a resurgence, not only in Canada but also throughout the world. We provided some reasons for this shift earlier, but it is important to recall that the interest in policy has been part of a larger effort at **public sector reform**. If reform has been the name of the game, can we expect that the type of policy analysis and the type of policy capacity that is being demanded will be the same as that of the 1960s and 1970s? Will old tools be adequate when the edifice is being drastically renovated?

This book's answer is no. Many of the tools remain useful, as do the concepts, but they are being revised and changed to come to terms with a situation where the role and nature of government is very different from what it was a generation ago, indeed, even very different from what it was only five years ago. Policymaking and policy analysis have to adapt to at least three fundamental shifts that have occurred in the last decade.

First, the nature of some perennial policy problems has changed, and they have been joined by some entirely new issues. The challenge of stimulating economic growth has always been with us, but what to do now in the face of a global economy teetering on the edge, and the U.S. economy (Canada's major export market) on life-support? New problems crowd in on the agenda almost endlessly: climate change, energy depletion, healthcare system collapse, the impact of social media on education.

Second, many key policy processes have changed. It is almost universally acknowledged that citizens today want a more direct say in both policy development and program implementation. The Internet gives people, nongovernmental organizations, and the private sector unprecedented and instant access to materials and information that previously would have been primarily in government hands. Government departments themselves are different from what they were before—they are generally smaller, more knowledge based, and focused more on evaluation of results and outcomes. Government responsibilities have been shuffled as well: in most provinces, notably Ontario and Quebec, major provincial responsibilities have been shifted to municipalities and vice versa. Today, policy analysis for a major urban centre in Canada is likely to include issues that previously would have been provincial or even federal responsibilities. And almost all "domestic" policy now has some sort of international dimension, from advocacy groups protesting energy development to the constraints of international standards.

Third, there has been a subtle but important change in the way governments view their relationship with the private sector and civil society. Whereas a generation ago it might have seemed normal for the state to dominate both these sectors, today there is a sense that government actions should, in most instances, complement markets and collaboratively work with civil society. Until the financial crisis of fall 2008, there was an emerging consensus that in most policy areas, a light touch was better than heavy-handed intervention. The collapse of major private sector companies around the world forced governments to spend billions on bailouts and rescue packages, and opened a new debate about the appropriate role of government in shoring up capitalism. Activist and muscular government intervention may once more be on the public agenda, especially with regard to imposing austerity to please global financial markets, as well as coordinated efforts to regulate the international financial system.

At its best, policy analysis provides guidance to governments as they try to address public problems. In practice, of course, governments are political creatures interested in re-election and in power, and so they may eschew "guidance" in favour of more politically motivated behaviour. But from a citizen's perspective, governments are democratically elected to address public problems and provide core public services in the public interest, not in their own interest. The definition of the public interest will be contested, of course, but it is this formula that provides the foundation for policy analysis and civic dialogue around policy issues. Policy analysis can then pose its core questions: What is the nature of the problem? What are we trying to achieve? How shall we go about addressing it? And how will we know whether we have been successful? These questions have always been the key ones, but this book argues that the context in which they are asked—both in Canada and around the world—has changed dramatically in recent years. To these changes we now turn.

KEY TERMS

bounded rationality—a term invented by Herbert Simon to capture the idea that most human decisionmaking takes place under various constraints rather than ideal conditions of complete information and unlimited processing capacities

emergent strategies—consistent patterns of behaviour that emerge or form rather than being planned

empirical analysis—takes logical analysis one step further: not what might be the likely effect of policy X, but what was its actual effect?

gender-based analysis (GBA)—a process that assesses the differential impact of public policies, programs, and legislation (proposed or existing) on women and men in terms of their social and economic circumstances, as well as their relationships in key social institutions such as the family

gender mainstreaming—an organizational strategy to ensure that a gender perspective is reflected in all types of organizational activities; championed by the United Nations as a means for achieving gender equality internationally

general goals—policy goals that enjoy a majority consensus or that express the broadest objectives of the policy initiative as a whole

governance—the process of governing or steering complex systems in cooperation with a variety of other actors

horizontal consistency—consistency across policy fields, not just within them

incrementalism—decisionmaking that proceeds by small, successive comparisons rather than grand designs, and moves forward in small steps or "increments"

internal consistency—consistency among the three elements of problem definition, goals, and instruments

La Relève—the initiative started by the Clerk of Privy Council, Jocelyne Bourgon, during the mid-1990s to address the "quiet crisis" in the federal public service and rebuild motivation and pride

legal analysis—looks at public policy through the prism of law: constitutionality, consistency with statute, and the practices of legal convention

logical analysis—deals with questions of consistency and coherence: Is the policy internally consistent? Is it vertically consistent? Is it horizontally consistent?

normative analysis—measures some aspect of policy against an ethical standard: secular morality, the Bible, the Koran, the Canadian Charter of Rights and Freedoms, or the UN Universal Declaration of Human Rights

policy analysis—the disciplined application of intellect to public problems

policy capacity—the institutional ability to conduct policy analysis and implement its results effectively and efficiently

policy consistency—agreement between the different elements of public policy, embracing horizontal, vertical, and internal consistency

policy development—the process of shaping policy initiatives, from problem recognition to implementation and evaluation

policy framework—a guide to a range of related actions and decisions in a given field

policy goals—the objectives to be achieved by a given public policy

policy instruments—means chosen on how to address the problem and achieve the policy goals

Policy Research Initiative—an initiative directed at developing a sustained demand for policy among a community of collaborating federal departments and the wider research community focused on long-term, research-based, and reflective issues

policy space—the wider field within which a given, single policy operates in relation to others that tackle different elements of the problem

policy-specific goals—goals related to the broader ones but more directly connected to the programs that give the policy effect

policy statement—defines the problem, sets the goals that are to be achieved, and indicates the instruments or means whereby the problem is to be addressed and the goals achieved

policy studies—the broad range of research literature that is relevant to the study of and reflection upon public policy

problem definition—indicates what the problem or issue is and some of the causal factors behind it

public policy—a course of action or inaction chosen by public authorities to address a given problem or interrelated set of problems

public sector reform—attempts to change management practices and institutional design in the public sector to enhance efficiency and effectiveness

rational model—a systematic approach to problem solving that lays out the problem, reviews options, and makes recommendations based on the intersection between goals and factual circumstances

rationalism—the characteristic form of knowing in the West that emphasizes empirical knowledge, science, objectivity, and systematic analysis

satisficing—the objective in most human decisionmaking to find a workable rather than a perfect solution to problems

vertical consistency—consistency between the broad policy framework and the specific programs that implement that framework

FURTHER READINGS

Anderson, J. E. (2006). *Public policymaking: An introduction*. Boston, MA: Houghton Mifflin.

Bardach, E. (2000). *A practical guide for policy analysis: The eightfold path to more effective problem solving*. New York, NY: Chatham House.

Bevir, M. (Ed.). (2011). *The Sage handbook of governance*. Los Angeles, CA: Sage.

Clemons, R. S., & McBeth, M. K. (2001). *Public policy praxis: Theory and pragmatism: A case approach*. Upper Saddle River, NJ: Prentice-Hall.

Dobuzinskis, L., Howlett, M., & Laycock, D. (Eds.). (2007). *Policy analysis in Canada: The state of the art*. Toronto, ON: University of Toronto Press.

Dunn, W. N. (2008). *Public policy analysis: An introduction* (4th ed.). Upper Saddle River, NJ: Prentice-Hall.

Howlett, M., Ramesh, M., & Perl. A. (2009). *Studying public policy: Policy cycles and policy subsystems* (3rd ed.). Don Mills, ON: Oxford University Press.

Moran, M., Rein, M., & Goodin, R. E. (Eds.). (2006). *The Oxford handbook of public policy*. Oxford: Oxford University Press.

Orsini, M., & Smith, M. (Eds.). (2007). *Critical policy studies*. Vancouver, BC: UBC Press.

Parsons, W. (1995). *Public policy: An introduction to the theory and practice of policy analysis*. Aldershot, UK: Edward Elgar.

Radin, B. (2000). *Beyond Machiavelli: Policy analysis comes of age*. Washington, DC: Georgetown University Press.

Weimer, D. L., & Vining, A. R. (2011). *Policy analysis* (5th ed.). Boston, MA: Longman.

REFERENCES

Aboriginal Affairs and Northern Development Canada. (2010). *Working guide on gender-based analysis.* Retrieved from http://www.ainc-inac .gc.ca/eng/1100100028541

Allison, C. R., & Saint-Martin, D. (2011, February). Half a century of "muddling": Are we there yet? *Policy and Society, 30,* 1–8.

Anderson, J. E. (2006). *Public policymaking: An introduction.* Boston, MA: Houghton Mifflin.

Arndt, C., & Oman, C. (2006). *Uses and abuses of governance indicators.* Paris: OECD, Development Centre Studies.

Bakker, I. (2006). *Gender budget initiatives: Why they matter in Canada* (Alternative Federal Budget 2006, Technical Paper 1). Ottawa, ON: Canadian Centre for Policy Alternatives.

Bakvis, H. (2000, January). Country report: Rebuilding policy capacity in the era of the fiscal dividend: A report from Canada. *Governance, 13,* 71–103.

Bird, M., & Stoney, C. (2006). Government approaches to the regulation of sin. In G. B. Doern (Ed.), *How Ottawa spends, 2006–2007* (pp. 247–265). Montréal, PQ: McGill-Queen's University Press.

Birkland, T. (2005). *An introduction to the policy sciences: Theories, concepts, and models of public policy making* (2nd ed.). Armonk, NY: M.E. Sharpe.

Bourgon, J. (2010, June). The history and future of nation-building? Building capacity for public results. *International Review of Administrative Sciences, 76,* 197–218.

Buduru, B., & Pal, L. A. (2010, November). The globalized state: Measuring and monitoring governance. *European Journal of Cultural Studies, 13,* 511–530.

Canadian Institute for Health Information. (2011, March). Wait times in Canada: A comparison by province, 2011. Retrieved from http://www.cihi.ca/CIHI-ext-portal/internet/EN/SubTheme/health +system+performance/access+and+wait+times/cihi010647

Cochran, C. L., & Malone, E. F. (2005). *Public policy: Perspectives and choices* (3rd ed.). Boulder, CO: Lynne Rienner.

Chase, S. (2011, September 21). Sweeping Conservative crime bill "only the beginning." [Toronto] *Globe and Mail.* Retrieved from http:// www.theglobeandmail.com/news/politics/sweeping-conservative-crime- bill-only-the-beginning/article595730/

Colebatch, H. K. (1998). *Policy.* Minneapolis, MN: University of Minnesota Press.

deLeon, P. (1988). *Advice and consent: The development of the policy sciences*. New York, NY: Russell Sage.

deLeon, P. (1997). *Democracy and the policy sciences*. Albany, NY: State University of New York.

deLeon, P. (2006). The historical roots of the field. In M. Moran, M. Rein, & R. E. Goodin (Eds.), *The Oxford handbook of public policy* (pp. 39–57). Oxford: Oxford University Press.

Dobuzinskis, L., Howlett, & M., Laycock, D. (Eds.). (2007). *Policy analysis in Canada: The state of the art*. Toronto, ON: University of Toronto Press.

Dryzek, J. S. (1990). *Discursive democracy: Politics, policy and political science*. Cambridge, MA: Cambridge University Press.

Dunn, W. N. (2008). *Public policy analysis: An introduction* (4th ed.). Upper Saddle River, NJ: Prentice-Hall.

Dye, T. R. (2010). *Understanding public policy* (13th ed.). New York, NY: Longman.

Fellegi, I. P. (1996). *Strengthening our policy capacity: Report of the task force on strengthening the policy capacity of the federal government*. Ottawa: Queen's Printer. Retrieved from http://www.csps-efpc.gc.ca/pbp/pub/pdfs/actionb_e.pdf

Fischer, F. (1980). *Politics, values, and public policy: The problem of methodology*. Boulder, CO: Westview.

Fischer, F. (1990). *Technocracy and the politics of expertise*. Newbury Park, CA: Sage.

Fischer, F. (1993, September). Citizen participation and the democratization of policy expertise: From theoretical inquiry to practical cases. *Policy Sciences, 26*, 165–187.

Fischer, F. (2003). *Reframing public policy: Discursive politics and deliberative practices*. New York, NY: Oxford University Press.

Fischer, F. (2009). *Democracy and expertise: Reorienting policy inquiry*. Oxford: Oxford University Press.

Fischer, F., & Forester, J. (Eds.). (1987). *Confronting values in policy analysis: The politics of criteria*. Newbury Park, CA: Sage.

Fischer, F., & Forester, J. (Eds.). (1993). *The argumentative turn in policy analysis and planning*. Durham, NC: Duke University Press.

Giddens, A. (1999). *The third way: The renewal of social democracy*. Malden, MA: Polity Press.

Government of Canada. (2007). *Cabinet directive on streamlining regulation*. Ottawa. Retrieved from http://www.tbs-sct.gc.ca/ri-qr/directive/directive-eng.pdf

Graham, G. (1988). "The policy orientation" and the theoretical development of political science. In E. Portis & M. Levy (Eds.), *Handbook of political theory and policy science* (pp. 150–161). New York, NY: Greenwood Press.

Hajer, M. A., & Wagenaar, H. (Eds.). (2003). *Deliberative policy analysis: Understanding governance in the network society* (Theories of Institutional Design). Cambridge: Cambridge University Press.

Hawkesworth, M. E. (1988). *Theoretical issues in policy analysis.* New York, NY: State University of New York.

Hofferbert, R. I. (1990). *The reach and grasp of policy analysis: Comparative views of the craft.* Tuscaloosa: The University of Alabama Press.

Hoppe, R., & Jeliazkova, M. (2006). How policy workers define their job: A Netherlands case study. In H. Colebatch (Ed.), *The work of policy: An international survey* (pp. 35–60). Boulder, CO: Lexington Books.

Hoppe, R. (2010). *The governance of problems: Puzzling, powering and participation.* Bristol, UK: The Policy Press.

Howlett, M., Ramesh, M., & Perl, A. (2009). *Studying public policy: Policy cycles and policy subsystems* (3rd ed.). Don Mills, ON: Oxford University Press.

Janowitz, M. (1972, July). Professionalization of sociology. *American Journal of Sociology, 78,* 105–135.

Kingdon, J. W. (1995). *Agendas, alternatives, and public policies* (2nd ed.). New York, NY: HarperCollins.

Kirschen, E. S., et al. (1964). *Economic policy in our time.* (3 vols.). Amsterdam, Netherlands: North-Holland.

Kraft, M. E., & Furlong, S. R. (2007). *Public policy: Politics, analysis, and alternatives.* Washington, DC: CQ Press.

Lasswell, H. (1951). The policy orientation. In D. Lerner & H. Lasswell (Eds.), *The policy sciences* (pp. 3–15). Stanford, CA: Stanford University Press.

Lasswell, H. (1970, March). The emerging conception of the policy sciences. *Policy Sciences, 1,* 3–13.

Levy, B. (2007). *Governance reform: Bridging monitoring and action.* Washington, DC: The World Bank.

Lindblom, C. (1979, November–December). Still muddling, not yet through. *Public Administration Review, 39,* 517–526.

Lindblom, C. E. (1959, Spring). The science of muddling through. *Public Administration Review, 19,* 79–88.

Linder, S., & Peters, B. G. (1989, January–March). Instruments of government: Perceptions and contexts. *Journal of Public Policy, 9*, 35–58.

Lindquist, E. (2006). *A critical moment: Capturing and conveying the evolution of the Canadian public service.* Ottawa, ON: Canada School of Public Service.

MacNair, M. D. (2006, February). In the name of the public good: "Public interest" as a legal standard. *Canadian Criminal Law Review, 10*, 175–204.

McCool, D. C. (Ed.). (1995). *Public policy theories, models, and concepts: An anthology.* Englewood Cliffs, NJ: Prentice-Hall.

Mantel, H. (2010). *Wolf Hall.* Toronto, ON: HarperCollins Canada.

Mintzberg, H. (1994). *The rise and fall of strategic planning: Reconceiving roles for planning, plans, planners.* New York, NY: The Free Press.

Mintzberg, H., & Jørgensen, J. (1987, Summer). Emergent strategy for public policy. *Canadian Public Administration, 30*, 214–229.

OECD [Organisation for Economic Co-operation and Development]. (1995). *Governance in transition: Public management reform in OECD countries.* Paris: OECD.

OECD. (2003). *Public sector modernisation.* Paris: OECD.

OECD. (2005a). *Public sector modernisation.* Policy Brief. Paris: OECD.

OECD. (2005b). *Modernising government: The way forward.* Paris: OECD.

OECD. (2011a). *Secretary-General's report to ministers 2011.* Paris: OECD. Retrieved from http://www.oecd.org/dataoecd/56/6/48066007.pdf

OECD. (2011b). *Government at a glance.* Paris: OECD.

Oliphant, S., & Howlett, M. (2010, August). Assessing policy analytical capacity: Comparative insights from a study of the Canadian environmental policy advice system. *Journal of Comparative Policy Analysis: Research and Practice, 12*, 439–445.

Pal, L. A. (Ed.). (1999). *How Ottawa spends: 1999–2000: Shape shifting: Canadian governance toward the 21st century.* Toronto, ON: Oxford University Press.

Pal, L. A., & Maxwell, J. (2004). *Assessing the public interest in the 21st century: A framework.* Ottawa, ON: Canada Policy Research Networks.

Pal, L. A. (2011, February). Assessing incrementalism: Formative assumptions, contemporary realities. *Policy and Society, 30*, 29–39.

Pal, L. A. (2012). *Frontiers of governance: The OECD and global public management reform.* New York, NY: Palgrave Macmillan.

Parsons, W. (1995). *Public policy: An introduction to the theory and practice of policy analysis*. Aldershot, UK: Edward Elgar.

Policy Horizons Canada. (2011). *About us*. Retrieved from http://www .horizons.gc.ca/page.asp?pagenm=pri_index

Privy Council Office (Canada). (1995). *Third annual report to the Prime Minister on the public service of Canada*. Retrieved from http://www.pco-bcp.gc.ca/index.asp?lang=eng&page=clerk-greffier &sub=AnnualReports

Privy Council Office (Canada). (1996). *Fourth annual report to the Prime Minister on the public service of Canada*. Retrieved from http://www .clerk.gc.ca/eng/feature.asp?mode=preview&pageId=140

Privy Council Office (Canada). (2007). *Fourteenth annual report to the Prime Minister on the public service of Canada*. Retrieved from http://www.clerk. gc.ca/local_grfx/docs/reports/14th_annual_report-eng.pdf

Privy Council Office (Canada). (2011). *Fifth report of the Prime Minister's Advisory Committee on the public service: A public service for challenging times*. Retrieved from http://www.clerk.gc.ca/eng/feature. asp?featureid=19&pageid=272

Quirk, B. (2011). *Re-imagining government: Public leadership and management in challenging times*. New York, NY: Palgrave Macmillan.

Radin, B. (2000). *Beyond Machiavelli: Policy analysis comes of age*. Washington, DC: Georgetown University Press.

Rochefort, D. A., & Cobb, R. W. (1994). Problem definition: An emerging perspective. In D. A. Rochefort & R. W. Cobb (Eds.), *The politics of problem definition: Shaping the policy agenda* (pp. 1–31). Lawrence, KS: University of Kansas Press.

Sanderson, I. (2009, December). Intelligent policy making for a complex world: Pragmatism, evidence and learning. *Political Studies, 57,* 699–719.

Scott, J. C. (1998). *Seeing like a state: How certain schemes to improve the human condition have failed*. New Haven, CT: Yale University Press.

Simon, H., Smithburg, D. W., & Thompson, V. A. (1958). *Public administration*. New York, NY: Alfred A. Knopf.

Stewart, J. (2009). *Public policy values*. New York, NY: Palgrave Macmillan.

Stone, D. (2001). *Policy paradox: The art of political decision making* (Rev. ed.). New York, NY: W. W. Norton and Co.

Surowiecki, J. (2005). *The wisdom of crowds*. New York, NY: Anchor Books.

Sutherland, S. L. (1993). The public service and policy development. In M. M. Atkinson (Ed.), *Governing Canada: Institutions and public policy* (pp. 81–113). Toronto, ON: Harcourt Brace Jovanovich.

Task Force on Public Service Values and Ethics. (2000). *A Strong Foundation: Report of the Task Force on Public Service Values and Ethics* (Tait Report). Ottawa, ON: Canadian Centre for Management Development.

Thomas, P. (1987). The use of social research: Myths and models. In M. Bulmer (Ed.), *Social science research and government: Comparative essays on Britain and the United States* (pp. 51–60). Cambridge, UK: Cambridge University Press.

Treasury Board of Canada Secretariat. (2003). *Values and ethics code for the public service.* Retrieved from http://www.tbs-sct.gc.ca/pubs_pol/hrpubs/TB_851/vec-cve-eng.pdf

United Nations, Entity for Gender Equality and the Empowerment of Women. (2011). *Gender mainstreaming.* Retrieved from http://www.un.org/womenwatch/osagi/gendermainstreaming.htm

United Nations Framework Convention on Climate Change. (2010, March 30). *Copenhagen Accord.* Retrieved from http://unfccc.int/resource/docs/2009/cop15/eng/11a01.pdf

Weiss, A., & Woodhouse, E. (1992, August). Reframing incrementalism: A constructive response to critics. *Policy Sciences, 25,* 255–273.

Weiss, C. H. (1983). Ideology, interest, and information: The basis of policy positions. In D. Callahan & B. Jennings (Eds.), *Ethics, the social sciences, and policy analysis* (pp. 213–245). New York, NY: Plenum Press.

Wildavsky, A. (1979). *Speaking truth to power: The art and craft of policy analysis.* Boston, MA: Little, Brown & Co.

World Bank. (1997). *World development report 1997: The state in a changing world (summary).* Washington, DC: The International Bank for Reconstruction and Development/The World Bank.

World Bank. (2000). *Reforming public institutions and strengthening governance.* Washington, DC: The International Bank for Reconstruction and Development/The World Bank.

CHAPTER

Modern Governance:
The Challenges for Policy Analysis

Policy analysis, in the service of the public interest, makes its contributions by asking certain questions and using certain tools. It cannot make those contributions in a vacuum, however, and the nature of policy work depends on context. As the last chapter suggested, that context has been changing in the last decades. This chapter reviews the key forces underpinning this change: globalization and the financial crisis, political culture, and governance. They are closely entangled, and sometimes conflicting, but with broad consequences that make a substantial difference to the nature of policymaking and analysis. Globalization involves deeper and more intense economic and political interdependencies and challenges fundamental assumptions about sovereignty and the role of the nation-state. In Canada as well as other industrialized countries, political culture is less deferential and more individualist and participatory. Changing notions of governance reflect these forces but also have their own dynamic that stresses new forms of governance and public management. Subsequent chapters take up the detailed implications of these forces for problem definition, policy design, implementation, agenda-setting, evaluation, policymaking in turbulent times, and policy communication.

In Chapter 1, public policy was defined as a course of action or inaction undertaken by public authorities to address a problem or interrelated set of problems. Policy analysis was defined as the disciplined application of intellect to public problems. If the nature of public problems changes, and if the broad context within which problems arise and are addressed is altered, then both public policy and policy analysis should change as well. This kind of change is precisely what has been happening in the past decades in industrialized countries, and a revitalized policy analysis has to come to terms with what is different about modern governance. It is a cliché, of course, that our times (like all times!) are marked by change. But it is in the nature of clichés to expose important truths, and no truth is more obvious than that we are surrounded and affected by changes of unparalleled magnitude and scope. On a global level, recent years have seen the collapse of the Soviet empire and of apartheid in South Africa, the rise of new security threats and global terrorism, the implosion of the American economy and that country's role on the world stage, the rise of China and India as global military and economic players, European Union turbulence and threats to the Euro, Internet viruses that spread around the world in minutes, the rising threat of pandemics such as SARS, devastating crises in our food supply such as mad cow disease and avian flu, wars in Iraq and Afghanistan.

These changes are massive and unrelenting, but the trick is to try to make some sense of the broad pattern and to tease out the implications for policy analysis and governance. This chapter argues that there are three powerful undercurrents beneath the waves of political turmoil and **policy reversal** evident in Canada and throughout the industrialized world. They are globalization, shifts in **political culture**, and evolving ideas about governance and **public management**. Each of these is multi-faceted, of course, and connected intimately to the others. Nonetheless, it is possible to outline at least a few of their most important features. They have been building for more than 25 years and, in some respects, are so much a part of our political, economic, and social environment that we take them for granted. A policy analysis that fails to come to grips with these forces and their implications for policy and governance is doomed to irrelevance.

Globalization

ECONOMIC GLOBALIZATION

The modern phenomenon of globalization has to be carefully distinguished from the mere fact of international connectedness. The British empire was global in scope, and other imperial systems like the Romans' covered enormous tracts of territory. The Moors extended their empire as far as Spain, and the Portuguese, in turn, established outposts as far away as Goa, India. Marco Polo travelled from the Mediterranean to China in the late 1200s. The city states of medieval Europe had extensive trade connections of their own to the Orient, and vast, complex, and virtually global systems of trade developed by the 1700s around raw materials, sugar, spices, and slaves (Brook, 2007). In short, human history in the last 1000 years has been clearly marked by internationalism that sometimes came close to embracing the entire planet. What is different about the present situation?

American journalist Thomas L. Friedman (1999, 2007) is one of the most popular exponents of what we can call the "extreme globalization" camp—the view that, since the Cold War, an inexorable **globalization system** has arisen. Globalization has several important features. It is not a static system but a dynamic process of the inexorable integration of markets and nation-states. Its driving idea is **free market capitalism**—the more countries integrate with the world economy and allow global economic forces to penetrate domestic economies, the more they will prosper. It has its own dominant culture—largely American or Western—and so tends to be homogenizing at a certain level (and thus generates reactions against that homogenization). It has its own defining technologies organized around computerization, digitization, satellites, the Internet, mobile communications, and global transportation systems. It has its own international balance of power—between nation-states (the traditional geopolitical balance, but wherein the United States is still the only global superpower, though increasingly challenged by China and Russia); between nation-states and markets (global investment markets driven by the "Electronic Herd"); and between individuals and nation-states (the ability of individuals to act directly on the world stage). Friedman argues that a "globalization 3.0" has emerged around new, converging digital technologies and global supply chains that both empowers individuals and shatters borders and boundaries. Companies from anywhere can compete everywhere, creating a "flat world." Friedman has been criticized for overstating how flat the world really is (in fact, it remains "spiky" with major differences among countries and economies), and while he is guilty of exaggeration and vivid imagery, the forces that he describes are undeniable. Globalization may not be inexorable—aspects of it can be and are being reversed or stalled—but it has a powerful set of dynamic drivers that make the world different today from what it was 20 years ago.

In understanding globalization, it is important also to understand what it is not. Scholte (2003) identifies what he calls four cul-de-sacs in conceptualizing globalization: globalization-as-internationalization ("the growth of transactions and interdependence between countries"); globalization-as-liberalization ("a process of removing officially imposed restrictions on movements of resources between countries in order to form an 'open' and 'borderless' world economy"); globalization-as-universalization ("a process of dispersing various objects and experiences to people at all inhabited parts of the earth"); and globalization-as-westernization ("social structures of modernity [e.g., capitalism, industrialism, rationalism, urbanism] are spread the world over, destroying pre-existent cultures and local self-determination in the process"). Scholte sensibly argues that understanding globalization in these terms is redundant—the phenomena of internationalization, liberalization, universalization, and westernization have existed much longer than contemporary globalization, and simply redefining these phenomena as globalization does not add anything to our understanding. "Arguments that only build on these conceptions fail to open insights that are not available through pre-existent vocabulary. Deployed on any of these four lines, 'globalization' provides no distinct analytical value-added" (Scholte, 2005, p. 54). Contemporary globalization, for Scholte, is characterized by **globality,** or the sense that the entire planet is a single social space, that people carry on conversations and movements within that space irrespective of territoriality, that they pay collective attention to "global events"—that there is a quality of simultaneity. Information and communications technologies, as well as modern transport (air travel and containers), are a crucial foundation for globality. Transportation systems make global supply chains possible, while digital communications means that billions of people on the planet can simultaneously listen to the same song or watch reports on a natural disaster.

At the same time, globality in the sense of a single space and time continuum that we all occupy collectively is complemented and complicated by disjunctures in the flows and networks that surround us. Appadurai (1996, 2001), for example, proposes that we explore contemporary globalization in terms of five "scapes": ethnoscapes (the movements of people as tourists, migrants, refugees, exiles), technoscapes (Internet and transportation technologies), financescapes (unpredictable financial flows), mediascapes (global media in all its forms, TV, videos, movies, audio), and ideoscapes (global flows of ideas and ideologies that are generated locally but then spread globally). For Appadurai, the key to understanding contemporary globalization is the increasing disjuncture among these scapes, the hybridity and plurality of personal experience. The disjuncture among these scapes is created through the absence of any coordinating entity or body—the logic of each scape is coupled only loosely to the others. Take the example of an Inuit teenager living in Iqaluit. She listens to Jamaican reggae on her made-in-China iPod while reading Jane Austen, and eats Florida oranges for breakfast as the snows swirl outside her home. Globality is the sense that these scapes—despite their heterogeneity—merge seamlessly and simultaneously, in an almost ordinary way.

We return to globality later in this section. For many, contemporary globalization is not about scapes and culture, but primarily about major economic transformations in the last 50 years. First, of course, has been the development of a complex international trading system. After World War II, a host of international institutions and conventions were established to create the beginnings of a true international economic system:

the General Agreement on Tariffs and Trade (GATT—now superseded by the World Trade Organization, or the WTO), the International Monetary Fund (IMF), the World Bank, and the Bretton Woods Agreement on currency transactions. The logic behind these initiatives was twofold: first, to create a set of supranational decision-making bodies that would create stable and harmonized international regimes dealing with a host of issues from trade to communications; second, to knock down those major barriers between countries that impeded or prevented interactions or communication. The postwar efforts were largely successful on both counts. Figure 2.1 shows the increased volume in global trade from 1950 to 2009. The key point is that, despite dips, the long-term trend for world trade has been steadily upward. In 2001, due in large part to the terrorist attacks on the World Trade Center, international trade declined and only began to improve after 2002. The 2008 global recession marked another substantial, and persistent, dip. However, the trend line seems clear: as borders become more porous, goods, services, and information can travel more freely across political lines. As well, in an often-ignored development, people move as well, and human migration is a major component of contemporary globalization (International Organization for Migration, 2010; Sassen, 1998). This migration is not simply one-way, but circular. People move from home countries to new ones for economic opportunities, but then back again, and back and forth. People have roots, but—at least for those with education and skills—they can increasingly be global nomads. It is clear that the world economy is subject to

Figure 2.1 World Merchandise Trade Volume by Major Product Group, 1950–2009 (Volume Indices, 1950 = 100)

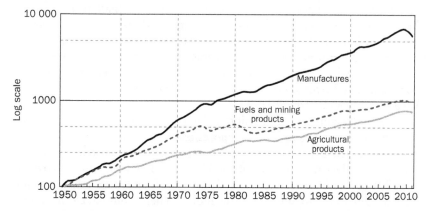

Source: International Trade Statistics 2010. © 2010 World Trade Organization. Reprinted with permission. www.wto.org.

turbulence as well, and there are reversals as well as advances in international economic integration. In 2008, the U.S. economy entered a stubborn recession due, among other things, to the housing credit collapse, and that recession, along with the European sovereign debt crisis, continues to threaten recovery in the global economy. However, in a sense the crisis illustrates the advance in economic globalization—integration is so deep now in trade and financial markets that turbulence in one part affects all the others.

In a pre-globalized world, lines on maps mark territories where, through public policy as well as forces of history, society, economy, and governance, "national systems" coincide. At the most elementary economic level, for example, national boundaries marked coherent economic systems. International trade in goods and services could be blocked through public policies that protected domestic markets. The whole idea of a national economy presumes that there is more internal than external trade. In a globalized world, as barriers between and within local markets fall, markets get integrated globally. The current financial crisis has not changed that—companies still hunger for global markets. Companies sell locally, regionally, and internationally, wherever anyone is willing to buy the product. They have **global supply chains,** or "global value chains," that distribute the different aspects of the production of a commodity or service to different parts of the world, with the end-product magically appearing at market.

Canada, always a trading nation, crossed an important threshold in the 1990s. Interprovincial trade through the 1980s was as important to the country as international trade, both growing yearly at about the same rate. In 1990, however, interprovincial trade flattened and increased only slightly each year, while international exports continued to make gains. By 1996, only Prince Edward Island, Nova Scotia, and the Northwest Territories were exporting more to other provinces than to the rest of the world. As Figure 2.2 shows, total exports flattened between 2000 and 2003, but since that period the country has been relying more and more on international trade. The recession has made that dependence fragile—Statistics Canada reported a drop of 25 percent in Canada's exports in 2009 over 2008, though they bounced back by 10 percent in 2010 (Statistics Canada, 2011).

A second economic dimension of globalization is the well-known phenomenon of **transnational corporations** (TNCs). This phenomenon too has evolved over the postwar period. Multinational companies are not in themselves new—think of the Hudson's Bay Company (chartered in 1670) or the British East India Company (founded in 1600 to trade with Mogul kings in what is now India). These companies, however, were instruments of an imperial system of mercantilism, tools of imperial governments. What is different about modern multinational commercial

Figure 2.2   Interprovincial and International Exports, Canada, 1997–2006 (Billions of Canadian Dollars)

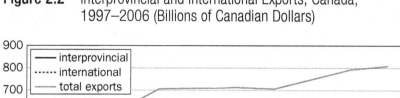

Source: Adapted from Statistics Canada, (2007, April), Provincial Economic Accounts, 2006 Preliminary Estimates (Catalogue no. 13-213-PPB), pages 324–326. Reproduced on an "as is" basis with permission from Statistics Canada.

firms is that their commercial interests are primary, they operate across the globe, and their national home base is relatively unimportant. As was the case with international trade, the 1990s were a boom period for TNCs and foreign direct investment (FDI). In 1998, foreign direct investment rose by almost 40 percent to over $640 billion, most of which was in developed countries. In 2007, global foreign direct investment peaked at US$1.9 trillion. But, according to the World Bank (2010, p. 2),

> The economic crisis slashed global FDI flows by about 40% in 2009, affecting all economies, sectors, and forms of investment. Mergers and acquisitions in high-income economies contracted the quickest after the 2007 subprime mortgage crisis in the United States contributed to banking and fiscal crises in Western Europe and Japan. The contagion gradually spread, affecting new investment in emerging markets and developing economies. Developing economies fared marginally better during the crisis. FDI in developing economies fell 35% in 2009, compared with 41% in high-income economies.

But TNCs continue to be important players in the international economy. The World Bank estimates that, in 2010, there were some 80 000 controlling at least 800 000 foreign affiliates, employing hundreds of millions of people abroad. Thus, a good part of what we think of as economic globalization in terms of economic interdependencies among countries is really due to a network of huge corporations and the investments they make and the goods and services they sell.

Country of origin mattered at one time, but in the contemporary phase of economic globalization, it is less important. The reason is because of a shift in the way in which these firms operate. The first phase of multinational development entailed exports to foreign markets of goods produced domestically (e.g., cars made in the United States or Japan exported elsewhere). The second phase was the establishment of production facilities in these foreign markets, facilities that were still quite dependent on the parent corporation for services, inputs, and strategies. A third phase has seen multinational firms begin to operate as transnational firms, that is, to organize their production processes into global chains. A computer or TV or car that seems to have a national label is actually assembled from parts that are outsourced to different manufacturers in different countries, assembled in one place, and then shipped. This development represents a significant change in the nature of globalization, since it implies a much more tightly integrated international market. As Thurow (1996) noted when the phenomenon first became visible, "For the first time in human history, anything can be made anywhere and sold everywhere" (p. 113). Global sourcing means that companies will shift production to the most attractive sites, either in terms of expertise or labour costs. It is important to remember that local markets continue to exist, and local or national markets have institutional advantages (e.g., similar languages or social customs) over international ones. But it does mean that as firms relentlessly relocate to build the cheapest supply chains, they abandon higher cost labour markets. The hollowing out of American manufacturing in favour of China has been one of the grim consequences of globalization.

A final aspect of economic globalization is the increase in capital flows and mobility, dramatically illustrated by the American subprime meltdown and its reverberations throughout global financial markets that had bought toxic mortgages as financial investments. Large financial institutions such as banks, insurance companies, and investment brokers have gradually developed systems to allow virtually instantaneous transfers of capital anywhere in the world. This capability is based, in part, on new technology and in part on the emergence of international institutions and the multinational corporations mentioned above, as well as the gradual dismantling of exchange barriers so that capital could move unimpeded—and increasingly erratically—around the world. On top of this, millions of individuals now invest in stocks, bonds, and currencies, further adding to volatility and risk. Companies such as Standard and Poor's provide rating services on countries and state enterprises that provide crucial information for international investors. Shifts in capital based on this information have deep consequences for domestic interest rates, stock prices, and exchange rates. The "PIGS"—Portugal, Italy, Greece, and Spain—felt the lash of markets in 2011, and responding to that lash led to deep spending cuts and street riots.

What does all this mean? Details will be explored in subsequent chapters, but economic globalization has had several consequences that, together, change the terrain of modern policymaking and analysis. Primarily, the development of international trading regimes means that governments have fewer policy instruments at their disposal to protect domestic markets, or what Porter (1990) called the "home base." In part this weakness is because governments have deliberately entered into agreements to increase trade and investment that constrain their own powers to discriminate in favour of their domestic industries or workforce. The North American Free Trade Agreement and the General Agreement on Tariffs and Trade (GATT, administered by the WTO), along with a host of new international trade agreements on intellectual property and trade in services, are prime examples. Dealing with trade disputes around the clash between domestic law and international agreements is now a small governmental cottage industry. As of 2011, for example, Canada was involved in WTO trade disputes with the European Union (use of hormones in livestock and over the seal hunt), Japan, and the United States (World Trade Organization, 2011). In some cases, Canadian legislation is a target of other countries under WTO rules (e.g., in the long-running dispute with Brazil over subsidies to Bombardier airplanes); in other cases, Canada uses international agreements as the basis for its own complaints (e.g., the softwood lumber case). International agreements of this sort are swords that cut both ways—that is why governments sign them—but they undeniably shift key decisionmaking powers over policy to international organizations. Moreover, the discipline of the global marketplace, exercised through massive and almost instantaneous capital flows, gives governments less and less room to manoeuvre, and less and less capacity to go it alone. It may drive them to a **race to the bottom** as they try to attract international capital through lower and lower standards. Yet another reason that governments have a harder time of going it alone is that globalization induces mutual interdependence and integration. Again, the global financial crisis illustrated the intimate entanglement of markets all around the world. The G20 emerged as a crucial global economic steering mechanism, and the crises in the Euro zone compelled EU countries, the European Central Bank, and the International Monetary Fund (the so-called "Troika") to launch bailout funds to prevent sovereign debt defaults (e.g., Greece) that could disrupt the entire continent.

Does this interdependence and economic integration mean that the state will wither away? Hardly. Earlier discussions of the impact of globalization assumed that interdependence would reduce government capacity, shift responsibilities upward to global institutions, and make states less important actors both globally and within their domestic spheres (Ohmae, 1990, 1995). To the degree that states assume authority over territory, and as we have noted, as territory becomes less and less important as an organizing principle for economic and social life, it would seem that states would become weaker. The story is more complicated than that, however. For one thing, states remain key institutions in responding to issues that matter to people—social security, economic prosperity, and more recently, the global financial recession, the environment, natural and man-made disasters (a stunning combined example of which was the 2011 earthquake, tsunami, and the resulting crisis at the Fukushima nuclear plant). States continue to have massive—if depleting—financial and personnel resources at their disposal, much more than any single corporation. For another thing, globalization itself creates an imperative for states to act internationally to pursue the interests of their citizens—climate change, telecommunications regulation, food and safety standards, and the "dark side of globalization"— international terrorism, human trafficking, drug and arms smuggling, organized crime, illegal immigration (Heine & Thakur, 2011)—all require states as the key players in international institutions. Finally, the post 9/11 security state has seen massive growth, not withering, of state capacities in defence, policing, and surveillance. Add all these together and states remain large—in 2009, the OECD average for the proportion of gross domestic product (GDP) accounted for by state spending was 46 percent, with some countries, such as France, at over 50 percent (Organisation for Economic Co-operation and Development [OECD], 2011, p. 65).

In this more complicated story, states, rather than withering away, are joined by a wider array of actors through international networks of governmental and nongovernmental organizations. Together they form a "multi-centric" (Scholte, 2005, Chapter 6) or "multi-scalar" (Mahon, Andrew, & Johnson, 2007) world system where networks provide global governance without a global government as such.

> In a world of government networks, by contrast, the same officials who are judging, regulating, and legislating domestically are also reaching out to their foreign counterparts to help address the governance problems that arise when national actors and issues spill beyond their borders. Global governance, from this perspective, is not a matter of regulating states the way states regulate their citizens, but rather of addressing the issues and resolving the problems that result from citizens going global—from crime to commerce to civic engagement. (Slaughter, 2004, p. 16)

Indeed, it is important to recall that many aspects of the global economy have been deliberately created by states, even if at the end of the day they cannot completely control them (Pauly, 1997). Moreover, globalization theorists often assume a hypermobility or hyperfluidity of capital and trade that belies the degree of concentration of material facilities and work processes in territorial sites—globalization is, in fact, "managed" through a small number of "global cities" or sites such as London, Tokyo, Frankfurt, and New York (Sassen, 1998, Chapter 10), and these cities are located in states that still have the capacity to regulate them in various ways. It is an open question as to whether these cities, and their growing interconnectivity around functions like financial investment flows, are the real backbone of economic globalization as opposed to states (Sassen, 2002a). Note that global cities such as Shanghai are now emerging in the developing world and linking up to previous leading cities, creating a truly global network (Sassen, 2002b).

Another important issue is whether economic globalization is inevitable and unidirectional. The trade and investment figures provided earlier might create an impression of steady growth and steady integration, with only minor and temporary reversals. There are several reasons why this perception needs to be treated cautiously. First, there is always the possibility of a major downturn that will induce countries to put up protective barriers. It happened in 2008, and again in 2011, and it appears that the global recession may last for several more years. Second, while it might be that **trade liberalization** is in everyone's interest, countries nonetheless try to protect their economies as much as they can, especially in the face of destabilizing capital flows. Third, while economic globalization has been accompanied by growing prosperity, it also exposes countries and economies to the cold winds of competition and consequently can engender resistance. As the Pew Global Attitudes survey found in late 2007:

> the publics of the world broadly embrace key tenets of economic globalization but fear the disruptions and downsides of participating in the global economy. In rich countries as well as poor ones, most people endorse free trade, multinational corporations and free markets. However, the latest Pew Global Attitudes survey of more than 45 000 people finds they are concerned about inequality, threats to their culture, threats to the environment and threats posed by immigration. Together, these results reveal an evolving world view on globalization that is nuanced, ambivalent, and sometimes inherently contradictory. (Pew Global Attitudes Project, 2007)

The global financial crisis simply intensified this ambivalence, to the point that in April 2011, the managing director of the International Monetary Fund—usually considered a one-sided cheerleader for free-market globalization—called for a rethinking of macroeconomic policy and greater attention to social cohesion and inequality (International Monetary Fund, 2011).

In response to the argument that globalization inevitably leads to a race to the bottom, analysts like Vogel (1995) pointed to the "California effect": trade can lead to higher environmental standards as political jurisdictions with higher standards "force foreign producers in nations with weaker domestic standards either to design products that meet those standards or sacrifice export markets" (p. 261). Foreign producers then have incentives to force their own countries' governments to increase standards. The California effect—counterintuitive as it might appear—has been observed in other jurisdictions and other policy areas (Vogel & Kagan, 2004), and the reasons are diverse: Western-based social movements agitating in developing countries; the disinclination of many low-income countries to passively accept damaging corporate policies; the penetration and acceptance of international standards.

Another example of counterintuitive forces at play in modern globalization is what Florida discerns as the rise of the "creative class" (2002, 2005, 2008). His argument highlights two important aspects of contemporary globalization. The first is that it is linked to, if not driven by, fundamental changes in economic production. Obviously, primary resources, manufacturing capacity, availability of capital, and scientific skill matter a lot in the modern economy. But for an increasing number of key goods and services, the primary element is not old-fashioned labour or resource investment, but creativity, often scientific, and just as often cultural or aesthetic. Creativity is the essential element behind the development of new ideas, new products and services, new forms of packaging old products, and is a blend of research, taste, and sensibility. It is what distinguishes products like Apple's iPad. To the degree that city planners respond to the creative class, they create urban spaces far from the Dickensian horrors of the industrial revolution. Again, in a counterintuitive development, globalization in this dimension drives standards up, not down.

In short, globalization is not an implacable and impersonal juggernaut. Despite its reality, it is both less extensive and intensive than the extreme globalizers would have us believe. It takes place in real space, often in quite limited spaces, and those spaces are subject to some form of policy intervention. Moreover, globalization is not merely an economic phenomenon but, in large part, is politically driven as countries decide that integrating more closely is in their interests. However, it is true that the financial crisis made it less a matter of choice than of necessity. Countries such as Iceland found themselves tethered to mortgages in Idaho. Frugal middle-class Germans woke up to find that they were funding—to the tune of more than 400 billion Euros—their European Union cousins, the unhappy PIGS.

y, citizens will not soon cease to demand the core services and
s of the contemporary welfare state, nor will they hesitate to
protection from the worst excesses of globalization. The trajec-
all these forces are difficult to predict, but it is clear that while
ation has created new channels through which geopolitics might
has not banished geopolitics. As well, the idea that globaliza-
essarily means relentless and implacable convergence toward the
" (low wages, deregulation, job loss), or a world without policy
is without solid foundation. In fact, what is striking is how pat-
onvergence and divergence appear simultaneously—even as trade
and G8 or G20 summits are held, major differences over policy
arise between the United States, the European Union, Russia, China, and
Southeast Asia. The challenge is to mount policy responses that highlight
the positive aspects of globalization and limit the "dark side."

CULTURAL GLOBALIZATION

Globalization is about more than economics, however (see Box 2.1). It
relies, for instance, on technologies of communication that also have had
a dramatic effect on culture. Once again the central issue is the degree to
which borders matter less as an element of cohesion in defining national
cultures and societies. We have already noted how markets have become
uncoupled from territorial boundaries, and the same is increasingly true
of culture and communications. One line of argument about this phenomenon is that all around the world people are rapidly becoming the
same. To some extent this is true. The massive penetration of American
culture through icons such as Coke, McDonald's, Hollywood, and Nike
means that there is a pervasive sameness in culture and consumption—
despite local differences—to major cities no matter where one goes on
the planet. Taste and style are increasingly global—iPads and jeans are as
fashionable in Doha as they are in Durban or Dallas.

However, this does not mean the consumers want identical products;
it means that with the erosion of barriers, products can be blends of
cultural traditions and expectations, and be available anywhere through
the "invisible global economy" (Ohmae, 2004). Local cultures do have
a resilience and carve out niches for themselves even in the shadows
of what Barber (1995) famously called "McWorld." Indeed, the coun-
terargument to this view that globalization means sameness is that it
portends a growing awareness of differences and an emphasis on particu-
larities (Rethmann, Szeman, & Coleman, 2010). In this scenario, which
seems supported by the tenacity of ethnic differences and conflicts around
the world, people retain their local cultural idioms, but globalization no
longer makes it possible for them to conceive of their own culture as
somehow "natural" and the only single possible world. Global trends

BOX 2.1   THE GLOBALIZATION INDEX

The Globalization Index, which is developed by the Centre for the Study of Globalisation and Regionalisation at Warwick University, measures the economic, social and political dimensions of globalization for countries on an annual basis over the period 1982 to 2004, and combines these into an overall globalization

Table 1
THE TWENTY MOST SOCIALLY GLOBALIZED COUNTRIES IN 2004

Unit: Score (max. 1)

Country	Score	Rank
Bermuda	1.000	1
Singapore	0.985	2
Hong Kong, China	0.781	3
Switzerland	0.776	4
New Zealand	0.712	5
Austria	0.684	6
Canada	0.683	7
Netherlands Antilles	0.658	8
Sweden	0.643	9
Denmark	0.641	10
United Kingdom	0.630	11
Malta	0.626	12
Iceland	0.622	13
Belgium	0.605	14
Australia	0.595	15
Finland	0.576	16
Netherlands	0.552	17
United States	0.551	18
Barbados	0.504	19
Ireland	0.473	20

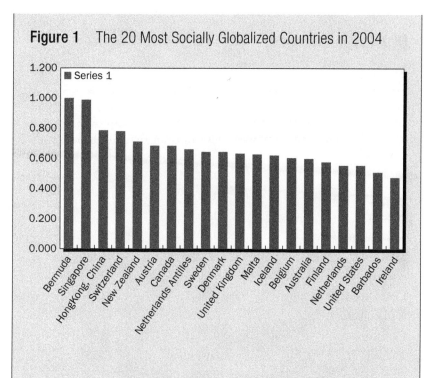

Figure 1 The 20 Most Socially Globalized Countries in 2004

index, or score. The overall globalization index and the economic, social, and political globalization indices are constructed to be consistent over time and across countries. The same variables are used to calculate the index for each year and country, and the variables are normalized to be comparable. The social globalization index is constructed from nine variables, of which four are included in the people globalization sub-index, and five are included in the ideas globalization sub-index. It is worth noting that on the website of the CSGR, there are data available only for the overall globalization index and the economic, social, and political globalization indices (no data available for specific sub-indices and variables).

1. *People globalization sub-index:* (i) foreign stock [stock of foreign population as proportion of total population]; (ii) foreign flow [inflows of foreign population as proportion of total population]; (iii) worker remittances [worker remittances (receipts) as a proportion of GDP].

(continued)

BOX 2.1 (continued)

Table 2

THE TWENTY LEAST SOCIALLY GLOBALIZED
COUNTRIES IN 2004

Unit: Score (max. 1)

Country	Score	Rank
Myanmar	0.002	134
Ethiopia	0.005	133
Nigeria	0.005	132
Madagascar	0.005	131
Mali	0.006	130
Bangladesh	0.008	129
Central African Republic	0.010	128
Mozambique	0.012	127
Cameroon	0.012	126
Malawi	0.013	125
Yemen, Rep.	0.016	124
Chad	0.019	123
Bhutan	0.019	122
Pakistan	0.020	121
Algeria	0.020	120
Nepal	0.022	119
Zambia	0.022	118
Sri Lanka	0.023	117
Papua New Guinea	0.023	116
Djibouti	0.025	115

2. *Ideas globalization sub-index:* (i) phone calls [international outgoing telephone traffic (minutes) per capita]; (ii) Internet users [Internet users as a percentage of population]; (iii) films [number of films imported and exported]; (iv) books and newspapers [sum of value of books and newspapers imported and exported per capita (US$)]; (v) mail [number of international letters delivered and sent per capita].

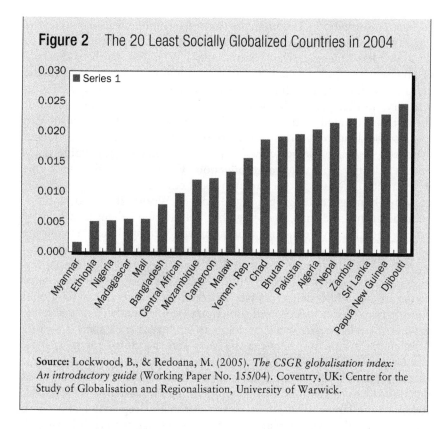

Figure 2 The 20 Least Socially Globalized Countries in 2004

Source: Lockwood, B., & Redoana, M. (2005). *The CSGR globalisation index: An introductory guide* (Working Paper No. 155/04). Coventry, UK: Centre for the Study of Globalisation and Regionalisation, University of Warwick.

and tastes articulate with local traditions and customs in a sort of cultural mash-up.

The telecommunications and information revolution has taken a giant leap forward with the Internet and social media. The Internet cuts through traditional debates about the effects of telecommunications and broadcasting on community and culture because it has the potential to globalize and localize at the same time. Accurate numbers are hard to come by, but according to estimates, there were as many as 1.3 billion Internet users around the world in December 2007, and as many as 2.1 billion in 2011 (Internet World Stats, 2011). North America accounted for 13 percent, Europe for 22.7 percent, and Asia for 44 percent. All of Africa accounted for only 5.7 percent, once again showing how uneven globalization is. Nonetheless, it has reach and power. The impact of social media such as Twitter was clearly displayed in the Arab Spring of 2011—protesters in Tunisia and Egypt organized and collaborated and shared with the world through their cellphones.

The convergence of computers and telecommunications and the plummeting costs of the technology suggest that the predicted "death of distance" has indeed arrived (Cairncross, 1997). The death of distance is precisely the policy challenge that contemporary states face in the cultural field. Cultural affinity has traditionally tended to coincide with territory, so that people defined their relevant communities in terms of the territory defined by the state. Under healthy circumstances (insularity can also be dangerous), this symmetry of territory and culture produces a desired degree of **social cohesion** and a foundation for stable community identity and cultural production. Globalization threatens this in a variety of ways. It can threaten local cultural traditions in favour of some homogeneous global standard—McWorld. It can destabilize cultural norms and understandings by "relativizing" them to a host of others and thereby reducing their apparent weight. It can encourage people to define their relevant communities in nonterritorial ways, and thereby weaken national bonds and support for national projects and policies. Governments therefore find themselves with distinctive policy conundrums: while many people welcome increased access to global culture, many resist fiercely and sometimes even violently. This challenge is what Castells means when he refers to the networked society and its "systematic disjunction between the local and the global for most individuals and social groups." The effects of globalization are so corrosive that the "search for meaning takes place then in the reconstruction of defensive identities around communal principles" (Castells, 1997, p. 11). Religious fundamentalism, militias, eco-terrorists, deep ecologists—these disparate social movements are symptoms of resistance to the globalized, networked society.

If culture depends on communication, the communications and information revolution mean that communication is now global, suggesting the emergence of certain global understandings or standards. This is the third aspect of globalization; the development of **international standards** of conduct.

INTERNATIONAL STANDARDS

The best example of these emerging standards is the **human rights** conventions that have evolved since 1945. The United Nations (UN) came into being on October 10, 1945, and its Economic and Social Council was instructed to establish a commission to draft an international bill of rights. The UN Charter referred to the "principle of equal rights" and the importance of universal respect for "human rights and fundamental freedoms for all." The Council established a Commission on Human Rights that produced the Universal Declaration of Human Rights, which was passed in December 1948. The Universal Declaration was nothing more than that—a declaration without force of international law and without any enforcement mechanism. It recognized the "inherent dignity of and the equal and inalienable rights of all members of the human family" and proceeded to list virtually every conceivable human right from traditional civil and political ones to newer ones such as social security, work, rest, leisure, the right to an adequate standard of living, education, and free participation in the cultural life of the community. At the time these ideals were lofty, and in one document were brought together two sets or generations of rights that coincided with the emerging global divisions around the Cold War: civil and political rights central to liberal democracies and social and economic rights championed by socialist and communist states.

The history of human rights since 1948 has seen the progressive elaboration of both standards and institutions to monitor and enforce those standards (Montgomery, 1999; United Nations, 2003). The Universal Declaration, for example, was followed by two International Covenants that did have the force of treaties rather than being mere declarations: the International Covenant on Civil and Political Rights and the International Covenant on Economic, Social and Cultural Rights. These were both passed by the UN in 1966 and came into effect in 1976. In addition to these covenants, the UN has passed Conventions for the Suppression of the Traffic in Persons and of the Exploitation of the Prostitution of Others (1951), the Status of Refugees (1954), the Elimination of All Forms of Racial Discrimination (1969), the Elimination of All Forms of Discrimination against Women (1981), against Torture and Other Cruel, Inhuman or Degrading Treatment or Punishment (1987), and on the Rights of the Child (1990). These UN initiatives have been complemented by similar regional conventions; for example, in the European Union, there has been a gradual development of citizens' rights through the 1950 Treaty of Rome, the 1961 European Social Charter, and the 1989 Community Charter. The 1997 Amsterdam Treaty gave the European Court of Justice the power to enforce fundamental rights. On July 1, 2002, a permanent International Criminal Court was established at The Hague (although the Rome Statute, which is the foundation for the court, was not signed until 1998). The globalization of international human rights standards has led to a "justice cascade" of legal prosecutions of political leaders around the world, effectively erasing their immunity (Sikkink, 2011).

Critics often dismiss this dense system of overlapping covenants and declarations as largely meaningless posturing by governments, many of which are energetic violators of the very agreements they have signed. But events such as the 1993 Vienna World Conference on Human Rights and the 1995 Beijing World Conference on Women demonstrate that a global moral community has emerged from these efforts. In the Arab Spring uprisings in Tunisia and Egypt in 2011, street protesters vividly appealed to international standards of human rights and democracy.

As with the other elements of globalization, the implications of the emergence of international standards, many of them contained in conventions and treaties that Canada has willingly signed, are that the policy process and the principles by which it is made are no longer delimited by purely domestic considerations. In most policy fields—from the environment to Aboriginal affairs—governments have to take note of international standards, international agreements that may bind them to those standards, and international reactions to their behaviour. Having said that, governments are not necessarily at the mercy of these standards and agreements; they can still find ways around them if they need to. The simple point is that these standards have a reality that can no longer be ignored, and when mobilized by international actors or institutions, can have a potentially powerful effect.

Any policies Canada develops will be measured against what other governments have done. In addition to standards and international institutions to monitor them, of course, is the emergence of what some have called a **"global civil society"** of activist NGOs that can be mobilized quickly around domestic policy issues (Keck & Sikkink, 1998). Canada's environmental policies, for instance, are closely watched by various groups around the world such as the Sierra Club and Greenpeace. The Yearbook of International Organizations conservatively estimates that, in 2012, there were some 63 589 such bodies (Union of International Associations, 2012).

In short, the traditional connection between public policymaking and the territorial boundaries of the nation-state has been severely challenged in the last decade. Both the source of policy problems and their potential solutions now lie as much outside the boundaries of the state as they do within. There was a time in the late 1990s when this seemed to signal a decline of the state in favour of markets and the mobility of people and ideas. Then came 9/11 and a decade-long buildup of security apparatuses in all developed states. Then came the financial crisis in 2008. The paradox is that nation-states are both weaker and stronger. They have vast security arsenals unimaginable 20 years ago. They are the last resort to bail out banks and corrupt and astoundingly unaccountable financial systems. They have to impose disciplines (slashing public sector jobs and social security programs, while raising taxes.) And yet, they are wounded giants that face ignited opposition on the streets and on the Tweets. They find that they cannot easily tame domestic economic turbulence except in concert with other countries and international agencies. The solutions to many key problems lie in developing international standards and regulation. The comfortable instruments they once had at their disposal are sometimes irrelevant, ineffective, or weak.

The Politics of Difference

Globalization helps us conceptualize changes that have occurred at the international level, along with their effects on domestic politics and policymaking. It would be surprising, however, if these international changes were not accompanied with equally significant changes in the ways in which domestic political communities see themselves and their relations to government. For example, how could international human rights regimes strengthen over the past 50 years without human rights simultaneously becoming more important as standards of civil conduct on the domestic level?

Political culture across the industrialized democracies has indeed changed significantly, no less in Canada than elsewhere. This section will briefly sketch three developments that set the backdrop to important shifts in political culture: the rise of **postmaterialism,** the increased salience of rights, and the new emphasis on "difference." Together, these comprise what some have called the **"postmodern condition"** of contemporary governance: "some state responses to globalization are fashioning a weaker kind of citizenship" (Jenson, 2003, p. 313).

Postmaterialism in the West consists of a shift away from deference, away from concern with purely material gain, toward a greater emphasis on lifestyle concerns and social, even spiritual issues, all conducted in a much more participatory mode. "Although individuals still value economic and physical security, they increasingly emphasize the need for freedom, self-expression, and improving the quality of their lives" (Abramson & Inglehart, 1995, p. 9). According to Inglehart, this gradual and long-term process will become evident through generational replacement. The trend is not inevitable, but there is considerable evidence that it has affected most industrial countries in the world. The consequences of a shift to postmaterialist values are potentially profound: greater support for democratic institutions through a new emphasis on self-expression values and human autonomy and, in particular, greater support for participatory democracy and a politics of identity and recognition. Cultures are, of course, resilient, and depending on socio-economic circumstances (a risk to survival), the trajectory of human development can be toward authoritarianism and xenophobia (Inglehart & Welzel, 2005).

The growth of postmaterialism has links to the development of what Mary Ann Glendon called the dominance of **"rights talk"** as a mode of political discourse. In the previous section we discussed the development of international human rights regimes. This development has been mirrored at the domestic level in the elaboration of human rights documents, institutions, and political discourse. Glendon argues that while rights talk is impervious to other more complex languages whereby we regulate our social and political lives, it "seeps into them, carrying the rights mentality into spheres of American society where a sense of personal responsibility and of civic obligation traditionally have been nourished" (1991, p. x). The Canadian version of this analysis was driven by the patriation of the Constitution in 1982 and its incorporation of a far-reaching Charter of Rights and Freedoms. Along with the traditional liberal-democratic rights of association, expression, and so on, the Charter contains modern clauses on equality and group rights. Canadian courts were granted a constitutionally entrenched power to review all federal and provincial statutes to ensure that they do not violate the Charter. Unsurprisingly, constitutional rights-based litigation mushroomed, foreshadowing a rights revolution (Cairns, 1991, 1992, 1993; Ignatieff, 2000).

The third element of the changed political culture in industrialized democracies is a tension between individual and group rights. The former consist of the traditional collection of civil and political rights that aim to treat individuals roughly the same, regardless of their social and economic differences. The original objective was to build a political community that, for the purposes of public policy, ignored group differences and concentrated instead on equal rights of **citizenship**. This noble political ideal still commands substantial support. However, this type of **liberal individualism** was vulnerable to the argument that differences did matter, particularly economic differences, and they impeded the practical achievement of real political equality.

The contemporary version of the argument about difference shifts ground, however. The old argument with liberalism was that differences mattered but essentially that they should somehow be overcome. The objective for **liberal universalism** was still the same. The modern argument of difference challenges the core assumptions of liberal individualism by insisting that differences matter in a positive way, that equal treatment of individuals as abstract citizens ignores fundamental social and cultural characteristics that define identities (though there is a line of thought that special treatment for minorities *as protection* against majorities, is consistent with liberalism; see Kymlicka, 2007). It encourages a policy of **multiculturalism**, which Canada pioneered, and which aims both to protect and celebrate diversity. This **politics of difference** argues that many important differences are routinely and systematically oppressed. Indeed, it is the fact of oppression that gives these groups special claims within the political system. Note that a "difference perspective" emphasizes **collective identities** as a basis for claims and urges the importance of those identities in making public policy. It explicitly privileges **cultural identity** as a normative base for making specific, countermajoritarian rights claims on behalf of individuals who are members of specific groups. This cluster of ideas leads to the conclusion that the application of universal rules will serve only to further disadvantage these groups and suppress their legitimate differences. Multiculturalism policy has, from its beginnings, been a program that recognizes and celebrates differences (Pal, 1993; Ryan, 2010).

From a policy perspective, the impact of postmaterialism, rights talk, and cultural pluralism is complex and often contradictory. For one thing, it has contributed to the widely noted **decline of deference** among the Canadian population and democratic citizenry in other countries. Citizens trust their governments and politicians less than they used to. If they trust less, they inevitably demand a different type of policy process. They want to be consulted, they want to participate, and they want their voices to be heard (Norris, 2011). Another consequence has been a new emphasis on identity and the politics of recognition. Demographics play an important role in this, and Canadian society is increasingly ethnically and racially diverse, indeed, one of the most ethnically diverse countries in the world. But new sensibilities abound as well, some of them encouraged through government policies such as multiculturalism, bilingualism, and equity employment, and recent court and human rights tribunal decisions. People increasingly identify themselves strongly with nonterritorially based groups—religious, ethnic, gender, linguistic, sexual, generational, or some exotic combination.

From a policy perspective, this kind of identification raises two challenges. One is the potential for **social fragmentation** and the importance of supporting some sort of social cohesion. Pluralism and diversity are certainly to be valued in any society, but by the same token, the balance between the two needs to be carefully managed. This is not simply an abstract philosophical principle, since social solidarity underpins the willingness of citizens to share burdens and benefits with each other, most notably through the redistribution of the welfare state (Barry, 2001). The second challenge is dealing with thorny issues of "ways of life" and collective rights. Both citizens and policymakers are often willing to compromise on material interests, but ways of life are intrinsically more precious and less negotiable.

These issues may sound somewhat abstract, but can be illustrated with two concrete issues: Quebec's appointment of a commission to investigate the scope of "reasonable accommodation" to minority groups in the province; and the controversy over *The Western Standard*'s decision to reprint the notorious Danish cartoons that caused Muslims to riot across Europe in 2006.

The reasonable accommodation issue was precipitated by public complaints in Quebec about insufficient integration of immigrants, particularly Muslim immigrants. In Quebec the issue of immigration is more challenging than in other provinces because of the sense, among both separatists and federalists, that Quebec is a nation (indeed, that sentiment was ratified by a successful motion before the federal Parliament in November 2006), usually defined in terms of its society, history, territory, and the French language. Integration of immigrants into the French language did not pose problems, but if those immigrants had significantly different social and religious practices, and at the same time demanded that those practices be accommodated by the majority, there could be difficulties. Isolated cases of accommodation demands (e.g., to shade gym windows to obscure the sight of women in skimpy exercise clothes) ignited Quebec public opinion. Premier Jean Charest struck the Consultation Commission on Accommodation Practices Related to Cultural Differences (CCAPRCD) in February 2007. The Commission decided to interpret its mandate broadly: it "would be to perceive the debate on reasonable accommodation as the symptom of a more basic problem concerning the socio-cultural integration model established in Québec since the 1970s. This perspective calls for a review of interculturalism, immigration, secularism and the theme of Québec identity." This mandate is a direct echo of the theme of cultural pluralism discussed earlier. Headed by two distinguished academics, and supported by a 15-member advisory committee, the Commission undertook consultations across the province beginning in 2007 and ending in February 2008 (CCAPRCD, 2008a). It received 901 briefs and released its report on May 22, 2008.

The Commission's basic conclusion was that "the foundations of collective life in Québec are not in a critical situation" (CCAPRCD, 2008b, p. 13). The real problem was one of perceptions, where due to a series of events and isolated cases, there was a broad but erroneous perception that Quebec was facing a crisis of numerous accommodations and major institutional revision. The number of accommodation cases that had found their way to the courts was small, and there was little evidence of any threats to social order or even to basic values. Nonetheless, the Commission pointed out that "interculturalism" as a principle of public policy in Quebec had a special role in balancing integration of immigrants into a French-speaking society with reasonable accommodation for ethnic and religious differences. The balancing act would not be simple: "To summarize, we could say that Québec interculturalism a) institutes French as the common language of intercultural relations; b) cultivates a pluralistic orientation that is highly sensitive to the protection of rights; c) preserves the creative tension between diversity and the continuity of the French-speaking core and the social link; d) places special emphasis on integration; and e) advocates interaction" (ibid., p. 42). The Commission's recommendations emphasized the development of economic opportunities and support for immigrants as much as it did interculturalism in terms of accommodations and institutional changes. A sign of the challenge in translating these philosophical principles into policy practice was the Commission's recommendation that the cross that is prominently displayed in the Quebec National Assembly be removed as an affront to the state's neutrality on matters of religion. The government immediately introduced a motion to keep the cross, and it was passed unanimously by all three political parties. The question of interculturalism continues to be debated in Quebec today (Adelman & Anctil, 2011).

In 2006, the now defunct magazine *The Western Standard*, under publisher Ezra Levant, decided to reprint the Danish cartoons depicting Mohammed, which had generated riots across Europe and in other parts of the world on account of the blasphemy of representing the Prophet in an image. The publication of those cartoons in Denmark offended no Danish law, nor did they offend any Canadian law prima facie. However, Syed Soharwardy lodged a complaint with the Alberta Human Rights Commission, alleging that the cartoons were designed to incite hatred against Islam, and so constituted hate speech, which is a violation of the human rights code. Levant was questioned by the Human Rights Commission (he filmed what he termed his "interrogation" and posted it on YouTube), but the complaint was eventually withdrawn. The human rights code provisions in this instance are designed to protect groups against speech that would incite hatred and ordinarily that would fall into the category of direct statements intended to accomplish that end. In this instance, the offending material was offensive to the complainant as a religious matter, and so the Commission was actually wading into the waters we discussed above—accommodation of specific minority group practices and characteristics as against the wider society's norms (the cartoons are only offensive to Muslims).

These cases illustrate the challenges of managing diverse democratic societies that try to balance individual rights, group rights, social and community obligations, and a broad rule of law that treats everyone equally. Canada, far from alone in dealing with these issues, may have some advantages through a long history of immigration and an early adoption (1971) of a formal policy of multiculturalism. France, Germany, the Netherlands, and the United Kingdom have been grappling with the same issues, and have called multiculturalism and immigration into question.

> In much of the Western world, and particularly in Europe, there is a widespread perception that we are failing this test. We are witnessing a backlash against immigration in many countries. There is also a strong sense that multiculturalism policies have "failed," a reaction that is strongest perhaps in the Netherlands but is felt in many other countries as well. This disenchantment with multiculturalism is driven by fears about economic costs, perceived threats to liberal values, challenges to historic cultures, anxieties about Islam and fears about security. But the reaction is also fueled by a fear that immigration and ethnic diversity are eroding social solidarity. (Banting, 2010, p. 797)

The politics of difference, as we have termed it, is a complicated cluster of ideas (rights talk, decline of deference, emphasis on identity), demographics linked to immigration, and institutions (courts). It is important not to exaggerate its impact on contemporary Canada or other industrialized states, but it is also important to take its full measure. For example, Banting, Johnston, Kymlicka, and Soroka (2006, p. 83) argue that there is no evidence of countries that have adopted strong multicultural programs seeing an erosion of their welfare states, primarily in terms of social welfare redistribution. The mere fact of demographic diversity and difference does not necessarily lead to a decline in political trust or social cohesion, or a willingness to share burdens and benefits through the redistributive welfare state, nor does it automatically mean minorities lack a sense of belonging. In the Canadian case, the main differences in social cohesion are not primarily due to ethnic differences but to how recent the immigrants' arrival has been. "The longer new immigrants are in Canada, the more their sense of pride and, to a lesser extent, of belonging comes to equal or exceed that of the largest ethnic group" (Soroka, Johnston, & Banting, 2007, p. 23). In comparative terms, the Canadian experience with plurality and multiculturalism has generally been quite successful (Adams, 2007; Banting, 2010). But the paradox remains that broad-scale measures of public opinion can mask the complications at the operative level of public policy (Myles & St-Arnaud, 2006). In that arena, groups may mobilize and articulate discourses of rights and difference that pose substantial challenges to democratic polities. It is clear that things have changed in important ways. The way that Canadians discuss rights, and how they frame policy issues in terms of rights, is vastly different today from a generation ago. There has been an undeniable decline in trust, deference, and engagement with conventional political institutions. All of this is new.

Governance and Public Management

The third major change in the context of policymaking and analysis has been in our concepts of the proper scope of governance by the state and the nature of public management. These are, of course, entangled with the changes described above in the domestic economy, globalization, and culture shifts, and probably represent the results of outcomes of these changes more than they do independent forces in their own right. Nonetheless, it is a crucial category for policy analysis since it cuts closest to what governments see themselves as properly doing, and the new politics of governance and public management rapidly developed their own dynamics, however much they might be a consequence of deeper factors.

Ideas about governance operate at several distinct levels. The most general is the view of the proper scope and nature of government activity.

The 1990s was a decade where policymakers across the ideological spectrum lost confidence in the capacity of government to do things. Conservatives retained less faith than liberals or those on the left, but generally the centre of gravity on these issues shifted perceptibly to the right and in favour—at least rhetorically—of smaller governments (the federal Conservative government actually increased spending in its first two terms and then dramatically after 2008 for its stimulus package). The differences were more a matter of tone, but tone sometimes matters. The federal Tories cut the GST in 2006 when most economists and the opposition parties objected. They decided on a universal child-care benefit rather than federally funded daycare centres. But nonetheless, many of the key questions in the debates over governance in the 1990s have not disappeared (in part because of austerity and the need to make the public sector more efficient), even as they have shifted dramatically because of the global financial crisis. Should governments provide services directly, or should they develop mechanisms for the delivery of these services through either for-profit or nonprofit agencies? How much should governments regulate banks and financial services? How much should they spend to stimulate, or how to cut to avoid soaring deficits? More philosophically, to what extent should government encourage the pursuit of what are basically private interests, such as child care or a university education, through the public sphere in the form of either services or legal structures that support such pursuits?

Another, more specific level concerns the tools that governments realistically have at their disposal for policy development and implementation. Can governments control unemployment and inflation through monetary policy? Can they "create jobs"? Can they solve poverty and eradicate racism? Can they provide adequate housing? Obviously, if one believes that the market can and should do this, the question of policy instruments will not arise. However, even in cases where one thinks that the role of government should be minimal, there can be disputes about appropriate tools for governance. The final aspect of governance concerns management practices. Given a certain vision of the role of government and the feasible tools at its disposal for dealing with public problems, how best to organize the administrative machinery of government to achieve those ends?

Ideas about governance and public management have been changing radically in the last two decades. The movement has coincided with the political ascendancy of the right in most liberal democracies, starting with Ronald Reagan in the United States (elected president in 1980) and Margaret Thatcher in Britain (who became prime minister in 1979). In Canada, the Progressive Conservatives were elected for terms in 1984 and again in 1988, before being almost wiped out in 1993. Interestingly, the Liberals accepted many key elements of the Tory agenda: **deficit reduction** and **government restructuring** being most prominent. This adoption mimics a pattern in other countries such as New Zealand, where the change in public administration and management was led by left-wing parties. But the gospel of smaller government, balanced budgets, reduced public debt, and new management practices gained converts from both left and right in the 1990s, under the banner of **new public management** (NPM). It became hardwired into most developed democracies, including Canada, but has since been overlaid with other management priorities.

What were its main features? Primarily, there was a belief that what Barzelay (1992, p. 5) calls the "bureaucratic paradigm" of carefully defined roles, reliance on rules and procedures, line and staff distinctions, tight financial control, and central agency oversight, should be replaced with a more client-focused, service-oriented system. Bevir, Rhodes, and Weller (2003) highlighted the following features of new public management:

> The term refers to a focus on management, not policy, and on performance appraisal and efficiency; disaggregating public bureaucracies into agencies which deal with each other on a user pay basis; the use of quasi-markets and of contracting out to foster competition; cost-cutting; and a style of management that emphasizes, among other things, output targets, limited term contracts, monetary incentives and freedom to manage…. It is said to be a global phenomenon. (pp. 1–2)

One of the most widely read gospels of NPM thinking was a 1992 book entitled *Reinventing Government*, by David Osborne and Ted Gaebler. The most important aspect of the book's argument was its rejection of the hierarchical architecture of most government bureaucracies. Close accountability requires close scrutiny and a minimum of bureaucratic discretion. This traditional system of public administration has many benefits, but it is also, in large part, responsible for the stereotypical inflexibility and unresponsiveness of government bureaucracy. The result very often is costly, lumbering organizations that are driven by rules rather than results. Creativity is stifled, problem solving is discouraged in favour of following routine, and significant resources are devoted simply to managing people within the system, rather than achieving policy goals. Osborne and Gaebler distilled 10 principles of reinventing government from the cases they reviewed. These principles were grounded in the assumption that government is necessary, but it does not necessarily have to act like government.

> Most entrepreneurial governments promote *competition* between service providers. They *empower* citizens by pushing control out of the bureaucracy, into the community. They measure the

performance of their agencies, focusing not on inputs but on *outcomes*. They are driven by their goals—their *missions*—not by their rules and regulations. They redefine their clients as *customers* and offer them choices—between schools, between training programs, between housing options. They *prevent* problems before they emerge, rather than simply offering services afterward. They put their energies into *earning* money, not simply spending it. They *decentralize* authority, embracing participatory management. They prefer *market* mechanisms to bureaucratic mechanisms. And they focus not simply on providing public services, but on *catalyzing* all sectors—public, private, and voluntary—into action to solve their community's problems. (Osborne & Gaebler, 1993, pp. 19–20)

Kenneth Kernaghan (2000) provides a useful list that contrasts what he calls "bureaucratic" with "post-bureaucratic" organizations. The list is presented in Figure 2.3 (page 74). Note that the characteristics on the postbureaucratic side lend themselves to a variety of different configurations—decentralized organizations, for example, could be completely privatized ones or public agencies with greater responsibility for their own actions.

In the United States, the Clinton administration launched a **National Performance Review** on government, headed by Vice-President Al Gore, in March 1993. Its first report contained 384 recommendations for improving federal governmental performance, touching on virtually every agency and program. Despite criticisms that the process was stalled within months of the release of the report, Kettl and DiIulio (1995) concluded that it led to real change, for example, in governmental culture, procurement practices, and cuts to some government agencies. By the second Clinton–Gore term, the effort had shifted to trying to imbed reinvention as a permanent feature of federal government agencies, and so the National Performance Review was rechristened as the National Partnership for Reinvention in Government. The priorities enunciated at the time included better service delivery, partnerships, and efficiency. These were joined by an emphasis on customer satisfaction and more online services. The election of George W. Bush in 2000 signalled a new direction in public management priorities for the U.S. government. Bush supported the mantras of efficiency and smaller government, but was much more ideologically enthused by reliance on market mechanisms to achieve public policy goals. Moreover, his one overarching public management initiative in the early part of his first term was more community-based delivery of public services and programs, but, in particular, with an emphasis on faith-based organizations (principally charities, but churches as well). This was new public management in the sense of community partnerships, and in the sense of a skepticism of traditional government bureaucracy, but with a new focus on charitable organizations. The 9/11 terrorist attacks eclipsed this initiative and, indeed, put the Bush administration on a completely different track with respect to public sector management. From a champion of small government, Bush was transformed into a champion of strong, robust, and, at least in connection with things pertaining to security, muscular and interventionist government. In the largest centralizing move in American peacetime, Bush released the National Strategy for Homeland Security, passed the Homeland Security Act, and created the Department of Homeland Security with 180 000 employees. Funding for homeland security tripled in the first two years to US$30 billion. The new department brought together the security services, Coast Guard, border control, emergency preparedness agencies, and immigration, along with several others. From that point on, the demands of fighting terrorism induced large and intrusive government at the national level, as well as massive spending to create the largest deficit in U.S. history.

It is difficult to track a clear line on public management reform for the Obama administration. Elected president in 2008 amid rare national euphoria, Obama was instantly confronted with two sets of legacy issues and one personal priority that swamped almost anything else in his first administration. The wars in Iraq and Afghanistan posed huge foreign policy challenges, and the collapse of the U.S. financial system and the accompanying recession matched them on the domestic front. Added to that was a determination to "fix" the U.S. healthcare system. All of these meant significantly larger government and more spending and more deficits, to the point that mid-term elections in 2010 gave Republicans and small-government "Tea Partyers" control of Congress and a shot at the presidency in 2012.

The wars, the security paranoia, the fiendishly complicated architecture of Obama's Affordable Care Act, all contributed to a massive expansion of the role of government in the United States. To take only one example, the Troubled Asset Relief Program, or TARP (which was signed into law by President Bush in October 2008): TARP was designed to address the market volatility precipitated by the subprime mortgage crisis, by allowing the U.S. Department of the Treasury to purchase (or insure) up to $700 billion of troubled assets. These troubled assets include residential or commercial mortgages, and any other financial instrument(s) necessary to maintain market stability. Essentially, the U.S. government would purchase these assets, hold them for a period of time, until the price of the assets recovers, and then sell them back (ideally at a profit to the Treasury and participating banks and financial institutions).

The significant point about TARP is that it essentially became a vehicle for the (temporary) nationalization of massive private assets, including buying General Motors and effectively running the company. The program will go on for as long as a decade, and while there have been some success stories (of assets rebounding and being sold at a profit), even in 2011 it was not clear (and this is from the agency that runs the program) that TARP would make money let alone break even (SIGTARP, 2011).

These are examples of unavoidable administrative reforms that have made the U.S. government even larger and more bureaucratic. However, President Obama did launch a public management reform initiative shortly after being elected: the Open Government Directive. In a memorandum to all Executive Departments and Agencies, the president articulated the three themes of the program: transparency, participation, and collaboration.

> Government should be transparent. Transparency promotes accountability and provides information for citizens about what their Government is doing. Information maintained by the Federal Government is a national asset....
>
> Government should be participatory. Public engagement enhances the Government's effectiveness and improves the quality of its decisions. Knowledge is widely dispersed in society, and public officials benefit from having access to that dispersed knowledge....
>
> Government should be collaborative. Collaboration actively engages Americans in the work of their Government. Executive departments and agencies should use innovative tools, methods, and systems to cooperate among themselves, across all levels of Government, and with nonprofit organizations, businesses, and individuals in the private sector. Executive departments and agencies should solicit public feedback to assess and improve their level of collaboration and to identify new opportunities for cooperation. (White House, 2009)

As a later extension of the plan in the 2011 budget, President Obama called for more specific performance targets (a set of 128 sub-goals that could be achieved in 18 to 24 months were identified), public dashboards (electronic, Web-based reporting widgets that provide clean, clear, and often real-time information about government services, spending, and so on), social media, and problem-solving networks that break down traditional bureaucratic boundaries (Kamensky, 2011). As we note below in our discussion of Canadian management developments and thinking about governance, these are hardly new ideas. An emphasis on performance and transparency (sometimes reinforced with an emphasis on accountability) has been part of the governance conversation for well

Figure 2.3 Bureaucratic versus Post-bureaucratic Organization/ Management

Bureaucratic Organization	*Post-bureaucratic Organization*
Policy and Management Culture	

Organization-centred
    Emphasis on needs of the
    organization itself
	Citizen-centred
	    Quality service to citizens (and
	    clients/stakeholders)

Position power
    Control, command and
    compliance
	Participative leadership
	    Shared values and participative
	    decision making

Rule-centred
    Rules, procedures and
    constraints
	People-centred
	    An empowering and caring milieu
	    for employees

Independent action
    Little consultation, cooperation
    or coordination
	Collective action
	    Consultation, cooperation and
	    coordination

Status quo-oriented
    Avoiding risks and mistakes
	Change-oriented
	    Innovation, risk taking and
	    continuous improvement

Process oriented
    Accountability for process
	Results oriented
	    Accountability for results

Structure	

Centralized
    Hierarchy and central controls
	Decentralized
	    Decentralization of authority and
	    control

Departmental form
    Most programmes delivered by
    operating departments
	Non-departmental form
	    Programmes delivered by wide
	    variety of mechanisms

Market Orientation	

Budget driven
    Programmes financed largely
    from appropriations
	Revenue driven
	    Programmes financed as far as
	    possible on cost recovery basis

Monopolistic
    Government has monopoly
    on programme delivery
	Competitive
	    Competition with private sector
	    for programme delivery

Source: From K. Kernaghan, "The Post-Bureaucratic Organization and Public Service Values," March 2000. International Institute of Administrative Studies, 2000, published by Sage Publications Ltd. Reprinted by permission of Copyright Clearance Center.

over a decade. Obama's embrace shows that despite tendencies (especially in the American case) for bigger government, the search for performance and results will not go away.

The British example is perhaps more relevant to the Canadian context because Britain too is a parliamentary democracy, and because it has not mixed NPM principles with religious fervour or a new massive security apparatus. Reforms began with Margaret Thatcher, but two initiatives, the **Next Steps** program and the **Citizen's Charter**, illustrate the early goals of the organizational revolution that took place in the United Kingdom (Doern, 1993; Jenkins & Gray, 1993). Tony Blair's "New Labour" victory in 1997 carried the government reform agenda forward with even greater vigour.

Next Steps had its origins in the Financial Management Initiative of 1982, which tried to underscore the importance of management in government by introducing better practices and giving managers greater autonomy over budgets and operations as long as they met certain performance and output targets. By the late 1980s the reform had bogged down, and so efforts were redoubled to take the "Next Steps" of the original Financial Management Initiative in decentralizing government services. The plan called for as many agencies as possible to be converted to "departmental executive agencies" that would essentially act as businesses delivering public services. The chief executive officer of each Next Step agency was to negotiate a contract with the department specifying performance goals and targets but would then have substantial freedom to operate the "business" as he or she saw fit. In a little over a year, eight agencies were created. By April 1993, 89 such agencies were employing almost two-thirds of the civil service. By 1998, 377 500 civil servants worked in 138 Next Steps agencies and four departments with Next Steps business lines.

This emphasis on decentralization was matched with a new emphasis on service and performance. The U.K. Citizen's Charter was introduced by John Major in 1991 after he had assumed the prime ministership from Margaret Thatcher. Whereas Next Steps introduced fundamental organizational changes, the Charter was designed to alter bureaucratic practices in order to raise the quality of public services. The Citizen's Charter applied across the British government and was joined to a program called "Service First." There was also an improved **Charter Mark** program. The Charter Mark program was a scheme to judge public sector organizations on their performance with customers and clients. Any agency that provided services directly to the public, and voluntary agencies that received at least 10 percent of their funds from public sources, could apply to receive a Charter Mark. Applications were made to assessors, based on six service standards (strong performance standards; serving customers; fairness, accessibility, and choice; continuous improvement;

effective resource management; and contribution to the quality of life in the community) and empirical evidence that customers agreed that those standards had been met.

The emphasis on service and, more important, the tailoring of services to citizens/customers, began in 2002 with the Blair government's new framework on social services delivery. The overarching goal of the strategy was customer satisfaction with the quality and variety of services, but also personalization of those services, on the understanding that the universalistic welfare state of the postwar period did not adequately respond to the different needs of individuals. The plan was premised on four key principles (national standards, devolution to the front line, flexibility to deliver diverse services, expanded choice for customers), which were to be buttressed with a new, more robust performance measurement and standards regime. Its vision was to create public service institutions that could develop responsively to citizen needs.

Prime Minister Cameron's "Big Society" is another attempted revolution in public sector thinking. He outlined it for the first time in the 2010 British election as the approach his government would take to dealing with social problems. The Big Society is "a society where the leading force for progress is social responsibility, not state control. It includes a whole set of unifying approaches—breaking state monopolies, allowing charities, social enterprises and companies to provide public services, devolving power down to neighbourhoods, making government more accountable" (Conservatives [U.K.], 2010). The state's role is to break public bureaucratic monopolies and galvanize and enable the "little platoons" of charities and neighbourhoods and towns and villages to tackle social problems themselves. The government would also provide funding channels for these social enterprises, but try to engage the private sector as well. The approach reflects a philosophy of decentralization, competition in the delivery of public services, and broad social engagement rather than a reliance on public bureaucracies. In July 2011 these early ideas were articulated in an Open Services White Paper (Cabinet Office [U.K.], 2011). Its core principles were to increase choice in public services, to decentralize them to the lowest appropriate level, to open them to a range of providers, to ensure fair access, and to make them accountable to users and taxpayers. The experiment is ongoing, but potentially radical. However, it faced the complication of the British government simultaneously launching the largest austerity exercise in recent history, leading observers to conclude that it was simply a way to offload services and cut government budgets ("Reshaping the State," 2011).

Canada did not go as far as the United Kingdom or other leaders in new public management, such as New Zealand and Australia, and its administrative practices diverged sharply from the Bush administration. At the provincial level, the governments of Alberta under Ralph Klein and

Ontario under Mike Harris attracted the most attention in the 1990s. The Alberta government passed a Deficit Elimination Act that committed it to that goal for 1996–97 but actually achieved a balanced budget a year earlier through deep spending cuts. It restructured its welfare services, closed hospitals, consolidated school boards, and privatized its liquor stores (Bruce, Kneebone, & McKenzie, 1997). A Conservative government was elected in Ontario in 1995 on the platform of its Common Sense Revolution, which promised virtually the same policy configuration as Alberta's (Ibbitson, 1997). In the words of Mike Harris, "I am not talking about tinkering, about incremental changes, or about short term solutions. After all, the changes we have all experienced in our personal lives have been much more fundamental than that. It's time for us to take a fresh look at government. To re-invent the way it works, to make it work for people" (Progressive Conservative Party of Ontario, 1995, p. 1). The high rhetoric, however, reflected massive changes under way in all the provinces. Lindquist and Murray (1994) concluded that all provincial governments in this period had been engaged in downsizing, delayering, and focusing on service quality. While Alberta and Ontario led the way, governments in British Columbia under Gordon Campbell and in Quebec under Jean Charest each implemented NPM principles.

At the federal level, the early vehicle of public sector reform was the **Program Review** exercise, launched in 1994. The scope and impact of the review hit home with Canadians only in the February 1995 federal budget statement. The language of that budget was as uncompromising as that in the Common Sense Revolution: "The Program Review will lead to long-standing structural change in what government does" (Department of Finance, 1995, p. 32). Program Review was guided by six tests or questions: "serving the public interest; necessity of government involvement; appropriate federal role; scope for public sector/ private sector partnerships; scope for increased efficiency; affordability" (Department of Finance, 1995, p. 34). These tests were explicitly linked to a deficit-reduction strategy that the federal government finally decided to embark upon seriously in 1995 (Greenspon & Wilson-Smith, 1996). Compared to some other countries, Canada's federal public-sector reform effort was at first primarily fiscally driven, something that set up two dynamics. The first was directly harnessed to the fiscal program and sought to implement wide-ranging public sector reforms to achieve more effective and efficient governance. The lead agency on this front was the Treasury Board, and it carried forward a program of management reform through the late 1990s under the rubric of **Getting Government Right**. The other dynamic was a reactive one, as the public sector sought to implement reforms to deal with the consequences of fiscal cuts; this effort was spearheaded primarily by the Clerk of the Privy Council, whose efforts under *La Relève* were briefly described in Chapter 1.

The *Getting Government Right* (1997) initiative was organized around several key themes. Together, they summarize Ottawa's reform efforts, which, while they were not structurally radical, did have a wide scope in covering both services and programs as well as their presentation to Parliament and to the public: modernizing program delivery (service clustering, transparency of regulatory procedures, cost-recovery where appropriate); alternative service delivery; partnering with other levels of government and the private sector; greater strategic oversight for central agencies like the Treasury Board; better accountability to Parliament and to the public.

The next phase of management reform from the Treasury Board was the president's 2000 report entitled *Results for Canadians*. The president pointed out that the management framework articulated in the document did not mark a departure from Getting Government Right, but a consolidation. The framework was to be guided by a four-step agenda: (1) recognize that the federal government must build a "citizen focus" into all its activities and services; (2) highlight the importance of public service values; (3) focus on achieving results for Canadians; and (4) promote "discipline, due diligence and value for money in the use of public funds" (Treasury Board of Canada Secretariat, 2000). *Results for Canadians* did not depart markedly from the 1997 approach, except that it emphasized structural changes in the federal government much less. In a sense, Ottawa had undergone whatever organizational changes it was prepared to stomach (indeed, federal employment began to grow again so that by 2003 it was at pre-Program Review levels). What was new was an emphasis on values and democratic accountability. As well, the focus on results was much greater—larger efforts were to go into developing indicators of program performance and reporting on them. In 2001 and 2002, the government produced government-wide performance reports for the country as a whole, taking the process beyond simply reporting at a departmental or agency level.

In its report *Plans and Priorities, 2003–2004*, the Treasury Board cited the importance of both *Getting Government Right* and *Results for Canadians* as the core of the federal government's management framework (Treasury Board of Canada, 2003). It highlighted again the importance of service quality improvements, particularly in reference to the Government On-Line initiative, an $880 million program over six years to make the most commonly used federal government services available and accessible to all Canadians online (Government On-Line, 2006). It also referred to the introduction of a comprehensive package of reforms to the federal public service—the Public Service Modernization Act. The core of this initiative was to encourage all federal managers (deputy heads) to use more flexible definitions of merit in their hiring decisions, and give them wider authority over hiring and staffing in their organizations. The intent was to streamline the often cumbersome human resource practices in the federal government.

By 2003, then, the public sector reform process at the federal level had emphasized performance, results, service, and a leaner, more partnered, and decentralized institutional framework—and these were all consistent with new public management. Accountability was a key item, but submerged within the overall emphasis on performance. This began to change in 2003, first with the alleged scandal of $1 billion lost in grants and contributions from Human Resources Development Canada (Good, 2003), and then with the sponsorship scandal and the Gomery Commission that investigated it (Commission of Inquiry into the Sponsorship Program and Advertising Activities [Gomery Commission], 2006; Perreault, 2006). Gomery, in particular, had fed the public imagination for almost two years with televised testimony of alleged kickback schemes, weeping and contrite corporate executives, and even former prime minister Chrétien pulling golf balls out of his briefcase. The Conservatives capitalized on this and made a new **Federal Accountability Act** the centrepiece of their election campaign. Once they won, the government moved quickly to put forward the new legislation.

The Federal Accountability Act is a sweeping piece of legislation that aims to change both political and public management practices in the Canadian federal government (Treasury Board of Canada, 2006). Among its highlights are new restrictions on party financing (a complete ban on contributions by unions, corporations, and other organizations; an annual limit of $1000 in donations by individuals); tougher conflict of interest guidelines (now enshrined in legislation with a new Conflict of Interest and Ethics Commissioner who can initiate formal investigations); a new independent Commissioner on Lobbyists, coupled with tougher standards on disclosure of contacts between lobbyists and decisionmakers; a new Parliamentary Budget Office to give objective analysis to Parliament on the nation's finances and economic trends, with the power to demand data from departments; a new Public Appointments Commission to oversee the selection process for government boards, commissions, agencies, and Crown corporations; tighter government procurement provisions; enhanced powers for the Auditor General to "follow the money"; and new whistle-blower provisions through the Public Servants Disclosure Protection Act with access to a more independent Public Service Integrity Commissioner as an officer of Parliament.

One of the more interesting if obscure provisions of the Accountability Act was the designation of deputy heads of departments as "**accounting officers.**" This convention has been used in Britain for more than one hundred years and is also accepted in Ireland, South Africa, and India. The basic idea is that deputy heads are personally responsible for the administration and management of their departments, and are accountable to Parliament and the public. This goes against the Canadian tradition of full ministerial responsibility for both policy and management of departments, a tradition that Gomery argued allowed ministers as well as officials to effectively avoid their responsibilities. The legislation fudged the issue by defining deputy heads as accounting officers consistent with the principle of ministerial responsibility, but Parliament (House of Commons, 2007) and the government (Privy Council Office, 2008) took a different view of what this meant in terms of the answerability of officials.

The state of public sector reform at the federal level in mid-2008 was therefore quite complicated. On the one hand, the NPM reforms in the mid-1990s and early 2000s had been hardwired into the system, institutionalized, and embedded in review and performance appraisal mechanisms. For example, the **Management Accountability Framework (MAF)**, developed in 2002, "sets out the Treasury Board's expectations of senior public service managers for good public service management. The MAF is structured around ten key elements that collectively define 'management' and establish the expectations for good management of a department or agency" (Treasury Board of Canada, 2007). Those 10 elements are summarized in Figure 2.4. Note that they include both "hard" and "soft" elements of new public management: risk management, accountability, results, and performance balanced against people, stewardship, accountability, and public service values.

Overlaying these NPM legacies are two new developments. One is a new public management regime with an unusually forceful emphasis on ethics and accountability. This development did not come about because Canada is especially corrupt (for amusing examples of U.S. federal government ethical lapses, see the Department of Defense's *Encyclopedia of Ethical Failure*, 2010); indeed, the Gomery Commission showed that overall the system worked quite well and that the scandal was due to a handful of rogue politicians and public servants. But the mood in Ottawa has changed (possibly across the country as well), and there is an extraordinary emphasis on probity. Ironically, an emphasis on probity and conduct translates into an emphasis on procedure and a web of formal and complex rules, and so this new overlay, to some extent, runs against the grain of the NPM optimism that government could become less bureaucratic, more nimble, agile, and responsive (Lépine, 2007).

A second development is a fresh emphasis on public sector renewal, particularly with respect to human resources. In November 2006 the prime minister appointed a blue-ribbon Advisory Committee on the Public Service. The committee's mandate was to focus on several key challenges for the federal public sector, primary of which were a major demographic shift (a huge wave of retirements due in the next five years)

Figure 2.4   Management Accountability Framework

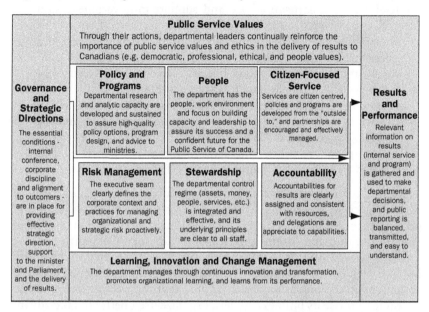

Source: *Management Accountability Framework,* URL: http:www.tbs.sct.gc.ca/maf-crg/ documents/booklet-livret-eng.asp, Department of Treasury Board of Canada Secretariat, 2005. Reproduced with the permission of the Minister of Public Works and Government Services Canada, 2012.

combined with a strong labour market that makes it imperative that the public service be competitive in attracting and retaining talent. Joined to this effort was the establishment of an associate secretary to Cabinet for public service renewal, a Deputy Ministers' Committee on Public Service Renewal, and an external Advisory Committee on Senior Level Retention and Compensation (it has existed since 1998). These changes all signalled a new, and somewhat un-NPM appreciation of the importance of a well-functioning public service. As the advisory committee on the public service put it in its first (2007) report:

> The first premise for our work as a committee is that a well-functioning and values-based public service is critical to the success of every country in today's complex and interconnected world. As a national institution, a high-quality, merit-based Public Service is part of Canada's comparative advantage and a key to competitiveness in the global economy. It also helps provide the foundation for sound democratic government, which is critical to a positive business climate in Canada.

The traditional mission of the Public Service is to provide professional, non-partisan advice and support to government, and high-quality programs and services that are responsive to the changing needs of Canadians. This means developing policies and programs that serve not just one sector or region but all Canadians, and not just for today but also for the longer term. The benefits—often unseen—that Canadians enjoy from the work of public servants include everything from effective regulation in various areas to border services, cultural institutions, and the federal contribution to Canada's broader criminal justice system. Federal programs touch Canadians in almost every facet of their daily lives. (Advisory Committee on the Public Service, 2007)

In its second report the committee continued to push the importance of excellence in the public service, more streamlined recruitment and performance measures, and a re-organized human resource management structure within the federal government (Advisory Committee on the Public Service, 2008). In its fifth report in 2011, it repeated that mantra, but also highlighted the impact of the financial crisis and coming cuts and reductions in the public service. It argued that the public service had to continue to revise its business models, organize itself better to take advantage of new technologies, and focus on its core business and shift the rest to the private sector (Advisory Committee on the Public Service, 2011).

New public management in the 1990s and early 2000s was a global phenomenon and argued to have similar characteristics no matter what the national context (Kettl, 2005; Lynn Jr., 2001). As Pollitt (1995) put it: "One senses an 'official line' advanced, with local inflections, by most national government leaders" (p. 204). This official line coalesced around a strong political emphasis on certain techniques: decentralization of budgeting, performance indicators, performance-related pay, an emphasis on quality and standards, the contractualization of relationships, and evaluation coupled with a concern about value for money. We should remember, however, that academic versions of new policy management, as well as some practical real-world examples, suggest a variety of sometimes inconsistent models (Peters, 1995). The emphasis on empowerment and the distrust of bureaucracy, for example, is just as likely to lead to a greater emphasis on broad political participation in policymaking as it is market-based prescriptions (Denhardt & Denhardt, 2000, 2003). And indeed, different models were implemented in different countries (Bevir, Rhodes, & Weller, 2003; Christensen & Laegreid, 2002, 2007).

The mix of public sector reform trends in Canada by 2012 consisted of some holdovers from the NPM movement—a continued emphasis on efficiency, somewhat smaller government if possible, and more work on service, performance, and results measurement. In the Canadian case, the sponsorship scandal changed political discourse and injected a high premium on accountability and ethics into discussions of public sector reform. Due to the financial crisis, the government launched a $50 billion stimulus program in 2008—the Economic Action Plan—promising to reduce the incurred deficits after 2011 (Pal, 2011). This reduction could come only from substantial cuts, the plan for which was announced in the 2010 Speech from the Throne. It involved a freeze on departmental operating budgets and an Administrative Services Review that would try to make "back office" services and platforms (e.g., human resource software) more efficient. These initiatives constituted yet another wave of public sector reform, but this one was completely driven by fiscal considerations.

A provincial counterpart to this deep search for public management reform in the light of fiscal pressures was the Commission on the Reform of Ontario's Public Services (2012), chaired by Don Drummond. The Commission's wide mandate (virtually unrestricted—it could examine anything it wished) made it more than a cost-cutting exercise and more of a review of government itself. Nonetheless, the report asserted that the only way to get out of deficits and to stay out was to reform, deeply, government programs. It offered 362 recommendations on health, educa- tion, social programs, employment and training, immigration, business support programs, infrastructure, electricity, environment, and justice, among others. While many of these recommendations were simply about cost-cutting (e.g., terminating full-day Kindergarten), many strove to suggest efficiencies and synergies (perhaps most comprehensively in the health field). And along with the cost-cutting and the efficiency was a motif of pursuing excellence in public service, in seeking profound reform in how government works as well as in how it spends.

The important point to keep in mind, however, is that these changes, however difficult they may be to align, do make for a very different public sector context for policymaking in the second decade of this cen- tury. There are greater pressures on performance, accountability, service, probity, and efficiency than ever before, which complicates the policy environment considerably. While governments continue to uphold the value of a professional public service, they are trying to balance that against enormous fiscal pressures. This situation poses challenges, but opportunities as well.

Conclusion

Are the forces described in this chapter stable, and will they last? Yes and no. Globalization, increasing cultural diversity, the decline of deference, and the information revolution are impossible to reverse and impossible to avoid. Governance, or our systems of public policy development and administration, are reactions to these forces, and can be expected to change and vary over time. Governing is about making choices, and choices are still very much available despite the inevitability of these forces. For example, the budget cutting, downsizing, and restructuring that characterized the mid-1990s and 2011–12 was indeed compelled, in part, by globalization, but governments handled it in different ways. In 2006 the Conservatives made key choices on implementing the Federal Accountability Act, on reducing the GST, and on changing course from an institutional daycare option favoured by the previous government to a Universal Child Care Benefit (giving parents $100 per month for each child under the age of six). The government of British Columbia introduced a carbon tax—the first in North America—in its 2008 budget. Each province in 2011–12 was facing a different fiscal situation, and the federal government was responding to shifting international forces; they had to make different choices based on their circumstances.

The changed context for policymaking does not mean the end of choices, simply different constraints, and different choices within those constraints. But those choices will not be made by governments of the type familiar in the 1990s; we have moved and continue to move from a bureaucratic model to something different and hybridized. Forms and processes of governance have changed, as have the problems they tackle and the means at their disposal. This book is about the new constraints, the new choices, and the new tools available to policymakers. The themes developed in this chapter will weave through the rest as we explore what it means to go beyond policy analysis. The next chapter looks more closely at the first key phase of policymaking, problem definition, and its link to the agenda-setting process.

KEY TERMS

accounting officer—designation of a deputy head of a federal department as personally responsible and accountable to Parliament for the administration and management of a department

Charter Mark (U.K.)—a scheme to engage independent assessors to judge and certify public sector organizations on their performance with customers and clients

Citizen's Charter (U.K.)—introduced by John Major in 1991 and designed to alter bureaucratic practices by publicly stating government service obligations to citizens

citizenship—traditional collection of civil and political rights that aim to treat individuals roughly the same, regardless of their social and economic differences

collective identities—widely shared characteristics such as race or language that are politically salient as a way of orienting oneself in politics

cultural identity—a normative base for making specific rights claims on behalf of individuals who are members of specific cultural groups

decline of deference—the decline in citizens' trust and confidence in their governments and increasing desire to be consulted, to participate, and to be heard in policy development

deficit reduction—a fiscal policy to reduce and eventually eradicate the budget deficit

Federal Accountability Act—major piece of public sector reform legislation introduced by the Conservative government in 2006 to deal with political party financing, lobbyists, and whistle-blowers, and to strengthen a host of institutions such as the Auditor General

free market capitalism—a type of capitalism that emphasizes smaller government, the minimum of controls and regulations, and wide scope for markets in the delivery of goods and services

Getting Government Right—a program of federal management reform led by the Treasury Board Secretariat through the late 1990s, which sought to implement wide-ranging public sector reforms to achieve more effective and efficient governance

global civil society—an emerging series of networks of activist NGOs and connected nongovernmental institutions that can be mobilized quickly around policy issues

global supply chain—also known as global value chain, represents the distribution of corporate functions (management, finances, communication, production) across the globe

globality—the sense that the entire planet is a single social space, that people carry on conversations in that space irrespective of territoriality, that they pay collective and simultaneous attention to "global events"

globalization system—the idea that globalization is not simply a matter of greater interdependence but is also a system with its own dynamics and logic

government restructuring—substantial and wide-reaching structural change in public administration and management, usually intended to reflect new public management objectives of efficiency and effectiveness

human rights—the recognition of the inherent dignity and of the equal and inalienable rights of all members of the human family

international standards—either formal or informal standards developed by the international community that are intended to supplement and sometimes override domestic standards

liberal individualism—insists that equality will best be achieved by treating people as individuals under a system of universally applicable and consistent rules

liberal universalism—the preference to treat individuals according to a universally applicable set of rules, not those tailored to specific group differences

Management Accountability Framework (MAF)—a set of 10 principles or measures against which the performance of senior federal public service managers' performance will be assessed

multiculturalism—a policy of protecting and celebrating the cultural diversity of different groups within a society, and ensuring that there is no discrimination on those grounds

National Performance Review (U.S.)—a program of public sector reform of the Clinton administration, headed by Vice-President Al Gore, in March 1993, touching on virtually every agency and program in the U.S. federal government

new public management—focus on performance appraisal and efficiency; disaggregating and decentralizing public bureaucracies; the use of market mechanisms and of contracting out to foster competition; financial management; partnerships

Next Steps (U.K.)—the plan in the late 1980s to convert many traditional departments into "departmental executive agencies" that would essentially act as businesses delivering public services

policy reversal—the changes in key policies during the early 1990s that have altered key social and political systems built up in the postwar period in both the developed and developing world

political culture—people's orientations of support and trust toward the political system

politics of difference—an emphasis on rights, discourse, culture, and group-specific differences as the foundation of politics and policy

postmaterialism—the broad cultural shift around the world but particularly in the West away from material concerns to questions of identity and lifestyle

postmodern condition—term used to describe the amalgam of conditions consisting of the rise of postmaterialism, the increased salience of rights, and the new emphasis on "difference"

Program Review—the federal Liberal government's policy in the mid-1990s of management reform and program-by-program assessment according to six criteria as a means for reducing the deficit and enhancing efficiency

public management—the process of directing the public sector as a whole as well as the specific agencies within it

race to the bottom—competition among countries for investment by lowering of standards

rights talk—a mode of political discourse that emphasizes the salience of individual and group rights

social cohesion—a sense of belonging to a community that shares values and a sense of purpose and commitment

social fragmentation—the process of losing social cohesion

trade liberalization—the process of lowering trade barriers of every sort such as duties and nontariff barriers, to encourage trade and investment flows

transnational corporations—commercial firms that operate in numerous countries, not simply for the sale of their products, but to organize production itself

FURTHER READINGS

Banting, K., Courchene, T. J., & Seidle, F. L. (Eds.). (2007). *Belonging?: Diversity, recognition and shared citizenship in Canada*. Montréal, QC: Institute for Research on Public Policy.

Barzelay, M. (2001). *The new public management: Improving research and policy dialogue*. Berkeley, CA: University of California Press.

Christensen, T., & Laegreid, P. (Eds.). (2007). *Transcending new public management: The transformation of public sector reforms*. Aldershot, UK: Ashgate.

Inglehart, R. (Ed.). (2003). *Human values and social change: Findings from the values surveys*. Leiden, Netherlands: Brill.

Kettl, D. F. (2005). *The global public management revolution* (2nd ed.). Washington, DC: Brookings Institution Press.

Norris, P. (2011). *Democratic deficit: Critical citizens revisited*. New York, NY: Cambridge University Press.

Ontario. Commission on the Reform of Ontario's Public Services. (2012). *Public services for Ontarians: A path to sustainability and excellence*. Retrieved from http://www.fin.gov.on.ca/en/reformcommission/chapters/report.pdf

Ritzer, G. (Ed.). (2007). *The Blackwell companion to globalization*. Malden, MA: Blackwell.

Scholte, J. A. (2005). *Globalization: A critical introduction* (2nd. ed.). Basingstoke, UK: Palgrave.

Stiglitz, J. E. (2003). *Globalization and its discontents*. New York, NY: W. W. Norton.

Stiglitz, J. E. (2006). *Making globalization work*. New York, NY: W. W. Norton.

REFERENCES

Abramson, P. R., & Inglehart, R. (1995). *Value change in global perspective*. Ann Arbor, MI: University of Michigan Press.

Adams, M. (2007). *Unlikely utopia: The surprising triumph of Canadian pluralism*. Toronto, ON: Viking Canada.

Adelman, H., & Anctil, P. (Eds.). (2011). *Religion, culture and the state: Reflections on the Bouchard-Taylor Report*. Toronto, ON: University of Toronto Press.

Advisory Committee on the Public Service (Canada). (2007). *Report to the Prime Minister, 2007*. Retrieved from http://www.tbs-sct.gc.ca/ren/cpmc/cpmc1-eng.asp

Advisory Committee on the Public Service (Canada). (2008). *Report to the Prime Minister, 2007*. Retrieved from http://www.tbs-sct.gc.ca/ren/cpmc/cpmc2-eng.asp

Advisory Committee on the Public Service (Canada). (2011). *Report to the Prime Minister, 2007*. Retrieved from http://www.tbs-sct.gc.ca/ren/cpmc/cpmc2-eng.asp

Appadurai, A. (1996). *Modernity at large: Cultural dimensions of globalization*. Minneapolis, MN: University of Minnesota Press.

Appadurai, A. (Ed.). (2001). *Globalization*. Durham, NC: Duke University Press.

Banting, K., Johnston, R., Kymlicka, W., & Soroka, S. (2006, December). Do multiculturalism policies erode the welfare state? An empirical analysis. In K. Banting & W. Kymlicka (Eds.), *Multiculturalism and the welfare state: Recognition and redistribution in contemporary democracies* (pp. 49–91). Oxford: Oxford University Press.

Banting, K. (2010, December). Is there a progressive's dilemma in Canada? Immigration, multiculturalism and the welfare state. *Canadian Journal of Political Science, 43*(4), 797–820.

Barber, B. R. (1995). *Jihad vs. McWorld*. New York, NY: Times Books.

Barry, B. (2001). *Culture and equality: An egalitarian critique of multi-culturalism.* Cambridge: Policy Press.

Barzelay, M. (1992). *Breaking through bureaucracy: A new vision for managing government.* Berkeley, CA: University of California Press.

Bevir, M., Rhodes, R. A. W., & Weller, P. (2003, March). Traditions of governance: Interpreting the changing role of the public sector. *Public Administration, 81*(1), 1–17.

Brook, T. (2007). *Vermeer's hat: The seventeenth century and the dawn of the global world.* New York, NY: Viking.

Bruce, C., Kneebone, R. D., & McKenzie, K. J. (Eds.). (1997). *A government reinvented: A study of Alberta's deficit elimination program.* Toronto, ON: Oxford University Press.

Cabinet Office (U.K.). (2011). *Open public services white paper.* Retrieved from http://www.cabinetoffice.gov.uk/resource-library/open-public-services-white-paper

Cairncross, F. (1997). *The death of distance: How the communications revolution will change our lives.* Boston, MA: Harvard Business School Press.

Cairns, A. C. (1991). *Disruptions: Constitutional struggle, from the Charter to Meech Lake* (ed. D. E. Williams). Toronto, ON: McClelland and Stewart.

Cairns, A. C. (1992). *Charter versus federalism.* Montréal, QC: McGill-Queen's University Press.

Cairns, A. C. (1993). The fragmentation of Canadian citizenship. In W. Kaplan (Ed.), *Belonging: The meaning and future of Canadian citizenship* (pp. 181–220). Montréal, QC: McGill-Queen's University Press.

Castells, M. (1997). *Economy, Society, and Culture: The power of identity* (Vol. 2). Oxford: Blackwell.

CCAPRCD [Consultation Commission on Accommodation Practices Related to Cultural Differences]. (2008a). *Home page.* Retrieved from http://www.accommodements.qc.ca/index-en.html

CCAPRCD. (2008b). *Building the future: A time for reconciliation.* Abridged report. Retrieved from http://www.accommodements.qc.ca/documentation/rapports/rapport-final-abrege-en.pdf

Christensen, T., & Laegreid, P. (Eds.). (2002). *New public management: The transformation of ideas and practice.* Aldershot, UK: Ashgate.

Christensen, T., & Laegreid, P. (Eds.). (2007). *Transcending new public management: The transformation of public sector reforms.* Aldershot, UK: Ashgate.

Conservatives (U.K.). (2010). *David Cameron: Our 'Big Society' plan.* Retrieved from http://www.conservatives.com/news/speeches/2010/03/david_cameron_our_big_society_plan.asp

Denhardt, R. B., & Denhardt, J. V. (2000, November). The new public service: Serving rather than steering. *Public Administration Review, 60*(6): 549–559.

Denhardt, R. B., & Denhardt, J. V. (2003). *The new public service: Serving, not steering.* Armonk, NY: M. E. Sharpe.

Department of Defense (U.S.). (2010). *Encyclopedia of ethical failure.* Washington, DC: Department of Defense. Retrieved from http://www.dod.gov/dodgc/defense_ethics/dod_oge/EEF_complete_10.doc

Department of Finance (Canada). (1995). *The federal budget.* Ottawa, ON: Ministry of Finance.

Doern, G. B. (1993, January). The UK Citizen's Charter: Origins and implementation in three agencies. *Policy and Politics, 21,* 17–29.

Florida, R. (2002). *The rise of the creative class: And how it's transforming work, leisure, community and everyday life.* New York, NY: Basic Books.

Florida, R. (2005). *The flight of the creative class: The new global competition for talent.* New York, NY: HarperBusiness.

Florida, R. (2008). *Who's your city? How the creative economy is making where you live the most important decision of your life.* Toronto, ON: Random House.

Friedman, T. L. (1999). *The Lexus and the olive tree: Understanding globalization.* New York, NY: Farrar, Straus, and Giroux.

Friedman, T. L. (2007). *The world is flat: A brief history of the twenty-first century.* New York, NY: Farrar, Straus, and Giroux.

Glendon, M. A. (1991). *Rights talk: The impoverishment of political discourse.* New York, NY: The Free Press.

Gomery Commission [Commission of Inquiry into the Sponsorship Program and Advertising Activities]. (2006). *Restoring accountability: Recommendations.* Ottawa, ON: Public Works and Government Services of Canada.

Good, D. (2003). *The politics of public management: The HRDC audit of grants and contributions.* Toronto, ON: University of Toronto Press.

Government On-Line. (2006). *Report.* Retrieved from http://publications.gc.ca/site/eng/290633/publication.html

Greenspon, E., & Wilson-Smith, A. (1996). *Double vision: The inside story of the Liberals in power.* Toronto, ON: Doubleday.

Heine, J., & Thakur, R. (Eds.). (2011). *The dark side of globalization.* Tokyo: United Nations University Press.

House of Commons (Canada). (2007). *Protocol for the appearance of accounting officers as witnesses before the Standing Committee on Public Accounts.* Retrieved from http://www.parl.gc.ca/HousePublications/Publication.aspx?DocId=2798921&Language=E

Ibbitson, J. (1997). *Promised land: Inside the Mike Harris revolution.* Scarborough, ON: Prentice-Hall.

Ignatieff, M. (2000). *The rights revolution.* Toronto, ON: House of Anansi.

Inglehart, R., & Welzel, C. (2005). *Modernization, cultural change, and democracy: The human development sequence.* New York, NY: Cambridge University Press.

International Organization for Migration. (2010). *World migration report 2010: The future of migration: Building capacities for change.* Geneva: International Organization for Migration.

International Monetary Fund. (2011, April 4). *Global challenges, global solutions.* An address presented by Dominique Strauss-Kahn at George Washington University, Washington, DC. Retrieved from http://www.imf.org/external/np/speeches/2011/040411.htm

Internet World Stats. (2011). *Internet users in the world.* Retrieved from http://www.internetworldstats.com/stats.htm

Jenkins, B., & Gray, A. (1993). Reshaping the management of government: The Next Steps initiative in the United Kingdom. In F. L. Seidle (Ed.), *Rethinking government: Reform of reinvention?* (pp. 73–109). Montréal, QC: Institute for Research on Public Policy.

Jenson, J. (2003). The frontiers of citizenship: Reflections. In T. J. Courchene & D. J. Savoie (Eds.), *The art of the state: Governance in a world without frontiers* (pp. 311–321). Montréal, QC: Institute for Research on Public Policy.

Kamensky, K. (2011). *Obama's performance revolution: Changing how government works (03-2010).* The IBM Centre for the Business of Government. Retrieved from http://www.businessofgovernment.org/brief/obamas-performance-revolution-changing-how-government-works-03-2010

Keck, M. E., & Sikkink, K. (1998). *Activists beyond borders: Advocacy networks in international politics.* Ithaca, NY: Cornell University Press.

Kernaghan, K. (2000, March). The post-bureaucratic organization and public service values. *International Review of Administrative Sciences, 66,* 91–104.

Kettl, D. F., & DiIulio, J. J., Jr. (Eds.). (1995). *Inside the reinvention machine: Appraising governmental reform*. Washington, DC: Brookings Institution Press.

Kettl, D. F. (2005). *The global public management revolution* (2nd ed.). Washington, DC: Brookings Institution Press.

Kymlicka, W. (2007). Ethnocultural diversity in a liberal state: Making sense of the Canadian model(s). In K. Banting, T. J. Courchene, & F. L. Seidle (Eds.), *Belonging?: Diversity, recognition and shared citizenship in Canada* (pp. 39–86). Montréal, QC: Institute for Research on Public Policy.

Lépine, G. (2007). *The web of rules: A study of the relationship between regulation of public servants and past public sector reform initiatives*. Toronto, ON: Public Policy Forum.

Lindquist, E. A., & Murray, K. B. (1994, September). Appendix: A reconnaissance of Canadian public administrative reform during the early 1990s. *Canadian Public Administration, 37*, 468–489.

Lynn Jr., L. E. (2001, June). Globalization and administrative reform: What is happening in theory? *Public Management Review, 3*, 191–208.

Mahon, R., Andrew, C., & Johns, R. (2007). Policy analysis in an era of "globalization": Capturing spatial dimensions and scalar strategies. In M. Orsini & M. Smith (Eds.), *Critical policy studies* (pp. 41–64). Vancouver, BC: UBC Press.

Martin, R. I. (2003). *The most dangerous branch: How the Supreme Court of Canada has undermined our law and our democracy*. Montréal and Kingston: McGill-Queen's University Press.

Montgomery, J. D. (1999, March). Fifty years of human rights: An emergent global regime. *Policy Sciences, 32*(1), 79–94.

Myles, J., & St-Arnaud, S. (2006). Population diversity, multiculturalism, and the welfare state: Should welfare state theory be revised? In K. Banting & W. Kymlicka (Eds.), *Multiculturalism and the welfare state: Recognition and redistribution in contemporary democracies* (pp. 339–354). Oxford: Oxford University Press.

Norris, P. (2011). *Democratic deficit: Critical citizens revisited*. New York, NY: Cambridge University Press.

OECD [Organisation for Economic Co-operation and Development]. (2011). *Government at a glance*. Paris: OECD.

Ohmae, K. (1990). *The borderless world: Power and strategy in the interlinked economy*. New York, NY: HarperBusiness.

Ohmae, K. (1995). *The end of the nation state: The rise of regional economies*. New York, NY: The Free Press.

Ohmae, K. (2004). *The next global stage: Challenges and opportunities in our borderless world.* Upper Saddle River, NJ: Wharton School Publishing.

Ontario. Commission on the Reform of Ontario's Public Services. (2012). *Public services for Ontarians: A path to sustainability and excellence.* Retrieved from http://www.fin.gov.on.ca/en/reformcommission/chapters/report.pdf

Osborne, D., & Gaebler, T. (1992). *Reinventing government: How the entrepreneurial spirit is transforming the public sector.* New York, NY: Penguin.

Pal, L. A. (1993). *Interests of state: The politics of language, multiculturalism, and feminism in Canada.* Montréal and Kingston: McGill-Queen's University Press.

Pal, L. A. (2011). Into the wild: The politics of economic stimulus. In C. Stoney & G. Bruce Doern (Eds.), *How Ottawa spends, 2011–2012: Trimming fat or slicing pork?* (pp. 39–59). Montréal and Kingston: McGill-Queen's University Press.

Pauly, L. W. (1997). *Who elected the bankers? Surveillance and control in the world economy.* Ithaca, NY: Cornell University Press.

Perreault, F. (2006). *Inside Gomery.* Toronto, ON: Douglas and McIntyre.

Peters, B. G. (1995). The public service, the changing state, and governance. In B. G. Peters & D. J. Savoie (Eds.), *Governance in a changing environment* (pp. 288–320). Montréal, QC: Canadian Centre for Management Development and McGill-Queen's University Press.

Peters, B. G. (2003). Democracy and political power in contemporary western governments: Challenges and reforms. In T. J. Courchene & D. J. Savoie (Eds.), *The art of the state: Governance in a world without frontiers* (pp. 81–108). Montréal, QC: Institute for Research on Public Policy.

Pew Global Attitudes Project. (2007). *World publics welcome global trade—But not immigration.* Retrieved from http://pewglobal.org/reports/display.php?ReportID=258

Pollitt, C. (1995). Management techniques for the public sector: Pulpit and practice. In B. G. Peters & D. J. Savoie (Eds.), *Governance in a changing environment* (pp. 203–238). Montréal, QC: Canadian Centre for Management Development and McGill-Queen's University Press.

Porter, M. E. (1990). *The competitive advantage of nations.* New York, NY: Free Press.

Privy Council Office (Canada). (2008). *Accounting officers: Guidance on roles, responsibilities and appearances before parliamentary committees 2007.* Retrieved from http://www.pco-bcp.gc.ca/index.asp?lang=eng&page=information&sub=publications&doc=ao-adc/2007/ao-adc-eng.htm

Progressive Conservative Party of Ontario. (1995). *The common sense revolution.* Toronto, ON: Progressive Conservative Party of Ontario.

Reshaping the state: Little platoons on a slow march. (2011, July 14). *The Economist.* Retrieved from http://www.economist.com/node/18958721/print

Rethmann, P., Szeman, I., & Coleman, W. D. (Eds.). (2010). *Cultural autonomy: Frictions and connections.* Vancouver, BC: UBC Press.

Ryan, P. (2010). *Multicultiphobia.* Toronto, ON: University of Toronto Press.

Sassen, S. (1998). *Globalization and its discontents.* New York, NY: The New Press.

Sassen, S. (2002a, April). Locating cities on global circuits. *Environment and Urbanization, 14*(1): 13–30.

Sassen, S. (Ed.). (2002b). *Global networks, linked cities.* New York, NY: Routledge.

Scholte, J. A. (2003). *What is globalization: The definitional issue—again* (Working Paper Series). Hamilton, ON: Institute on Globalization and the Human Condition, McMaster University.

Scholte, J. A. (2005). *Globalization: A critical introduction* (2nd ed.). Basingstoke, UK: Palgrave.

Slaughter, A.-M. (2004). *A new world order.* Princeton, NJ: Princeton University Press.

SIGTARP. (2011). *Quarterly report to Congress.* Retrieved from http://www.sigtarp.gov/reports/congress/2011/April2011_Quarterly_Report_to_Congress.pdf

Sikkink, K. (2011). *The justice cascade: How human rights prosecutions are changing world politics.* New York, NY: W. W. Norton and Company.

Soroka, S. N., Johnston, R., & Banting, K. (2007). Ties that bind? Social cohesion and diversity in Canada. In K. Banting, T. J. Courchene, & F. L. Seidle (Eds.), *Belonging?: Diversity, recognition and shared citizenship in Canada* (pp. 1–40). Montréal, QC: Institute for Research on Public Policy.

Statistics Canada. (2007). *Provincial economic accounts, annual estimates: Tables and analytical document* (Catalogue no. 13-213-PPB, pp. 324–326). Retrieved from http://www.statcan.ca/bsolc/english/bsolc?catno=13-213-P

Statistics Canada. (2011). *Imports, exports and trade balance of goods on a balance-of-payments basis, by country or country grouping.* Retrieved from http://www40.statcan.gc.ca/l01/cst01/gblec02a-eng.htm

Stiglitz, J. E. (2006). *Making globalization work*. New York, NY: W. W. Norton.

Thurow, L. C. (1996). *The future of capitalism: How today's economic forces shape tomorrow's world*. New York, NY: William Morrow.

Treasury Board Secretariat. (1997). *Getting government right*. Ottawa, ON: Minister of Public Works and Government Services Canada.

Treasury Board of Canada Secretariat. (2000). *Results for Canadians*. Ottawa, ON. Retrieved from http://www.tbs-sct.gc.ca/report/res_can/siglist-eng.asp

Treasury Board of Canada. (2003). *Plans and priorities, 2003–2004*. Ottawa.

Treasury Board of Canada. (2006). *Federal accountability action plan: Turning a new leaf*. Ottawa, ON. Retrieved from http://www.tbs-sct.gc.ca/faa-lfi/docs/ap-pa/ap-patb-eng.asp

Treasury Board of Canada. (2007). *Management accountability framework: Frequently asked questions*. Retrieved from http://www.tbs-sct.gc.ca/maf-crg/faq_e.asp

Union of International Associations. (2012). *Yearbook of international organizations, 2012/2013*. Retrieved from http://www.uia.be/ybvolall

United Nations. (2003). *The globalization of human rights*. Geneva: United Nations University Press.

Vogel, D. (1995). *Trading up: Consumer and environmental regulation in a global economy*. Cambridge, MA: Harvard University Press.

Vogel, D., & Kagan, R. (Eds.). (2004). *Dynamics of regulatory change: How globalization affects national regulatory policies*. Berkeley, CA: University of California Press.

White House (U.S.). (2009). *Transparency and open government*. Retrieved from http://www.whitehouse.gov/the_press_office/TransparencyandOpenGovernment/

World Bank. (2010). *Investing across borders 2010*. Retrieved from http://iab.worldbank.org/~/media/FPDKM/IAB/Documents/IAB-report.pdf

World Trade Organization. (2009). *International trade statistics 2010*. Chart 3. Retrieved from http://www.wto.org/english/res_e/statis_e/its2010_e/its10_charts_e.htm

World Trade Organization. (2011). *Dispute settlement: Chronological list of dispute cases*. Retrieved from http://www.wto.org/english/tratop_e/dispu_e/dispu_status_e.htm

Problem Definition in Policy Analysis

Policymaking is, in large measure, about trying to solve problems, and so the nature of those problems—how they are defined—is central to the entire process. But defining problems is not merely a technical exercise; it entails political and strategic manoeuvres, insofar as problem definition sets the tone for successive stages in the process. Framing problems draws on a wide variety of ingredients, from scientific expertise to conventional wisdom and rhetoric. In a democracy, it always means shaping arguments in ways that capture public attention and support. We discuss policy communication in Chapter 9, but in this chapter examine the nature and dynamics of problem definition. The second part of the chapter explores ways in which both the substance and the process of problem definition are changing in the face of the forces described in Chapter 2.

The core of any public policy is the triad of problem definition, goals, and instruments. Know them, and you know the policy. But if we view policy more dynamically, which of these elements comes first, or what is the prime mover in the policy response? There is almost universal agreement that the key factor is the problem or at least the definition of a situation considered problematic (Geva-May & Wildavsky, 1997, p. 1). As Dunn puts it: "Problem structuring is a central guidance system or steering mechanism that affects the success of all subsequent phases of policy analysis. Regrettably, policy analysts seem to fail more often because they solve the wrong problem than because they get the wrong solution to the right problem" (Dunn, 2008, p. 72). Policies are responses to problems, and so the character and shape of the problem will deeply affect the nature of the response. At the most extreme, if a problem is not widely recognized, there will be little or no policy response. The existence of widespread and systematic poverty in the United States in the late 1950s was largely ignored, for example, until the publication of Michael Harrington's *The Other America: Poverty in the United States* (1962). The same could be said of modern environmentalism: until Rachel Carson's *Silent Spring* (1962), the notion that what we were doing to the environment was a problem simply did not occur to many people. Al Gore's book and movie *An Inconvenient Truth* (2007) did the same for climate change. A striking Canadian example comes from research conducted by the Canadian Advisory Council on the Status of Women in 1987 on domestic abuse: the study *Battered but Not Beaten* by Linda MacLeod took something from the shadows of private family life and exposed it as a major social problem. In recent years there was a sudden burst of reports across North America about the looming "crisis" of obesity. While fat and dieting have been features of contemporary culture for years, obesity suddenly emerged as a policy problem; before it had been visible only as a personal issue. In March 2004, for example, the American Centers for Disease Control and Prevention announced that obesity would soon overtake smoking as the leading cause of preventable death, and media were festooned with stories about the connections between obesity and diabetes, and the impact on the young and the elderly. By 2010 the Organisation for Economic Co-operation and Development (OECD) had declared obesity to be a "global epidemic." It had launched its report on the subject in 2007 to probe the causes, effects, and remedies for an unfamiliar international health threat (OECD, 2010). All of these cases illustrate the fact that policy problems do not simply "exist out there"—they have to be recognized, defined, structured, and made visible.

It would seem that there should be another end of the continuum to complement problem invisibility, a point where problems are so well defined and understood that the policy response seems obvious and uncontroversial. There are very few of such problems, at least with respect to proposed solutions. On some issues, such as child pornography, consensus appears overwhelming about both the character of the problem (universally despised) and the solution (a strong prohibition), but even here there can be defences of artistic merit. Another instance is prostitution. While many would argue that prostitution is exploitative of those who sell their bodies, others argue that legal regimes to prohibit or severely restrict prostitution cause harm and danger. This thinking is behind the legalization of prostitution in jurisdictions such as Nevada and the Netherlands, and the partly successful challenge to Canadian prostitution laws in 2012 (the Ontario Court of Appeal decided that, for safety reasons, prostitutes may operate bawdy houses, but not solicit openly in public places). So clearly, there is more to problems than simply recognizing them or not: they have to be discerned, shaped, articulated, and defended. So many different elements can conceivably go into a problem definition—including both facts and values—that people may see the same situation quite differently, even if they agree on its general aspects. As a result, they will offer very different solutions.

The idea that people disagree in their perceptions of problems and solutions is hardly news, so it may come as a surprise to learn that there was and continues to be a strong stream of policy analysis that holds out the hope of trying to "get it right," in other words, to achieve the correct definition of the problem. As Stone (2012) put it:

> In conventional policy analysis textbooks, as well as in the larger rationality project, a problem definition is a statement of a goal and the discrepancy between it and the status quo. In this conception, problem definition is a matter of observation and arithmetic—measuring the difference between two states of affairs. (p. 128)

Almost 30 years ago, a leading text could refer to the possibility of making "mistakes" in the problem definition or initiation phase of policy design (Brewer & deLeon, 1983, p. 35). The idea of "making mistakes" would strike Stone (2012) as very odd since, to her, problem definition "is a matter of representation because every description of a situation is a portrayal from only one of many points of view ... [and it] is strategic because groups, individuals, and government agencies deliberately and consciously fashion portrayals so as to promote their favored course of action" (p. 145). When everything is open to interpretation, there is no clearly superior way of discerning a situation, and so all interpretations are equally valid. This insight explains the problem-saturated policy environment within which we live. The media, interest groups, experts, analysts, think tanks, and political parties subject us to a constant barrage of crises and problems. Not only is the number of problems apparently infinite, but the range of solutions seems bewilderingly wide.

Governments do not have infinite resources or time, however, and every government faces the ultimate test of having to choose among definitions and solutions and doing what it was elected to do: govern. It is this combination of epistemological variety and political reality that shapes the agenda of questions that occupy the literature on problem definition: (1) by what political and intellectual processes are problems defined, (2) what are the generic elements of a problem definition, (3) how are some problems chosen to be on the political/policy agenda while others languish in obscurity, and (4) what impact does problem definition have on subsequent stages of the policy process? The good news is that most of the answers to these questions are interesting and insightful. The bad news is that they are not systematic nor could we really expect them to be so. Problem definition has a strong socio-psychological dimension;

Chapter 3 Problem Definition in Policy Analysis

it is one component in the imaginative construction of reality, with heavy doses of professional skill, creativity, intuition, and serendipity. It is as much about "problem structuring" (problem finding, or puzzling about difficult problems) as it is about problem solving (Hoppe, 2010, p. 15; Winship, 2006). Moreover, problem definition is embedded in fluid political and policy processes, where accident and luck play a strong role. It is not surprising, therefore, that the literature is dominated by case studies that, while interesting, often conclude that "it all depends."

However, the questions, and some of the general answers to them, are worth exploring, if only because they do provide an organized way of thinking about problem definition and formulation. Contemporary policy analysis needs to go beyond this to recognize that some key elements of both the substance and process of problem definition have changed dramatically in the last decade in response to the forces described in Chapter 2. In terms of the substance of public policy problems, **globalization** and the global financial crisis have changed the agenda dramatically. While there might still be some **ideas in good currency**—that is, consensual standards of good governance and appropriate public policy—there has been tremendous turbulence in both policy problems and possible solutions in the last years. The tools needed to deal with these new policy problems in this altered environment are different from those in the past, and this chapter closes with a consideration of the demands this places on analysts.

Problem Definition: Key Issues

What constitutes a problem? A classic definition in the field is that a problem is a "substantial discrepancy between what is and what should be" (Dery, 1984, p. 17), or to put it another way, policy problems "are unrealized needs, values, or opportunities for improvement" (Dunn, 2008, p. 72). Hoppe builds on these definitions nicely: "Problems are experienced as non-acceptable discrepencies between real situations and desired future situations; between a socially constructed 'is' and 'ought'.... [T]hey vary in terms of consent on relevant, valid knowledge on what is and will or can be; as well as in terms of degrees of consent on values, norms and standards at stake in defining a desirable future situation" (Hoppe, 2010, p. 30). There are three components to these definitions: reality (what is—the unrealized needs or values), a desired state of affairs (what should be—the improvement), and the gap between them (the discrepancy). But why should the simple fact of a discrepancy or gap between reality and the ideal constitute a problem? Clearly it does not. Note that the definitions address what should be, not what could be. There have to be realistic opportunities for improvement. So, this is a first clue on the nature of problem definition—it is incomprehensible without some understanding of the goals being pursued or the standards being used to judge "what should be."

If standards are always involved in defining the desired state of affairs, the other key ingredient is discerning the gap or discrepancy. Indeed, discerning is the first phase in the process of problem definition. Before problems can be defined, they have to be recognized or sensed. This stage in problem definition is primordial in that it usually involves just a first tremor that something is wrong, a sense of unease that there is a difference between reality and our preferred standard. Strict constructionists like Deborah Stone (2012) see this as a highly unpredictable and strategic process and, moreover, one that is contingent on core assumptions, worldview, and social location. They see all problems as socially constructed. It is widely agreed, however, that values, perceptions, and interests play a huge role in this phase, since recognition depends on attention, and attention depends on relevance and an ability to notice and care about signals coming in from the environment around us. How likely is someone with a secure job who lives a middle-class lifestyle to notice or care about urban homelessness or Aboriginal suicide?

While the role of selective perception has a measure of truth to it, too strong an emphasis on mutually exclusive values tends to underestimate the degree to which some standards whereby we recognize nascent problems and public issues are widely shared and hardwired into the political process. **Problem recognition**, according to Kingdon (1995), is often stimulated by widely agreed-upon **indicators** and routine monitoring that turns up discrepancies or patterns that hint that something is amiss:

> Fairly often, problems come to the attention of government decision makers not through some sort of political pressure or perceptual sleight of hand but because some more or less systematic indicator simply shows that there is a problem out there. Such indicators abound in the political world because both governmental and nongovernmental agencies routinely monitor various activities and events: highway deaths, disease rates, immunization rates, consumer prices, commuter and intercity ridership, costs of entitlement programs, infant mortality rates, and many others. (p. 90)

Kingdon goes on to say that while pressure campaigns and dramatic events are certainly important in attracting notice to a problem, people pay attention "rather straightforwardly because there actually is a demonstrable problem that needs their attention" (p. 93). This response occurs in those instances where there is a reasonable degree of consensus about the indicators and what they mean. Canadian debates about poverty, for

Chapter 3 Problem Definition in Policy Analysis

example, are normally based on the low income cutoffs (LICO) developed by Statistics Canada. These cutoffs, however, were never intended to be a measure of poverty but rather an indicator of when the consumption of an "average" package of goods would become difficult (Sarlo, 1996, Chapter 2). Moreover, the LICO is a relative measure—it measures low income as a proportion of income spent on certain goods (20 percentage points or more of after-tax income on food, shelter, and clothing) above what other Canadian families of the same size spend. Another approach is an absolute measure of low income or poverty, which tries to determine what it would take at a minimum to survive. But even here, the definitions of these "market basket measures" can vary from bare necessities to something more elaborate. Nonetheless, despite debates and a variety of measures, when the number of Canadians who fall below the LICO increases, there are immediate concerns about possibly rising poverty in the country. Changes in other indicators such as the gross national product (GNP), the exchange rate, crime statistics, productivity rates, literacy, aging, teenage pregnancies, and smoking (to choose just a few) also convey messages. When the indicator shows a positive development (e.g., increases in GNP, productivity, and literacy), there is a general sense that "things are going well." When the indicator shows a negative development, this signals that perhaps there is a problem that needs attention.

Indicators come in various forms. Sometimes, they are routinely produced by programs and government departments—annual reports, unemployment statistics, Statistics Canada data, and government-sponsored research reports and studies. Interest groups, think tanks, and foundations, of course, have an interest in either highlighting indicators that support their cause or their orientation or in developing research that casts light on suspicions they have about a given issue or problem. These types of indicators are different from what Kingdon calls **"focusing events,"** which can be sudden catastrophes or crises that grab attention. One of the most chilling of these was the SARS (Severe Acute Respiratory Syndrome) epidemic. The first known outbreak occurred in Foshan City, Guangdong Province, China, on November 16, 2002. At that time it was not recognized as SARS, but simply as an unusual respiratory ailment. Almost two months later, the World Health Organization (WHO) received an email describing an unusual contagious disease that had left more than 100 people dead in Guangdong Province. In the next few days, Chinese authorities revealed that some 300 people were ill and five had died, but asserted that the cause was simply atypical pneumonia and that the outbreak was under control. Then followed a series of deaths and illnesses in Hong Kong that were ascribed to avian flu. By the end of the month, there were reports and rumours of as many as 50 hospitals in Guangzhou (in Guangdong Province) with ill patients. The mystery disease began to spread beyond China, as a Canadian woman and an American man both made their way homeward. The American man stopped over and became ill in Hanoi, and by March 5 the Canadian woman was dead in Toronto and five relatives were hospitalized. Still no one knew precisely what the disease was or where and how it was spreading. By mid-March the WHO had given SARS its name and issued a travel advisory on the suspicion that the disease was spreading through international flights. Not until mid-April was the causative agent in SARS identified—a completely new coronavirus, unlike any other human or animal member of the coronavirus family (World Health Organization, 2003). The 2003 epidemic affected 8098 people worldwide, of whom 774 died.

SARS was unusual in that it attracted worldwide attention very quickly. By themselves, most focusing events are not so mysterious and dramatic, and usually have to be supplemented by other factors such as a receptive public mood, energetic politicians, interest groups willing to push the issue, or some sense that trends are developing beyond acceptable thresholds. It is in the character of focusing events that they galvanize debate and discussion, but the most that happens at this stage is the development of a sense that there may be a problem that needs attention and further research. For example, the horrific footage of Robert Dziekanski, a Polish immigrant, being tasered and eventually dying on October 14, 2007, in the Vancouver airport sparked a national debate on police use of tasers. The topic had barely ever been mentioned before, but as more incidents of taser use occurred in the following months, a host of questions arose: How do tasers work? What voltage is safe? Are police overusing tasers? New Brunswick, Newfoundland and Labrador, and Nova Scotia all launched reviews of tasers. Amnesty International produced research purporting to show that 310 people had died in North America as a result of taser use ("Push-Button Policing," 2008, p. A17). The RCMP's Commission on Public Complaints also reviewed taser use in the force and recommended limits ("Restrict the Use of Tasers," 2007, p. A24). Even the UN got into the act, with its Committee Against Torture proclaiming that use of tasers constituted a form of torture.

Problem definition or structuring is the arduous process of taking some indicator that a problem exists—such as lagging productivity or average income—and answering three fundamental questions.

The first question is about the indicator itself and its relation to the phenomenon it is representing. This means being both clear about that phenomenon and about the "fit" between it and the indicator. We noted above that poverty can be defined in several ways, for example, as a lack of material resources (basic food and shelter) or as social exclusion, the inability to fully participate in one's community. A different concept of poverty demands a different measure or indicator, or perhaps some combination of several indicators to get a handle on the full complexity of the issue. The same problem comes up in the recent international interest in measuring "well-being" or happiness. It has long been obvious that material or monetary measures of well-being (e.g., income per capita, spending patterns, GDP) are limited. The OECD has led in developing a statistical compendium of measures of well-being, in 2011 publishing a report entitled *How's Life?* The indicators that the OECD chose incorporated economic measures, but also encompassed work–life balance, health, education, personal security, and the strength of community ties. The double trick was in coming up with plausible *categories* of measures, and then the numbers behind those categories.

The second question is also about the indicator but now shifts to causality. Why did this happen and how? What matrix of cause and effect is at work? In our examples above, the central question is "why." What is the cause of SARS or low productivity or poverty? In the SARS case it might be atypical pneumonia or a completely new strain of a pathogen. For poverty, it could be a lack of education or skills that bars people from good jobs. Each of these hypotheses would have to be considered and tested in some fashion.

The third question is about what action to take in the event that there is a "real" problem at stake. Is this a problem that can be solved, and who should solve it? Most important, is this a problem that government should solve? Is it in the public sphere, or is it a matter either for private initiative or nongovernmental collective action, or some sort of hybrid of government and nongovernmental intervention?

It is rare for these questions—particularly the first two on the nature of the phenomenon/indicator and the causal matrix that might underlie it—to be answered in detail except by specialists. The range of specialists that will be engaged in a policy issue will vary with the substance of that issue; economic problems will engage economists, environmental problems will engage experts in biology and environmental sciences, and so on. But policy problems are different from more general research problems in that the objective is to define and, if possible, resolve the problem in some practical way. Accordingly, a key aspect of determining these questions and developing answers to them is what Dunn (2008) calls "**problem structuring**" (p. 72). He points out that some problems are well structured (few decisionmakers and a small set of alternatives), while some are moderately or ill structured. Ill-structured problems are marked by high levels of uncertainty and competing objectives and alternatives (p. 79). In this case, policy analysis must rely on creativity, insight, and judgment in helping to shape a workable understanding of the problem. Nonetheless, there are generic techniques that can be used to help scope out the nature of a policy problem. Dunn outlines some common ones, such as **argument mapping, assumptional analysis, boundary analysis, brainstorming, classification analysis, hierarchical analysis, multiple perspective analysis,** and **synectics** (see Key Terms at the end of this chapter for definitions).These techniques and steps are far from infallible, but they do provide some conceptual tools to help move beyond the recognition stage to problem definition and problem structuring, particularly when there are a large number of stakeholders and a variety of different views, assumptions, and arguments about the nature of the problem.

Few of us, however, have the time to be that well acquainted with a problem definition or to apply these techniques independently. Most of us, even in cases where we are quite interested in a given policy issue, will tend to summarize it in what Baumgartner and Jones (1993) call "**policy images.**" Policy images are a "mixture of empirical information and emotive appeals" that explain the issue and justify the public policy response (p. 26). Moreover, since these images are shorthand, they convey more than information; they give a sense of the tone of the issue in positive or negative terms. Baumgartner and Jones cite the changing tone in the policy image surrounding civilian nuclear power from a largely positive association with economic progress to a negative connotation linked to environmental damage. A policy issue may be framed in various images, depending on the interests and actors in the field. Stable policy fields tend to coalesce around one dominant policy image, and policy challenge and change is largely about mobilization through the "redefinition of the prevailing policy image" (p. 239).

Problem structuring or definition therefore involves various techniques aimed at probing an issue that has been signalled in some way as a possible policy problem. The process of problem definition is one of shaping a persuasive argument about the nature of the problem and, of course, the solution. Of what does that argument consist? Rochefort and Cobb (1994) offer a scheme that captures some of the key elements, summarized in Box 3.1.

Not every problem definition or **policy argument** will contain all these characteristics, but most will be present. The definer has to deal with the question of causation. Without an idea of why the problem exists there is no way to figure out what to do about it. The **causal images** we use can differ in their emphasis on individual responsibility or systemic sources. Is poverty a result of individual decisions and choices or of larger economic forces? Definitions can also differ in the degree of complexity of their causal portraits. Inevitably, however, policy action can be taken only across a narrow range of factors so that the causal assumptions in most policy-relevant problem definitions are usually limited. The severity of the problem is another important characteristic. A problem may be acknowledged, but it might be innocuous enough not to matter in policy terms (e.g., the radiation effects of cellphones). This often gets connected to the incidence of the problem in the sense of how different groups in the population are directly affected. The debate of legalizing prostitution focuses on the problem effects on women; high

BOX 3.1   ASPECTS OF POLICY ARGUMENTS AND PROBLEM DEFINITION

Causality (What kinds of causal factors lie behind the problem?)

- Individual causation versus systemic (the former stresses choices and culpability; the latter stresses impersonal and unavoidable forces).
- Intentional versus accidental causes.
- Causes due to the nature of values systems.
- Complex causal systems versus simple causal agents.

Severity (How bad is the problem, and how bad is it likely to get?)

- This aspect distinguishes between the acknowledged existence of a problem (e.g., recession) and how serious it is likely to become.
- Severity is usually measured against some backdrop or context, such as trend lines ("this will soon go away" or "this is getting worse"), specific populations ("this is a big problem only for group X"), or what is considered normal or deviant.

Incidence (What is the scope and impact of the problem?)

- Who is affected generally?
- What subgroups are affected and how?
- What patterns of incidence are most important?

Novelty (Is this new?)

- Is the issue or problem new?
- Is it unexpected?

Proximity (How "close" is the problem?)

- This aspect refers to the degree to which a problem "hits home."
- Determining it depends on how "home" is defined. (Given that children are valued for any social group's survival, by definition, anything that affects children negatively is "close.")

Crisis (How pressing is the problem?)

- Largely a rhetorical device to signal severity and proximity.

Problem populations (Who will be targeted in the policy response?)	• Problem definitions can also define the people who are potential targets of policy interventions. • Deserving versus undeserving of assistance. • Sympathetic versus deviant definitions of groups. • Definitions that emphasize capacities versus those that emphasize dependency.
Instrumental versus expressive orientations (How important is the process of solving the problem in comparison to the solution itself?)	• Difference between focusing on ends (the instrumental intent to solve the problem) and the means (the degree to which what you do expresses an important symbol or value—e.g., refusing to negotiate with terrorists even if it harms hostages).
Solutions (What can be done?)	• Solutions sometimes precede the problem and help shape it (e.g., a commitment to vouchers as a policy instrument to deal with a host of problems). • Are solutions available—can something be done to solve a problem, or is action taken merely for its own sake or for symbolism?

Source: Adapted and amended from D. A. Rochefort and R. W. Cobb (Eds.), *The Politics of Problem Definition: Shaping the Policy Agenda*, "Problem definition: An emerging perspective," pp. 1–31. © 1994 University Press of Kansas.

school dropout rates focus on youth (especially boys, who drop out at much higher rates than girls).

Novelty, proximity, and crisis are all elements that help heighten the urgency of a problem. In recent years, the way in which a problem definition portrays potential target populations of policy interventions has received more attention (Schneider & Ingram, 1997, 2005) on the sound assumption that policies are more than just instruments for solving problems: "Public policies that serve democracy need to garner support, stimulate civic engagement, and encourage cooperation in the solution of problems" (Ingram & Schneider, 2006, p. 180). Policies also convey signals about how policymakers picture recipients of government programs.

Welfare programs are typically paternalistic, building on and conveying the image that welfare recipients cannot plan their own lives and must be watched carefully for fraud. Having a negative image of a target population (e.g., prostitutes, drug users) can interfere with clear-eyed policy responses to the problems faced by that population, another aspect of the symbolic or expressive dimension of policy. Often what matters most about a problem is not whether it *can* be solved or managed but *how* it will be solved or managed. What we do (in this case, collectively as a political community) says much about who we are.

We can apply some of these categories to our earlier example of SARS. Obviously, causality behind the crisis was a key element, but it was not simply a matter of a medical emergency, but an organizational one as well. This tension may seem odd in the SARS case, since the virus was eventually identified. Though the cause was epidemiological, the problem of the *epidemic* was due to how it was contained and dealt with, and this was more a matter of hospital, health, and immigration organization. China, for example, was widely blamed for not reporting the first cases for months. In Toronto, there were complaints about the emergency response system and the practice of rotating nurses among hospitals (thus potentially spreading the disease). The severity of SARS was acutely high, since people died and the economic impact was devastating. The incidence of SARS in North America was limited to Toronto in the end, but the fear at the time was that it might spread, and spread rapidly. Thus, while it remained a local problem, it had national and even international dimensions. In terms of novelty, the SARS tragedy was unexpected and frightening, which added to the sense of crisis. While it did not have a problem population per se, the elderly were more at risk with SARS. The SARS issue forced consideration of procedural questions—testing and the appropriate protocols for health authorities and the WHO. Finally, SARS was susceptible to a "solution" for two reasons. First, the pressure was intense because of the nature of the epidemic. The fact that it was an international crisis mobilized international resources through the WHO to track its source. Second, quarantine and immigration controls could plausibly contain the epidemic, even if they could not cure the disease. The problem dynamics around SARS are repeated virtually anytime there is a danger of a flu epidemic, as in H1N1 in 2009.

There is no science of problem definition, and providing the sort of checklist found in Box 3.1 is at best an approximation of the elements that go into the process of persuading others that a problem exists and that it should be addressed. What is clear, however, is that much of the time the process of problem recognition and definition is one of making arguments and persuading others (Fischer, 2003; Majone, 1989). **Constructivists** emphasize that there can be no absolutely conclusive proof of anything outside a shared paradigm of understandings. Within those worlds, of course, according to their own canons, it is possible to make a case that will be widely judged as "more true" than the next. Across those worlds, different values and standards of evidence and persuasion will make it difficult to come to firm and widely accepted conclusions. However, there is neither an infinite variety of conceptual paradigms nor of standards of what constitutes good argument. While rhetoric and presentation are always important, there are both inherent constraints within issues, as well as broadly shared understandings at any given point in time that form a common backdrop for the debate about public policy issues. Dunn's (2008) illustrations of **boundary analysis** show that, for example, in asking a group of 20 people what criteria they use to judge the severity of a problem (e.g., cost, social impact), the number of criteria is not infinite. The first person asked might list a dozen criteria. The second person, in adding new ones, might offer eight. And so on, until no one can think of any more to add. The "boundary" or complete set of criteria is reached fairly quickly. People will still disagree over weights and interpretation, but they do so on a foundation of commonly agreed criteria, which is an important first step.

Issue framing or problem definition consequently has two dimensions. The first is analytical and emphasizes the logical elements that make up an argument or claim. William Dunn (1993, 2008, Chapters 1, 8), for example, offers a schema to decipher the different statements that comprise any policy argument. *Policy-relevant information* (I) is the data or evidence at the policy analyst's disposal. A *policy claim* (C) is the conclusion of the policy argument, usually in the form of a recommendation on how to tackle the problem. A *warrant* (W) is an assumption that permits the analyst to move from the information to the claim. Warrants come in different forms—appeals to authority, to intuition, to values, and so on. *Backings* (B) are statements that provide support for warrants or neutralize possible criticisms or objections. Finally, *qualifiers* (Q) are statements that express the degree of confidence or certainty in the policy claim (e.g., "very likely" or "probably").

Take the question of legalization of marijuana, possession of which is currently a criminal offence in Canada and the United States. The policy-relevant information (I) in this instance would consist of medical evidence on the impact of marijuana use, the costs of enforcement, the rate of arrests for different groups, the effect of criminal records, the number of illegal grow houses, and so on. Those in favour of decriminalization would make that policy claim (C), based on several possible warrants (W): everyone uses it, whether it is legal or not; recreational use does not lead to addiction or impaired health, at least not any more than reasonable alcohol consumption; government has no role in regulating a substance like this. Backing (B) would come from statements producing evidence or arguments to support the warrant in question, and qualifiers (Q) would indicate the likelihood of a surge in addictions or drug use. Those opposing decriminalization would begin with much the same information (I), but, of course, make a completely opposite policy claim (C). The warrants (W) might be empirical (e.g., relaxation of controls will lead to a surge in use; the negative health effects are more than negligible; enforcing regulations is difficult) or moral (e.g., society is already too hedonistic). Backing (B) and qualifiers (Q) would be adduced to make the case stronger. As Dunn points out, understanding the structure of policy arguments helps us understand that often the same policy-relevant information (I) can lead to very different claims (C), based on different assumptions, values, and perspectives on the evidence (W). For example, there are provisions in Canada for the medical use of marijuana, a case where additional considerations about a specific population (those suffering ailments that marijuana can alleviate) are brought to bear. Making effective arguments is partly about assembling elements along these lines, but also combining them with powerful rhetorical tools such as **metaphors** and **labels**. This second aspect of issue framing or policy communication is discussed in detail in Chapter 9.

As Kingdon (1995) points out, getting people to see new problems or see old ones in new ways "is a major conceptual and political accomplishment" (p. 115). At any given time, there is a host of problems competing for public attention. Some are old and familiar, some are new twists on old issues, and a very few are completely new. The first hurdle is the one mentioned earlier, of providing persuasive indicators that something of importance is going on. The next step is a fuller description or definition that will likely take into account some or all of the elements outlined in Box 3.1. A critical aspect of this process is one that was briefly alluded to earlier: defining the problem as one that falls in the public sphere, and indeed as a problem to which the government can offer a credible and feasible response. Even if successful in all this, however, the problem still has to be positioned high enough on the public agenda to receive attention. Obtaining this normally entails neutralizing opposition to change, since any given status quo will have its supporters who will often fight vigorously to defend their benefits or reject what they see as wrong-headed policy (Cobb & Ross, 1997). This is the process of **agenda-setting**. Why do some problems or issues get onto the agenda when others do not, and what explains the relative positions of issues on that agenda?

We already have referred to the importance of issue-framing, and to the vague but important principle of some broad public consensus that determines which ideas (and issues) are plausible and important. At any given time, the number of such "ideas in good currency" as Donald Schon (1971) termed them, is quite limited. They change slowly and lag behind present circumstances, but provide a point of reference for policy debates. According to Schon, beneath every policy debate, "there is a barely visible process through which issues come to awareness and ideas about them become powerful" (p. 123). Some examples of ideas in good currency from the 1950s included competition with the Russians, the space race, and basic research. Certainly the 1990s list would have included competition, sustainable development, and fiscal prudence. The new millennium seems to have generated a few of its own ideas in good currency: tax cuts, investment in healthcare, innovation through investments in science and technology, the need to tackle climate change, the importance of security and defence against terrorists. Kingdon (1995) captures much the same idea with the notion of the **national mood**:

> People in and around government sense a national mood. They are comfortable discussing its content, and believe that they know when the mood shifts. The idea goes by different names— the national mood, the climate of the country, changes in public opinion, or broad social movements. But common to all of these labels is the notion that a rather large number of people out in the country are thinking along certain common lines, that this national mood changes from one time to another in discernible ways, and that these changes in mood or climate have important impacts on policy agendas and policy outcomes. (p. 146)

Baumgartner and Jones (1993; also see Jones, 1994; and True, Jones, & Baumgartner, 1999), emphasize the turbulence and change in American politics, but note also that periods of policy stability are marked by substantial consensus over policy images: "One of the clearest findings from our research is the extent to which a prevailing conception of a policy issue dominates both press coverage and official behavior during periods when policy subsystems are especially strong" (p. 238). Part of this stability is due to the need by decisionmakers to winnow the tremendous amount of information produced in the political system and in policy subsystems. Jones and Baumgartner (2005) argue that policy systems are typically "information rich" and so the problem that decisionmakers have is selecting relevant information, responding appropriately to signals conveyed by that information, and prioritizing decisions through prioritizing problems. Moreover, information is often ambiguous, incomplete, or contested, making the job even more difficult. Consequently, attention can be fixed only on a limited set of problems and information flows at any given time. Indeed, a coping strategy in this type of cacophonous environment is to deliberately ignore signals, to avoid paying attention. Combined with institutional structures in the political system that process information selectively (for example, the Canadian parliamentary system has fewer access points for interest groups than the American congressional system), the entire policy process—and agenda-setting—has a strong coefficient of drag, of stability: "If we put together the limits of human information processing and the characteristics of democracies that encourage error correction, we get a model of politics that is very static but reluctantly changes when signals are strong enough" (Jones & Baumgartner, 2005, p. 19).

Ideas in good currency and the policy images that dominate a given policy field at any given time help clarify the boundaries and constraints in agenda-setting, and facilitate information processing and the reduction of informational "noise." The political system as a whole can handle only a limited number of issues at one time (Soroka, 2007). It is rare for new ideas and new issues to come out of nowhere. Fresh policy proposals typically are framed in ways that resonate with existing ideas in good currency, but, if they fail, they drop off the agenda into a sort of twilight zone for policy innovations that might be mobilized again later, when the opportunity affords itself. This process of ideas struggling for attention and then fading away has supported the image of an agenda-setting cycle where issues arise, enjoy some intensive debate and perhaps success, and then gradually fall off. An early and influential example of this image was Anthony Downs's **issue attention cycle** (1972), but a cyclical image underpins most discussions of agenda-setting. Baumgartner and Jones (1993) borrowed the idea of **punctuated equilibrium** (which they have since subsumed under a broader theory they term "disproportionate information-processing"; see Jones & Baumgartner, 2005) to convey a process that simultaneously combines long stable periods of policy consensus followed by bursts of change around new issues and new policy images. Research on Canadian data shows little evidence for either an issue attention cycle or for punctuated equilibria, possibly because the parliamentary system gives "extensive agenda-setting powers to governments by, among other things, curtailing public and media access to information" (Howlett, 1997, p. 27; also see Soroka, 2002). Nonetheless, the work described in the previous paragraphs is as much about decisionmaking as a psychological state as it is about agenda-setting through institutions. Many of the informational-processing dynamics could still hold at the individual level, even while parliamentary institutions provide a more stable platform for the development and maintenance of policy priorities. And there are enough examples of surprises, reversals, and disequilibria in the Canadian and other systems to warrant some skepticism about their overall stability, especially since the turbulence of the global financial crisis. Even from the point of view of theory, there is growing interest in trying to understand policy change and growing conviction that policy is more evolutionary than static (Capano & Howlett, 2009; Genieys & Smyrl, 2008).

A great deal of the agenda-setting process is contingent on unpredictable factors and personalities, or as Kingdon puts it, the "opening of **policy windows.**" Windows sometimes open regularly (e.g., cabinet shuffles and budget speeches), but who jumps through successfully or not is still a matter of chance and skill. It is clear that some issues are driven onto the agenda by fundamental characteristics of a political community and economy: in Canada, for example, the perennial questions of Quebec and of our relationship to the United States. Modern welfare states have a wide range of important redistributive social programs that are of vital importance to recipient groups (e.g., pensions and the elderly), and so issues of this type are usually high on the public agenda. Massive changes in economic circumstances or powerful shifts in technology also have a way of rippling through the political system and generating issues for public discussion. But these structural explanations can illuminate only the broad shape of the public agenda. Much depends on political jockeying, **policy entrepreneurs**, and combinations of complex and unpredictable forces. The best that one can hope for in this field is a grasp of the institutions and the routines they generate (Howlett, 1998), the actors and their networks (Princen, 2009), and the opportunities, as well as the importance of shaping a coherent problem definition. As we will argue shortly, however, the dynamics and circumstances of problem definition have changed significantly in the last decade, and some of the old assumptions no longer apply.

What is the relation of problem definition to policy solutions? The conventional argument in the literature is that the way in which a problem is defined has a dramatic impact on the proposed solutions. At one level this makes sense: if you have to hit a nail, use a hammer, or something that hammers, which could just as easily be a shoe or a brick. Problem definition shapes solutions primarily because of the causal explanations that are its heart. Unemployment, for example, is a problem, but to deal with unemployment we need to know what causes it. If it is due to an international recession, there is not much the government can do to insulate the economy. If it is due primarily to a skills shortage, then the answer may be training programs. According to Statistics Canada (2005—the last time statistics on this issue were gathered), four out of 10 Canadians fall below the basic standard of literacy, but how to deal with this? Better early education? Better diagnosis of persons with reading disabilities? Adult literacy programs? The solution would depend on the fundamental causes at work.

There are, nonetheless, important variances between problem definition and solutions. First, as noted above, problems are not always so easily defined. Many social problems are "squishy" in that they don't lend themselves to mathematical formulation and are politically controversial (Strauch, 1976, p. 134), or "messy" in that they are deeply entangled with other problems (Ackoff, 1976, p. 21). In addition to being messy, some policy problems can be characterized as "wicked": among other qualities, they have no definitive formulation and no clear causal roots, no objective criteria to judge solutions, are adaptable and dynamic so that solutions just create waves of other consequences that become part of the problem matrix, and are entangled in inseparable and complex ways with other problems (Rittel & Webber, 1973). Some researchers have even coined the term "super wicked" for global policy problems like climate change (Levin, Cashore, Bernstein, & Auld, 2012). In this case, the problem is characterized by four key features: time is running out, and there are significant and acute consequences to not acting; there is no central authority to effect change (no global authority, in other words); there are no clear winning coalitions since even those who want to solve the problem contribute to it; and because no one can precisely predict the direct impact of non-action on any specific group, constituency, or region, decisionmakers adopt very short time horizons (the mentality is that if the world is going to end sometime soon, but we don't know when or for whom, let's enjoy ourselves).

The more squishy, messy, wicked, and super wicked policy problems are, the less likely unique and clear solutions can be derived from a problem definition. Sometimes, band-aid or incremental solutions are all that we have. Sometimes, the key, rather than large paradigmatic change, is strategic but small interventions that build coalitions and establish virtuous circles and pathways toward solutions. Just as there is no science of problem definition, there is no clear science of solutions.

Problem Definition: Beyond Old Categories

The preceding section sketched out the conventional theories of problem definition and agenda-setting. But, as Chapter 2 argued, the context within which policy analysis is practised today has changed substantially, and some of the key assumptions about the reality to which these theories apply—the substance as well as process of problem definition and agenda-setting—need to be reexamined. This section comes at problem definition and agenda-setting from this angle: what are the implications of globalization, culture shift, and governance for the ways in which we define public policy problems? Problem definition cannot be easily disentangled from the other phases of the policy process, but this chapter will concentrate on the emerging societal policy agenda and ideas in good currency. More detailed aspects of policy design, implementation, and evaluation will be taken up in subsequent chapters.

THE EMERGING POLICY AGENDA

With a new context for policymaking, we should expect both a new agenda and a new sense of the sources of policy problems. One of the most important changes in the sources of policy problems is that many of them are now generated beyond our borders due to globalization. As was argued in Chapter 2, the dynamics of globalization and internationalization mean that borders are much more permeable. But that permeability is coupled with a new level of integration and vulnerability within the international political economy. It is important not to exaggerate this phenomenon. There have been many areas of public policy in the past— finance, communications, foreign policy, agriculture, trade, to name a few—that have traditionally been highly exposed to international forces and tightly integrated into international systems. By the same token, there remain many policy areas today that will continue to be insulated from the direct influence of these international forces or systems, for example, healthcare, social security, and overland transportation. Rather, what has happened is that the intensity of international exposure has increased in many policy fields traditionally marked by global influences, and a host of other areas have been indirectly affected by these wider forces. As the financial crisis exploded in 2008, foreclosures in Nebraska were being felt by small investors in Norway and Iceland. By 2011, there were fears that if the European Union could not somehow salvage the Greek economy, the Euro might collapse and send the entire global financial system into chaos. Policymaking systems have essentially shifted away from a preponderant concern about problems generated domestically within national borders to problems generated internationally. The policy challenge is how to respond to these new types of problems. While globalization takes pride of place in the new pantheon of sources of policy challenges, it is not alone. Technology is another obvious candidate, both in its own terms and because of its close connection to economic competitiveness through innovation. The issue of international terrorism—itself connected to globalization—has been on the agenda since 9/11.

One window on the range of policy challenges posed by these and other phenomena is the 2010 Government of Canada report *Canada@150* (Government of Canada, 2010; the following discussion is based on this document). This report was an unusual exercise, launched by the Clerk of the Privy Council as part of public service renewal. One hundred and fifty early career public servants took part in a series of conferences, Web-based collaborations, mentoring, and training over two years, with the objective of increasing their policy analytical skills (especially "foresight methods"), learning how to work together in new ways, and exploring the policy challenges that the country will be facing as it turns 150 years old in 2017. As government processes go, this one was relatively open-ended and driven from below, by young public servants (who did much of the work for the report on their own time).

Initially, the project participants identified 40 policy challenges in the next decade, but these were winnowed down to 26, and then further to 13 (with two others on the public service and federal-provincial-municipal cooperation as cross-cutting through the 13). Work groups were then given the task of analyzing their specific policy challenge and outlining options. What follows is a list of those policy challenges, with excerpts from the report describing the challenge and possible policy responses.

Competing in a Multipolar World

What will be the impacts of the global economic recession, stalled trade talks, and shifts in who holds major economic levers (e.g. debt, currency holdings) and how they are likely to use those levers? Canada's traditional economic strengths—natural resources and manufacturing—will be significantly challenged in 2017 as the world pushes further towards knowledge-based economic activity. Canada can play to its strengths by harnessing its science and technology expertise to be first-to-market with regulatory and standards regimes; by engaging immigrant, diaspora, and foreign student communities to tap foreign market opportunities; and by maintaining strong ties with the United States, partly as a buffer in the event of sweeping global protectionism or a prolonged recession.

Maximizing Canada's Engagement in the Global Knowledge-Based Economy

Both advanced and developing economies are increasingly dependent on knowledge, information, and highly-skilled workers to improve productivity and their standard of living. Canada could become a "Northern Tiger" in terms of productivity and innovation if it takes advantage of its open economy, a diverse and innovative society, a strong regulatory framework, and its capacity for research and development. There are significant challenges to overcome, however. From a human capital perspective, Canada cannot out-compete emerging economies in terms of labour and production costs; its labour force will be smaller in 2017; there has been a decline in labour productivity compared to the United States; and nearly half of adult Canadians are estimated to be below the accepted literacy standard for coping in a modern society. In terms of research and development, persistent challenges, such as weak commercialization and low and declining research and development investments, are reflected in an immature venture capital market, relatively few "high science and technology" companies, and a lack of growth in patent filings. Meanwhile, regulatory systems are having difficulty keeping up with science and technology developments, consistent with broader complaints about their lack of predictability and timeliness. National frameworks for innovation and learning, as well as interjurisdictional collaboration to support lifelong learning and retraining, could help address these challenges. New institutions could be created to address specific gaps, including an Office of Commercialization for public research and a Venture Capital Fund to develop the market by providing seed money for high-risk, high-return proposals.

Canada's Place in a Changing Geopolitical Landscape: Leveraging Our Comparative Advantage

What is Canada's comparative advantage in the changing geopolitical landscape? In 2017, the world will be even more complex and unpredictable than today, making it even harder for Canada to maintain its reputation for "punching above its weight." With more voices and powers emerging while Canada's influence decreases according to traditional measures such as GDP, Canada will need to be realistic about the scope of its influence in 2017. It will be important to understand the heterogeneity of emerging powers and to maintain or strengthen ties to the United States, while at the same time recognizing its relative decline in power and fortifying other relationships. A stronger focus on Mexico—a key North American player and a window to other emerging powers—is recommended. On security issues, Canada should be well-placed for interventions abroad based on the mission in Afghanistan and our work in other fragile states.

Canada's North—Overcoming the Challenges to Leverage and Opportunities

The relationship of Canada's North with the rest of the country and the rest of the world is evolving, with climate change, resource exploration, and geopolitical factors around sovereignty and trade routes all expected to have major impacts. A small population that is geographically dispersed, low rates of education completion, and persistent infrastructure challenges will continue to affect socio-economic well-being for Northern Canadians. Some challenges, like road infrastructure, are exacerbated by climate change, with the North even referred to as the "canary in the coal mine." Indeed, one of the major challenges for the North is the multitude of domestic and international governing interests and the overlap and tension between policy areas such as resource development and climate change. In terms of policy options, more comprehensive funding arrangements would reduce the administrative burden of small communities that expend significant overhead to secure funding for different services. A long-term infrastructure plan, encompassing local job creation and training, could integrate community and regional-level needs to address persistent infrastructure issues.

Ensuring Our Regions Are at the Cutting Edge in 2017 and Beyond

The socio-economic challenges faced by vulnerable regions were highlighted by the financial crisis and will be exacerbated in the years ahead by ongoing globalization, urbanization, and environmental pressures. Strengthening regional and community capacity and institutions through a model of sustainable regional development would equip currently vulnerable regions to take advantage of domestic and international opportunities by 2017. Four types of vulnerable regions currently face a range of trade, human capital, environmental, and socio-demographic chal-lenges: single-industry regions; regions dependent on low value-added production; remote regions; and traditional, family-based business regions.

Healthy, Sustainable and Competitive Cities

In Canada, a small number of cities represent half or more of the country's population and economic activity. Against the world's largest urban centres, however, Canada's cities will have difficulty competing for talent and investment based on population or low wages and other costs. Furthermore, the combination of rising energy costs and urban sprawl will leave cities more vulnerable to price shocks. From a demographic perspective, immigration is expected to be the only source of population growth in 2017, at a time when the gap between the economic outcomes of recent versus earlier immigrant cohorts has grown and many neighbourhoods are becoming more expensive. Innovative proposals include allowing munici-palities to nominate candidates for immigration in order to tap into local needs and networks. Tax incentives could be used to encourage sustainable private development by addressing the negative externalities associated with suburban development (e.g., provide a revenue neutral feebate [sic] on GST for new residential construction or a sliding commercial land transfer tax based on the density of the zone).

Greening Canada's Transportation Systems

A number of environmental problems are associated with rising demand for cargo and passenger transport, an emissions-intensive trade model, and the strains on transportation systems due to urbanization and urban sprawl. Particular Canadian challenges—a vast geography and complicating jurisdictional factors—exacerbate a situation in which environmental costs are negative externalities, so there is little incentive for change. Producer and consumer (user) behaviour must change in order to create a greener and more efficient transport system in 2017. The key is to create an environment in which transportation users understand the full costs of their decisions and are rewarded for making sustainable choices. This means determining the full cost of transportation across the life cycle from construction to use to maintenance, putting a price on carbon, and providing complementary incentives to encourage green travel choices.

Reducing the Ecological Footprint of Urban Passenger Travel and Changing the Habits of Canadians

The contribution of passenger transportation to Canadian greenhouse gas emissions is rising. Persistent transport challenges such as Canada's vast geography, coupled with a growing and increasingly urban population and urban sprawl suggest that technology and infrastructure advancements alone will not counter rising transportation use and the associated environmental costs by 2017. Changes in the choices and habits of Canadians must therefore be a part of the solution. Obstacles to more sustainable passenger transportation include complex jurisdictional responsibilities and resulting funding gaps, inadequate research on passenger behaviour, and insufficient application of the polluter-pays principle. Investing in research to understand the motivations behind passengers' transit choices (including variations between different regions and urban centres) and initiating pilot projects to study local transport dynamics could lead to place-based transport solutions developed by all implicated stakeholders.

Building a Sustainable ECOnomic Model

The dominant global economic model is challenged by the limited supply of resources and the finite carrying capacity of the planet for waste and pollution. To get to the stage where the use of the planet's resources is attuned to its carrying capacity, the environmental costs of human activity must be internalized. Environmental and economic outcomes would then jointly define prosperity, resulting in an "ECOnomy" that is more shock-resistant. Building a more sustainable economy requires three things: a systems approach for understanding feedback loops, cascading effects, and trade-offs; carbon pricing; and diversified, distributed, localized production that features more redundancy and closer connections between producers and consumers.

Ensuring National Security While Protecting Human Rights

Security and human rights policies can and should be mutually reinforcing, rather than cast as opposing forces in a zero-sum game. Protecting human rights contributes to social cohesion, which is, in turn, an important element of security. In 2017, the Canadian population will be larger and more diverse, particularly through immigration, with resulting greater risks to social cohesion. In addition, there will be continuing security threats from familiar sources including weak states, radical Islam, and illegal arms trafficking, all set in the context of broader trends like the increasing influence of non-state actors and the proliferation of science and technology. Canada will need to strengthen its foreign intelligence capacity and reduce its reliance on information from its allies. The collection and use of data in support of the "discretionary decisions" made every day in the security domain will need to improve. An ethics code would be needed to govern the use of such data, and accountability and reporting regimes need to better reflect the integration of human rights and security interests.

Diversity, Identity, and the Social Cohesion Advantage

Canada's population will be more diverse in 2017, and increased diversity can affect the sense of fairness, inclusion, and common values in a society when there is inequality or when norms and institutions are not sufficiently robust. Conversely, social cohesion—strong bonds between individuals at a community and national level—generally leads to positive social outcomes.

Traditionally Canada has been seen as a leader with a "social cohesion advantage." In 2017, however, economic factors and changing demographics, increased diversity, ageing, and a younger Aboriginal population could contribute to challenges at the intersection of identity, diversity, and social cohesion. Particularly as other models of diverse society are being seen as having failed (e.g., in Europe), more attention is being paid to possible "weak signals" in Canada such as increasing economic disparity between recent and earlier immigrant cohorts; the Herouxville code and the debate over reasonable accommodation in Québec and to unfolding processes that could affect social cohesion like the reconciliation process around Residential Schools.

Unlocking the Potential of Marginalized Youth

Canada will need to improve its labour productivity by 2017 due to declining labour force growth as the baby boomer generation retires, the more educated and skilled workforce required for a knowledge-based economy, and the fact that labour markets rebound relatively slowly after a recession. The changing demographic make-up of Canada will create significant potential in a large Aboriginal and immigrant youth community that could become a very important part of the workforce. Unfortunately, these communities have traditionally faced systemic, legal, and institutional barriers to their full participation in the labour market, and their exclusion not only limits economic opportunity but also leads to higher social and justice spending. Seizing this opportunity in 2017 will require integrated, place-based approaches that account for interconnected social factors like housing, poverty, food, health, and safety, in part by ensuring better access to basic, necessary services.

Proactive Approaches to Health

Alongside its ageing population, Canada may be encountering the first instance of children having worse life expectancy than their parents. Factors like environmental stressors (e.g., air quality) and lifestyle and work behaviours (e.g., lack of exercise driven in part by urban planning decisions) may be countering medical advances that prolong lifespan. For some Canadians, socio-economic factors like being unattached to the workforce, have particularly negative effects on health. More broadly, the rising incidence of obesity and chronic diseases costs the economy tens of billions of dollars in lost productivity and health care utilization. The health system's focus on treatment rather than prevention is often identified as an important contributor to these challenges, leading to a recommendation of a long-term health promotion approach built around healthy living, with a focus on children and Canadians of lower socio-economic status.

This list is daunting, but while not every issue will appear on every policy wonk's personal agenda of challenges facing the country (and the world), a good deal of them would. The usual suspects are globalization (and its implications, as we noted in Chapter 2, for economic competition, shifts in economic power balances, and migration), demographic pressures (both youth and aging), the environment, security, diversity and social cohesion, and spatial or scalar problems (cities, regions, and geopolitical positioning). What the list and the process behind *Canada@150* also illustrate is the centrality of thinking about policy, analyzing problems, defining them as best as possible, and looking to future solutions.

Conclusion

No one should read this chapter as claiming that everything about our processes of problem definition and framing has suddenly shifted to the United Nations or consists of nothing more than carping about money. There are still plenty of policy problems bubbling at all levels that are primarily domestic in origins and solutions: drugs, crime, literacy, water quality, housing, waste disposal, cities, education—in short, things that matter to people on a daily basis. The simple point of this chapter is that the context and processes of problem definition are never set hard and that they have changed in important ways in the last decade and, indeed, dramatically since 2008. Some of the sources of policy problems have a completely different character today: globalization, technology, and the environment, for example. Others are quite new: the aging of society and falling productivity. Still others have affected the nature of traditional domestic problems, for example, international terrorism and epidemics. And as we argued in Chapter 2, there has also been a change in approaches to governance, in what we consider possible and acceptable for governments to do in addressing these problems. While there is still an emphasis on performance and service, that now has been coupled with the sheer necessity of broad government action to keep the economy and society afloat.

And yet several paradoxes are at the heart of these changes. One is that the nature of these issues (e.g., globalization and technology) is such that they are closely entangled. This understanding has led to laudable demands that policy thinking today be more "horizontal" and cross-cutting (as we see above with *Canada@150*), since the issues are more diffuse and interconnected. The aging of the population, for example, is linked to economic issues (productivity and training), to social programs (pensions), and to immigration. The danger, however, is that problem definition will become an exercise in thinking about everything at once. In addition to horizontality, there is also pressure on how to maintain both coherence and focus in problem definition. This pressure is reflected in an almost limitless range of problems and issues that governments could conceivably address. While on the one hand, governments are challenged to connect the dots between issues such as human capital, early childhood education, and immigration, or between terrorism, security, and human rights, on the other hand, there remains general skepticism about how effective in general and in particular government can be.

In practical terms, what does this all mean for doing policy work and developing coherent and workable policy problem definitions? It is important to re-emphasize the distinctions between problem recognition and problem definition. In countries like Canada, even though there is likely a greater degree of agenda control by government, there is a constant stream of data, information, and arguments about the range of existing and emerging problems that require a policy response. A crucial part of good policy work remains the analysis and development of those data into something more detailed—a problem definition that brings together data, research, analysis of causal links, and logical arguments. Moreover, there are techniques and guides (as described in the first part of the chapter and exemplified in the *Canada@150* exercise), to help this process along. However, the contemporary policy analyst must, at the same time, be aware of the changed context within which that work takes place. She requires an appreciation of existing research, international trends, and the broad domestic policy agenda. She must have a grasp of current and fundamental policy debates, as well as sensibilities about the nature of the "public" and the "private" and the appropriate role for government. She needs an understanding of the complex matrix of cause and effect that infuses almost any policy issue and, in particular, the nature of global forces and their effects on local problems. Finally, she has to be able to take her work beyond problem definition to policy design. That is the subject of the next chapter.

KEY TERMS

agenda-setting—the social and political process of determining what issues to address and in what priority

argument mapping—a technique to map and classify the different components of policy arguments made by stakeholders, such as arguments based on statistics, authority, values, intuition, or judgment

assumptional analysis—aims at developing a synthesis of the different assumptions that stakeholders have about the issue or problem. Involves canvassing the full range of solutions proposed for the issue or problem and using that as a vehicle for analyzing and challenging the assumptions that underlie the problem definition

boundary analysis—a technique to canvass the whole range of existing definitions and conceptualizations of a given problem

brainstorming—a family of techniques, more or less formal, to generate ideas, goals, and strategies; can involve informal and unstructured exchange to scenario writing

causal images—a shorthand conceptualization of complex cause-and-effect relationships

classification analysis—breaking down the policy problem phenomenon into logically distinct categories or classes

constructivism—philosophical position that there can be no absolutely conclusive proof of anything outside a shared paradigm of understandings

focusing events—sudden catastrophes or crises that grab attention

globalization—the progressive exposure of domestic economies and polities to a wide range of international forces, and the increased interdependence that comes with it

hierarchical analysis—a technique for identifying possible causes of a problem by classifying causes as possible causes, plausible causes, or actionable causes

ideas in good currency—broad ideas about public policy that are widely shared without much commentary or debate and that change slowly over time but form the backdrop for policy discussion

indicators—atypical or routine monitoring that turns up discrepancies or patterns that hint that something is amiss and lead to further development and analysis of the problem definition

issue attention cycle—a portrayal of public policy going through cycles of attention, reaction and action, and quietude

issue framing—a way of depicting a policy issue or problem in broad and understandable, if somewhat simplified terms

labels—summary words that convey subtle but powerful meanings: "homosexual" versus "gay," "vagrant" versus "homeless," "tax" versus "user fee"

metaphors—in a policy context, words or phrases that convey powerful meanings through an implicit comparison, such as the "Cold War," "Iron Curtain," or "social safety net"

multiple perspective analysis—a technique to review the problem situation from three perspectives: (1) the technical perspective: cost–benefit analysis, econometrics, and systems analysis; (2) the organizational perspective: focus on institutional rules and processes, and following standard operating procedures; and (3) the personal perspective: viewing problems and solutions in terms of individual perceptions and values

national mood—an inchoate, broad, but nonetheless real consensus among the population around some national issue

policy argument—an organized set of claims about a policy problem and recommended solutions that include such characteristics as causality, severity, novelty, crisis, instruments, and solutions

policy entrepreneurs—actors who shape the public agenda and can quickly and effectively mobilize around a policy issue when they see or sense an opportunity

policy images—a mixture of empirical information and emotive appeals that explain the issue and justify the public policy response

policy windows—unpredictable openings in the policy process that create the possibility for influence over the direction and outcome of that process

problem recognition—the stage at which there is an emerging sense that there may be a problem that needs attention and further analysis, usually based on indicators or some event that signals an issue

problem structuring—the intellectual process of shaping the problem definition

punctuated equilibrium—a process that simultaneously combines long stable periods of policy consensus followed by bursts of change around new issues and new policy images

synectics—a technique that relies on the use of analogies to see whether new policy problems have sufficiently similar characteristics to older ones that previous problem definitions and solutions can provide some guidance

FURTHER READINGS

Baumgartner, F. R., & Jones, B. D. (1993). *Agendas and instability in American politics*. Chicago, IL: University of Chicago Press.

Dery, D. (1984). *Problem definition in policy analysis*. Lawrence, KS: University Press of Kansas.

Dunn, W. N. (2008). *Public policy analysis: An introduction* (4th ed.). Upper Saddle River, NJ: Pearson Prentice Hall.

Hoppe, R. (2010). *The governance of problems: Puzzling, powering, participation*. Portland, OR: The Policy Press.

Jones, B., & Baumgartner, F. R. (2005). *The politics of attention: How government prioritizes problems*. Chicago, IL: University of Chicago Press.

Kingdon, J. W. (1995). *Agendas, alternatives, and public policies* (2nd ed.). New York, NY: HarperCollins.

Moran, M., Rein, M., & Goodin, R. E. (Eds.). (2006). *The Oxford handbook of public policy*. Oxford: Oxford University Press.

Soroka, S. (2002). *Agenda-setting dynamics in Canada*. Vancouver, BC: UBC Press.

REFERENCES

Ackoff, R. L. (1976). *Redesigning the future: A systems approach to societal problems*. New York, NY: John Wiley and Sons.

Baumgartner, F. R., & Jones, B. D. (1993). *Agendas and instability in American politics*. Chicago, IL: University of Chicago Press.

Brewer, G. D., & deLeon, P. (1983). *The foundations of policy analysis*. Homewood, IL: The Dorsey Press.

Carson, R. (1962). *Silent spring*. Boston, MA: Houghton Mifflin.

Capano, G., & Howlett, M. (Eds.). (2009). *European and North American policy change: Drivers and dynamics*. New York, NY: Routlege.

Cobb, R. W., & Ross, M. H. (Eds.). (1997). *Cultural strategies of agenda denial: Avoidance, Attack, and Redefinition*. Lawrence, KS: University Press of Kansas.

Conservative Party of Canada. (2004). *Platform 2004*.

Dery, D. (1984). *Problem definition in policy analysis*. Lawrence, KS: University Press of Kansas.

Downs, A. (1972, Summer). Up and down with ecology: The issue attention cycle. *Public Interest, 28*, 38–50.

Dunn, W. N. (1993). Policy reforms as arguments. In F. Fischer & J. Forester (Eds.), *The argumentative turn in policy analysis and planning* (pp. 254–290). Durham, NC: Duke University Press.

Dunn, W. N. (2008). *Public policy analysis: An introduction* (4th ed.). Upper Saddle River, NJ: Pearson Prentice Hall.

Fischer, F. (2003). *Reframing public policy: Discursive politics and deliberative practices*. New York, NY: Oxford University Press.

Genieys, W., & Smyrl, M. (Eds.). (2008). *Elites, ideas, and the evolution of public policy*. Houndsmills, UK: Palgrave Macmillan.

Geva-May, I., & Wildavsky, A. (1997). *An operational approach to policy analysis: The craft*. Boston, MA: Kluwer Academic Publishers.

Gore, A. (2007). *An inconvenient truth*. New York, NY: Viking.

Government of Canada. (2010). *Canada@150*. Retrieved from http://www.horizons.gc.ca/page.asp?pagenm=can150_index

Harrington, M. (1962). *The other America: Poverty in the United States*. New York, NY: Macmillan.

Hoppe, R. (2010). *The governance of problems: Puzzling, powering, participation*. Portland, OR: The Policy Press.

Howlett, M. (1997, March). Issue-attention and punctuated equilibria models reconsidered: An empirical evaluation of the dynamics of agenda-setting in Canada. *Canadian Journal of Political Science, 30*(1), 3–30.

Howlett, M. (1998, September). Predictable and unpredictable policy windows: Institutional and exogenous correlates of Canadian federal agenda-setting. *Canadian Journal of Political Science, 31*(3), 495–524.

Ingram, H., & Schneider, A. L. (2006). Policy analysis for democracy. In M. Moran, M. Rein, & R. E. Goodin (Eds.), *The Oxford handbook of public policy* (pp. 169–189). Oxford: Oxford University Press.

Jones, B. D. (1994). *Reconceiving decision-making in democratic politics: Attention, choice, and public policy*. Chicago, IL: University of Chicago Press.

Jones, B. D., & Baumgartner, F. R. (2005). *The politics of attention: How government prioritizes problems*. Chicago, IL: University of Chicago Press.

Kingdon, J. W. (1995). *Agendas, alternatives, and public policies* (2nd ed.). New York, NY: HarperCollins.

Levin, K., Cashore, B., Bernstein, S., & Auld, G. (2012). Overcoming the tragedy of super wicked problems: Constraining our future selves to ameliorate global climate change. *Policy Sciences, 45*(2), 123–152.

MacLeod, L. (1987). *Battered but not beaten: Preventing wife battering in Canada*. Ottawa, ON: Canadian Advisory Council on the Status of Women.

Majone, G. (1989). *Evidence, argument, and persuasion in the policy process*. New Haven, CT: Yale University Press.

OECD [Organisation for Economic Co-operation and Development]. (2010). *Obesity and the economics of prevention: Fit not fat*. Paris: OECD.

OECD. (2011). *How's life? Measuring well-being*. Paris: OECD.

Princen, S. (2009). *Agenda-setting in the European Union*. Houndmills, Basingstoke: Palgrave Macmillan.

Push-button policing: Why talk when you can shock? (2008, February 11). *The Globe and Mail*, p. A17.

Restrict the use of tasers. (2007, December 14). *Globe and Mail*, p. A24.

Rittel, H., & Webber, M. (1973). Dilemmas in a general theory of planning. *Policy Sciences, 4*(2), 155–169.

Rochefort, D. A., & Cobb, R. W. (1994). Problem definition: An emerging perspective. In D. A. Rochefort & R. W. Cobb (Eds.), *The politics of problem definition: Shaping the policy agenda* (pp. 1–31). Lawrence, KS: University Press of Kansas.

Sarlo, C. A. (1996). *Poverty in Canada* (2nd ed.). Vancouver, BC: Fraser Institute.

Schneider, A. L., & Ingram, H. M. (1997). *Policy design for democracy.* Lawrence, KS: University Press of Kansas.

Schneider, A. L., & Ingram, H. M. (Eds.). (2005). *Deserving and entitled: Social constructions and public policy.* Albany, NY: State University of New York.

Schon, D. A. (1971). *Beyond the stable state.* New York, NY: W. W. Norton and Company.

Soroka, S. (2002). *Agenda-setting dynamics in Canada.* Vancouver, BC: UBC Press.

Soroka, S. (2007). Agenda-setting and issue definition. In M. Orsini & M. Smith (Eds.), *Critical policy studies* (pp. 185–210). Vancouver, BC: UBC Press.

Statistics Canada. (2005). *Building on our competencies: Canadian results of the International Adult Literacy and Skills Survey 2003* (Catalogue no. 89-617-XIE). Retrieved from http://dsp-psd.pwgsc .gc.ca/Collection/Statcan/89-617-X/89-617-XIE2005001.pdf

Stone, D. (2012). *Policy paradox: The art of political decision making* (3rd ed.). New York, NY: W. W. Norton.

Strauch, R. E. (1976, Winter). A critical look at quantitative methodology. *Policy Analysis, 2,* 121–144.

True, J. L., Jones, B. D., & Baumgartner, F. R. (1999). Punctuated-equilibrium theory: Explaining stability and change in American policymaking. In P. A. Sabatier (Ed.), *Theories of the policy process* (pp. 97–116). Boulder, CO: Westview.

Winship, C. (2006). Policy analysis as puzzle solving. In M. Moran, M. Rein, & R. E. Goodin (Eds.), *The Oxford handbook of public policy* (pp. 109–121). Oxford: Oxford University Press.

World Health Organization. (2003). *SARS: Chronology of a serial killer.* Retrieved from http://www.who.int/csr/don/2003_07_04/en/

Policy Instruments and Design

Policy design is a mix of inspiration and technique. The inspiration comes in framing the policy issue (discussed in Chapter 3) in ways that make sense of the problem and provide a broad sketch of how to tackle it. The technique (though not without its creative side either) comes in the detailing of what tools to use, and in what combination, to achieve a given end. The tools will vary with the task at hand, sometimes involving expenditures, sometimes regulation, partnerships, or the exchange of information. Policy design usually will draw on all of these and more, and then be bundled into programs. The conventional discussion of policy instruments usually proceeds by laying out the basic categories and outlining some of the objective characteristics of each of the instruments; when and why, for example, regulation makes more sense than direct program provision by government. This chapter will honour that format in briefly describing the main categories, but it will also show how the menu of choices has changed. While the reality of instrument choice has always been more constrained than theory might suggest, the old, full menu of the past has been replaced with something closer to a table d'hôte with a more limited but, in some respects, more novel range of items. At the same time, there are new pressures on governments to do traditional things with traditional tools, intervene less, and also to intervene more with unprecedented instruments and interventions to forestall economic collapse. Choosing what to do, why to do it, and how has never been more interesting or more challenging.

Policies are best thought of as creative solutions to challenging puzzles rather than as dry legislation and programs. The creative dimension breaks through conventional definitions of the issue and comes up with something people have not thought of before. Of course, it cannot be assumed that those creative solutions are the correct ones, only that they offer an unanticipated or surprising approach. The harm reduction approach to severe addiction that we discussed in previous chapters with the Insite facility in Vancouver is one example.

Policy design is about choosing the most appropriate instrument to deal with the policy problem as it has been defined in order to achieve a given policy goal. This choice implies that a key criterion in instrument choice and policy design is effectiveness—getting the job done. Efficiency—getting the job done with the least resources—is typically considered another key criterion. The reality of politics means that popularity and re-election cannot be left out of the mix of motives; indeed, they may be overpowering at times. But if one adds the inevitably creative aspect of policy design to the range of criteria by which that design might be judged, it is clear that coming up with a list of tools is no easy task. In fact, while lists abound, and while some agreement on at least the major policy instruments and their characteristics exists, there is little agreement (or knowledge) of how and when particular mixes of instruments should be used in policy design. Like a list of the letters in the alphabet, the keys on a piano, or all the possible ingredients in five-star French cooking, the best that an inventory can provide is a sense of the possibilities of language, music, or cuisine. Choice and design are marked as much by art and circumstance as they are by technique.

Nonetheless, thinking through at least the major categories of ingredients is a useful exercise. The first section of this chapter will do this with brutal economy, splitting only enough hairs to make sense of major alternatives and some of the broad dynamics of choice. Policy instruments will be distinguished here from implementation, which we take up in Chapter 5. There is an overlap between the two, of course, but "policy instruments" usually refer to the technical means of achieving a goal, such as a **tax** or a **regulation**, while "implementation" refers to the organizational structure and processes to execute that instrument. Policy instruments and implementation overlap most obviously in cases where a particular organizational format is the technical means of achieving the policy goal, such as a **partnership** between a nongovernmental agency and a government department. We take this up in Chapter 6.

Thinking about instruments and policy design also helps clarify the relationship among policy, programs, and instruments. As we argued in Chapter 1, policy is a framework, a map, or a guide. It connects a problem definition (or clusters of problems) with goals and objectives, and a selection of instruments (means or tools) whereby the problem will be overcome and the objectives met. To be actualized or made real, policies have to be expressed or implemented through programs, and any given policy (if it is broad enough) will likely have several programs, which, in combination, will tackle different aspects of the broader problem (something that also raises the issue of horizontal consistency). These programs, in turn, consist of bundles of instruments or policy tools (expenditures, taxes, regulations). In 2011, for example, Agriculture and Agri-Food Canada had a list of 186 distinct programs, such as the Manure Management Plan (available only in Alberta) and the Canada Brand Program (available for exporters). These programs are embedded in a policy framework adopted in 2008, *Growing Forward* (Agriculture and Agri-Food Canada, 2011).

The theme of this book is that the world of policymaking is changing, and so the bulk of the chapter will take up these new dynamics and also link the question of **instrument design** to a question that increasingly troubles policymakers: how to fashion democratic and cooperative social institutions as vehicles for the other things that a people might wish to accomplish collectively.

Inventory and the Dynamics of Instrument Choice

The technical means whereby we pursue goals are a reflection of the ways in which we perceive problems and the goals we are pursuing. For example, income security programs made their appearance as full-blown policy instruments only when Western governments (grudgingly) came around to the view, during the Great Depression in the 1930s, that income inequality was a problem and that it was a legitimate goal of government to try to redistribute income. Any inventory of policy instruments will therefore be a snapshot of what is considered legitimate and efficacious at any given time. There is a sense of appropriateness or legitimacy to the use of policy instruments that will change from time to time. This sense of what is legitimate rests on several ethical foundations and, in a country like Canada, principally on a cluster of ideas such as equality, equity, liberty, and rights. There is no point in trying to define these ideas, since they are constantly contested, but it is fair to say that at this point in Canadian history, most of us look to the Charter of Rights and Freedoms and the courts for inspiration as to the proper scope and limits of government action in our lives. Policy analysts have to know which way the wind is blowing in these areas, or instruments that they may recommend for good policy reasons may turn out to have little or no legitimacy among the wider public. The government of Singapore, for example, has had a ban on chewing gum as part of its Regulation of Imports and Exports, though since 2004, it has allowed the import of chewing gum with therapeutic value. Visitors to Singapore will see this on the government's website: "The import of chewing gum classified under HS code

1704 1000 into Singapore is absolutely prohibited under the Regulation of Imports and Exports (Chewing Gum) Regulations"(Singapore Customs, 2011). This regulation would be considered ridiculous in Canada, but in Singapore, with a history of addiction to natural gums with hallucinogenic qualities, it makes sense. Context matters. After the July 7, 2007, subway terrorist bombings, the City of London massively increased its on-street video surveillance network, to the point that almost everyone is being recorded every second. Again, 20 years ago, this level of government intrusion would have been strenuously resisted.

The history of attempts to classify governing policy instruments begins with Kirschen (1964). His system presented 62 different types of economic policy instruments, and the various contributors to the field since have tried various ways of combining aggregate categories with the more finely grained instruments within them. Doern and Phidd (1992, p. 97), for example, argued that there are really only five broad categories: (1) **self-regulation**, (2) **exhortation**, (3) **expenditure**, (4) regulation (including taxation), and (5) public ownership. Based on earlier work by Doern and Wilson (1974), this typology assumed that as one moves from the first category to the last, one moves roughly along a continuum of **legitimate coercion**. The argument was that all government in a liberal democracy involves some degree of imposition or coercion and that politicians generally prefer to use the least coercive instrument possible. Within these broad categories, Doern and Phidd (1992) identified as many as 26 finer "graduations of choice" such as grants and subsidies, **guidelines**, and speeches (p. 112).

Another well-known typology by Hood (1983; Hood & Margetts, 2007) developed what he called the "NATO scheme," standing for the different resources that governments have at their disposal to effect policy change. N stands for **nodality** or information resources; A, for authority; T, for treasure or money; and O, for organization or personnel. These struck Linder and Peters (1989) as too broad, and in their article on the question, they developed their own schema that drew on several existing schemes, including Hood's. Four basic classes appeared over and over again in the literature they reviewed, but not always the same four, and so they combined them into a group of seven major categories of policy instruments: "(1) direct provision, (2) **subsidy**, (3) tax, (4) contract, (5) authority, (6) regulation, (the only consensus class), and (7) exhortation" (p. 44). They too provide a finer gradation of choice, based on their view that what really matters is the way in which policymakers subjectively perceive the choices that they have before them. The problem is that this gradation does not mesh very well with other attempts at classification (e.g., Howlett, Ramesh, & Perl, 2009; McDonnell & Elmore, 1987; Schneider & Ingram, 1990), all of which adopt a different classificatory principle (e.g., government resource versus impact or ends).

Yet another classification system for policy tools or instruments comes from Lester Salamon (2002). He defines a policy tool or instrument as "an identifiable method through which collective action is structured to address a public problem" (p. 19). Salamon is particularly interested in the degree to which modern governments are third-party governments. "What is distinctive about many of the newer tools of public action is that they involved the sharing with third-party actors of a far more basic governmental function: the exercise of discretion over the use of public authority and the spending of public funds" (p. 2). His list includes government enterprises; economic and social regulation; government insurance; public information; taxes, charges and tradable permits; procurement contracting; purchase of service; and tort liability (giving people rights in law to seek compensation for wrongs).

Given this rich variety of classifications and lists, how to proceed? Vedung (1998) defined policy instruments as the "set of techniques by which governmental authorities wield their power in attempting to ensure support and effect or prevent social change" (p. 21). The important thing about this definition is that it reminds us that policy, programs, and ultimately the policy instruments that give them effect are about *deliberately achieving some desired outcome*, and that moreover, social change is ultimately a result of human behaviour. The question of instruments, therefore, is really about the resources and techniques that governments have at their disposal to achieve certain outcomes through affecting human behaviour. In a phrase, it often involves making people do things or stopping them from doing some other things. For this reason most classifications of policy instruments stress the degree of coercion involved. Salamon (2002) defines coercion as the most salient dimension in understanding policy tools and suggests that it "measures the extent to which a tool restricts individual or group behaviour as opposed to merely encouraging or discouraging it" (p. 25). Stewart (2009, p. 90) argues that a basic distinction in instruments is between "tough" (coercive and sanction-based) and "tender" (relying on incentives, persuasion, and capacity building). The state has the monopoly of legitimate force in most societies, as well as the capacity to issue **binding rules** and **prohibitions**. It is useful therefore to consider the degree of state involvement and the degree of state coercion embedded in any policy instrument, as long as we understand that the choice of instrument assumes some grasp of what level of coercion will be accepted as legitimate in society. As we noted earlier, that line of legitimacy will shift. The financial crisis induced governments to use much more coercive instruments (e.g., virtual nationalization of banks and auto companies, heavy regulation on the financial sector, and draconian pressures on countries such as Greece and Italy to get their fiscal houses in order). 9/11 made citizens in all democracies more tolerant of invasions of privacy, and the growing costs of lifestyle choices like obesity have resulted in more scolding and shaming.

Since there is no universally accepted typology, and since most typologies of instruments emphasize different criteria, the one offered in this chapter (see Figure 4.1) is deliberately eclectic. We begin by presuming that the policymaker's purpose is to achieve an outcome in terms of (1) the behaviour of individuals; (2) political, social, or economic conditions; or (3) services provided to the public. It would be possible to state the latter two in terms of behavioural changes as well; for example, the desired outcome of reducing poverty could be achieved through changed behaviours, such as employers paying higher wages due to increased minimum wage levels or the poor being able to purchase more necessary goods and services because of tax breaks or subsidies. As Stewart (2009, p. 87) notes: "Behavioural change is strongly implicated in policy implementation. This is because, when public policies are implemented, they involve relationships between agents of the state and those outside it." However, since much policy discussion takes place around conditions (e.g., poverty, unemployment, productivity, crime) and services (e.g., health, education, water quality monitoring), there seems little benefit in jettisoning the terms. Now, given the fact of some desired outcome or policy objective (based on an assessment of the problem), what tools are at the policymaker's disposal for achieving it?

Figure 4.1 provides three broad categories, the first of which is to do nothing. In a sense, the option of doing nothing is not really a choice of instrument—it is simply inaction. As we noted in Chapter 1, we refer here to deliberate inaction, a conscious choice. We discuss this in more detail below, but the logic of highlighting this as a choice is to underscore the point that doing nothing often makes sense when it turns out that a perceived policy problem was not really a problem at all, or that the cost of intervention exceeds the benefits, or that other forces will achieve the desired outcome in the absence of government action.

The next two categories contain the two broad families of interventions or policy instruments that governments can choose to achieve their objectives. The first entails acting indirectly in the sense that the objectives are being pursued through the actions and behaviour of citizens, organizations, or firms. This kind of intervention can be made through affecting the information or values that underpin behaviour (information or exhortation instruments); influencing the calculus of monetary costs, benefits, and resources (expenditure instruments); or stipulating rules and sanctions attached to certain behaviours (regulatory instruments). Within this family of instruments, information-based tools are generally considered to be less coercive than expenditure-based tools, and both of these are considered less coercive than regulation-based tools. The continuum is not perfect—as we note below, taxes are probably

Figure 4.1 Policy Instruments: A Classification

GOVERNMENTS CAN...

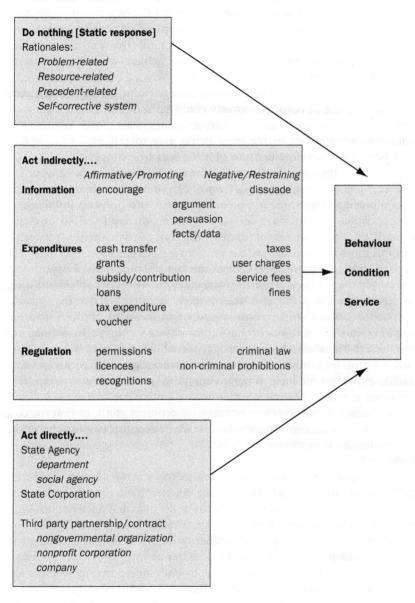

Do nothing [Static response]
Rationales:
Problem-related
Resource-related
Precedent-related
Self-corrective system

Act indirectly....

	Affirmative/Promoting	Negative/Restraining
Information	encourage	dissuade
	argument	
	persuasion	
	facts/data	
Expenditures	cash transfer	taxes
	grants	user charges
	subsidy/contribution	service fees
	loans	fines
	tax expenditure	
	voucher	
Regulation	permissions	criminal law
	licences	non-criminal prohibitions
	recognitions	

Behaviour

Condition

Service

Act directly....
State Agency
department
social agency
State Corporation

Third party partnership/contract
nongovernmental organization
nonprofit corporation
company

more coercive than self-regulation through **voluntary codes**. As well, in some respects, acting indirectly in our sense involves quite coercive state powers (e.g., the criminal justice system). However, it captures a rough scale effect as we move from one category to the other. The other axis, borrowing from Vedung (1998), is between affirmative/promoting and negative/restraining (p. 26). Tools drawing on information, expenditures, and regulation can either promote certain behaviours or outcomes, or prohibit or restrain them.

In the last family of instruments, the state acts directly and is ultimately accountable for achieving its objectives. The most obvious and conventional way to do this is through the use of the state's own resources to change conditions or provide services. For example, Revenue Canada, as a department, used to collect taxes for the federal government. Now taxes are collected through the Canada Revenue Agency, which, however, is still an agency (though at arm's length) of government. Many provincial and municipal governments, in dealing with the housing problems of poor people, directly provide social housing through special agencies. Canada used to have a large number of public enterprises or state corporations, most notably Air Canada and Petro-Canada before they were privatized, but also the still-surviving Canadian Broadcasting Corporation. Whatever the form—a department, agency, or corporation—in all three instances, the government is achieving its policy objective through the marshalling of its own resources and organizational capacity and not working through citizens, nongovernmental organizations (NGOs), or the private sector. It is doing the work itself. However, another form of direct action is through partnerships or **contracts** with third parties such as NGOs, nonprofit agencies, or companies. This subcategory admittedly stretches the definition of direct action slightly, but it is included here because the state is still formulating its objectives, determining acceptable outcomes, signing the contract for service delivery, providing the funds, and monitoring performance. It is also ultimately responsible for those outcomes.

It is important to understand that in the run of normal or routine politics, the range of instrument choice is generally limited by the existing array that is already embedded in the policy field. Policymakers think through their options on the basis of what is currently in the field or underpinning policy efforts. If evaluation shows that some instruments are not working, they can be amended, but as long as normal politics is incremental politics, the temptation is to build upon already existing and fairly finely graduated policy instruments. In periods of greater policy turbulence, policymakers will begin to think in broader instrument categories, because in turbulent times policies are often fundamentally restructured, forcing a consideration of instrument types. We discuss the new dynamics of instrument choice in the second half of this chapter;

the changes in governance in the past decade and especially the past five years have, indeed, been turbulent, and with them have come new debates and new approaches to instrument choice. In the sections below, we briefly outline the key characteristics of each instrument. We begin, however, by briefly outlining the logic of "doing nothing."

DOING NOTHING

"Doing nothing" may appear as a nondecision, which indeed it is if it has no rationale beyond either ennui or a simple desire to remain unengaged. As we argued in Chapter 1, however, a deliberate choice not to intervene, made after an analysis of the problem, should be considered a policy decision—what we will call here **"static response."** There can be several good rationales for declining to intervene. Together, they comprise a coherent set of considerations that should be part of any systematic process of instrument choice, even though doing nothing does not seem intuitively to fit the notion of an instrument or tool. The four rationales that follow presume that a potential problem or opportunity has presented itself to policymakers in some fashion and that a careful analysis was undertaken about the nature of the problem and the appropriate response.

Problem-related rationales: The analysis indicates that there is either no problem after all or a problem not within the government's current priorities, jurisdiction, or capacities. In May 1999, for example, the Canadian Radio-television and Telecommunications Commission (CRTC) announced that it would not extend its regulation to the Internet because it "concluded that the new media on the Internet are achieving the goals of the Broadcasting Act and are vibrant, highly competitive and successful without regulation" (CRTC, 1999). This decision was reversed less than 10 years later, in May 2008, when the CRTC concluded that the Internet was no longer a distinct technology and delivery channel, and that the lines between it and broadcasting were increasingly blurred. Another example of static response was Canada's refusal to join the war against Iraq. Prime Minister Chrétien and his Cabinet did not believe that Iraq had weapons of mass destruction, nor did they believe that the invasion would defeat terrorism. Theirs was a deliberate decision not to act (Chrétien, 2007, pp. 317–318). The debate over climate change, and the evident reluctance of some governments to do very much, is not necessarily a denial of the problem, but a recognition of the sheer range of causes behind the problem and the mass effort that would realistically be required to address those causes.

Resource-related rationales: The analysis indicates that there is indeed a problem and that it falls within the government's general priorities and jurisdiction. Nonetheless, given resource constraints and other more pressing demands, the government cannot allocate resources for the problem. The tension between pressing problems and resource restraints has become much sharper with the global financial crisis. Governments around the world have had to wrestle with stimulus packages, rising deficits, sovereign debt crises (Greece and Italy), and austerity programs. The irony is that with the continued pressure to stimulate their economies, this excuse not to spend because of strained resources is less and less defensible.

Precedent-related rationales: A problem exists, but the analysis raises the concern that a policy intervention might set a precedent that could place unmanageable demands on government. In the tainted blood scandal, for example, Ottawa refused to compensate hepatitis-C victims who had contracted the disease from blood products before 1986 in the fear that doing this would open a floodgate of compensation claims that would go beyond the $1.1 billion the federal and provincial governments were already paying out (Orsini, 2002). The same worry has been behind Ottawa's careful approach to "redress" policies for ethnic groups that endured historical injustices (e.g., the Japanese, the Chinese, Ukrainians, Aboriginal peoples) (James, 2007). Some critics of same-sex marriage argued that the government should leave the traditional definition of marriage as it was because of the possibility of a precedent leading to the legalization of polygamy (in November 2011 the British Columbia Supreme Court ruled that anti-polygamy laws were constitutional, but that decision is likely to be appealed to the Supreme Court of Canada).

Self-corrective system rationales: In this case, while it is accepted that there may be a problem, it is also assumed that there is a coherent system (e.g., social, cultural, religious, economic, even natural) at work that, over time, may correct it spontaneously, without the need for government intervention. Market-based rationales are the most familiar example of this: the argument is that market competition, over time, will correct the problem. This rationale is wearing thin in the face of financial market collapses, real-estate bubbles, and the apparent ability of markets to "correct" themselves only with government bailouts and various other protections. The Occupy Wall Street movement, which we discuss in Chapter 6, was an expression of frustration over the idea that markets would self-adjust and benefit society at large. From a policy perspective, this option is more about creating frameworks for self-correction, rather than doing nothing at all. In environment policy, for example, it might involve protection of habitats so that species can come back from possible extinction.

Static response appears like an empty category, a nullity or absence of action, but is important as part of the instrument selection or policy analysis process. The term is slightly misleading—"doing nothing" does require analysis and a decision not to respond directly. More subtly, it may require a careful balance of some action (setting a framework of constraints and boundaries) and inaction (allowing forces within those boundaries to calibrate themselves). Governments are constantly pressed to "solve" problems, and static response—appearing to do nothing—is politically difficult. But sometimes there are good grounds for inaction.

INFORMATION-BASED INSTRUMENTS

Information-based policy instruments include government-directed "attempts at influencing people through transfer of knowledge, communication of reasoned argument, and **moral suasion** in order to achieve a policy result" (Vedung & van der Doelen, 1998, p. 103). Of course, all serious policies and programs depend on information in the minimal sense of making people aware of their existence, but Vedung (1998) makes the useful distinction between information as an independent policy instrument and information as a metapolicy instrument that supports others (p. 49). Information-based policy instruments can include flyers, pamphlets, booklets, training, advertisements, reports, websites, and portals. Information-based instruments are considered the least coercive of all policy instruments since there is no obligation to act on the information and no supplementary inducement or penalty. Some forms of information can be designed to dissuade behaviours—a good example is the graphic health warnings on cigarette packages—while others are designed to encourage or promote certain behaviours—for example, *Canada's Food Guide* helps us know how many legumes to consume per week. Other forms of information are just that: information that citizens require in order to make decisions and take actions. Government now places on the Web enormous quantities of information that is useful to citizens—information about programs, about services, and forms and applications. In 2011 the federal government launched an "Open Data Pilot Project" that would make hundreds of official datasets available to citizens, groups, and businesses without cost for their own use (Government of Canada, 2011). Most interestingly, since many government services are essentially exchanges of information (applying for licences, paying taxes, making inquiries), information instruments can also be interactive, with information flowing both ways. We discuss information in relation to services in Chapter 5; we discuss information in the sense of policy communication in Chapter 9; here we will focus on information as an instrument to tackle policy problems.

A key principle behind information-based instruments is that human behaviour is largely based on knowledge, beliefs, and values. Assume that the government's policy objective is to reduce smoking. If knowledge, in the sense of facts at the smoker's disposal, is incorrect or incomplete (e.g., the addictive qualities of nicotine), or beliefs are wrong (e.g., that smoking has no ill-health effects), or values are counterproductive (e.g., it's "cool" to smoke), then smoking behaviour will continue unabated. Presumably, an information campaign that would enlighten smokers would change their behaviour, since it would appear to be manifestly in their interest to reduce or quit smoking. But of course we know that this is not always the case, and it alerts us to the fact that information-based policy tools work best when knowledge, beliefs, and values are consistent with direct and immediate self-interest. Even when "enlightened" by government information campaigns, smokers may continue to smoke because they like it, because they discount the negative health effects far into the future, because they struggle with temptation even though they know and try better (Schelling, 1984), or because they want to defy what they perceive as a hectoring, paternalistic government program (the boomerang effect).

There is a paradox about information-based instruments—as benign as they might appear, ultimately the most powerful way to change behaviour is to change the knowledge, beliefs, and values upon which it is based. Autocratic regimes understand this very well, though they keep a "big stick" in reserve in case propaganda does not work. The use of information or exhortation in democratic states can seem much less objectionable; it is remarkable, for example, how public attitudes toward the environment have changed in only one generation and have become the foundation for acquiescence to blue-box programs, anti-littering campaigns, and picking up after your dog in the park. This is all to the good. But there can be concerns. In Canada, the federal government has for decades been the country's single largest advertiser. There is a fine line between promoting public policies and programs, and self-promotion for the government of the day (we discuss this in Chapter 9). Other levels of government in Canada have not been left behind. And information can be used in a somewhat discomfiting way as a **shaming** instrument—in a sense, this is the use of information *about* rather than information *for*. Our behaviour might be changed not because our beliefs have been affected by an information campaign but because of information about us that has been provided publicly to others (e.g., the publication of the names of "johns"). The use of shaming as a policy instrument is more widespread than we might assume; it relies on prevailing social norms and the understandable desire of most people to seek esteem and approbation (Bogart, 2011). Product labelling, for example, can be used to induce companies to remove ingredients that are deemed harmful to the consuming public. Regulatory agencies can issue lists of "worst offenders" (e.g., polluters), deliberately using the publicity as a way of inducing change. Graham describes this as "democracy by disclosure": "Stated simply, such strategies employ government authority to require the standardized disclosure of factual information from identified businesses or other organizations about products or practices to reduce risks to the public" (Graham, 2002, p. 138). The interesting thing about the new disclosure instruments is that unlike warning labels that tell people what to do or articulate a harm or risk, mandatory disclosure simply puts factual information in the public domain (e.g., nutritional labelling) and lets people make up their own minds about risk. It can also be used as an instrument to increase transparency, as is the case in the federal government's proactive disclosure policy, where travel and hospitality expenses of senior officials and contracts over $10 000 are posted on department websites. The combination of public disclosure laws (and the United States is considerably ahead of Canada in this respect), assiduous researchers and critics, and modern media give information a potency that is sometimes underestimated. We address some new aspects of information as exhortation in the second part of the chapter.

EXPENDITURE-BASED INSTRUMENTS

From the policymaker's point of view, virtually every policy instrument involves expenditure—even giving a speech will entail the cost of speechwriters and distribution of materials. So money is a ubiquitous and universal resource that governments use to affect policy, and rarely, if ever, can expenditure as an instrument be avoided. The point about expenditure-based policy instruments, however, is that money itself is the direct instrument. In this instance, governments are not trying to achieve their objectives or outcomes by changing the information that undergirds behaviour, but rather the calculus of costs, benefits, and financial resources that individuals or organizations undertake before they do something. Producing Canadian films, for example, is risky because of the high probability of not making a profit due to a small domestic market. Government subsidies and tax breaks can change that equation and encourage more Canadian filmmaking. Canadians who live in poverty and who might not be able to afford a proper diet or housing can be aided through **cash transfers** in the form of income security or assistance payments.

In December 1998 the Auditor General of Canada undertook a special audit of the **grants** and **contributions** practices of several departments, primarily Industry Canada and Heritage Canada. As the report pointed out, the "provision of grants and contributions to individuals, businesses and not-for-profit organizations is one of the most important ways that the Government of Canada pursues its program objectives" (Auditor General of Canada, 1998). The report defined grants as "unconditional transfer payments for which eligibility and entitlement may be verified" and contributions as "subject to performance conditions that are specified in a contribution agreement. The recipient must continue to show that these conditions are being met in order to be reimbursed" (Auditor General of Canada, 1998, Chapter 27.1).

In Figure 4.1 we have distinguished between cash transfers, grants, and subsidies or contributions. In Canadian usage, transfers usually apply to payments by government to individuals or other governments that do not involve any form of exchange and have only minimal conditions attached to them. Equalization payments and the Canada Health and Social Transfer (CHST) are prime examples of cash transfers from the federal government to the provinces. Provincial governments also transfer cash to their municipalities to support a wide range of programs. Old Age Security and the Canada Child Tax Benefit are examples of transfers to individuals. The key point is that a cash transfer tends to be provided for broad support rather than in connection with a specific project or endeavour. Grants, even while they have few if any performance conditions attached, are usually provided in connection with a more specific endeavour (e.g., student educational grants). However, in a technical sense grants tend not to be too closely calibrated to the actual costs of engaging in that endeavour. Contributions and subsidies, on the other hand, have more numerous and detailed conditions, usually demand some measure of performance, and are more carefully calculated to defray some specific proportion of the cost of the endeavour. They differ from loans in that the latter must be repaid. **Tax expenditures** accomplish much the same thing as contributions or subsidies, but through the mechanism of reducing taxes for specific activities and thereby increasing the benefits. Perhaps the most publicly visible tax expenditure in Canada is the Registered Retirement Savings Program (RRSP), where interest in special accounts is tax free and contributions are tax deductible, though the device is used routinely to support everything from small businesses to **investments** in high technology and research. The 2008 federal budget introduced the Tax-Free Savings Account (TFSA) which is similar to the RRSP, but where contributions are not tax deductible, interest can grow tax free, and withdrawals are not taxed either. **Vouchers** are typically "coupons" for stipulated amounts of money that may be redeemed under certain conditions—the best known example is Food Stamps in the United States, although vouchers are increasingly being used to provide educational services, housing, child care, transportation, and healthcare (Steuerle & Twombly, 2002). In the United States, vouchers have become the dominant form of federal housing assistance (Center on Budget and Policy Priorities, 2007). The Organisation for Economic Co-operation and Development (OECD) points out that vouchers can be in the form of coupons—an "explicit" voucher—or in the form of reimbursements or direct payments for goods or services from approved suppliers. "The extent of use of these three forms of vouchers is significant in some sectors in OECD member countries, with their use being mainly focused on housing, education (primary and secondary), childcare (nursery education), and care for the elderly" (OECD, 2005, p. 146). Vouchers have even been recommended in the fight against obesity. Instead of "naming and shaming" the obese, some have suggested "healthy living" vouchers that people could use as they see fit to improve their health and lifestyles (Seeman & Luciani, 2011).

Expenditure instruments pose substantial management challenges in terms of ensuring that conditions are met and monies are spent appropriately, with some result. The Auditor General has been evaluating grants and contributions by the federal government for more than 20 years, and as early as 1984 identified eight critical management processes for grant and contribution programs: "stating objectives clearly; establishing unambiguous terms and conditions; informing potential applicants of program guidelines; reviewing and approving applications diligently; making payments properly; monitoring individual grants and contributions appropriately; providing good information to management; and assessing program effectiveness" (Auditor General of Canada, 1998).

The sponsorship scandal, which broke in early 2004 and involved the Ministry of Public Works and contracts with the Quebec communications firm Groupaction, simply illustrated that the government still was challenged in handling the spending instrument. The Auditor General's review of the matter found "an appalling disregard for the Financial Administration Act, the Government Contracts Regulations, Treasury Board policy, and rules designed to ensure prudence and probity in government procurement" (Auditor General of Canada, 2002, p. 1). The Gomery Commission agreed: "Many factors contributed to what has been described as the 'sponsorship scandal': inappropriate political interference in administrative matters, acceptance by public servants of such interference, excessive concentration of power in the Prime Minister's Office, carelessness and incompetence and blatant disregard of Treasury Board policies, greed and venality" (Gomery Commission, 2005, p. 438). To be fair, public sector financial management is complex, and because of its political/bureaucratic environment, is susceptible to all sorts of gameplaying (Graham, 2007, especially Chapters 6 and 8, and Appendix 1). As well, many of the challenges to managing large spending programs are systemic—ironically, in 2000, the Human Resources Development Canada "scandal" over a billion dollars lost in employment training funds (eventually determined to be only $85 000) might have been, in part, caused by new public management practices that led to decentralized decisionmaking and little oversight and information (Good, 2003). Since then, the machinery designed to manage public money has become even more complex. Whereas once the expenditure process could be summarized as a struggle between "spenders" (most departments) and "guardians" (the Department of Finance and Treasury Board), it now is characterized by "spenders, guardians, priority setters (the Prime Minister's Office and the Privy Council Office) and financial watchdogs (the

Office of the Auditor General) ..." (Good, 2007, p. 4). On top of that, the Federal Accountability Act, introduced in 2006, created audit committees for each department and gave sharper responsibilities to deputy ministers to act as "accounting officers." Then came Canada's Economic Action Plan, spending billions of dollars on hundreds of projects across the country, that demanded both rapid roll-out and prudent management. An austerity plan that was introduced in 2011 now demands spending reductions of 5 to 10 percent.

The negative/restraining side of expenditures is to increase the costs of some activities. Governments tax, of course, to get revenue. They can have policies about taxation, in terms of the fairness and incidence of the tax regime. They can also use taxes as deliberate policy instruments. For example, **sin taxes** on alcohol and cigarettes are a means of discouraging their use (Bird & Stoney, 2006). The distinction between taxes and other types of government levies such as user charges or fees is increasingly blurred, but, in principle, taxes have a compulsory aspect and generally are not connected to any specific service. Income and property taxes do have a discretionary component in that if someone decided not to work or live in a dwelling, he or she would not be liable for those taxes—but in practice, of course, they are almost unavoidable. Nonsmokers do not pay cigarette taxes, but smokers who do pay those taxes do not receive any specific government service in return. Both **user charges** and **service fees** have a service component in them and so are not usually viewed as taxes. In the case of user charges, the service component is quite general and the charge therefore is levied on a category of person or user. Examples include access to and use of facilities such as airports (many now levy an "improvement charge") or municipal dumps. A service fee usually is connected to some specific service rather than general use, for example, receiving a passport. In practice, the terms are often interchangeable, and for cosmetic reasons policymakers often prefer to use the term "fee" rather than "tax." Whatever term is used, the precise amounts of any levy and its attendant conditions (e.g., when, how, and on which payers) are complex questions of public finance.

REGULATION

Regulation draws on the most fundamental resource a government has: its capacity to command and prohibit. "Regulatory instruments are used to define norms, acceptable behavior, or to limit activities in a given society. The law, backed up with the threat of sanction, represents the 'stick' used to prescribe or prevent certain types of human behavior" (Lemaire, 1998, p. 59). That capacity depends on a blend of legitimacy and effective sanctions for disobedience, with the greatest weight on legitimacy. If governments merely have power without authority, they will have little capacity to command and have citizens obey. It is the legitimacy of their commands as perceived by the majority of citizens that permits them to efficiently use sanctions against the minority that disobey. A great deal of public policy is about achieving outcomes through ensuring certain actions or behaviours. Regulatory instruments rely on rules to prohibit or promote selected actions or behaviours. This technique has an admirable directness to it—"thou shalt" or "thou shalt not"—but we have classified them here under "indirect" instruments since, in most cases, regulation is understood to involve government rules aimed at certain activities undertaken by individuals, organizations, or firms to achieve certain outcomes.

Regulation is therefore a distinct type of rule making available to governments. It is termed **secondary legislation** because, unlike simple rules or codes or guides, it requires a statutory basis. As the 2003 *Cabinet Directive on Law-Making* makes clear,

> Canada's system of responsible parliamentary government is based on the rule of law. This means that laws must be made in conformity with the Constitution. The Crown retains very few regulatory powers that are not subject to the legislative or law-making process. For example, regulations governing the issuance of passports or medals and honors are still made under the royal prerogative. Parliament may delegate regulatory authority to Cabinet (the Governor in Council), a person (such as a Minister of the Crown) or a body (such as the Atomic Energy Control Board). However, this authority remains subject to the will of Parliament and regulations made under this delegated authority are referred to as subordinate legislation. (Privy Council Office, 2003)

Affirmative/promoting uses of regulation include permissions, licences, recognitions, and self-regulation. **Permissions** are simply permits or enablements with few if any conditions attached—for example, a hunting permit or a city declaration that bars can stay open later for a special event. **Licences** are more complicated in that they involve a mix of prohibition, permission, and condition—the classic formula of the regulator. To regulate, first, generally prohibit some action (e.g., broadcasting TV signals, driving a vehicle, fishing for salmon, doing brain surgery); second, specifically permit that action for individuals or organizations that will respect some predefined criteria or conditions. The licence conditions can be as detailed or as scant as the regulator likes. Of course, a key ingredient is defining sanctions for the unlawful (or unlicensed) practice of the regulated act. Use of "regs," as seasoned policy analysts like to call them, is a marvellously flexible instrument in that it can define prohibited acts quite precisely and can attach equally precise conditions to the licensee. Keeping track of regulations can be difficult, and the Standards Council of Canada has made "RegWatch" available on the Web to identify

Canadian, foreign, and international standards referenced in Canadian federal law.

Regulation can also entail **recognition** or defining the bona fide actors in a policy field. The most benign is simply to recognize certain individuals or organizations for some policy-relevant quality that they have or have achieved. Under the Indian Act, for example, the federal Department of Indian Affairs and Northern Development keeps a registry of all Indians so defined for purposes of the legislation (essentially those individuals descended from Indian bands with whom the federal government struck treaties in the 19th and 20th centuries). Appropriately enough, they are known as status Indians, and other Indians are described as non-status or non-treaty Indians. For the purposes of the Indian Act and what it permits, prohibits, and provides, it matters a great deal if one is status or non-status. Another example is the Energuide program from Natural Resources Canada. Appliances, buildings, heating and cooling equipment, new homes and vehicles must, by law, display a label that shows the amount of energy consumed.

A species of regulation is government-sanctioned self-regulation, where the state delegates its regulatory power not to a state agency but to a nongovernmental organization or association. The professions (medicine, law, engineering) are the main examples and involve the delegation of government powers to set mandatory standards and discipline infractions. The assumption policymakers have made is that these professions can be trusted not to take the short-term view or operate primarily for economic gain. In other cases, government accredits organizations to conduct official activities and may incorporate the results into legislation, thereby giving those activities the force of law. A good example is the National Standards System, which is managed by the Standards Council of Canada, a Crown corporation. The Council accredits organizations to develop, test, and apply standards. Most standards (and there are thousands, covering almost every conceivable product and many services) are voluntary, though some are incorporated by reference into international law. In another strategy, government can help organizations develop their own voluntary codes of conduct. Voluntary codes also go by other names: codes of conduct, codes of practice, voluntary initiatives, guidelines, and nonregulatory agreements. Successful codes are said to have the following characteristics: (1) buy-in from leaders of the relevant organizations; (2) rank and file support; (3) a clear statement of objectives, obligations, and rules; (4) transparent development and implementation; (5) regular flow of information; (6) an effective dispute-resolution system; (7) meaningful incentives to participate; and (8) negative repercussions for failure to join or comply (Industry Canada, 1998, pp. 7–8). The government's role in voluntary codes is that of a catalyst, facilitator, and sometimes endorser. In those cases where voluntary codes affect business or industrial sectors, government is also interested in the degree to which the codes may impede competition.

Regulations can broadly be classed as economic, social, or environmental, though each of these will have subsets based on the object (e.g., prices, safety) or targets (e.g., specific industries). Economic regulation typically addresses such factors as pricing, advertising, and labelling, competition, some aspects of production, profits, and disclosure of financial information. The classic rationale for economic regulation is that markets are not working efficiently. Problem cause may be due to monopolies (the historical case for public utility regulation), oligopolies (hence, competition regulation), or the simple occurrence of various forms of behaviour designed to maximize profits at the expense of workers and consumers (e.g., collusion, false advertising, union busting). Social regulation is designed to protect us less as consumers than as persons or citizens. This somewhat vague formulation is fairly clear when it comes to health and safety standards such as fire regulations. Though these frequently apply to products and services, they also affect our use of spaces and buildings as citizens. It is a lot less clear what criteria regulators have in mind as they move into the cultural realm with broadcasting regulations (e.g., Canadian content, nonstereotyping) and social justice regulations such as employment equity or speech codes. Environmental regulation struggles with the standards issue as well, since the science is often not precise enough to determine what the allowable limits of many toxic substances might be. Nor can we easily know the effects of the interaction of hundreds of thousands of substances in the air, land, and water.

ACTING DIRECTLY

The preceding categories of instruments are indirect in that they involve working through citizens or organizations to achieve public goals. Governments can decide to achieve the conditions or service goals they have in mind by marshalling their own resources toward those ends. A good example is education. Parents need to have their children educated, but governments can elect to provide that education directly through a state-run system or to provide parents with the funds (usually through some form of voucher) that they can then redeem for services as they see fit, from either government providers, the private sector, or some mix. Any service directly provided by government, from garbage collection to education, will involve the expenditure of often very substantial amounts of money. In 2009 (latest data), for example, provincial and territorial governments spent a total of $259 billion on health ($115.5 billion), social services ($61.7 billion), and education ($81.8 billion). These combined amounts represented 74 percent of total expenditures of the governments in that year (Statistics Canada, 2009).

So, "direct provision" is less an alternative to spending money than it is a means of spending money that reflects a different policy logic. It is a logic reflected in the questions listed in Box 4.1 (see on the next page). Take municipal garbage collection as an example. The need in this case is the removal of refuse, and municipal governments have traditionally provided this service directly by raising general tax revenues to cover the cost. Traditionally, no fees have been attached. Municipal governments have had both the authority and the fiscal capacity to deliver the service. The nub of the issue is in questions 4 and 5. Are there alternative service providers? Absolutely. The garbage business in North America is huge. What is the compelling policy reason to directly collect garbage with city workers rather than through a contract for service with a private company? Typically, the argument from public sector unions has been that the level of service (and the wages and working conditions of sanitary workers) will decline if private companies get into the act. Apart from that, most people care only that the can at the curbside is emptied weekly—this is essentially a question of efficiency. If public sector workers can collect the garbage as efficiently as a private sector company can, there usually is little reason to change. Question 6, however, has risen with a vengeance in recent years. As the costs of garbage collection and recycling have increased dramatically across North America, and as pressure to hold the line on taxes has mounted, more and more municipal governments have decided to charge some sort of fee for collection. Doing this can get quite creative, from charges per can or bag to limits on the number of bags one can put out. The logic in both cases is the same: what was once a "free" service now has a direct cost attached to it. The other questions deal with the ways in which government can either support or regulate the private provision of services. As we shall see in Chapter 5, **alternative service delivery** or some variant of the term has become an important issue in the implementation of public policy. More and more jurisdictions are answering question 4 in the affirmative, but question 5 in the negative, and then the game turns into one of deciding how to structure a private sector–public sector partnership. Another implementation issue is, if the service is to be provided through a public agency, how should that agency be designed? Should it be a direct-line department, or an arm's-length entity like a public or Crown corporation?

As the list of questions on service delivery suggests, governments can either provide the service directly or regulate the provision of the service by third parties, or they can do a mix of both. Policy instruments are not mutually exclusive but are usually combined in packages to deal with the different dimensions of the problem.

The preceding has covered most of the major categories of instruments. What can we conclude from the discussion? First, no list is ever complete, and there are some instruments that some authors would include as

BOX 4.1   QUESTIONS TO ASK ABOUT DIRECT PROVISION OF SERVICE INSTRUMENTS

1. What is the need or the problem, and what service or bundle of services will meet that need?
2. Do we have the legal capacity to provide the service?
3. Do we have the resources to provide the service?
4. Are there alternative service providers?
5. Is there a compelling policy reason to provide the service directly (e.g., safety, uniformity of standards, recipients cannot choose appropriate service levels, retaining agency capacity in the program field)?
6. If the service is provided publicly, should there be fees attached?
7. If the service is provided privately, will recipients be able to pay for it, or should there be some subsidy?
8. If there is a subsidy, should it be paid to providers or recipients?
9. If the service is provided privately, by what sort of entity? (Examples: For-profit or nonprofit.)
10. If the service is provided privately, what oversight or regulation should government provide?

separate categories (e.g., Crown corporations) and others would place under a broad category such as direct provision. Second, the sliding scale of authority idea is only moderately helpful in distinguishing these instruments. A high government charge on a service I need to use regularly will seem a lot more coercive to me than even the most detailed regulations covering a service I rarely access. Equally, a persistent series of hectoring ads about what the government believes to be naughty behaviour may seem more paternalistic than the income tax I am forced to pay once a year. This point takes on even greater force when we consider a third conclusion: no instrument is an island. Since they tackle clusters of problems, government policies use clusters of programs. These program clusters, in turn, bundle together groups of instruments. Education, for example, mixes big spending, direct service delivery, taxation (special education taxes), and lots of regulations.

This crude inventory has shown us what instruments we can choose and some of the rationales behind their choice. But what explains instrument choice? Theoretically, some instruments are substitutable, meaning that from the point of view of cost and at least the major outcome desired by policy, it makes little difference which instrument you use. Postsecondary education is currently funded in part by federal government transfers to the provinces. For years, federal ministers have mused about converting that transfer into vouchers that would go directly to students. The money would be exactly the same, and it could flow only into postsecondary institutions. The big difference would be the change from a cash transfer to governments to a voucher for students. The other aspect of this issue is comparing the pattern of instrument choice across governments. Expenditures across the OECD countries on health, education, and income security are much closer than the means used to provide these services.

Linder and Peters (1989) provided an early model for understanding the links between the broad policy system variables and decisions that policymakers undertake in given situations. They emphasized the importance of systemic variables, organizational characteristics, problem features, and the profile of individual decisionmakers. Systemic variables include such broad factors as national policy style, political culture, and prevailing social cleavages. Organizational variables include the way that the sponsoring department is structured, its history, and its connections with its relevant policy communities. The problem context embraces questions such as how crowded the policy domain is, the political constraints of using a specific instrument, and the requirements of political support (Bressers & O'Toole, 2005). Finally, individual-level variables comprise perceptions, values, and experience of the policymaker. This schema operates almost like a funnel, channelling these larger forces down from the systemic level to the individual decisionmakers. Of course, national policy style and political culture are not actors on the policy stage; they have influence only through the decisionmaker's implicit or conscious application. The current debate in some provincial jurisdictions over the use of private management companies (or private-public-partnerships—PPPs) to run public hospitals is an interesting illustration: this is contracting out to a third party in a policy area that jealously protects its public character. The decision to use this instrument will certainly depend on cost considerations and effectiveness (the problem context), but also on what is feasible or acceptable in that political regime (style and political culture).

New Dynamics

As we have argued throughout this book, the nature of governance is changing because of globalization, technology, culture, and new approaches to public management and statecraft. While the impacts on problem definitions are powerful, as we saw in Chapter 3, they are still somewhat difficult to conceptualize because problem definition and agenda-setting are such complex processes in their own right. In this chapter and in Chapter 5, we see clear evidence for new ways of making policy.

Spending Instruments

The first edition of this book appeared in 1997, when governments across Canada were in the midst of seriously attacking deficits that had built up over almost a quarter century. From 1998 to 2008, the federal government ran a string of large surpluses. In 2006–07, all provincial/territorial governments were in surplus as well. Given the angst in the mid-1990s over deficits (which had been a constant feature of federal budgets since the early 1970s, piling up the national debt annually) this position was a singular achievement and one that distinguished Canada from most other OECD countries. Much of this achievement came from a sustained U.S. economic boom in the same period, and in 2006–07, a spike in resource prices. As we argued in the previous chapter, the global financial crisis in 2008 raised the spectre of deficits once again. Starting in 2008, the federal government ran a string of deficits that started at $5.7 billion in 2008–09 and climbed to $55.5 billion the next year (Department of Finance, 2011a). It projected continued, but diminishing deficits until 2015 (Department of Finance, 2011b). But in addition, new pressures stemming from global and continental competition have induced new configurations and new types of spending instruments. In order to understand this, we need to briefly review the political background to Canadian fiscal policy in the last decade.

Serious fiscal restraint began for the federal government in the mid-1990s with program review that forced policymakers to ask six fundamental questions (see Chapter 2) about each program they administered and to reconsider modes of delivery, that is, their instruments. Provincial governments went through similar exercises, under different guises, and took somewhat longer to achieve balance. At the federal level, total expenditures in 1992–93 were $161 billion; by 1997, they dropped to $149 billion. Much of that drop was achieved through cuts in transfers to the provinces, particularly in health and social services, with predictable results across the country. Federal spending started to increase again after 1997, stemming from an unbroken string of surpluses.

During the late-1990s period of restraint, the magnitude and imperative of the cuts faced by most spending departments in most jurisdictions across Canada demanded a fundamental re-evaluation of lines of business. When funding drops by 20 percent or 30 percent in two years, something has to change, and that change cannot be incremental. Another consequence of this period of restraint was a greater interlinkage in designing policy. In part, this stemmed as well from the growing appreciation of the interconnectedness of policy fields. Sustainable development, for example, can be defined to include health and social stability, in which case, almost anything becomes relevant as "environmental policy." And as fiscal concerns permeated policymaking over the past decade, almost everything came under the purview of departments of finance. Added to this were shifts in economic theory that highlighted the importance of human capital for competitiveness in high-technology, information-based industries—encouraging social policy to merge to a large extent with economic policy. Nonetheless, reduced spending capacity helped this new appreciation of linkages and leverage to emerge as well.

In this period of restraint, most government departments had to reassess their priorities, cut some programs, reduce spending on others, and downsize their staff and other resources. They had to focus their programs more tightly, budget carefully, and try to demonstrate results. Then came a happy decade of surpluses in many jurisdictions (Ottawa, in particular) and annual increases in spending. The financial crisis changed all this, and governments around the world found themselves spending to stimulate their economies, and in the face of declining revenues due to a severe economic downturn, plunging into a sea of debt—in some cases, like Greece, so severe that they threatened a sovereign debt default and an exit from the Euro. There is now a substantial debate about the right course to take: continue spending to stimulate the economy, or begin the long, hard process of deficit reduction. That debate has been waged politically in Washington, in Brussels, in London, and in most other capitals in the world.

In Canada at least, there now seems to be solid, emerging cross-political orthodoxy against running deficits, if at all possible, an orthodoxy that goes back to the searing deficit decade of the 1990s (Campbell, 1999, p. 141). All federal parties in the 2004, 2006, and 2008 elections promised not to run deficits, and only the global financial crisis opened the door to the newly elected Conservatives in November 2008 to contemplate running a "temporary" deficit. Equally significant, while the newly elected McGuinty government in Ontario brought down a deficit budget in May 2004, it also committed itself to a four-year plan to reach balance—which it achieved, with some pride. By 2011, of course, in the face of economic downturn, the province was running a projected annual deficit of $16.7 billion (though most observers agreed that it would have been higher without the earlier efforts (Province of Ontario, 2011)).

Several things appear to have happened over time. First, countering previous economic orthodoxy, deficits did not seem necessary to stimulate the economy. Second, once large surpluses were achieved, they were much more congenial from the point of new spending programs. Third, from a political perspective, actively avoiding deficits became a mark of solid financial management—all parties have celebrated the importance of prudent financial management. The pull of this orthodoxy was evident in the federal government's grudging willingness to entertain a deficit in 2009, but not "structural deficits," as well as a determined plan to get back to a balanced budget (Pal, 2011).

Nonetheless, there continues to be an appetite among the Canadian public for focused spending in various areas, particularly in healthcare and defence, and governments cannot be blind to spending pressures that are associated with changing demographics and a certain minimum maintenance of infrastructure and core services, not to mention economic survival. As we noted earlier, about 70 percent of all provincial government spending is on health, education, and social services, and not surprisingly, these are the top priorities for citizens as well. After the shocks of transfer cuts in the mid-1990s, and facing a constant barrage of criticism from provincial leaders and rising concerns from ordinary Canadians about the quality of healthcare, the federal government began to respond in various ways. It started to put money back into the system: in 2001, Ottawa established the Commission on the Future of Health Care in Canada (the Romanow Commission), which paved the way for the Health Care Renewal Accord of February 2003 ($34.8 billion over five years). In the June 2004 election, all three national parties pledged to support the Accord and to add even more money. In 2007, federal government spending on healthcare was up by nearly 5 percent over 2006, in part because of new expenditures for the Patient Wait Time Guarantee Trust (Department of Finance, 2007b, p. 57).

The issue therefore is not spending per se. Even the allegedly fiscally phobic Conservative Party of Canada has increased spending each year since being elected in 2006 and was resigned to a deficit for 2009. Another interesting indication that spending is viewed more carefully these days is the emphasis on making "investments." Almost all major government spending initiatives are now described as "investments." An investment implies a return of some sort, a benefit or a profit, and so is rhetorically more useful to contemporary policymakers. This emphasis on investments and boutique spending programs marked the government's policies until late 2008, but the spending instrument has come back with a vengeance. Defence and healthcare were givens for increased spending, but new financial demands to support the ailing automotive industry, and even mining and forestry, put new pressures on government coffers. The 2008 Speech from the Throne clearly indicated a reluctance to engage in long-term or "structural" deficits, but it looked like big spending was back, and indeed, some respected economists argued that sustained deficit spending was needed to save the Canadian and global economies from collapse.

There is likely to be continued pressure on the spending instrument, though it will be used cautiously and somewhat reluctantly (at least in Canada—Europe faces an economic crisis so severe that austerity has been rejected by almost all EU members except Germany). There has been another important change in public attitudes and public policy discourse, however, which might upset this equation: the popularity of tax cuts. It should be remembered that a good part of the success in erasing deficits and achieving balanced budgets in the late 1990s was through increased tax rates and increased tax revenues. Alberta led the way in first reducing taxes after it had achieved balanced budgets, and then in 2001 moving to a flat tax rate of 11 percent on taxable income and substantially increased personal exemptions. Tax cuts were a major feature of federal budgets between 2000 and 2003, and again all three national parties offered some degree of tax relief in the June 2004 election (the Liberals, with only minor reductions for seniors and those with disabilities; the Tories, with major personal and corporate cuts; the NDP, with increased taxes on the wealthy combined with reductions for middle- and lower-income groups). It is clear, however, that tax-cutting as an economic strategy is more comfortable for the right, whereas the left will emphasize "fairness" in taxation with targeted and relatively minor reductions. The federal Conservatives carried on in 2006 and 2007 with successive cuts to the GST and major cuts to income taxes (the government's 2007 Economic Statement proudly proclaimed $60 billion in cuts over six years to individuals, families, and businesses).

The pressure for tax reductions may not disappear entirely, at least as an instrument for economic stimulus, but given demands for higher spending, the scope for reductions is likely to be smaller. To this might be added a strong sense that government grants and contributions are often badly managed, and that money is wasted in hundreds of small and large ways in Ottawa and provincial capitals. This perception stemmed in large part from the HRDC and sponsorship scandals discussed earlier, and this shift in public mood was the foundation for the Federal Accountability Act, as well as the new policy on grants and contributions announced in 2008.

The government established the Independent Blue Ribbon Panel (BRP) on Grant and Contribution Programs in June 2006. The Panel's report, *From Red Tape to Clear Results*, became the catalyst for a three-year government action plan to reform the administration of grants and contributions. The Panel noted that the federal government annually spends over $27 billion on more than 800 grant and contribution programs, spread over 50 departments and agencies (Blue Ribbon Panel, 2006). Its report was intended to suggest changes that would make those programs more efficient and effective, while at the same time ensuring accountability. To that end, its recommendations were geared to making the programs more responsive to clients, clarifying objectives, providing better service, and simplifying—without compromising—reporting, accountability, and audit functions.

The government received the report enthusiastically and launched an action plan in 2008 to implement the Panel's recommendations over a three-year period (Treasury Board of Canada Secretariat, 2008). The first part of the plan was the development of a new policy on transfer payments, to go into effect on October 1, 2008. The next steps included the development of a new service policy for the departmental administration of grants and contributions, and the designation of six "vanguard" departments to develop business plans (Canadian Heritage, Canadian International Development Agency, Economic Development Agency of Canada for the Regions of Quebec, Health Canada, Human Resources and Social Development Canada/Service Canada, Indian Affairs and Northern Development). Their common areas of focus were "simplification of funding programs and agreements; streamlining, standardization, and harmonizing of the application process; introduction of flexible risk management practices; establishment of service standards; identification and implementation of best practices; improved access to information via technology; and enhancement of stakeholder engagement" (Treasury Board of Canada Secretariat, 2008, p. 5).

TAXATION

Canadian governments tackled their deficits in the 1990s by cutting some expenditures, but they also benefited from increased tax revenues. As Purchase and Hirshhorn (1994) show, total tax revenues in Canada "increased from 31.3 percent in 1983 to 37 percent in 1992" (p. 36). Moreover, while corporate taxes actually declined in this period, "taxes on individuals have increased sharply" (p. 37). Federal government revenues were $116 billion in 1993–94; in 2000–2001 they were $162 billion; and in 2002–03, they were $177 billion. In 2007–08, they were projected to total $245.5 billion, up 4 percent from 2006–07, and up 10.5 percent from 2005–06 (Department of Finance, 2008, pp. 199–202). While most Canadians welcomed the eradication of government deficits in the 1990s, they were not entirely pleased with the high taxes they had to pay to achieve it. Taxes did begin to decline from that period, but even in 2007 the federal government admitted: "Personal and corporate income taxes as a percentage of GDP are higher in Canada than in all other G7 countries" (Department of Finance, 2007a, p. 19). As we noted above, all three major national parties favour tax reductions of some sort, with the key difference being their magnitude and incidence, and the Conservative government has moved aggressively to cut both corporate and personal income taxes, not to mention the GST, a signature slash. By 2012, the federal corporate tax rate had been reduced to 15 percent, one of the lowest among the G-7. Personal federal income tax was projected to rise from 7.0 percent of GDP in 2010–11 to 7.4 percent in 2016–17 (Department of Finance, 2011b).

A countertrend to reduced income taxes is an increase in user charges and service fees. The deepest reasons for this are also the murkiest, and perhaps the most controversial: as citizens become more resistant to redistributive government, they become more resistant to redistributive (general) taxation. Fees and charges seem to link services more directly to beneficiaries. Through user charges and service fees, special benefits enjoyed by only a minority of citizens are paid for in whole or in part by that minority. In the 1990s, studies showed that user fees accounted for as much as 17 percent of Ontario's government revenues and that reliance on them, by at least Ontario municipal governments, was increasing (Sproule-Jones, 1994, p. 7). A June 2000 report of the federal Standing Committee on Finance noted that while user charges contributed a negligible amount to Ottawa's revenues (about 2.4 percent), some 391 of them were spread over 47 departments and agencies (Standing Committee on Finance, 2000). The government had encouraged departments to rely more on user charges and cost recovery in its 1997 Cost Recovery and Charging Policy, which was changed to the External Charging Policy in 2003. In 2003, there were "400 external charging programs in 47 departments and agencies resulting in thousands of different fees" (Treasury Board of Canada Secretariat, 2003). In 2004 the External Charging Policy was superseded by the User Fees Act and an accompanying Policy on Service Standards for External Fees. In 2008, these were supplemented by a Guide to Establishing the Level of Cost-Based User Fee or Regulatory Charge. The intent behind all these new policy frameworks was to improve "accountability, oversight, and transparency in the management of user fee activities" (Treasury Board of Canada Secretariat, 2007a). In 2005–06, federal government revenue from user charges was $1.9 billion, spread out across 51 departments (Treasury Board of Canada Secretariat, 2007b).

The latest taxation twist has been **carbon taxes**, linked to new and more aggressive action to counter climate change caused by greenhouse gas emissions. As we noted earlier, a tax—used as a policy instrument and not simply to raise revenue—is a device to make targeted behaviours more expensive and hence, less attractive. In this broad sense, a tax (as a charge that is a disincentive) can be levied on almost anything, assuming that it cannot be easily evaded. Carbon taxes have an additional quality in that they are designed to both expose and levy the costs of externalities on those who produce them. A company that pollutes the air or water does not usually have to take into account the cost of this external effect on others when it prices its products.

In February 2008, British Columbia was the first North American jurisdiction to levy a full, revenue-neutral carbon tax—a tax not focused on one type of emission. It followed Quebec, with its 2007 tax on hydrocarbons. The idea is not new: Finland has had a carbon tax since 1990, Sweden since 1991, the United Kingdom since 2001, and New Zealand since 2005 (Carbon Tax Center, 2011); Australia introduced a plan in 2011 for a carbon tax and eventually a market-based emissions trading scheme ("Pushing for a Carbon Tax," 2011a). It is the carbon in fossil fuels that contributes to climate change, and proportions of carbon in different fuels are known quite precisely (e.g., coal emits more carbon than natural gas). This knowledge is the platform for taxing emissions or developing other measures such as **cap and trade.**

The B.C. carbon tax was a trendsetter in several respects (British Columbia, 2008). The tax hit all fossil fuels, initially at a rate of $10 per tonne of greenhouse gas emissions, tripling by 2012. The tax was to be revenue neutral, meaning that whatever was raised would be returned to taxpayers. This point is an important one since a carbon tax is regressive—it hits low-income consumers of gas, oil, and electricity the hardest. The B.C. budget introduced a low-income Climate Action Tax Credit of $100 per adult and $30 per child (paid quarterly) and promised to reduce both personal and corporate income taxes. On top of this, it introduced a Climate Action Dividend of $100 in June 2008 for each provincial resident to offset the lifestyle changes that they were being asked to make. The government projected revenues from the carbon tax of $1.85 billion over three years, all of which it said would be returned to taxpayers through off-setting tax reductions and credits.

The pressure to deal with climate change through some form of taxation or regulation has been building steadily. In January 2008, the National Roundtable on the Environment and the Economy concluded that Canada could substantially reduce its carbon emissions by 2050 through either carbon taxes or a cap and trade scheme (National Round Table on the Environment and the Economy, 2008). The federal Standing Committee on Finance recommended, in 2008, that the federal government develop tax incentives to encourage truck owners and operators to reduce their greenhouse gas emissions (Standing Committee on Finance, 2008). The federal government responded to these pressures and to the B.C. example in March 2008 by choosing to regulate rather than tax. Its *Turning the Corner* strategy on greenhouse gas emissions (first announced in 2007) had regulated caps for industry that it claimed would result in a 20 percent overall reduction by 2020. The tar sands were specifically targeted with requirements that all new plants starting after 2012 would have to use carbon capture and storage (beneath-the-ground) technologies. New regulations would apply to 16 sectors, "including oil sands, oil and gas, power plants, refineries, chemical and fertilizer plants, pipelines, cement, metals, smelters, and pulp and paper" (Government of Canada, 2008). The government also proposed a one-time carbon credit for firms that had taken past actions to reduce emissions, as well as the establishment of a carbon trading market. The financial crisis in 2008 took new taxes off the table, and in any case, the Harper government preferred carbon capture and storage as a policy option. As well, rather than taxes, the government, in 2010, adopted a regulatory approach in one area—motor-vehicle fuel-efficiency standards—adopting American standards that would reduce greenhouse gas emissions by 25 percent by 2016 (Macdonald, 2011).

REGULATION

Just as the character of expenditures and taxes as policy instruments has changed, so has regulation. The pressures on regulatory instruments have been somewhat contradictory. Initially, as part of downsizing government in the 1990s and related to cuts in spending, there was also a movement to deregulate on the grounds that excessive regulation did as much harm to the economy as deficits did, if not more. The OECD noted, for example, a strong trend among its members to "reforming and reviewing" regulation (OECD, 2007). Regulatory instruments rely on the use of authority, and to the extent that government lost some legitimacy in the late 1990s, so it lost its authority, and with that came an increasing distaste for government "red tape." As well, in the same period, both international agreements and economic and technological forces constrained the use of regulatory instruments in many traditional areas such as telecommunications and broadcasting, utilities, foreign investment, and marketing boards. On the other hand, especially after 9/11, SARS, the collapse of Lehman Brothers, and turmoil in financial and sovereign debt markets, and even debates about what to do about lifestyle-related major health problems (e.g., obesity and diabetes), the public appetite for re-regulation has begun to grow. Public discourse also shifted to recognizing the need for regulations in a complex, risk-saturated modern world to even recognizing that effective regulatory systems can be a competitive advantage. This idea of effective systems was driven home by the financial crisis: countries like Canada weathered the storm better not because of markets but because of more effective financial regulatory systems. We will try to make sense of these contradictory pressures by addressing constraints on regulation, demands for regulation, and shifts in regulatory venues.

The constraints on the use of regulatory instruments come principally from four sources: international trade agreements, technology, economics, and cost. A large subset of economic regulatory instruments has been devoted in one fashion or another to the protection of domestic industries from excessive internal or foreign competition. Classic examples include regulations that prevented foreign banks from operating in Canada, regulations that gave domestic Canadian oil companies advantages over foreign-owned competitors, foreign investment guidelines, broadcasting rules that protected Canadian advertisers and cable companies, and agricultural marketing boards for everything from milk to potatoes. International trade agreements, on the other hand, want to reduce these kinds of protective, regulatory instruments in favour of freer markets. The 1989 Free Trade Agreement, and its successor, the North American Free Trade Agreement (NAFTA), with Canada, the United States, and Mexico, expressly forbids some forms of regulation that would advantage domestic industries over competitors from the partner countries. Agricultural marketing boards, for example, faced pressures under the NAFTA provisions on agriculture and food products, but managed to survive. By 2011, with serious discussions under way to establish a free-trade agreement called the Trans-Pacific Partnership, Canada was once again opening the discussion on marketing boards. While environmental, health, and cultural regulations are, in principle, shielded from NAFTA, the larger free-trade logic of the agreement increasingly puts these provisions under pressure. The World Trade Organization (WTO), the successor to the GATT (General Agreement on Tariffs and Trade), was explicitly designed to establish clearer and more efficient institutional mechanisms to deal with a wider variety of trade issues (e.g., services, farming, and manufactured goods); it has a major focus on technical barriers to trade (regulations).

The Technical Barriers to Trade Agreement (TBT) tries to ensure that regulations, standards, testing and certification procedures do not create unnecessary obstacles. However, the agreement also recognizes countries' rights to adopt the standards they consider appropriate—for example, for human, animal or plant life or health, for the protection of the environment or to meet other consumer interests. Moreover, members are not prevented from taking measures necessary to ensure their standards are met. But that is counterbalanced with disciplines. A myriad of regulations can be a nightmare for manufacturers and exporters. Life can be simpler if governments apply international standards, and the agreement encourages them to do so. In any case, whatever regulations they use should not discriminate. The agreement also sets out a code of good practice for both governments and non-governmental or industry bodies to prepare, adopt, and apply voluntary standards. Over 200 standards-setting bodies apply the code. The agreement says the procedures used to decide whether a product conforms with relevant standards have to be fair and equitable. It discourages any methods that would give domestically produced goods an unfair advantage. The agreement also encourages countries to recognize each other's procedures for assessing whether a product conforms. Without recognition, products might have to be tested twice, first by the exporting country and then by the importing country (World Trade Organization, 2011)*.

As we note below, however, internationalization has also provided a fresh context for **re-regulation** that brings domestic policy targets into a wider, international regime. This new context can actually strengthen domestic regulation, not constrain it. A decade ago, Doern and colleagues pointed out that there had been an increase in some business framework and environmental regulation, and that, in contrast to the conventional view that the previous two decades had been primarily an era of **deregulation**, "it is evident that, overall, the density and extent of rule making by, or on behalf of, the state has increased" (Doern et al., 1999a, p. 5). This increase is in part due to pressures in health and safety regulation, often driven by technology. Food products, clean air standards, water quality, and the impact of biotechnology across a host of areas drive a demand for more, not less, regulation (Doern & Prince, 2012). Another important change to regulation as a governing instrument and as part of policy design has been the internationalization of regulatory regimes. If we think of regulation in its broadest sense—rules and standards about conduct, backed by sanctions of some sort—then many of our domestic regulatory regimes are becoming linked with international ones. This development reflects one side of the process of globalization discussed in Chapter 2. As the forces and factors important to policy shift to the international level, governments increasingly have to cooperate at that level in order to continue to have some influence on their domestic practices. A perfect example is the Financial Stability Board (FSB) established by the G20 in 2009. It brings together national authorities, central banks, and other international financial institutions to provide better international regulation and oversight of financial institutions and markets around the world. In the face of the financial crisis, domestic regulation of financial institutions that effectively operate in global markets simply was inadequate to the problem at hand.

These organizational constraints on regulatory instruments mirror the constraints that some of these instruments face as a result of technological and economic changes. The key to conventional regulatory instruments is the government's ability to first, forbid some activity or outcome, and then, permit it under certain conditions. These conventions assume that the activity or outcome in question can indeed be controlled and monitored. When regulatory authorities can be bypassed, then the regime collapses or becomes irrelevant. Substantial changes in technology

---

*Understanding the WTO, "Technical Regulations and Standards." © 2012 World Trade Organization. Reprinted with permission. www.wto.org.

and competitive markets were the foundation for the massive deregulation movement in trucking, airlines, and energy in the 1980s (Schultz, 1994). Before the advent of satellite dishes, for example, what Canadians watched on TV could be controlled by the regulator. It was less clear what the CRTC could do about what Canadians watched in a 500-channel TV universe, where most of those channels are being broadcast by entities beyond the CRTC's control. This situation explained the CRTC's initially cautious approach to new, Internet-based media (CRTC, 1999). As noted above, in the last decade the lines between the Internet and broadcasting have become increasingly blurred, and so, in 2007, the CRTC launched its New Media Project "to examine the cultural, economic, and technological issues associated with new media broadcasting and what actions, if any, the CRTC should take to ensure that the Canadian new media broadcasting environment meets the objectives of the Broadcasting Act" (CRTC, 2008). This initiative was followed in May 2008 with a public notice for comments on the scope of future regulatory activity in this field.

These forces help us understand the constraints and limits on regulatory instruments, forces that lie behind much of what has been labelled "deregulation" in the past decade. However, there are countervailing pressures that make regulatory instruments attractive and that, in fact, mean that what has been going on is better described as "re-regulation" in some areas and even an intensification of the state's regulatory role in others. Ironically, the argument that government should be reduced and restructured can work to the advantage of regulatory instruments. The downsizing comes principally in expenditures and direct service provision, leaving a stronger role for governments in the establishment of framework legislation or regulation: "Deregulation in Canada has resulted in a more focused and likely more robust regulatory role by government. Case studies of deregulation in various sectors show that major deregulatory actions have been accompanied by refinements and creations of new regulatory instruments" (Doern, Schultz, & Hill, 1999b, p. 394). Governments, so the argument runs, should steer, not row, and this role draws them toward regulatory instruments that focus more on frameworks and outcomes than minute rules. As well, key areas of regulation are supported by the public: public health and safety, transportation, food, and infectious diseases. Indeed, even as major areas of economic regulation were cut back in the the last 10 years, social regulations have, in some cases, been increasing. Human rights legislation, regulations against discrimination, and efforts to control violence and pornography have enjoyed continuing support. Moreover, the forms of regulation may adapt. Prince (1999) reminds us of the importance of what he calls civic regulation: rule-making "with respect to numerous social aspects of human behaviour and needs, moral conduct and standards, intergovernmental relations, and human rights and civil liberties" (p. 204). He agrees that this arena of state regulation is probably expanding due to pressures for "intervention and protection from citizens, interest groups, social movements, and governments" (p. 221). But there are odd juxtapositions: in 2011, the Harper government killed the long-gun registry, admittedly hugely expensive and probably not effective, but at the same time, it was thinking about classifying energy drinks such as Red Bull or Monster as stimulant drugs that should be sold only under the supervision of pharmacists (Schmidt, 2011).

The trends in regulation are therefore complicated. First, it is undeniable that there has been a combination of pressures in the last two decades to reexamine the effects and the management of economic regulations (Ireland, Milligan, Webb, & Xie, 2011). This has been driven in part by technological changes (e.g., in communications and in financial services) and partly by deliberate decisions to deregulate taken by conservative governments around the world. The Canadian variant was several reviews of regulation undertaken in the 1970s, which eventually yielded the Regulatory Impact Assessment Statement regime of the mid-1980s (Mihlar, 1999) and the government's 1999 Regulatory Policy, which has since been replaced by the Cabinet Directive on Streamlining Regulation (Government of Canada, 2007). The Strategic Review exercise of 2011–12 will press departments with major regulatory responsibilities to find ways of reducing their regulatory budgets. Second, while some regulatory agencies and their oversight have been weakened, for instance, in transportation, resources, and utilities, they have also become, in some instances, more focused and strategic. Third, there have arisen new areas of civic and environmental and even economic regulation that are being managed by all three levels of government, sometimes alone but sometimes in concert. As we noted above, the federal government's response to climate change was deliberately regulatory and not based on carbon taxes. The regulatory regime for carbon trading will be one of the most complex ever attempted in Canada:

> To be eligible to generate offset credits, projects must be within the scope of the Offset System, and must achieve real, incremental, quantified, verified and unique reductions of greenhouse gases.
>
> The credit creation process is as follows:
>
> - A Protocol Developer creates a quantification protocol for the project type and Environment Canada approves the protocol.
> - A Project Proponent applies to have their project registered.
> - Environment Canada registers the project.
> - A Project Proponent reports the greenhouse gas reductions achieved from a registered project and ensures that a verifier has provided a reasonable level of assurance on the reductions claim.

- Environment Canada certifies the reductions and issues offset credits.

Each offset credit will represent one tonne of carbon dioxide equivalent. Offset credits will be tradable and bankable within the unit tracking system. The proposed industrial air emissions regulations will set out the conditions under which regulated entities will be able to use offset credits for compliance. (Government of Canada, 2008)

Fourth, domestic regulation is increasingly affected by international factors, institutions, and decisions, and, in many cases, "bridges" between domestic and international regulatory agencies are being constructed in order to facilitate harmonization of standards. This dynamic is evident in climate change policy, for example, where standards are being harmonized around the Copenhagen agreement. Canada has, since 9/11, tried to harmonize border controls with the United States to ensure that goods and people between the two countries can continue to move smoothly (Doern & Johnson, 2006). Fifth, the rhythms of regulation and deregulation vary considerably by country. We have already noted the different financial regulatory regimes in Canada, the United States, and Europe, with Canada's being stronger and more stable. On the other hand, the United States is often (through California and the federal Environmental Protection Agency) a world leader in environmental regulation. Regulations around smoking, while converging internationally, still do vary. All this reflects the point made earlier that instrument choice is in part a function of what is considered both efficacious and legitimate by governments and their citizens.

A perfect illustration of these complexities can be seen in the federal government's attempt to rethink regulation in the early 2000s. It established the External Advisory Committee on Smart Regulation in 2003 and asked it to develop a regulatory strategy for the 21st century, based on a sense that the context for regulation was increasingly challenging: "the speed of modern society has resulted in an explosion of new technologies, the rapid flow of commerce and instant access to information. Businesses are continually innovating to meet changing consumer needs, cut production costs and increase their market shares. In a knowledge-based economy, regulatory regimes have to adapt quickly to sustain effective protection and keep pace with innovation and entrepreneurship" (External Advisory Committee on Smart Regulation, 2004).

The concept of "smart regulation" has several components. Possibly the most important is a sense of rising competitive pressures, particularly international ones, a more rapid cycle of innovation and technological development, coupled with public concerns about health, safety, and consumer choice. The basic saw-off is between providing companies with light, flexible, and responsive regulatory regimes that allow them to bring products to market quickly and capitalize on a clear, consistent, but not overbearing regulatory system, and making sure that the regulatory system continues to protect consumers while not patronizing them. This vision of "smart regulation" as articulated by the advisory committee became the foundation for the 2007 *Cabinet Directive on Streamlining Regulation*. It was largely a procedural document on the various steps that should be followed (e.g., the range and scope of consultations; respecting international obligations). In 2011 the federal government published *Mid-term Evaluation of the Implementation of the Cabinet Directive on Streamlining Regulation* (Treasury Board of Canada Secretariat, 2011). As the report noted, the changes introduced by the Cabinet Directive were intended to "support a sound and effective regulatory system providing consistency, fairness, and transparency, and supporting innovation, productivity, and competition." The most important changes were as follows:

- a process to address the full regulatory life cycle, with specific requirements for the development, implementation, evaluation and review of regulations;
- better coordination across governments and jurisdictions to address overlap and duplication;
- enhanced guidance where gaps were identified (e.g., cost-benefit analysis and performance measurement) to enhance the transparency, quality, analytic rigour and utility of regulations for decision making;
- early assessment in order to focus resources on regulatory proposals having the highest impact; and service standards and reporting on results. (Treasury Board of Canada Secretariat, 2011)*

Seeking the appropriate balance between protecting the public interest in health, safety, and security and the need to support competitive and innovative markets remains the key challenge in designing and using the regulatory instrument.

New Emphases: Information, Partnerships, Internationalism, and Institutional Design

The mark of the inventive policy designer is the ability to come up with new ways of doing things, and there have been some fresh techniques

---

Mid-term evaluation of the implementation of the Cabinet directive on streamlining regulation, URL: http://www.tbs-sct.gc.ca/report/orp/2011/cdsr-dcrr01-eng.asp, Department of Treasury Board of Canada Secretariat, 2011. Reproduced with the permission of the Minister of Public Works and Government Services Canada, 2012.

or devices both discussed and implemented in some countries in recent years (e.g., tradable pollution permits). This section will focus, however, on four categories of policy instruments and how emphasis has shifted to make them comparatively more important than ever before.

As we noted above, information is typically considered to be a weak and relatively unobtrusive instrument in the government toolkit. We also noted, however, somewhat less benign uses of information through "regulation by shaming" and the robust use of advertising, exhortation, and public awareness campaigns. In fact, information as a technique in delivering policy outcomes may be gaining importance for at least four reasons.

The first reason is that spending, regulatory, and taxation instruments have been under pressure in the new governance and fiscal environment. By comparison, information is often less expensive as an instrument and gives the impression of being less invasive.

The second reason is somewhat more complex, but reflects the new approaches to public management discussed in Chapter 2, and which we will take up again in Chapter 5 in greater detail. Two major emphases in this new thinking are **citizen engagement** and better accountability mechanisms from government to the public. While these are clearly related, the first refers to bringing citizens and groups into the decision-making process, while the second refers more to techniques of providing **transparency** in public decisionmaking. The Federal Accountability Act has several provisions for transparency and reporting, such as proactive disclosure, whistle-blowing legislation, and greater powers for public watchdogs. As we will note in Chapter 5, the emphasis in recent years on performance measurement and results is also part of a new emphasis on stronger accountability regimes. It is now widely assumed that engagement, transparency, and accountability may become key factors in policy development. In short, if governments promise to do certain things, and their promises and their performance are a matter of public record, sooner or later that information will be used to hold them accountable.

The third reason that information is becoming a more important resource and instrument for governments is due to the explosion of information and communications technologies (ICTs). ICTs are important drivers changing the way that citizens and consumers get goods and services from government and the private sector. Every level of government across the country is experimenting with ways of using information in new ways to manage program delivery and handle policy problems. It is simply a given now that information technology is a major economic driver and that knowledge and innovation are the key comparative advantages for firms as well as national economies. The federal government's vision of "e-government" or "government on-line" is also emblematic of a focus on information as a main conduit of interaction between governments and citizens. The federal government, for example, launched its Government On-Line initiative in 1999, with the objective of converting 130 of its most widely used services to an electronic platform, where they could be accessed 24/7 by all Canadians, anywhere in the country or the world. The project was declared a success in 2006 and was ended. The project had been such a success that the Canadian government was ranked first internationally for its electronic service delivery five years in a row by Accenture in its global survey (Brown, 2007). Thirty-four departments and agencies were involved in the project. Many of these services were simply informational, but many also were "transactional" in the sense that there would be two-way communication between clients and government, and interactive access to services online that would previously have been available only at a government office. The Canada Revenue Agency, for example, provides "the following on-line services to its business clients: filing a return; registering a business; getting information on corporations, sole proprietors and partnerships, e-commerce, GST/HST Netfile; keeping records; making requests; payroll services; making an electronic payment; downloading or ordering forms and publications." As we will discuss in more detail in Chapter 5, e-government or government online is more than just about the delivery of services; it has broader implications for public management and public policy as a whole. "E-government has had a significant impact on public administration, changing the environment in which the public service operates, adding new concepts and methods to its operations and changing the relative weight and relationships among established elements of public administration" (Brown, 2005, p. 247). This is a case of information as a policy instrument both being used by government, but also fundamentally changing the practice and organization of government itself. The Open Data project is the latest (somewhat tentative) attempt to put government information or databases online and make them accessible to citizens. Once databases like this are available, "crowd-sourcing" can take over and create mash-ups never anticipated by the creators of the databases. The mySociety initiative in the United Kingdom (www.mysociety.org) provides an example of a nonprofit group that builds websites to enable local groups or neighbourhoods to deliver information to government, perhaps to members of parliament, and to ask for services. One of these websites is FixMyStreet (www. fixmystreet.com), which allows citizens to identify local street problems and send them directly to responsible local authorities. mySociety fosters transparency and democracy.

Information has become more important for a fourth reason as well. As governments have become more active in the realm of civic regulation, such as antidiscrimination, they inevitably get into the persuasion game, since the policy problems here are primarily attitudinal (Hood & Margetts, 2007). Policy concerns about health and lifestyle in this period also contributed to the importance of changing hearts and minds on key issues such as exercise and eating habits. Contemporary concerns about violence, stereotyping, and abuse ensure that policy instruments that both convey information and try to exhort certain behaviours will remain important. In addition, however, governments increasingly find themselves working with partners for the delivery of programs, as will be explained in Chapter 5. This interdependency depends on the exchange of information and the building up of relationships. The more that government finds itself operating in networks, relying on partners, and enhancing and facilitating the capacities of societal actors to do things, the more its primary role is to provide critical information, help circulate it, and encourage policy learning. This effort can go beyond simple distribution of information to calling attention to new policy problems—providing leadership, in short.

A new emphasis on partnerships is another development in policy targets and hence, policy instruments. Partnerships will be discussed in greater detail in Chapters 5 and 6, but the basic logic is that government can either get out of some of the things that it has traditionally done and leave them to the private or nonprofit sectors, or it can continue to do those things in partnerships with those sectors. An example is care for the elderly, which is provided primarily by for-profit and nonprofit organizations that receive the bulk of their funding from provincial governments. The first mode suggests an oversight capacity for government once the service has been devolved. The second implies a direct partnership with a community association, industry group, or nongovernmental organization. If partnerships are conceived of as a policy instrument, then they will not simply appear; they will have to be created. Doing this requires some skill, as well as a grasp of the different types of partnering that can be undertaken (e.g., one of consultation versus a roundtable format or working together to implement programs). As we discuss in greater detail in Chapter 5, this new reality implies a new form of public administration, one in which citizens and governments "co-produce" policy (Bourgon, 2011). An interesting and new example of creative partnerships are "social impact bonds" ("Who Succeeds Gets Paid," 2011). Government social service agencies issue the bonds, which are bought by private investors. The money is then used to support nonprofit agencies and charities in a variety of areas, such as education and law enforcement. Repayment to investors is contingent on performance and success standards for the programs. If services perform well, investors receive a return; if they do not, they simply receive their principal. Thus, three sectors are involved (government, nonprofits, and financial investors), and all have an incentive to encourage performance. The Obama administration set aside $100 million for pilots in its 2012 federal budget (White House Office of Management and Budget, 2011).

The third new emphasis in policy is the international system itself. The traditional organization of the foreign policy dossier called for a single foreign affairs department that would channel issues from domestic departments into the international system. With the internationalization of so many policy fields, and with the substantive policy expertise lodged in "domestic" departments, more and more of these departments are engaged in international negotiations. The Department of Foreign Affairs and International Trade tries to coordinate this at the national level, but the sheer scope of international representations by every government body, from local municipalities to federal departments, makes it a difficult task. Yet, international agreements and international negotiations are becoming a routine instrument in the pursuit of domestic policy. Moreover, it is not simply a matter of single policy fields being projected upward to the international level but linkages across policy fields being developed by international agencies and communities of practice (Slaughter, 2004).

A final, unconventional category that seems to be attracting increasing attention is **procedural** (Howlett, 2000) or institutional instruments (Kirschen, 1964). Governments "increasingly come to rely on the use of a different set of 'procedural' tools designed to indirectly affect outcomes through the manipulation of policy processes" (Howlett, 2000, p. 413). Many of these instruments are aimed less at delivery of policy and programs than at the restructuring of relationships either within the state or between the state and social partners. Webb offers a vision of what he calls "sustainable governance" that highlights not only the institutional dimension of policy instruments, but the combination of institutions and actors and instruments that are active within a given policy field: "… sustainable governance involves a combination of governmental and nongovernmental institutions, processes, instruments, and actors, it entails more than simply a question of instrument choice…. Sustainable governance is a concept that attempts to recognize and draw on the largely untapped potential of the private sector, the third (voluntary) sector, and individual citizens to assist in governing in the public interest" (Webb, 2005, p. 243).

Another way to see this category of instruments is as focusing on organization or network-type targets. Organizational instruments take the state itself—its structure and management—as a target of public policy. As Osborne and Gaebler (1993) famously argued, there is a continuing role for government but not in its bureaucratic guise. It is necessary to restructure government so that incentives to perform efficiently and well are clear and pervasive. **Performance indicators** and pay linked to performance help do that. Other mechanisms are designed to introduce market forces into the provision of public services, from contracting out to full privatization.

Network targets are primarily groups and individuals in civil society, outside the state. The role of government is to facilitate and empower rather than to deliver and direct. Adjustment programs, capacity building, the dissemination of information, participation and partnerships, rights enforcement, funding of interest groups, and development of stakeholder networks—all of these make sense only if organizations and individuals are granted high levels of autonomy and legitimacy as policy actors in their own right, not merely as recipients of government programs. As McDonnell and Elmore (1987) argued, policy instruments in this category have the character of "inducements" rather than mandates and hinge on "how much variation policymakers are willing to tolerate in the production of things of value" (p. 15). If individuals, organizations, and communities are to have choice and autonomy, then the tolerance for variation has to increase substantially. Framework policy, decentralization, and information policy instruments clearly presume that policy outcomes will depend on a degree of "co-production" with other actors. Of course, **co-production** also means a greater degree of mutual interdependence—governments cannot control all processes and outcomes. Therefore, this approach requires a greater tolerance for potential failure and the possibility that partners will both make mistakes and have to learn from them. It puts the policy designer less in the position of being an "engineer" than an "animateur," relying primarily on process values and politics (Linder & Peters, 1995). We will return to these types of instruments in the next chapter.

Conclusion

We should address two questions in closing this chapter. First, is there a uniform tilt to the new toolbox of policy instruments? Second, what does the evolution of the toolbox tell us about modern governance?

Readers will have noticed that there does appear to be a tilt—though only a slight one and with some contradictions—to the way in which instruments and policy design have been going. At one time we might have said the tilt was toward smaller and leaner and less intrusive government. Now, the reality is probably something closer to prudential caution, sobriety about the influence of government, coupled with strong and even expansionist actions in certain sectors with retreats in others. New pressures on spending and pump-priming now seem insurmountable. The rhetoric of cutting back on government reached a high point in the early 2000s, but after 9/11 and the global economic crisis, it became more muted. For reasons that we explored in Chapter 1, there has been a renewed appreciation of the importance of governance for economic performance and social stability—the subprime and financial sector crisis in fall 2008, for example, led to nationalizations of mortgage lending institutions and banks in the United States and United Kingdom, along with massive financial bailouts in other countries (including Canada) to keep the financial system solvent. We would argue that legacies remain from the NPM era, but that they have been overlaid by a new willingness to use government policy instruments more robustly, to align with civil society and the private sector where possible, and to explore ways to be more open and agile in serving the public interest. It is important to distinguish between what governments do and how they do it. There is no doubt that the "what" has been expanding inexorably in the last five years—more regulation, more taxation, more spending, and more information campaigns. The "how" is more subtle. There are new ways to regulate (although these vary across sectors and policy types), to subsidize, to tax, to provide information, and to structure social interactions and partnerships.

Other factors lie behind this complicated shift in governance. First, as we noted in Chapter 2, postmaterialist values are not uniformly pro-market, for example, when it comes to the environment. Second, there is substantial angst about some major social policy questions such as youth crime, violent pornography, decaying family structures, racism, school behaviour, and educational performance, not to mention a host of health and safety concerns. In these areas it is far from clear that governments or citizens are prepared to accept the old nostrums of minimal government and market mechanisms. Third, the challenges of contemporary capitalism pull governments in every direction. The venality and greed of Wall Street financial firms has fed a deeper aquifer of public resentment. People want controls, regulation, punishment, and support. At the same time, governments will not abandon (quasi) free market capitalism, and so have to balance those public demands against measures that simultaneously sustain and discipline those markets ("The Visible Hand," 2012). Finally, it is important not to overestimate the ease with which global pressures penetrate national social, economic, and political systems. The institutional configuration of these systems can make it more or less easy for global pressures to be channelled through to governments (Neville, 2002). For example, despite globalization and two free trade agreements with the United States, Canadian and American health and social policy systems remain very different, relying on different instruments and approaches.

The policy literature is coming to recognize this, principally by urging the importance of values in public policy. Though this is a larger issue than instrument choice, the discussion in this chapter has shown that the tilt of the toolbox is to maximize individual choice in programming and societal co-production with more careful, if possibly more extreme, government intervention than anything seen in the recent past.

But public policy is not purely instrumental; it sends signals to citizens about who they are and how they should behave. For better or worse, it gives them a picture of appropriate social and political relations. Policy implementation that depends on market mechanisms and pure individual choice will encourage citizens to see their relations to government and to each other as primarily ones of exchange—a set of quasi-economic transactions for individual benefit. As Aaron, Mann, and Taylor (1994) pointed out: "In the jargon of the social scientists, analysts have begun to recognize that values and norms are not 'exogenous,' or independent of public policy. And the idea that values can change, combined with the recognition that responses to policies depend on people's preferences— that is, their values—leads to thinking about how public policy might change values directly or indirectly and thereby change the responses of public policies themselves" (p. 3). Their point is twofold: (1) effective public policies depend on a certain temperament of cooperation and support from citizens, and to neglect the nurturing of that temperament would be a major mistake, and (2) governments have a legitimate, though carefully balanced, role in supporting and developing some key social values, such as trust, community, and empathy. This role can extend to policy designs that might have an element of paternalism to them. For example, most people discount the future in relation to the present, and most people weigh current losses more heavily than future benefits. These are among the reasons why many people, absent any external mechanisms, find it hard to quit smoking or drinking, stick to diets, save for their retirement, and invest in their education. There is a case to be made that the government has an admittedly, paternalistic role in combating these tendencies through health information campaigns and regulatory regimes, or public pension systems that force people to save ("Nudge, Nudge, Think, Think," 2012; Thaler & Sunstein, 2003, 2008).

These are ultimately questions of policy design for democracy, an issue that the literature on policy instruments often avoids and that practising policymakers usually sidestep. But it is worth asking these questions. What effect will downsized government or oversized government have on citizenship? How far should we go in encouraging individual self-reliance or dependency before eroding common bonds and a public space? Schneider and Ingram (1997) are concerned about "degenerative policy designs" that, in their view, "send different messages to different target populations, but these messages encourage most of the target groups to take only their own interests into account in their expectations of government thereby leading to irresponsible citizenship and the demise of community" (p. 197).

This argument sounds soft when compared to the tough talk usually associated with developing economic competitiveness. Recent thinking about what truly makes economies competitive, however, suggests that these softer policy targets may be vitally important. Work on **social capital**, for example, seeks to explain both efficient government and competitive economies in terms of social bonds of association and trust. The phenomenal success of Robert Putnam's *Making Democracy Work* (1993) and *Bowling Alone* (2000) suggests that concerns about social capital cut across ideological lines. Francis Fukuyama (1995) has argued that economic performance depends on social capital and is a function of trust, which he defines as the "expectation that arises within a community of regular, honest, and cooperative behaviour, based on commonly shared norms, on the part of other members of that community" (p. 26). Both economic and political performance can be seen as forms of "collective action" problems, where what is rational from a collective point of view (say, a clean environment) runs up against incentives for individuals to free-ride and maximize their self-interest (say, the profits that can be made when all your competitors install antipollution equipment but you do not). If people cooperate, they are all better off. Community and social cohesion have become watchwords for government policy throughout North America and Europe, and have faced specific challenges in the face of soaring unemployment rates and souring attitudes toward both business and government.

The above should help provide the answer to our second question about what the toolkit tells us about modern governance. As has been mentioned many times in this book, modern governments have had their hands tied by fiscal pressures, internationalization, and ideological debates that simultaneously demand less and more intervention. There seems to be limited tolerance for deficit spending, and there is pressure to at least hold the line on taxes, if not reduce them. Internationalization means that the domestic economy is much more exposed to global competition, and investors sit ready to judge government policy by pulling out of currency and bond markets if they see something they dislike.

This is not the whole story, however. As we noted earlier in this chapter, the same forces of globalization that constrain governments create powerful pressures for them to act on behalf of their domestic constituencies. Governments remain massively involved in health, education, infrastructure, innovation, and social security. New issues such as public security, climate change, Aboriginal self-government, information technologies, and building and maintaining social capital also demand attention. Information resources and technologies of power (e.g., surveillance) have also improved considerably. We noted above that governments may be forced to use more informational policy instruments to change hearts and minds around lifestyle issues. But it is not simply information we are talking about. If one takes seriously the notion that the modern welfare state should be redefined to become a more positive instrument in supporting personal autonomy and self-development, and that lifestyle circumstances can undermine these qualities, then "policy must be interventionist, rather than just of the safety-net type … positive outcomes will presume lifestyle change" (Giddens, 2007, p. 122). This kind of intervention, which we see around issues such as smoking regulations, bans on trans fats, and carbon capture, mixes instruments in novel and more muscular ways.

What is different is that policymakers have to be a bit more clever than they once were. A perfect example is former U.S. president Clinton's book *Back to Work*. Clinton (2011) offers no less than 35 "smart" policy prescriptions to remake America—suggestions that touch on virtually every key policy area. Without the easy option of throwing money at a problem (even the financial crisis has its limits), and with these new demands, policy suddenly requires more imaginative use of available instruments. If internationalization threatens an important domestic industry, the trick is to find a way, within the rules, to help. If government cannot do something on its own, it needs to create the conditions to work with others to achieve the objectives. Both of these are tricks about converting policy tools into implementation, the subject of the next chapter.

KEY TERMS

alternative service delivery—the use of nontraditional means to deliver public services (e.g., commercialized firms, partnerships, single-window service centres)

binding rules—rules or regulations that have the coercive power of law behind them

cap and trade—a regulatory tool that caps carbon emissions and then allows companies over their limit to purchase allowances on markets that have been made available by companies below their limit

carbon tax—a tax on the carbon content of fossil fuels

cash transfer—money provided by the government for broad support rather than in connection with a specific project or endeavour

citizen engagement—bringing citizens and groups directly into the decisionmaking and policy implementation process

contract—a binding agreement between two or more parties

contributions—cash transfer subject to performance conditions that are specified in a contribution agreement

co-production—production of goods or services jointly by various partners

deregulation—the process of reducing the number, incidence, and cost of regulations

exhortation—the use of information resources to make direct appeals

expenditure—disbursement of monies

grants—cash transfers with few if any performance conditions attached, though other requirements may be built into the grant

guidelines—codes or frameworks to guide action, without coercive support

instrument design—the generic term for the selection and calibration of different policy instruments through programming to achieve policy objectives

investment—a cash payment that implies a return of some sort, a benefit, or a profit

legitimate coercion—the application of force backed by law

licence—permit to engage in activities that may involve a mix of prohibition, permission, and conditions

loan—cash transfer that requires eventual repayment

moral suasion—the ability to persuade others based on one's institutional prominence or authority

nodality—the generic category of information resources at the disposal of governments

partnership—working jointly and cooperatively with others, in some formal arrangement, for the production and delivery of goods and services

performance indicator—some measure of how well a service or activity is doing, either through financial or output measures, or client satisfaction

permission—regulatory device that permits a certain activity under specific conditions

policy design—the process of choosing the most appropriate instrument to deal with the policy problem as it has been defined in order to achieve a given policy goal

procedural policy instrument—instrument that alters institutional rules and arrangements to try to induce behaviour

prohibitions—regulatory device that forbids certain activities under certain conditions

recognition—regulatory device that uses the government's capacity to recognize certain qualities or achievements as a "sign of approval"

regulation—the generic category of policy instruments that rely on the government's capacity to command and prohibit

re-regulation—a process of developing new regulatory regimes for arenas that had been previously regulated in more traditional formats

secondary legislation—regulations announced under the regulatory powers of a statute and that therefore have the force of law without necessarily being passed by the legislature

self-regulation—the delegation of the state regulatory power to a nongovernmental organization or private association

service fee—fee attached to the provision of some service, such as issuing a passport

shaming—publication of unwelcome information in order to force targets to change their behaviour in order to protect their reputations

sin tax—traditionally, taxes levied on cigarettes and alcohol

social capital—the degree to which members of a community trust each other and engage in reciprocal relations based on that trust

static response—a deliberate choice not to intervene, made after an analysis of the problem

subsidy—cash transfers that are closely calibrated to the costs of engaging in an activity that the government regards favourably

tax—a compulsory levy that is not generally connected to any specific service and is intended to provide general purpose revenues to the government

tax expenditure—the technique of forgoing certain owed taxes (and hence losing or "spending" tax dollars) in order to subsidize an activity

transparency—clear accountability, reporting, and publication provisions for the provision of services as well as the decisionmaking process

user charge—the charge levied on a category of person or user of a service, not the service itself

voluntary code—standards or codes developed by private sector organizations; sometimes known as codes of conduct, codes of practice, voluntary initiatives, guidelines, and non-regulatory agreements

vouchers—"coupons" for stipulated amounts of public financial support attached to a service that may be redeemed under certain conditions

FURTHER READINGS

Bardach, E. (2000). *A practical guide for policy analysis: The eightfold path to more effective problem solving.* New York, NY: Chatham House.

Bemelmans-Videc, M.-L., Rist, R. C., & Vedung, E. (Eds.). (1998). *Carrots, sticks and sermons: Policy instruments and their evaluation* (pp. 59–76). New Brunswick, NJ: Transaction.

Bogart, W. A. (2011). *Permit but discourage: Regulating excessive consumption*. Oxford: Oxford University Press.

Bourgon, J. (2011). *A new synthesis of public administration: Serving in the 21st century*. Montréal and Kingston: Queen's School of Policy Studies and McGill-Queen's University Press.

Eliadis, P., Hill, M. M., & Howlett, M. (Eds.). (2005). *Designing government: From instruments to governance*. Toronto, ON: University of Toronto Press.

Hood, C. (1984). *The tools of government*. London, UK: Macmillan.

Hood, C., & Margetts, H. Z. (2007). *The tools of government in the digital age*. New York, NY: Palgrave Macmillan.

Howlett, M. (2011). *Designing public policies: Principles and instruments*. New York, NY: Routledge.

John, P. (2011), *Making policy work*. New York, NY: Routledge.

Salamon, L. M. (Ed.) (2002). *The tools of government: A guide to the new governance*. New York, NY: Oxford University Press.

Schneider, A. L., & Ingram, H. (1997). *Policy design for democracy*. Lawrence, KS: University Press of Kansas.

REFERENCES

Aaron, H. J., Mann, T. E., & Taylor, T. (Eds.). (1994). *Values and public policy*. Washington, DC: Brookings Institution Press.

Agriculture and Agri-Food Canada. (2011). Growing forward agricultural policy framework. Retrieved from http://www4.agr.gc.ca/AAFC-AAC/display-afficher.do?id=1200339470715&lang=eng

Auditor General of Canada. (1998). *Annual report 1998. Grants and contributions: Selected programs in Industry Canada and Department of Canadian Heritage*. Ottawa, ON: Office of the Auditor General.

Auditor General of Canada. (2002). *Report to the Minister of Public Works and Government Services on three contracts awarded to Groupaction*. Ottawa, ON: Office of the Auditor General.

Bird, M., & Stoney, C. (2006). Government approaches to the regulation of "sin." In G. B. Doern (Ed.), *How Ottawa spends, 2006–2007: In from the cold—The Tory rise and the Liberal demise* (pp. 247–265). Montréal, QC: McGill-Queen's University Press.

Blue Ribbon Panel on Grant and Contribution Programs. (2006). *From red tape to clear results*. Ottawa, ON: Treasury Board of Canada Secretariat. Retrieved from http://www.brp-gde.ca/pdf/Report_on_Grant_and_Contribution_Programs.pdf

Bogart, W. A. (2011). *Permit but discourage: Regulating excessive consumption*. New York, NY: Oxford University Press.

Bourgon, J. (2011). *A new synthesis of public administration: Serving in the 21st century*. Montréal and Kingston: Queen's School of Policy Studies and McGill-Queen's University Press.

Bressers, H. Th.A., & O'Toole, L. J. (2005). Instrument selection and implementation in a networked context. In P. Eliadis, M. M. Hill, & M. Howlett (Eds.), *Designing government: From instruments to governance* (pp. 132–153). Toronto, ON: University of Toronto Press.

British Columbia. (2008). *Budget and fiscal plan, 2008/09–2010/11*. Retrieved from http://www.bcbudget.gov.bc.ca/2008/bfp/default. aspx?hash=2

Brown. D. (2005). Electronic government and public administration. *International Review of Administrative Sciences, 71*(2), 241–254.

Brown, D. (2007). The government of Canada: Government on-line and citizen-centred service. In S. Borins et al., *Digital state at the leading edge* (pp. 37–68). Toronto, ON: IPAC and the University of Toronto Press.

Campbell, R. M. (1999). The fourth fiscal era: Can there be a "post-neo-conservative" fiscal policy? In L. A. Pal (Ed.), *How Ottawa spends, 1999–2000: Shape shifting: Canadian governance toward the 21st century* (pp. 113–149). Toronto, ON: Oxford University Press.

Carbon Tax Center. (2011). *Where carbon is taxed*. Retrieved from http://www.carbontax.org/progress/where-carbon-is-taxed/

Center on Budget and Policy Priorities. (2007). *Introduction to the Housing Voucher Program*. Retrieved from http://www.cbpp.org/5-15-03hous.pdf

Chrétien, J. (2007). *My years as prime minister*. Toronto, ON: Alfred A. Knopf.

Clinton, B. (2011). *Back to work: Why we need smart government for a strong economy*. New York, NY: Alfred A. Knopf.

CRTC [Canadian Radio-television and Telecommunications Commission]. (1999). *Public notice CRTC 1999–84*. Retrieved from http://www.crtc.gc.ca/eng/archive/1999/PB99-84.HTM

CRTC. (2008). *New media project initiative*. Retrieved from http://www.crtc.gc.ca/eng/media/media3.htm

Department of Finance (Canada). (2007a). *Advantage Canada: Building a strong economy for Canadians*. Retrieved from http://www.fin.gc.ca/ec2006/plan/pltoce.html

Department of Finance (Canada). (2007b). *Annual financial report of the government of Canada—Fiscal year 2006–2007*. Retrieved from http://www.fin.gc.ca/toc/2007/afr2007_-eng.asp

Department of Finance (Canada). (2008). *The budget plan 2008: Responsible leadership*. Retrieved from http://www.budget.gc.ca/2008/pdf/plan-eng.pdf

Department of Finance (Canada). (2011a). *Fiscal reference tables 2011, tables 3 and 7.* Retrieved from http://www.fin.gc.ca/frt-trf/2011/frt-trf-11-eng.asp

Department of Finance (Canada). (2011b). *Update of economic and fiscal projections—2011.* Retrieved from http://www.fin.gc.ca/efp-pef/2011/efp-pef-01-eng.asp#highlights

Doern, G. B., & Phidd, R. W. (1992). *Canadian public policy: Ideas, structure, process* (2nd ed.). Toronto, ON: Nelson.

Doern, G. B., & Wilson, V. S. (Eds.). (1974). *Issues in Canadian public policy*. Toronto, ON: Methuen.

Doern, G. B., Schultz, R. J., & Hill, M. M. (1999a). Canadian regulatory institutions: Converging and colliding regimes. In G. B. Doern, R. J. Schultz, & M. M. Hill (Eds.), *Changing the rules: Canadian regulatory regimes and institutions* (pp. 3–26). Toronto, ON: University of Toronto Press.

Doern, G. B., Schultz, R. J., & Hill, M. M. (1999b). Conclusions. In G. B. Doern, R. J. Schultz, & M. M. Hill (Eds.), *Changing the rules: Canadian regulatory regimes and institutions* (pp. 389–406). Toronto, ON: University of Toronto Press.

Doern, G. B., & Johnson, R. (2006). Multilevel regulatory governance: Concepts, context, and key issues. In G. B. Doern & R. Johnson (Eds.), *Rules, rules, rules, rules: Multilevel regulatory governance* (pp. 3–26). Toronto, ON: University of Toronto Press.

Doern, G. B., & Prince, M. (2012). *Three bio-realms: Biotechnology and the governance of food, health, and life in Canada*. Toronto, ON: University of Toronto Press.

External Advisory Committee on Smart Regulation. (2004). *Smart regulation: A regulatory strategy for Canada*. Retrieved from http://epe.lac-bac.gc.ca/100/206/301/pco-bcp/committees/smart_regulation-ef/2006-10-11/www.pco-bcp.gc.ca/smartreg-regint/en/index.html

Fukuyama, F. (1995). *Trust: The social virtues and the creation of prosperity*. New York, NY: Free Press.

Giddens, A. (2007). *Over to you, Mr. Brown: How Labour can win again*. Cambridge, UK: Polity Press.

Gomery Commission [Commission of Inquiry into the Sponsorship Program and Advertising Activities]. (2005). *Who is responsible? Fact finding report*. Ottawa, ON: Minister of Public Works and Government Services.

Good, D. A. (2003). *The politics of public management: The HRDC audit of grants and contributions.* Toronto, ON: University of Toronto Press.

Good, D. A. (2007). *The politics of public money: Spenders, guardians, priority setters, and financial watchdogs inside the Canadian government.* Toronto, ON: University of Toronto Press.

Government of Canada. (2007). *Cabinet directive on streamlining regulation.* Retrieved from http://www.tbs-sct.gc.ca/ri-qr/directive/directive00-eng.asp

Government of Canada. (2008). *Turning the corner: Taking action to fight climate change.* Retrieved from http://www.ec.gc.ca/default.asp?lang=En&n=4891B242-1

Government of Canada. (2011). *Open data pilot project.* Retrieved from http://www.data.gc.ca/default.asp?lang=En&n=F9B7A1E3-1

Graham, A. (2007). *Canadian public-sector financial management.* Kingston, ON: School of Policy Studies, Queen's University, and McGill-Queen's University Press.

Graham, M. (2002). *Democracy by disclosure: The rise of technopopulism.* Washington, DC: Brookings Institution Press.

Hood, C. (1983). *The tools of government.* London, UK: Macmillan.

Hood, C., & Margetts, H. Z. (2007). *The tools of government in the digital age.* New York, NY: Palgrave Macmillan.

Howlett, M. (2000, Winter). Managing the "hollow state": Procedural policy instruments and modern governance. *Canadian Public Administration, 43,* 412–431.

Howlett, M., Ramesh, M., & Perl, A. (2009). *Studying public policy: Policy cycles and policy subsystems* (3rd ed.). Toronto, ON: Oxford University Press.

Industry Canada. (1998). *Voluntary codes: A guide for their development and use.* Retrieved from http://www.ic.gc.ca/epic/site/oca-bc.nsf/vwapj/volcodes.pdf/$FILE/volcodes.pdf

Ireland, D., Milligan, E., Webb, K., & Xie, W. (2011). Regulatory agency budget cuts: Public interest support through a better approach. In C. Stoney & G. Bruce Doern (Eds.), *How Ottawa spends, 2011–2012: Trimming fat or slicing pork?* (pp. 106–124). Montréal and Kingston: McGill-Queen's University Press.

James, M. (2007). The permanent-emergency compensation state: A "post-socialist" tale of political dystopia. In M. Orsini & M. Smith (Eds.), *Critical policy studies* (pp. 321–346). Vancouver, BC: UBC Press.

Kirschen, E. S., et al. (1964). *Economic policy in our time* (3 vols.). Amsterdam, Netherlands: North-Holland.

Lemaire, D. (1998). The stick: Regulation as a tool of government. In M.-L. Bemelmans-Videc, R. C. Rist, & E. Vedung (Eds.), *Carrots, sticks and sermons: Policy instruments and their evaluation* (pp. 59–76). New Brunswick, NJ: Transaction Publishers.

Linder, S. H., & Peters, B. G. (1989). Instruments of government: Perceptions and contexts. *Journal of Public Policy, 9*, 35–58.

Linder, S. H., & Peters, B. G. (1995). The two traditions of institutional designing: Dialogue versus decision? In D. L. Weimer (Ed.), *Institutional design* (pp. 133–160). Dordrecht, Netherlands: Kluwer.

Macdonald, D. (2011). Harper energy and climate change policy: Failing to address the key challenges. In C. Stoney & G. Bruce Doern (Eds.) *How Ottawa spends, 2011–2012: Trimming fat or slicing pork?* (pp. 127–143). Montréal and Kingston: McGill-Queen's University Press.

McDonnell, L. M., & Elmore, R. F. (1987). *Alternative policy instruments*. Santa Monica, CA: Center for Policy Research in Education.

Mihlar, F. (1999). The federal government and the "RIAS" process: Origins, need and non-compliance. In G. B. Doern et al. (Eds.), *Changing the rules: Canadian regulatory regimes and institutions* (pp. 275–292). Toronto, ON: University of Toronto Press.

National Round Table on the Environment and the Economy. (2008). *Getting to 2050: Canada's transition to a low-emission future.* Retrieved from http://nrtee-trnee.ca/climate/getting-to-2050/getting-to-2050-convene

Neville, A. (Ed.) (2002). *Policy choices in a globalized world.* New York, NY: Nova Science Publishers.

Nudge nudge, think think. (2012, March 24). *The Economist.* Retrieved from http://www.economist.com/node/21551032

OECD [Organisation for Economic Co-operation and Development]. (2005). *Modernising government: The way forward.* Paris: OECD.

OECD. (2007). *Cutting red tape: Comparing administrative burdens across countries.* Paris: OECD.

Orsini, M. (2002, September). The politics of naming, blaming and claiming: HIV, Hepatitis C and the emergence of blood activism in Canada. *Canadian Journal of Political Science, 35*, 475–498.

Osborne, D., & Gaebler, T. (1993). *Reinventing government: How the entrepreneurial spirit is transforming the public sector.* New York, NY: Penguin.

Pal, L. A. (2011). Into the wild: The politics of economic stimulus. In C. Stoney & G. Bruce Doern (Eds.), *How Ottawa spends, 2011–2012: Trimming fat or slicing pork?* (pp. 39–59). Montréal and Kingston: McGill-Queen's University Press.

Prince, M. J. (1999). Civic regulation: Regulating citizenship, morality, social order, and the welfare state. In G. B. Doern et al. (Eds.), *Changing the rules: Canadian regulatory regimes and institutions* (pp. 201–227). Toronto, ON: University of Toronto Press.

Prince, M. J. (2005). From welfare state to social union: Shifting choices of governing instruments, intervention rationales, and governance rules in Canadian social policy. In P. Eliadis, M. M. Hill, & M. Howlett (Eds.), *Designing government: From instruments to governance* (pp. 281–302). Toronto, ON: University of Toronto Press.

Privy Council Office (Canada). (2003). *Cabinet directive on law-making.* Retrieved from http://www.pco-bcp.gc.ca/index.asp?lang=eng&page=information&sub=publications&doc=legislation/cabdir-dircab-eng.htm

Province of Ontario. (2011). *2011 Ontario Budget.* Retrieved from http://www.fin.gov.on.ca/en/budget/ontariobudgets/2011/papers_all.pdf

Purchase, B., & Hirshhorn, R. (1994). *Searching for good governance.* Kingston, ON: Queen's School of Policy Studies.

Pushing for a carbon tax in Australia: An expensive gamble. (2011, July 14). *The Economist.* Retrieved from http://www.economist.com/node/18959030/print

Putnam, R. (1993). *Making democracy work: Civic traditions in modern Italy.* Princeton, NJ: Princeton University Press.

Putnam, R. (2000). *Bowling alone: The collapse and revival of American community.* New York, NY: Simon and Schuster.

Salamon, L. M. (Ed.) (2002). *The tools of government: A guide to the new governance.* New York, NY: Oxford University Press.

Schelling, T. C. (1984). The intimate contest for self-command. In T. Schelling, *Choice and Consequence* (pp. 57–82). Boston, MA: Harvard University Press.

Schmidt, S. (2011, September 27). Energy drink report causes dilemma. *Ottawa Citizen.*

Schneider, A., & Ingram, H. (1990). Behavioral assumptions of policy tools. *Journal of Politics, 52,* 510–529.

Schneider, A. L., & Ingram, H. (1997). *Policy design for democracy.* Lawrence, KS: University Press of Kansas.

Schultz, R. (1994). Deregulation Canadian-style: State reduction of recasting? In I. Gow & L. Bernier (Eds.), *A downsized state? Canada and Québec compared* (pp. 129–147). Montréal, QC: Presses de l'Université du Québec.

Seeman, N., & Luciani, P. (2011). *XXL: Obesity and the limits of shame.* Toronto, ON: University of Toronto Press.

Singapore Customs. (2011). *Singapore Customs—Chewing gum (HS CODE 17041000)*. Retrieved from http://www.customs.gov.sg/leftNav/trad/TradeNet/Singapore+Customs+-+Chewing+Gum+(HS+CODE+17041000).htm

Slaughter, A.-M. (2004). *A new world order*. Princeton, NJ: Princeton University Press.

Sproule-Jones, M. (1994). User fees. In A. M. Maslove (Ed.), *Taxes as instruments of public policy* (pp. 3–38). Toronto, ON: University of Toronto Press.

Standing Committee on Finance (Canada). (2000). *Challenge for change: A study of cost-recovery*. Retrieved from http://cmte.parl.gc.ca/cmte/CommitteePublication.aspx?COM=158&Lang=1&SourceId=36476

Standing Committee on Finance (Canada). (2008). *Taxing to prosper: Canada's system of taxes, fees and other charges*. Retrieved from http://cmte.parl.gc.ca/Content/HOC/committee/392/fina/reports/rp3253372/finarp03/04-toc-e.htm

Statistics Canada. (2009). Table 385-0002—Consolidated federal, provincial, territorial and local government revenue and expenditures, annual (dollars). Retrieved from http://estat.statcan.gc.ca/cgi-win/cns-mcgi.pgm?Lang=EESTAT/&C2DB=EST&CII_DDSect=376&CII_Blurb=DIRBLURBS&ResultTemplate=ESTAT/CII_Dir#H2_9

Steuerle, C. E., & Twombly, E. C. (2002). Vouchers. In L. M. Salamon (Ed.), *The tools of government: A guide to the new governance* (pp. 445–465). New York, NY: Oxford University Press.

Stewart, J. (2009). *Public policy values*. New York, NY: Palgrave Macmillan.

Thaler, R. H., & Sunstein, C. R. (2003). Libertarian paternalism. *American Economic Review, 93*, 175–179.

Thaler, R. H., & Sunstein, C. R. (2008). *Nudge: Improving decisions about health, wealth, and happiness*. New Haven, CT: Yale University Press.

Treasury Board of Canada Secretariat. (2003). *External charging policy*. Retrieved from http://www.tbs-sct.gc.ca/archives/opepubs/tb_h/2004/crp-eng.asp

Treasury Board of Canada Secretariat. (2007a). *Report of the president of the Treasury Board on the provisions and operation of the User Fees Act*. Retrieved from http://www.tbs-sct.gc.ca/report/orp/2007/ufa-lfu/ufa-lfu_e.asp

Treasury Board of Canada Secretariat. (2007b). *User fees: Implementation*. Retrieved from http://www.tbs-sct.gc.ca/fm-gf/ktopics-dossiersc/fms-sgf/uf-fu/menu-eng.asp

Treasury Board of Canada Secretariat. (2008). *The Government of Canada action plan to reform the administration of grant and contribution programs.* Retrieved from http://www.tbs-sct.gc.ca/gcr-esc/docs/2008/ragcp-rapsc-eng.asp

Treasury Board of Canada Secretariat. (2011). *Mid-term evaluation of the implementation of the Cabinet directive on streamlining regulation.* Retrieved from http://www.tbs-sct.gc.ca/report/orp/2011/cdsr-dcrr01-eng.asp

Vedung, E. (1998). Policy instruments: Typologies and theories. In M.-L. Bemelmans-Videc, R. C. Rist, & E. Vedung (Eds.), *Carrots, sticks and sermons: Policy instruments and their evaluation* (pp. 21–58). New Brunswick, NJ: Transaction.

Vedung, E., & van der Doelen, F. C. J. (1998). The sermon: Information programs in the public policy process—Choice, effects, and evaluation. In M.-L. Bemelmans-Videc, R. C. Rist, & E. Vedung (Eds.), *Carrots,sticks and sermons: Policy instruments and their evaluation* (pp. 103–128).New Brunswick, NJ: Transaction.

[The] visible hand. (2012, January 21). *The Economist.* Retrieved from http://www.economist.com/node/21542931/print

Webb, K. (2005). Sustainable governance in the twenty-first century: Moving beyond instrument choice? In P. Eliadis, M. M. Hill, & M. Howlett (Eds.), *Designing government: From instruments to governance* (pp. 243–280). Toronto, ON: University of Toronto Press.

White House Office of Management and Budget (United States). (2011). *Paying for Success Bonds—2012 budget.* Retrieved from http://nffsib.org/resources/pay-success-bonds-2012-budget

Who succeeds gets paid: Barack Obama imports a big idea from Britain. (2011, February 17). *The Economist.* Retrieved from http://www.economist.com/node/21542931/print

World Trade Organization. (2011). *Technical regulations and standards.* Retrieved from http://www.wto.org/english/thewto_e/whatis_e/tif_e/agrm4_e.htm#TRS

Policy Implementation

S ay "implementation" and you say "organization." Whereas Chapter 4 dealt with policy instruments—the means or techniques of getting things done—this chapter addresses the challenges of organizing and delivering outcomes through those instruments. The policy literature sometimes states that no one paid serious attention to implementation until the 1970s, but this view is wrong. Policy analysts themselves did not pay much attention to it, but the field of public administration has concentrated on implementation for most of its history, since a good deal of administrative science, or management, as it is now called, deals with harnessing personnel and other resources in order to get things done. The subject of implementation brings public administration and public policy analysis about as close as they ever come. Even then, the policy literature has paid less attention to organizational details than the political and intellectual constraints in implementation. This chapter will pick up the discussion from Chapter 4 and look at design questions (how we achieve our objectives) from the point of view of organizing services and programs. Implementation studies have the reputation of being the dismal science of policy studies, since much of the work here tends to emphasize how tough it is to get anything accomplished. However, in contrast to theory, the practice of public administration and policy implementation has been undergoing a revolution in recent years. With **decentralization**, partnerships, client focus, quality service standards, performance and results, subsidiarity, special operating agencies, privatization, commercialization, accountability, and ethics, the list of new management practices and emphases is long. As one would expect, there is considerable debate whether these new forms of policy implementation represent improvements or decline, and whether there are uniform trends.

Implementation and policy design are conceptually distinct, though they overlap in practice. Think of design as the blueprint for the policy and implementation as its execution. Looked at in this way, the relationship between the two aspects of the policy process raises an interesting question: is it possible for badly designed policies to be well implemented, and good policy designs to be badly implemented? Box 5.1 illustrates a rough set of relationships that can exist between implementation and design. A well-designed policy with good implementation is almost a definition of success: a good idea well executed. There is another degree of success, however, which might be thought of as implementation failure—a good idea that suffers from inadequate execution. It must be said that this explanation of failure is the refuge of many a policy designer. The idea was fine, but the follow-through was responsible for less than spectacular results. More on this in a moment. One point to keep in mind is that there is still hope: since the design is sound, failure is a matter of organization, personnel, or resources. It is also possible to have design failure—the policy is badly designed in terms of problem definition or instruments or goals, but is executed reasonably well. Total failure—and total misery—occur when both design and implementation are seriously flawed. To be realistic, most policies will have shortcomings in design and in implementation; what we are considering here is very weak design combined unhappily with very weak implementation.

We can see from these crude categories that implementation makes a distinct contribution to the success or failure of a policy.

> The study of policy implementation is crucial for the study of public administration and public policy. Policy implementation is the stage of policymaking between the establishment of a policy, such as the passage of a legislative act, the issuing of an executive order, the handing down of a judicial decision, or the promulgation of a regulatory rule, and the consequences of the policy for the people whom it affects. If the policy is inappropriate, if it cannot alleviate the problem for which it

was designed, it will probably be a failure no matter how well implemented. But even a brilliant policy poorly implemented may fail to achieve the goals of its designers. (Edwards, 1984, p. ix)

The design phase is about determining the problem, the goals, and the most appropriate instruments for a solution. Even if all of that goes well, and the conceptualization of the policy problem is broadly correct, the follow-through can fail. Knowing this, of course, the smart designer builds considerations about implementation into the policy design from the beginning; however, this too can raise problems if we presume that there should be both some degree of flexibility in the way policies are implemented as well as input from below. In this chapter we will assume that the policies are well designed and concentrate on principles and mechanisms of implementation. The first section quickly reviews some of the conventional wisdom of the policy literature, while the second reviews the exploding world of new forms of public management and service delivery.

Implementation Theory

Recall the discussion of instruments and policy design in the last chapter. In elaborating a set of programs that combine various instruments in order to put the policy into effect, what would one want in order to ensure success?

Box 5.2 (page 188) draws on Hogwood and Gunn's (1984, Chapter 11) classic list of requirements. The image of the successful implementer that arises from this list of requirements is someone or some organization that has brains, strong planning capacity, resources, authority to act, and complete understanding of the goals. It is, in short, a world without friction, without scarcity, without confusion, miscommunication, conflict, or misunderstanding. It is also a world of hierarchy and power, where the implementer decides and those decisions cascade down to the final point of delivery without obstruction or misinterpretation. Little wonder, then, that perfect implementation almost never happens, and, as Hogwood and Gunn (1984) conclude, some degree of failure "is almost inevitable" (p. 198).

While the Hogwood and Gunn list of requirements is developed from the point of view of the administrator or implementer, there is another approach that incorporates some system-level considerations. Offered by Sabatier and Mazmanian (1981), this list picks up many of the same variables as Hogwood and Gunn. Box 5.3 summarizes the framework, which hinges on three broad categories of variables. First, the tractability of the problem: Some issues, for example, traffic congestion, are easier to deal with than others, disposal of nuclear waste among them. A good

BOX 5.2   ELEMENTS FOR SUCCESSFUL IMPLEMENTATION

No insurmountable external constraints	• Usually organizations and individuals that will not cooperate, but can include acts of nature
Adequate time and sufficient resources	• Time, money, and people
Required combinations	• Time, money, and people in the right order and mix
Valid theory	• Good design, especially cause-and-effect relationships
Causal connections are reasonable, clear, and direct	• Focus on causal variables that can realistically be addressed by public policy, rather than, for example, large systemic ones that are resistant to intervention
Dependency relationships are minimal	• Authority is not fragmented or dispersed
Agreed objectives	• Everyone sings from the same song sheet; no dispute about ends
Correct sequence of tasks	• Doing first things first, and so on
Communication	• Clear communication and understanding
Compliance	• No sabotage, recalcitrance, or rebellion

Source: Hogwood, B. W., & Gunn, L. A. (1984). *Policy analysis for the real world* (Oxford: Oxford University Press), Chapter 11.

causal theory, a relatively narrow range of targeted behaviour, a small population target group, and a small desired change in behaviour as a result of policy make implementation more successful, all other things being equal. Second, Sabatier and Mazmanian also incorporate legislative and institutional variables. The statute should be clear, and the implementing agency well resourced. Linkages to cooperating agencies should be designed with a minimum of veto points and strong lines of accountability. The statute should be implemented by agencies or individuals sympathetic to its goals, and outside access to the decisionmaking process should be skewed toward supporters rather than critics.

BOX 5.3   A CONCEPTUAL FRAMEWORK OF THE IMPLEMENTATION PROCESS

TRACTABILITY OF THE PROBLEM

1. Availability of valid technical theory and technology
2. Diversity of target-group behaviour
3. Target group as percentage of the population
4. Extent of behavioral change required

ABILITY OF STATUTE TO STRUCTURE IMPLEMENTATION	NONSTATUTORY VARIABLES AFFECTING IMPLEMENTATION
1. Clear and consistent objectives	1. Socioeconomic conditions and technology
2. Incorporation of adequate causal theory	2. Media attention to the problem
3. Financial resources	3. Public support
4. Hierarchical integration with and among implementing institutions	4. Attitudes and resources of constituency groups
5. Decision-rules of implementing agencies	5. Support from sovereigns
6. Recruitment of implementing official	6. Commitment and leadership skills of implementing officials
7. Formal access by outsiders	

Source: Sabatier, P. A., & Mazmanian, D. A. (1981). The implementation of public policy: A framework of analysis. In D. A. Mazmanian & P. A. Sabatier (Eds.), *Effective policy implementation* (p. 7). Lexington, MA: Lexington Books.

A third category is broad socio-economic and political variables that determine the fate of implementation. These overlap in part with forces discussed in Chapter 3, maintaining the sense in the public and the political system that the problem to which the policy is being directed is important and requires attention. In sum, the chances of successful implementation, which Sabatier and Mazmanian define as "the translation of statutory objectives into the policy decisions of implementing agencies," are maximized if there are clear objectives, sympathetic agencies, authority, resources, fidelity to statute and rules, leadership, and public support—such a daunting list that it illustrates why the study of implementation appears to be the dismal science of policy analysis, or "misery research" (Hill & Hupe, 2009, p. 107).

The book that arguably kicked off interest in implementation by policy analysts was by Jeffrey L. Pressman and Aaron Wildavsky. First published in 1973 (3rd ed., 1984), it had an appropriately pessimistic title: *Implementation: How Great Expectations in Washington Are Dashed in Oakland: Or, Why It's Amazing That Federal Programs Work at All, This Being a Saga of the Economic Development Administration as Told by Two Sympathetic Observers Who Seek to Build Morals on a Foundation of Ruined Hopes*. The book examined an urban employment scheme, called the Oakland Project, announced in 1966. At the time, Oakland had an unemployment rate of 8.4 percent, concentrated among inner-city blacks. The program was to spend $23 million on a variety of public works projects and would be administered by the Economic Development Administration (EDA). As Pressman and Wildavsky pointed out, the Oakland Project enjoyed wide political support and was well funded, with monies in place. Yet three years later, only $3 million had been spent, most of that for a freeway overpass and architects' fees. Why did the Oakland Project fail?

From the beginning, "the success of the EDA program depended on agreement among a diverse group of participants with differing organizational objectives" (p. 30). The project had, at minimum, 15 different sets of actors, some within the same agency. They included, among others, five different sets from within the EDA itself: the Department of Health, Education, and Welfare; the Department of Labor; the U.S. Navy; the City of Oakland; and African-American community leaders. Beyond this there were all the private sector actors who were supposed to create jobs with the help of EDA funds. Levels of commitment, perceptions of urgency, and capacity varied enormously among these actors. Moreover, the implementation process was marked by a sequence of tasks that had to be completed or agreements struck before the process could move on. Pressman and Wildavsky called these "decision points" that required "clearance" by multiple sets of actors in order for implementation to go forward. They hypothesized that 30 decision points required a cumulative total of 70 clearances. Assuming an 80 percent probability of agreement on each clearance point, the chances of completion were one in a million. Even if one assumed an unrealistically high probability of 99 percent for each clearance, the odds for successful implementation were only about one in two. "However you look at it, the ultimate probability of success is very low" (p. 107).

One might argue that the Oakland Project succumbed to the fragmentation that characterizes the American political system. It is true that parliamentary systems like Canada's have a higher degree of executive dominance and institutional capacity to implement from the top down (Atkinson, 1993; Pal & Weaver, 2003). But Canada's is also a federal system, which reduces the executive dominance to some degree at the centre. The other notable feature of the Oakland Project was the high consensus around it. In cases where principles differ, where problem definitions are widely divergent, or where actors have incentives to impede, delay, or frustrate, it could be expected that policies will face even greater odds against implementation.

Fortunately, things are not so grim. Subsequent work has shown that the probability of successful implementation increases if one adopts assumptions that are plausible, but only slightly different from those held by Pressman and Wildavsky in their study. After all, things do get accomplished, however imperfectly. The Pressman–Wildavsky implementation model consists of a chain of statistically independent nodes or clearance points with an attached probability. Relax the model in five ways and the probability for clearance increases substantially (Alexander, 1989). First, it is unrealistic to assume that actors will make only one attempt at clearance. They may persist in multiple tries. Second, clearance points are not always independent; they might be packaged or bundled in ways so that one clearance ripples through several others. Third, there is a bandwagon effect at times where previous clearances increase the probability of future clearances. This momentum usually develops in threshold decisions where a certain number of agreements are necessary before a large payoff can be received, which puts pressure on holdouts. A good example is labour negotiations, where both sides try to "build momentum" on a series of minor issues before they tackle the larger ones. Fourth, program-reduction strategies may be used to shorten the **decision chain**. If the proposed program is being held hostage at one clearance point because of some feature that requires agreement from reluctant supporters, it is possible to cut out that component and proceed to the next decision point. Finally, one can assume higher probabilities of clearance than 99 percent in some instances, and this has a marked effect on overall clearance probabilities.

All of these techniques, in one way or another, involve trying to make the implementation process more controlled. But what if, as Eugene Bardach (1977) asked, "the character and degree of many implementation problems are inherently unpredictable" (p. 5)? Bardach took the dynamic conceptualization of implementation first developed by Pressman and Wildavsky—dynamic in the sense that it occurs over time—and arrived at the notion of "games" as a way of understanding the essentially defensive nature of implementation: games involve players, strategies, resources, rules, and uncertainty about outcomes. In reflecting on what makes the implementation game successful, what enables implementers to deal with its inevitably unpredictable character, Bardach offered several strategies. First, avoid implementation designs that rely on complex management systems, large organizations, and lots of clearances. Implement through the market, if possible; deliver cash directly to people rather than services that require elaborate bureaucracies, and aim at small and feasible targets. Second, engage in scenario-writing to work out different possible consequences of a string of actions and interactions. Third, and most important, fix the game in the sense of "repairing" it when it goes awry and in the sense of "adjusting certain elements of the system of games ... so as to lead to a more preferred outcome" (Bardach, 1977, p. 274). Doing this amounts to paying attention to the policy-formation process (Winter, 1990, pp. 25–26).

If the prospects for implementation were as bleak as some of the earlier literature suggested, then policymaking would seem a hopeless enterprise. It may be that we have unrealistically high notions of what constitutes policy success. Ironically, because perceptions of government became more negative over the 1970s and 1980s, the public sector may be presumed to be doing worse than it actually is: "by adopting new ways of looking at and evaluating public policymaking, we have ourselves constructed a significant number of the fiascoes we subsequently 'observed'" (Bovens & t'Hart, 1996, p. 146). However, the lessons of implementation cannot be ignored. It is difficult to make things happen, and it becomes increasingly difficult the further removed the situation is from the preconditions identified by Hogwood and Gunn. It can also be more difficult than it need be, if we expect perfect implementation through control. If top-down control is our standard, if we see implementation as the formal elaboration of some unitary design, then, almost by definition, that is unlikely to happen, given what we know about the limits of organizations and the impact of politics on decisionmaking. Majone and Wildavsky (1984) urged an image of implementation as evolution, not as control:

> Implementation is evolution. Since it takes place in a world we never made, we are usually right in the middle of the process, with events having occurred before and (we hope) continuing afterward.... When we act to implement a policy, we change it. When we vary the amount or type of resource inputs we also intend to alter outputs, even if only to put them back on the track where they were once supposed to be. In this way, the policy theory is transformed to produce different results. As we learn from experience what is feasible or preferable, we correct errors. To the degree that these corrections make a difference at all, they change our policy ideas as well as the policy outcomes, because the idea is embedded in the action. (p. 177)

Implementation is therefore an execution process, an elaboration, a realization of schemes and conceptions, the building of links in often long chains of decision and agreement. It can also be seen as a process of communications, an "implementation subsystem full of messages, messengers, channels, and targets" (Goggin, Bowman, Lester, & O'Toole, 1990, p. 33). It takes place in a world of multiple powers and authorities, organizations, and personalities, and therefore is inevitably a struggle. Even this fails to capture the reality, since it still implies an evolution from the design or blueprint, when what may be happening is closer to the loop or cycle mentioned in the preceding quotation, where implementation is a function of combined top-down and bottom-up processes. Indeed, some students of implementation have been so impressed by the degree to which the fortunes of policies are determined at the final point of delivery that they have urged a **backward mapping** technique to work out what the policy should actually be, as opposed to more conventional **forward mapping**.

> Forward mapping ... begins at the top of the process, with as clear a statement as possible of the policymaker's intent, and proceeds through a sequence of increasingly more specific steps to define what is expected of implementers at each level. At the bottom of the process, one states, again with as much precision as possible, what a satisfactory outcome would be, measured in terms of the original statement of intent.... [Backward mapping] begins, not with a statement of intent, but with a statement of the specific behavior at the lowest level of the implementation process that generates the need for a policy.... Having established a relatively precise target at the lowest level of the system, the analysis backs up through the structure of implementing agencies, asking at each level two questions: What is the ability of this unit to affect the behavior that is the target of the policy? And what resources does this unit require in order to have that effect? In the final stage of analysis, the analyst or policymaker describes a policy that directs resources at the organizational units likely to have the greatest effect. (Elmore, 1982, pp. 19, 21)

In sum, the conventional work on implementation has tended to highlight its multidimensionality, difficulty, ambiguity, and a growing realization of its importance. The multidimensionality arises from the understanding that implementation can be viewed as an organizational process, something internal to bureaucracies and focused on the challenge of balancing discretion with accountability. Implementation can also be viewed primarily as a political process of bargaining among actors who, while not necessarily equal in resources, can each affect outcomes. It can also be seen from the perspective of individuals, personalities, and leadership capacities, either in organizations or political structures. The difficulty of implementation lies in the high demands for success. As Hogwood and Gunn (1984), as well as Sabatier and Mazmanian (1981), illustrate, it is a lot easier to outline the requirements for successful implementation than to fulfill them. The challenge of implementation reflects the complex symbiosis between theory and practice: policy is initially nothing more than ideas or conceptualizations, while implementation is the specific means of execution and elaboration in practice. Theory guides practice, but practice must, of necessity, add details that were never contemplated in the origins of the policy. Finally, the importance of implementation comes through precisely this contribution of practice—it is, in effect, the test of the policy theory (assuming it goes well). By testing, we learn. So a properly designed implementation process should provide a mechanism for monitoring, **policy feedback**, learning, and improvement. Eggers and O'Leary (2009, pp. 133–134) propose that implementers adopt a "project management" mindset or discipline, and recommend the following tools and techniques:

1. Task and milestone management: Set goals and timelines.

2. Stakeholder management: Identify stakeholders and their needs and expectations.

3. Change management: Develop a transition strategy to increase support.

4. Technical management: Use the technology you need, but nothing on the "bleeding edge."

5. Risk mapping: Identify the probability of significant risks.

6. Set up a war room: This is a sort of "command centre" to manage implementation.

7. Scenario plan: Develop scenarios of how and why things might go wrong.

8. Segment your customers: Divide the universe of potential "customers" into similar and more tractable groups.

9. Chunk your projects: Try to break large projects and initiatives into more manageable "chunks" that are less complex and less risky.*

Implementation, however, is not a matter of merely empirically deciding what works and then developing checklists of factors to consider as one tries to realize it. As Linder and Peters (1990) noted, looking at policy from the top down, the "implementation solution" criterion seems to be clarity, so that compliance can be ensured down the line. From the bottom up, however, the main criterion appears to be flexibility and discretion, and hence, policy design should emphasize simplicity (pp. 64–65). The factors that we consider to be important in

---

*Eggers, W. and O'Leary, J., *If We Can Put a Man on the Moon: Getting Big Things Done in Government*, Harvard Business Publishing, 2009, pp. 133–134. Reprinted with permission.

implementation, in other words, depend on the way in which we perceive governance. To take an extreme example, if the scope of government were to be reduced to its 19th-century proportions of maintaining public safety and infrastructure such as roads and sewers, it is unlikely that any student of public policy would dream of implementation as a major issue. Implementation is a concern only when there are lots of complex policies to implement. Moreover, the nature of the issues and challenges we confront in implementation also depend on the modes of implementation that we characteristically use. When governments deliver services like education directly, accountability and compliance are more or less presumed to flow from the line relationships that extend down from the ministry or department to the local schools. Imagine a situation where all educational services were delivered by third parties, and the government's only role was to develop curricula and distribute support to parents in the form of vouchers. Key implementation issues would suddenly become related to compliance with curricular guidelines and fraud in the use of the vouchers.

Like everything else in policymaking, the practical world of implementation has changed significantly in the last two decades. The main trend in the 1980s and 1990s and into the early 2000s was new public management (NPM), briefly described in previous chapters. This kind of management involved the downsizing of the state, decentralization, a focus on performance and results as well as on service orientation, partnerships, and an emphasis on market mechanisms. Again, as previously mentioned, the specific pattern of reforms varied by country, and Canada's version was considerably less enthusiastic than some others. Nonetheless, many key principles were adopted and implemented at all levels of government. There is no clear successor to the NPM model as a broad management philosophy, but some developments in management theory and practice in the last decade have overlayed this kind of management and created yet another distinctive environment for the implementation and management of public policy in Canada, with similar tendencies evident in other OECD countries.

Public Management Developments: The NPM Model and Beyond

The broad outlines of the philosophical premises of new public management were sketched in Chapter 2. These premises imply a different form of governance and different types of agencies and accountability relationships. Not surprisingly, to the degree that the NPM model took root in Canada, it had an influence on mechanisms of implementation. Although new public management has been overtaken by other developments in public management thinking, it has left an imprint on how governments in Canada and elsewhere act.

The sources of the NPM model are various. Politically, the first wave of radical governmental reform came with the Thatcher regime in Britain in the late 1970s and early 1980s. According to Savoie (1994), these initiatives became one of the key inspirations for the Mulroney-era changes to the public service (p. 231). The massive changes undertaken by the New Zealand government in the mid-1980s were another harbinger of things to come. Intellectually, the management revolution was led by gurus such as Peters and Waterman (1982) and Osborne and Gaebler (1993). While the political roots of new public management were initially in the conservative end of the political spectrum, gradually governments of every political stripe accepted at least part of the message and reformed their internal structures and connections with social partners. In New Zealand, change was initiated by a Labour government. In Canada, the Saskatchewan NDP government was the first to balance its budget, ahead of Conservative Alberta. In the United Kingdom, Tony Blair's "New Labour" government spearheaded substantial public sector reforms focusing on performance.

The broad appeal of NPM ideas (despite the variable uptake among different countries) suggests that deeper forces were at work: the bundle of factors described in Chapter 2 that links globalization, technology, and shifts in postwar paradigms to the nature of the nation-state. In May 2000, for example, the Clerk of the Privy Council argued that globalization would force more public involvement, more partnerships, and more focus on service delivery (Privy Council Office, 2000). It is important to note the conflicting pressures behind these forces since they help explain some of the confusing characteristics of the NPM model. On the one hand, new public management was all about re-organization and restructuring and relied heavily on market terminology such as **quality management** and **client satisfaction**. On the other hand, it also emphasized the need for fundamental governance changes that would involve more participation, citizen control, democracy, and responsiveness.

What were the key principles of the NPM model? First, as we noted in Chapters 1 and 2, it is critical of traditional bureaucracies. Bureaucracy in this perspective is inflexible, slow, rule bound, and clumsy. Second, a basic question is posed as to whether government should be involved in the policy area in the first place. This position seems like much more than a management issue, and it is. But it represents a sea change in thinking that presumes that the lines between state and civil society are drawn in different ways, ways that return substantial responsibilities to nongovernmental actors. Third, if it is determined that a government policy response is appropriate to the problem, the mode of delivery or broad implementation strategy stresses a strong focus on nongovernmental actors (communities, private corporations, citizens) as primary partners in delivery. Fourth, there is greater attention to outcomes and **performance**, with a special emphasis on clear standards of service to which agencies can be held accountable. Agencies are encouraged to think of service recipients as customers or clients. Fifth, organizationally, the NPM model looks to new hybrid forms of delivery that may have greater flexibility and also to a sharper distinction between policymaking functions in the executive and service functions that can be delivered on a contractual basis by some entity, either at arm's length or in the department. (The latter is known as "disaggregation.")

These principles permit a fairly wide variation in practice, and governments that moved in this direction did so to different degrees and in different configurations, though there is no doubt that new public management was a broad global movement (Christensen & Laegreid, 2002; Kettl, 2005). Moreover, there are important ideological differences that still surface, whatever the similarities in approach. Scandinavian countries took a more citizen-centred, service delivery orientation to new public management than did the Anglo-democracies, and the pace of reform differed among countries (Christensen & Laegreid, 2011). In Canada, at the federal level, the inauguration of new ways of thinking about management and program delivery came with the 1989 initiative entitled **PS2000**, and then was followed by successive waves of reform, each broader and more intense. According to Paul Tellier (1990), who was then the Clerk of the Privy Council and responsible for launching PS2000, the program had three core objectives: better service, improved personnel management, and flexibility. Together, these objectives would shift public sector thinking away from a philosophy of control to a philosophy of **empowerment.**

The 1994 federal budget announced the successor to PS2000, the Program Review (though PS2000 was never formally abandoned). Linked to a deficit-reduction strategy, Program Review's "main objective was to review all federal programs in order to bring about the most effective and cost-efficient way of delivering programs and services that are appropriate to the federal government's role in the Canadian federation" (Department of Finance, 1995, p. 33). As described in Chapter 2, ministers were asked to review all their programs in light of the six tests or questions: serving the public, necessity of government involvement, the federal role, scope for partnerships, efficiency, and affordability. Note that the first four of these speak directly to the issue of implementation or how government programs are delivered to the public. Coupled with large budget cuts, the effect of the Program Review was a major downsizing of the federal civil service, some 15 000 full-time-equivalent positions in 1994, and 45 000 the next year. The average decline in departmental spending between 1994 and 1999 was 20 percent.

Just as important as the financial impact of Program Review, however, was its impact on and reflection of a new way of thinking about government services. The most extensive presentation of the new vision came in the government's blueprint entitled *Getting Government Right: A Progress Report* (Treasury Board of Canada, 1996a). Its strategy had four objectives: (1) clarification of federal roles and responsibilities, (2) better targeting of resources on high priority social and economic issues, (3) better and more accessible government "involving clients more in decision making and using modern and practical service delivery tools," and (4) more affordable government. Overarching these goals was a fundamental rethinking of services and the best ways of delivering them: "A central thrust of the renewal agenda has been to determine where the federal government is best placed to deliver programs or services and where these programs and services are more appropriately delivered by others" (Treasury Board of Canada, 1996a, p. 7). Program Review officially ended in March 1999, but the management approach outlined in *Getting Government Right* continued. In horizontal terms, the government launched an **Alternative Service Delivery** (ASD) initiative in 1996, which was then supplemented by a **Quality Services Initiative** and finally an approach that stressed **citizen-centred service delivery** (Treasury Board of Canada, 2000a).These changes demonstrated an unusually firm commitment not only to deal with the deficit and spending, but also to move more fundamentally and deeply on a public sector reform agenda. *Getting Government Right* was followed four years later with *Results for Canadians,* with a new emphasis on performance and results measurement. *Results for Canadians* made four management commitments: (1) citizen focus in service delivery and broader partnerships; (2) ethical values; (3) reporting on results; and (4) responsible spending (Treasury Board of Canada, 2000b).

These commitments were followed up with two other developments. The first was the Public Sector Modernization Act (PSMA) of 2003. The act was designed to modernize human resources management in the federal government of Canada by giving deputy heads more flexibility in hiring, redefining the merit principle to, again, introduce more flexibility and enhance human resources management and support throughout the government, for example, by redesignating the Canadian Centre for Management Development as the Canada School of Public Service, and creating a new agency, the Public Service Human Resources Management Agency of Canada (PSHRMAC). That agency was subsequently renamed as the Canada Public Service Agency and designated as the central agency responsible for human resources management in the government of Canada (later reabsorbed into the Treasury Board Secretariat, although human resources management is under the Office of the Chief Human Resources Officer within the Secretariat). Another development that stemmed from

Results for Canadians and the Public Sector Modernization Act was the Management Accountability Framework (MAF), introduced in 2005. The MAF was designed to integrate 10 key management expectations, bringing together the principal elements of modern comptrollership, human resources modernization, service improvement, and Government On-Line. The MAF is reproduced in Figure 2.4 (p. 81). Each of the elements is accompanied with specific indicators as well as measures for those indicators. These include both process measures (e.g., completed plans or reviews) and improvement measures (e.g., staff and service satisfaction or audit findings).

As bold as these NPM measures might have seemed in the 1990s and early 2000s, the Canadian approach was somewhat tepid in comparison with that of other countries: the "style of these reforms was generally moderate, as was the substance" (Gow, 2004, p. 11; also see Cheung, 1997). In the earlier phases of both PS2000 and the subsequent reforms of the cabinet system, for example, there was never the same level of public political commitment and leadership to management change in Canada as there was in the United Kingdom, Australia, or New Zealand. The PS2000 exercise was driven primarily by the mandarinate, with little interest from the executive. Aucoin (1995) cites the Auditor General of Canada's 1993 study to the effect that "Canadian reforms under the Conservatives had met with less than the desired success precisely because the required political and public service leadership had been lacking" (p. 13). In the other Westminster democracies, leadership on management change had come directly from the top, from prime ministers and senior cabinet ministers. The fundamentals of new public management as experienced in New Zealand and the United Kingdom required a combination of rather radical restructuring around the separation of policy from operations, with a determined focus on service that, in turn, demands the development and application of performance standards. In Canada, at both federal and provincial levels, restructuring did not go as far, with the main organizational vehicle remaining the department or ministry.

In all countries where NPM variants were implemented, there were moves to change the nature of executive agencies and their relations to service or delivery agencies that went considerably beyond what Canada tried. The logic behind this was that mixing policy development functions with delivery of services in a traditional, hierarchical, civil service bureaucracy would not be conducive to efficiency and flexibility. If the objective is the highest standards of service to the public, then these functions should be clarified and distinguished in some way so that service delivery need not be hobbled by considerations that are more appropriate to policy development and advising the executive. The clearest and earliest example of this approach to the organization of government functions was the U.K.'s Next Steps initiative, formally launched in 1988 with the release of *Improving Management in Government: The Next Steps*, a report from the prime minister's Efficiency Unit. The Blair government continued these early efforts on public sector reform through its Service First program, which was replaced in 2002 with the Office of Public Services Reform, guided by the Principles into Practice document. The emphasis was on tailored public services to citizens, something that continued with the Brown government. The recent "Big Society" initiative of the Cameron government (discussed in Chapter 2) is still in pursuit of better service, but through partnerships with civil society organizations and local governments.

The U.K. model restructured government through a division between policy advice (or development) and delivery. The New Zealand model, launched in the mid-1980s, was similar in principle but quite different in design. Launched by Labour governments, the reforms were remarkable for their boldness, rigour, and scope. New Zealand became the poster child for new public management around the world and, indeed, in 1993 was ranked first by the World Competitiveness Survey for the quality of its government. The objectives and principles behind the reforms were also enunciated with admirable clarity. The objectives were to improve effectiveness, efficiency, and accountability; to reduce expenditures and the size of the public sector; to improve transparency and quality of services. Three key principles in achieving these objectives were that ministers be responsible for selecting outcomes while department executives be responsible for determining inputs (with minimum interference) for achieving those outcomes; that, wherever possible, publicly funded services be open to tender and competition; and that decisionmaking powers be as decentralized and as close to the consumer as possible (Boston, Martin, Pallot, & Walsh, 1996, pp. 4–5).

New Zealand, at the time of its reforms, had retained many more commercial and quasi-commercial functions within departmental structures than was characteristic of other Commonwealth countries, and so the first step in the government re-organization was the establishment of "state-owned enterprises" to act as commercially viable providers of government services. This was common in some European countries— Sweden is an example of the **"functional model"** in "which the tasks of policy advice and implementation are generally carried out by separate agencies" (Boston et al., 1996, p. 69). The alternative, which still characterizes most OECD countries, including Canada, is a **"sectoral model"** that vertically integrates advice and delivery within a ministry or department (though this may be changing; see the discussion of Service Canada later in this chapter). The change in New Zealand was dramatic: by 1995, fewer than half of government departments had any significant service delivery functions (Boston et al., 1996, p. 78). This model of governance was retained, with modest changes, as part of a "managing for results" framework, but has been changed in the most recent public service development plan to 2015 (see discussion later in this chapter on post-NPM developments).

These U.K. and New Zealand examples are only part of a larger international trend that in one form or another aimed to restructure the public sector to more sharply define services, agencies that provide them, and accountability relationships both to government and to clients. We addressed this international "policy movement" in Chapter 1. The Organisation for Economic Co-operation and Development (OECD) (2004) highlighted several reform priorities in 2004: budgeting in the public sector, connecting government and citizens, ethics and corruption, human resources management, public sector statistics, regulatory reform, and strategic policymaking. Whereas the emphasis in the mid-1990s seemed to be more on structural reform of governments, recently there has been a shift in attention toward strategic management, particularly of **horizontal issues** that cut across various policy areas, public sector culture (ethics), human resources management, and continued focus on regulation in the broadest sense of both law and rule-making by other agencies. The OECD reinforced these findings in its 2005 *Modernising Government: The Way Forward*. The highlights of public sector modernizing were open (transparent) government, enhanced public sector performance, accountability and control, reallocation of expenditures, the use of market-type mechanisms, and improved human resources management.

> In the period under review, many of the assumptions about the extent of direct government responsibility as a service provider have been challenged and, in some countries, radically changed. Governments have progressively withdrawn from commercial activities, ownership of industries and service provision in, for example, communications and energy and water supply. These are explicit governance changes. (OECD, 2005, p. 16)

Figure 5.1 illustrates the rich range of reforms undertaken by OECD members in the mid-2000s. The data are self-reported and do not give a sense of magnitude or depth, but they do demonstrate that public sector reform is a global phenomenon. The key question is whether it is still useful to characterize it as an NPM phenomenon, or whether we have moved to a post-NPM stage of reforms (Christensen & Laegreid, 2011). This is tricky, since few governments around the world (at least those in the OECD) have given up on the language of new public management and its emphasis on performance, efficiency, service, and market mechanisms. However, if the NPM model is not dead, then it has certainly been overshadowed or layered over with several new developments in public management reform, none of which amounts to a new "paradigm" but which together suggest a substantially changed orientation. Of the OECD's *Modernising Government* priorities (open, or transparent, government, enhanced public sector performance, accountability and control, reallocation of expenditures, the use of market-type mechanisms, and improved human resources management), most were dedicated to principles that were not part of the NPM core of the 1980s and 1990s. As well, new public management had been in large part—to be blunt—about downsizing government, reducing expenditures, and making the public sector work more like the private sector. Some large forces in the last years have upset that agenda, and we mentioned them in previous chapters. One was the impact of 9/11, which revived a sense that strong government, at least on the public security side, was important and necessary. The financial crash in 2008 and its ongoing effects (at time of writing) have created a schizophrenia in the public mind about government. Italy and Greece are presented as examples of feckless politics and public sectors Swiss-cheesed with energetic corruption and languid incompetence. Corporations and the private sector, as partly responsible for the crash, are in bad odour, as is the mantra of "private sector efficiency." Good government remains the only life raft in these turbulent times.

Because Canada did not go as far as other countries in adopting new public management, it did not need to roll back any of its major reforms. In other countries, however, that is exactly what happened. Dunleavy et al. (2005) argue that the NPM model was marked by three broad themes: disaggregation (splitting up large public sector hierarchies), competition (introducing purchaser/ provider separation into public structures), and incentivization (moving to specific performance incentives rather than rewards based on a public sector professional ethos). In terms of our earlier discussion, these themes capture only part of new public management, but Dunleavy and colleagues go on to specify 34 reform components within those three broad themes and argue that most of these are either stalled or reversed. The disaggregation theme has seen the greatest reversal, particularly with respect to purchaser–provider separation, **agencification**, and growth of quasi-government agencies. Only the following NPM components have continued to spread and enjoy support: improved performance measurement, league tables of agency performance, customer-tagged financing, user control, and service charges. The United States, the United Kingdom, and New Zealand—all early NPM leaders—have recently moved to consolidate or **re-governmentalize** certain functions. In the United Kingdom this was trumpeted as **"joined up government"**; the U.S. example was the creation of the Department of Homeland Security. In the Canadian case, an example is the creation of the Canadian Air Transport Security Authority after 9/11. Previously, airport security had been contracted out to private

Figure 5.1 Management Reform in the OECD

Summary of country recommendations[a]

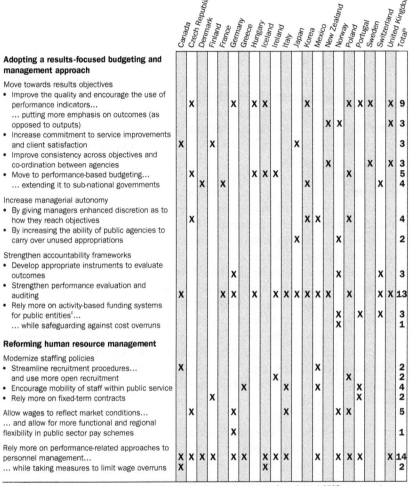

Adopting a results-focused budgeting and management approach

Move towards results objectives
- Improve the quality and encourage the use of performance indicators... — 9
  ... putting more emphasis on outcomes (as opposed to outputs) — 3
- Increase commitment to service improvements and client satisfaction — 3
- Improve consistency across objectives and co-ordination between agencies — 3
- Move to performance-based budgeting... — 5
  ... extending it to sub-national governments — 4

Increase managerial autonomy
- By giving managers enhanced discretion as to how they reach objectives — 4
- By increasing the ability of public agencies to carry over unused appropriations — 2

Strengthen accountability frameworks
- Develop appropriate instruments to evaluate outcomes — 3
- Strengthen performance evaluation and auditing — 13
- Rely more on activity-based funding systems for public entities[c]... — 3
  ... while safeguarding against cost overruns — 1

Reforming human resource management

Modernize staffing policies
- Streamline recruitment procedures... — 2
  and use more open recruitment — 2
- Encourage mobility of staff within public service — 4
- Rely more on fixed-term contracts — 2

Allow wages to reflect market conditions... — 5
... and allow for more functional and regional flexibility in public sector pay schemes — 1

Rely more on performance-related approaches to personnel management... — 14
... while taking measures to limit wage overruns — 2

a) These policy recommendations are derived from the public spending chapter for individual OECD country reviews published in 2000 for Japan and Mexico; 2001 for Canada and Czech Republic; 2002 for Denmark, Germany, Greece, Hungary, Italy, New Zealand, Norway, Poland, Sweden, Switzerland, and the United Kingdom; 2003 for Finland, France, Iceland, Ireland, Korea, and Portugal.
b) Number of countries for which these recommendations were spelled out among the 21 countries for which in-depth public expenditure chapters in final form are available.
c) In the case of Portugal and Switzerland, this recommendation applies to the hospital sector.
Source: Individual country in-depth chapters on public expenditure.

Source: Adapted from Table 5: Reforming budgeting and management practices to improve public spending effectiveness, OECD Economic Studies No. 37, 2003/2, www.oecd.org/oecdeconomicstudies. Reprinted with permission.

firms, and the creation of the Authority was part of a five-year, $2.2 billion plan announced in 2001. New Zealand, because it was perhaps one of the most radical innovators in terms of functional differentiation, agencification, and decentralization, is the most interesting. Many of the early NPM enthusiasms have been rolled back and by the early 2000s "combating the vertical siloing of agencies came to be identified by the country's State Services Commission as a key priority" (Dunleavy et al., 2005, p. 471). Starting in 2005, and building through to 2008 with the latest articulation of its development goals for the public service by 2015, the New Zealand government has increasingly focused on joining up what had once been sundered—networked delivery of services through IT, but also more coordination and integration around horizontal policy themes (Fancy, 2007a, 2007b; State Services Commission [New Zealand], 2005, 2007).

While new public management as a movement has been stalled, we need to be clear that it has left a strong mark on public sectors around the world—what Hood and Peters referred to as NPM's "aging" and entrance into the "age of paradox" (Hood & Peters, 2004). First, there remains (as the OECD shows) a powerful impulse toward public sector modernization. There is now, in most countries, a public sector culture of continuous improvement, in part based on the NPM assumption that the public sector should try to be as efficient and as responsive as possible. Second, as Dunleavy et al. (2005) and Christensen and Laegreid (2007) point out, some key NPM components such as a focus on performance, results, client service, and incentivization, have taken root and continue to be part of public sector practice around the world. Third, some NPM aspects have been institutionalized and hence are difficult to reverse—in the Canadian context, the **Public Service Modernization Act (PSMA)** is part of the legislative basis for human resources management in the federal government.

At the same time, as we noted above, many countries that introduced strong NPM-inspired changes either in part or in whole have reversed them. Others, including Canada, never went as far and so have not had to roll back as much. In some measure, of course, the financial crisis has created a completely different tone around public sector reform and implementation practices: "getting government right" is an even more important priority today than it was a decade ago, but it is much more driven by fiscal pressures. This situation is not so different from the mid-1990s experience of Canada, for example, where reform took essentially two tracks: tackling the deficit and downsizing the public service, but trying at the same time to create new sinews of public management and service delivery. In our view, while reform in most OECD countries is indeed being driven by similar forces, those forces do not amount to a coherent philosophy of the public sector in the same sense that new public management did. We explore at least three of these drivers in the Canadian context in the concluding section to this chapter.

Implementation and a Changing Public Service

We can conclude from the previous section that something indeed has changed about the organization and delivery of public services at every level of government in Canada, first through an extended phase of new public management, and then a more recent focus on post-NPM improvements. Moreover, these changes were part of a global pattern of public sector reform, even though tone and colour differed across different countries. The Canadian experience through the 1990s was, in comparative terms, less far-reaching or radical than was true of the United Kingdom or New Zealand. In the first half of the 1990s, management reform, while defended in terms of higher standards of service to the public, was driven largely by fiscal constraints at both the federal and provincial levels of government. But the fiscal constraints should be given their due: as we noted in Chapter 4, without those constraints it would have been easy to continue doing business as usual.

Things have changed. As an example, whereas in the 1990s and the early 2000s the federal government and management thinkers used the term "alternative service delivery," or "ASD," to reflect the sort of change they had in mind—alternatives to traditional bureaucracy—the phrase was hardly mentioned by 2008 (the 1996 Treasury Board policy on ASD was replaced in 2002, and then effectively mothballed). Nonetheless, the conviction that government services should be delivered imaginatively and with a constant eye to innovation remains largely accepted, and as we noted above, has been reinforced in some ways by fiscal pressures. One example of how conventional this thinking has become within the profession is represented by the Institute of Public Administration of Canada (IPAC): the Institute has handed out Innovation Management Awards annually since 1990. IPAC's description of the program nicely illustrates the synergy between innovation and financial pressure: "Governments are facing challenges that are increasingly complex and often spread across ministerial mandates and jurisdictions. These issues affect citizens and stakeholders in both predictable and unintended ways. Although resources are increasingly limited, citizens still have expectations and assume that governments will work together to address them through new and creative approaches.... In an era of economic restraint, the timing, leveraging, and funding of these programs are more crucial than ever. We collectively demand new approaches to public services that are relevant, cost effective, efficient, transparent and are especially ... innovative" (IPAC, 2012).

Box 5.4 lists the annual themes for which IPAC has invited applications, and it is striking how the notions of reform, service, collaboration, partnership, performance, and technology dominated over the years. The examples in Box 5.4 are Canadian, but the **innovation networks** that now appear to bind together public administrators, managers, consultants, and academics have ensured that examples of public sector innovation in program delivery are as widely available as possible—in fact, there is a Global Innovators Network explicitly designed to encourage sharing experiences in innovation. The leading node in this network of innovation is the John F. Kennedy School at Harvard University, which sponsors *Innovations in American Government* (John F. Kennedy School, 2012). The program has recognized innovations in public management since 1986, initially in the United States but then expanding to include Brazil, Chile, China, Mexico, the Philippines, Peru, South Africa, the east African region, and Native American tribes in the United States. It provides annual awards for innovation in American government and 10 countries and regions around the world. Award winners can be searched in the program's database according to theme: accountability, collaboration, participation, social justice, social services, sustainable development, and technology, among others. Whereas a good deal of the academic analyses of NPM innovations have been critical—in part because of its borrowing from private sector models, its emphasis on public sector process constraints over efficiency, and its skepticism about unaccountable public service manager "innovators"—the Kennedy innovations awards program was and is inspired by an optimistic view that public servants can be entrepreneurial in their efforts to create public value, and can achieve "micro-improvements" that collectively add up to substantial and positive changes in governance (Borins, 2008, pp. 5–6).

As we argued above, there are clearly strong traces of NPM themes in these awards programs, and they echo many of the realities of public sector management and reform efforts today. However, that is not the whole story. At least with respect to Canada, several broad developments have occurred that overshadow some of the NPM skepticism of the public sector, even while amplifying some NPM elements, such as service and performance. We will highlight three major shifts that have occurred in the last five years.

The first shift is a renewed appreciation of the special nature of the public sector, of public sector values, and of how public institutions (government, but the para-public sector as well) serve the public interest. This appreciation is, in part, due to the impact of 9/11 and the continuing financial crisis, but also has more complicated roots in the realization (discussed in Chapter 2) that in a global, knowledge-based economy,

BOX 5.4   IPAC INNOVATIVE MANAGEMENT AWARD THEMES, 1990–2011

2011: The Leading Edge
2010: Collaboration at Work
2009: Turn Around
2008: Managing the Green Workplace/Innovations in Greening
2007: New Service Breakthroughs with Technology
2006: Sharing Governance: Citizens, Partners and Networks
2005: Public Service without Borders
2004: Pulling against Gravity: Horizontal Collaboration
2003: In the Know: Knowledge Management
2002: Outside-in: Changing Government to Meet Client Needs
2001: Developing the Public Service of Tomorrow
2000: Collaboration: New Approaches to Policy and Management
1999: Measurement and Recognition
1998: [Not available]
1997: Breakthroughs: Connecting Citizens and Government
1996: Mastering Change
1995: Making Diversity Work
1994: Re-Shaping Government
1993: Better with Less
1992: Partnership Management
1991: Empowerment: Employees, Managers and Organizations
1990: Service to the Public

Source: Reprinted by permission of the Institute of Public Administration of Canada (IPAC) www.ipac.ca

good governance and a well-functioning public service comprise a key competitive advantage.

The second shift is a new emphasis on accountability and ethics. While this emphasis is not specific to Canada, the Federal Accountability Act that the newly elected Conservatives passed in 2006 represented a signature policy and one with extraordinary scope. It is not that the NPM model ignored ethics; it simply did not place it at the centre of thinking about governance. As the OECD (2005) noted, accountability and ethics had emerged as key themes, in combination with transparency and openness, in many public sector reforms.

The third shift is not really a shift at all, but contains the seeds of potential radical change. A core NPM theme was enhanced service to citizens. Critics of new public management dismissed this as reducing citizens to clients or customers, but it was more far-reaching than that, and impelled by a genuine desire to make government more responsive to public needs. This emphasis on service coincided with the revolution in information and communication technologies, just as governments were moving into the digital age. The impact of digital technology on governance is already profound and promises to have even more dramatic effects in the next decade.

We can describe these themes as "governance themes" and so they are in one sense broader than implementation as such. However, to the degree that they affect the structure and direction of the public services that do the work of implementation, they do have profound impacts on that work.

RETHINKING THE VALUE OF THE PUBLIC SERVICE

New public management, despite variations that celebrated the importance of citizen engagement and client service, had a strong undercurrent of skepticism about the public sector. There were good grounds for this in the 1980s and 1990s in terms of practical politics: the public sector had grown for decades without much restraint, and public bureaucracies were stereotypically unresponsive and leaden. By the late 1990s, as we noted in Chapter 1, there was a growing realization that the public sector and governance were critical ingredients to economic competitiveness. What some called the "public domain" was being rediscovered as a balancing mechanism for the failure of markets, and a large part of that public domain consisted of government and government services (Drache, 2001). That realization was amplified with the 9/11 attacks, and perhaps even more dramatically with the global meltdown in 2008. A new sense of the importance of public sector values gradually grew through the early 2000s (Aucoin, 2002) and was possibly reinforced through a reaction to crude NPM assertions that governments had no higher purpose than efficiency (Jørgensen & Andersen, 2011).

Denhardt and Denhardt (2000, 2003), for example, have made the case for a "new civil service" rooted in the responsibility that public servants have to serve and empower citizens, to help them discover their shared interests by building trust and collaboration. Their seven principles: (1) serve, rather than steer, (2) the public interest is the aim, not the by-product, (3) think strategically, act democratically, (4) serve citizens, not customers, (5) accountability isn't simple, (6) value people, not just productivity, and (7) value citizenship and public service above entrepreneurship.

Their ideas reflect a view of public administration and public service that emphasizes its distinct characteristics in contrast to the private sector: the primacy of the rule of law, the generation of public value, and the key importance of public services to modern life. As we mentioned earlier, fiscal pressures are forcing a more narrow focus on cuts to the public service and to services, but at the same time, they are forcing a realization of the indispensability of a strong, effective, and dedicated public service to managing this world of turbulence, complexity, and crisis. As the Clerk of the Privy Council put it in his 2011 report to Prime Minister Harper, noting the increasing complexity of government and the problems it has to deal with: "In adapting to meet these new realities we will be guided by the enduring values of the Public Service—respect for democracy, respect for people, integrity, stewardship and excellence. They will continue to define our role and our duties as public servants. A strong values-based approach to our work will make it easier to deal with complexity. It will also support efforts to create a culture of innovation and intelligent risk taking in government" (Privy Council Office, 2011a).

The emphasis on public sector renewal since 2006 reflects this new appreciation of both the importance of the public service and the impending changes due simply to demographic shifts (Privy Council Office, 2007, 2008, 2011b). While it might be too much to suggest that this shift entails a "new public administration theory," Bourgon is certainly correct to highlight a change in perspective from NPM's emphasis on markets, productivity, managerialism, and the emulation of private sector practices (Bourgon, 2007, p. 2011). Her argument is that a new approach to public administration should begin with a focus on citizen-centred services (see below), value for taxpayers' money, and a flexible public service workforce. Its fundamental building blocks would be citizen involvement, the public interest, service to citizens, and collaborative approaches to the development of public policy. Even a critic of her 2007 article noted that "the state does not simply provide services, it also carries deep responsibilities for law and order and security, the discharge of which will sometimes bring the public authorities up against the expressed wishes of significant communities or groups, and which will often require the restraining and prevention of individuals from pursuing their preferred courses of action. The re-conceptualization of the 'public interest' that Bourgon refers to needs to accommodate these more coercive and regulatory aspects of the government's role" (Pollitt, 2007, p. 39). Neither Bourgon nor Pollitt is envisioning the sort of stripped-down state imagined in new public management. They are both suggesting, as is the Clerk of the Privy Council, a model of governance where the public service and the public sector are distinct in terms of their values as well as their contributions to society. More evidence for this comes from the recent, renewed emphasis on public service ethics and accountability.

Ethics and Accountability: New Benchmarks

Heintzman (2007a) notes: "One of the most important things that has taken place in public services right across the country, over the last ten years is a reawakened awareness of the democratic, professional, ethical and people values inherent in public service, and of their importance, both to public service institutions, and to the daily lives of individual public servants." He also argues that the concern for public-service values has been a "prominent feature of public-service reform and renewal in many countries over the past decade" (Heintzman, 2007b, p. 574). Similar to the point we made above about the rediscovery of the special qualities of the public service, the renewed emphasis on ethics and values was driven by a reaction to new public management and prompted "another careful look at the first principles of public administration ... a rediscovery of public-service values was intended to address and remedy the confusion resulting from the initial, over-eager embrace of private-sector ideas, ideas that could not be imported indiscriminately into the public sector without great damage to the profession, institutions and practice of public administration" (Heintzman, 2007b, p. 576).

In the Canadian case, this rediscovery stemmed initially from one of several Deputy Minister task forces established in 1995 by Jocelyne Bourgon (then Clerk of the Privy Council). In *A Strong Foundation*, first published in 1996, the Task Force on Values and Ethics highlighted the importance of the "the public good, and ... related values (such as equity and balance), for public service. The notion of the public interest is a touchstone of motivation for public servants. It is for the public service what justice and liberty are for the legal profession, or what healing and mercy are for the medical profession" (Task Force on Public Service Values and Ethics, 2000, p. 37). The Task Force report, or Tait Report as it is commonly known, then became the basis for the 2003 Values and Ethics Code for the Public Service (Government of Canada, 2003). That Code highlighted four clusters of values: (1) democratic values (helping ministers, under law, to serve the public interest; (2) professional values (serving with competence, efficiency, and transparency); (3) ethical values (behaving with integrity, objectivity, and impartiality); and (4) people values (respect for human dignity). Creation of the Code was then followed by a new program linking ethics to democratic reform during the Martin government (Langford & Tupper, 2006). The innovations we mention in the next paragraph led to further revisions to the Code under the Harper government, and a new one was introduced on April 2, 2012. It listed five basic values, as well as behaviours that should flow from those values: (1) respect for democracy (serving the public interest through a nonpartisan public service); (2) respect for people (treating all people with respect, dignity, and fairness); (3) integrity (honesty, fairness, and impartiality); (4) stewardship (care for public resources); and (5) excellence (in the design and delivery of policy, programs, and services). These values are to guide public servants "in all activities related to their professional duties" (Treasury Board of Canada, 2011).

The salience of ethics and accountability only grew in the mid-2000s and became the centrepiece of the new Conservative government's election campaign in 2006. The Federal Accountability Act, the first piece of legislation introduced by the government, brought with it a heightened ethics and accountability regime at the federal level. The legislation, extremely complicated, is too detailed to discuss here, but its highlights included new restrictions on the financing of political parties (e.g., a complete ban on contributions by unions, corporations, or other organizations, and a contribution limit of $1000 to parties annually by individuals); a new Conflict of Interest and Ethics Commissioner with enhanced powers, and a new Conflict of Interest Act enshrining codes on conflict of interest and post-employment provisions; tougher rules on lobbyists; a Parliamentary Budget Office; tighter government procurement regulations (e.g., public disclosure of contracts over $10 000); a Public Servants Disclosure Protection Act; and the designation of deputy heads as "accounting officers" (Federal Accountability Act, 2006).

The animus behind this renewed emphasis on ethics and accountability is complicated. In part, as we noted, it stems from a genuine sense of rediscovery of unique public service values and characteristics that hinge on the protection and promotion of the public interest. At the same time, some of it is driven by scandals, distrust, and a suspicion that the public sector needs careful oversight and scrutiny. It has been a strange combination of drivers. The first is a genuinely positive commitment to a broader and deeper sense of the value of the public service, exemplified by Bourgon, Tait, and the last two Clerks of the Privy Council. But this has largely been an internal discourse within the profession. The second driver has tended to overwhelm the first—it is a ramped-up suspicion of malfeasance throughout the public sector (including politicians), coupled with a determination to "fix it." The ironic result of this oil and water has been a heightened sense of the importance of public service, its values, its ethical fibre, and its accountability to the public interest. This sense was muted in NPM days, but it is loud and clear today.

DIGITAL GOVERNANCE AND QUALITY SERVICE

The mid-1990s was a period of structural reform (however modest in the Canadian case), coupled with a focus on citizen-centred service, satisfaction, and quality. A network of Canadian public servants and policymakers became concerned about the "service gap" or the distance between what citizens expect from their governments and the level of satisfaction that they have with what they get. They launched a national survey called Citizens First to probe what Canadians thought about public services and what they wanted from those services. The first survey was conducted in 1998, with follow-ups in 2000, 2002, 2005, and 2008. The surveys showed that for some specific services, Canadians found the public sector more efficient and responsive than the private sector. At the same time, the surveys showed that citizens are dissatisfied with phone service (still the main channel of communication with government) and expect same-day responses for most inquiries. The five drivers of citizen satisfaction with services are timeliness, staff, positive outcome, ease of access, and recent experiences with services (Institute for Citizen-Centred Service, 2012). The methodology behind these surveys has been criticized, but even critics agree that the surveys have had a powerful influence in putting customer service and single windows at the centre of the service transformation agenda (Howard, 2010).

The seriousness with which this dimension of implementation was taken is illustrated by the Service Improvement Initiative that was launched in 2000 and then regalvanized in 2004. Forty-seven departments and agencies were required to participate in the initiative, whose target was a minimum 10 percent increase in client satisfaction by 2005. It required measurements of client satisfaction, benchmarks, annual improvement plans, and public progress reports. This initiative was then replaced with Service Canada (discussed below), which was launched in 2005.

This emphasis on quality and service would be largely empty if there were no way of assessing the success of achieving quality and service goals, and finding out what clients and citizens actually think about the services that they receive. Hence, the emphasis on service is almost inevitably linked to an emphasis on performance assessment, measurement, and results. We will take up the question of performance measurement in Chapter 7, but it can be noted here that there are many ways of assessing outcomes and performance, from program impacts on specific targets to levels of satisfaction with services. The important thing is that it is being done, and that in comparison with the older tradition of public administration, it is new. In the past, the reporting function focused primarily on the appropriate administration of resources, while policy evaluation took care of cost-benefit analyses of impact analyses. Performance and satisfaction matter now because citizens matter more, not purely from an altruistic or "feel-good" posture by governments and public officials, but because the financial crisis required emergency measures that had to work well, and work quickly (e.g., Canada's Economic Action Plan, with hundreds of projects across the country). Citizens are also, because of the impact of the crisis on jobs, mortgages, pensions, and other services, angry.

Another clear characteristic of the federal government's approach to public sector reform is the centrality of partnerships. We will discuss this in Chapter 6 in the context of policy communities and networks, and we provided the broader context for this shift in Chapter 2 in terms of shifting governance regimes. Today, implementation is neither primarily about doing it alone nor shifting public responsibilities completely to the private sector. It is about doing it in concert with partners from the voluntary sector, from interest groups and NGOs, from the private and not-for-profit sectors. The range of available modes and partners in service delivery is virtually limitless, with various permutations and combinations of commercialized, voluntary, and purely public services, and every hybrid in between. The main dimensions are commercialization, private/public partnerships, and independence from government. Combined with initiatives to improve the quality of services, enhance performance, and publicize results, it is clear that the world of implementation and policy instruments has changed significantly.

This emphasis on service and quality is now more than two decades old. What has stimulated new thinking, however, is the merging of digital technology and service. As we mentioned earlier, some (Dunleavy et al., 2005) see this as a new public service paradigm. We do not go that far. Many things in government are still delivered in old-fashioned ways, from garbage removal to meals-on-wheels. Moreover, rule-bound bureaucracies are likely to simply shift their rules to be embedded in software as opposed to codes and guidelines in the hierarchy (Fountain, 2001). But, as we noted in Chapter 4, it is undeniable that the "digital state" is a qualitatively different animal from what preceded it, and that has certain consequences for the organization of government and the delivery of services. According to Borins, "The most significant change that could flow from IT-enabled government, however, is a reshaping of the public service that consolidates many common functions previously located separately in each department. Three aspects ... are integrated service delivery organizations, joined-up policy development and knowledge management, and integrated support organizations" (Borins, 2007, p. 16). From a service provision perspective, this new IT environment—Web 2.0 governance—adds new channels (Web, email) for citizens to register their preferences and new modes of delivery of services, especially ones that are primarily information based, and new forms of collaboration among public agencies, private and nonprofit organizations, and citizens (Tapscott & Williams, 2006). A particularly important development is allowing citizens access to either general information or personal information (e.g., medical records, tax files) that previously would have been available only with great difficulty or not at all. Another development is the sharing of service delivery data in real time with citizens, for example, GPS data on snow removal operations in a city. Within governments, Web 2.0's enhanced capabilities are allowing (mostly younger) public servants to organize their own communities using blogs, wikis, and social networking tools analogous to Facebook, and most governments are wrestling with how to provide these tools both internally, and in ways that will allow public servants to connect with wider constituencies of stakeholders.

The Service Improvement Initiative described above was what is known in the literature as an "integrated service delivery" (ISD) model that is "multi-channel and multi-jurisdictional" (Flumian et al., 2007, p. 558). Integrated service delivery "is the result of bringing together related government services so that citizens can access them in a single seamless experience based on their wants and needs. A seamless service delivery system is 'fluid, agile, integrated, transparent, connected'" (Kernaghan, 2007, p. 103). Service Canada was launched in the 2005 federal budget, building on the successes of the Government On-Line initiative that ran from 1999 to 2006. Service Canada is a single window for federal government services, provided through several channels such as in-person, telephone, Internet, and mail delivery. It has more than 20 000 employees, operates in over 600 in-person points of service across Canada, and has millions of unique website visits per year. Just as important, it is "working with a growing number of federal departments, the majority of provinces and community partners to bring services and benefits together in a single service delivery network" (Flumian et al., 2007, p. 559). Services are available by subject (e.g., education, pensions) but also by categories of citizens (e.g., Aboriginal peoples, newcomers to Canada, people with disabilities). It is clear that integrated service delivery of this nature—other examples include Canada's BizPal, which "provides Canadian businesses with one-stop access to permit and licence information for all levels of government," and Australia's Centrelink (Halligan & Wills, 2008)—does hold important implications both for services and how they are delivered, as well as government organization. Service Canada's ambition is to provide Canadian citizens and organizations with the bulk of federal as well as provincial and community-based services 24/7 through multiple channels. Just as important, in many instances it lets those citizens and organizations have access to data (e.g., the status of an immigration or passport application) that previously would have been available only to government officials. On the organizational side, Service Canada is becoming the ISD mechanism for most federal departments, which will eventually focus more of their efforts on policy development and program design, and away from implementation of programs and services. Doing this will not be easy:

> Striking a new balance between hierarchy and flexibility, between vertical and horizontal dimensions of accountability, is the

nexus of technological and organizational interoperability and innovative leadership. Strengthening the capacities of the public service in this regard, via initiatives such as Service Canada, entails more than incremental modifications to existing structures and processes. A more networked and collaborative mindset must take hold in order to loosen the forces of bureaucratic and political tradition that are intertwined with vertical hierarchy and control. (Roy, 2006, p. 284)

The challenge is especially acute in a federal state like Canada's. Whereas networking and collaboration seem, by definition, to be good things and almost certainly are when departments at one level of government work together, an overemphasis on the technical efficiency of service delivery can undermine federal division of responsibilities and jurisdictions if the only goal is a "single window" (Fafard, Rocher, & Côté, 2009).

Conclusion

It is easy enough to see what is different about implementation—new organizational forms, clearer standards, use of information technology for integrated service delivery, partnerships, a service orientation, and public exposure of plans and performance. Partnering in some format is becoming a critical aspect of governance and service delivery. This reality poses fresh challenges for public managers and policy analysts, since our traditional paradigms of service delivery have relied on a top-down, centralized control model. When governments act as partners, providing support and frameworks rather than services directly, and when they move to integrated service delivery, it changes the nature of the implementation game quite dramatically, for example, through highlighting accountability issues, monitoring, and learning loops. In terms of the theory discussed in the first part of this chapter, modern implementation practices seem to combine strategies of decentralization and integration (the Service Canada model) to reduce blockages in decisionmaking and strategies of interdependency that will demand greater attention to communication and cooperation (e.g., partnerships; Savoie, 2004, p. 7).

It should also be clear from this chapter that while the world of policy implementation has changed, the tableaux of those changes are confusing and difficult to trace. The NPM movement dominated public sector and service reform for two decades, with a focus on service quality, results, performance, and fidelity to private sector efficiencies. The post-NPM period has overtaken those initiatives with new stresses on ethics and accountability, and the unique character of public services, better integration or reintegration of governmental agencies (a "whole-of-government" perspective), but the NPM instinct for change, innovation, service, and quality has not disappeared. Indeed, what is possibly new about the current context is a marriage of NPM and post-NPM philosophies (Christensen & Laegreid, 2011)—though whether they can be blended (the web of rules that comes from the Accountability Act is not entirely consistent with a nimble service orientation) is not clear.

We have argued that many of these changes are being driven by deep forces that are difficult, if not impossible, to avoid, and that these changes in governance cut across ideological lines. Certainly, the first wave of NPM reforms reflected a combined sense that government could and should be leaner and more efficient, and that it could and should capitalize on emerging information technologies. The human cost was in public sector jobs, with literally thousands of people let go (though in the case of Ottawa, employment increased steadily after 1999 to bring levels back to where they had been in 1995; Statistics Canada, 2004, 2008). Those who remained standing in the rubble of public sector institutions in the late 1990s had little choice but to seek partners and support. A big part of the equation had thus been determined: a smaller public sector, doing fewer things with fewer resources. It was only a matter of time before circumstances demanded innovation, though as we noted, NPM rhetoric also placed a premium on innovation and service directly.

This initial NPM enthusiasm for disaggregation, competition, and incentivization has, as we argued earlier, been eclipsed for various reasons. Governments post 9/11 have not become smaller, and indeed have continued to grow—with the financial crisis, exploding in terms of spending. There were some policy failures due to NPM ideas (especially in the United Kingdom, the United States, Australia, and New Zealand), and that contributed to rolling back some initiatives (Gregory, 2002). This change was accompanied by a new appreciation of the specific qualities of the public sector and the public service, which has led to fresh preoccupations with probity (ethics and accountability) and service (ISD). Overlaying all this, of course, is the pressure on almost all OECD governments to slash expenditures in the face of ballooning deficits and volatile bond markets. Brutal austerity measures, for example, are being taken in Britain, Spain, Italy, and Greece, and in the runup to the 2012 U.S. presidential election, the debate was almost entirely about taxes and spending and the debt. Canada's version was announced in the 2012 federal budget. In the previous year, the government had reviewed $75 billion in direct program spending and identified over $5 billion in potential savings. It projected moving from an annual deficit of $33 billion in 2010–11 to a balanced budget by 2014. This effort involved inflicting some considerable pain through public sector job cuts, but coupled with actual expenditure increases in innovation and research (Department of Finance, 2012). By European standards, this was "austerity lite."

We also need to be wary of the interests that are served, and those that are not, by catch phrases such as "citizen-centred service delivery" and "partnerships." There is always the danger, for example, that surveys that seem to be searching for citizens' views on services might in the end be used more as legitimizing instruments to support what governments are doing anyway. The same can be said of performance and results reporting. What should be honest attempts at transparency can easily become weapons of government propaganda, skewing the numbers in such a way as to declare perfection. As well, it cannot be lost on many observers that the craze for quality and service exploded just at the time that many services were either being reduced or eliminated. The energy and resources flowing into measurements, benchmarks, surveys, reports, and indicators may serve to persuade the citizenry that governments care about what they are doing, when, in fact, much of government may steam along as usual. Most analyses of quality service initiatives and performance measurement are well aware of these human and political dynamics, and so consequently stress leadership, organizational commitment, and culture change as key ingredients in achieving genuinely different outcomes. This emphasis is especially true of integrated service delivery, which does pose fundamental organizational challenges for the way government conventionally operates.

The core issue is one that has been touched on repeatedly in this chapter and which has surged in importance in recent years: accountability. The traditional governance model under a parliamentary regime like Canada's assumes that monies are spent by government departments and agencies that are accountable to their ministers, and through them to the government as a whole, and ultimately to the legislature and the people. The new forms of service delivery, either through ISD channels such as Service Canada or through horizontal partnerships, pose challenges for these conventional practices of democratic accountability. In late 1999, for example, the Auditor General released a report on new governance arrangements that had been developed in the mid-1990s in response to budget cuts and new management thinking. He found 77 such new arrangements that collectively spent $5 billion of taxpayers' money annually. "Under these arrangements, the federal government involves external partners in the planning, design and achievement of federal objectives, replacing delivery by federal employees, contractors or agents. These partners are not accountable to ministers and Parliament" (Auditor General of Canada, 1999). The infamous 2003 review of the sponsorship program that eventually led to the Gomery Inquiry also pointed out problems in accountability relationships because of the nature of the program. Even in 2005, the Auditor General found that while there had been improvements, federal central agencies had "not developed enough specialized tools for the governance, accountability, and co-ordination of federal efforts in such initiatives and have made little progress in developing means of funding horizontal programs" (Auditor General of Canada, 2005).

In many respects, these are broad questions of governance and not merely technical ones of implementation. Our discussion of integrated social delivery and the increasing impact of IT in government showed that there are substantive organizational impacts that go well beyond simply changing delivery channels from in-person to electronic. We will address these larger governance issues in our conclusions in Chapter 10. Chapter 7 will take up the difficult question of asking how we might measure whether all this innovation, alternative service delivery, and quality actually result in efficiencies and positive impact. The next chapter, however, considers the question of the participants in the policy process.

KEY TERMS

agencification—breaking up government departments into quasi-autonomous agencies with more flexible management practices, and usually contractual relationships with political authorities based on performance requirements

Alternative Service Delivery—a term used in the 1990s, but less so now, to describe attempts to deliver government services outside a traditional departmental format, in partnership for example with the private sector or NGOs, or through contracting out

backward mapping—a technique to work out what the policy will look like in terms of delivery of programs at the final point of service, and hence what the implementation needs are at that point

citizen-centred service delivery—ensuring that clients get what they want and that resources are allocated accordingly by focusing on citizens first and assessing their needs and their levels of satisfaction

clearances—the number of agreements required by multiple sets of actors in order for implementation to go forward

client satisfaction—degree to which customers or clients of a service are happy with that service

decentralization—devolution of responsibilities to other government jurisdictions or third parties, and restructuring accountability relationships within government departments

decision chain—the sequence of agreements, decisions, or clearances that have to be surmounted in order for the implementation process to move forward

decision points—a single stage in a decision chain requiring clearances and agreements before movement to the next point is possible

empowerment—the provision of real powers and authorities to the government's other partners in the policy process

forward mapping—the conventional technique of implementation analysis that starts with as clear a statement as possible of the policymaker's intent and proceeds through a sequence of increasingly specific steps to define what is expected of implementers at each level

functional model—the model in which the tasks of policy advice and implementation are generally carried out by separate agencies

horizontal issues—issues that cut across various policy areas

innovation networks—networks that bind together public administrators, managers, consultants, and academics to ensure that examples of public sector innovation in program delivery are as widely available as possible

joined-up government—the U.K. term for horizontal coordination across government departments and agencies

performance—empirical indicator of how well a program or organization is operating with respect to clearly articulated goals

policy feedback—information about the consequences or impacts of a policy that goes back into its improvement and redesign

PS2000—a 1989–93 federal public-sector reform initiative inaugurated in 1989, which had three core objectives: better service, improved personnel management, and flexibility

Public Service Modernization Act (PSMA)—federal legislation introduced in 2003 to make human resources management in government departments more flexible and decentralized

quality management—managing programs and services with a high priority placed on quality, performance measures, and reporting

Quality Services Initiative—the late 1990s federal initiative that stresses citizen-centred service delivery

re-governmentalize—the opposite of agencification—pulling agencies or activities back into the public sector from the private sector

sectoral model—a model that vertically integrates advice and delivery within a ministry or department

service delivery—procedures and organizational resources devoted to getting services to clients

FURTHER READINGS

Aucoin, P. (1995). *The new public management: Canada in a comparative perspective*. Montréal, QC: Institute for Research on Public Policy.

Bardach, E. (1977). *The implementation game: What happens after a bill becomes a law.* Cambridge, MA: MIT Press.

Borins, S., et al. (2007). *Digital state at the leading edge.* Toronto, ON: Institute of Public Administration of Canada and the University of Toronto Press.

Borins, S. (Ed.). (2008). *Innovations in government: Research, recognition, and replication.* Boston, MA, and Washington, DC: Ash Institute for Democratic Governance and Innovation, and Brookings Institution Press.

Christensen, T., & Laegreid, P. (Eds.). (2011). *The Ashgate research companion to new public management.* Burlington, VT: Ashgate.

Hill, M., & Hupe, P. (2009). *Implementing public policy: An introduction to the study of operational governance* (2nd ed.). Thousand Oaks, CA: Sage.

Pressman, J. L., & Wildavsky, A. (1984). *Implementation: How great expectations in Washington are dashed in Oakland: Or, why it's amazing that federal programs work at all, this being a saga of the economic development administration as told by two sympathetic observers who seek to build morals on a foundation of ruined hopes* (3rd ed.). Berkeley, CA: University of California Press.

Roy. J. (2006). *E-government in Canada: Transformation for the digital age.* Ottawa, ON: University of Ottawa Press.

REFERENCES

Alexander, E. R. (1989). Improbable implementation: The Pressman–Wildavsky paradox revisited. *Journal of Public Policy, 9,* 451–465.

Atkinson, M. (1993). Public policy and the new institutionalism. In M. Atkinson (Ed.), *Governing Canada: Institutions and public policy* (pp. 17–45). Toronto, ON: Harcourt Brace Jovanovich.

Aucoin, P. (1995). *The new public management: Canada in a comparative perspective.* Montréal, QC: Institute for Research on Public Policy.

Aucoin, P. (2002). Beyond the "new" in public management reform in Canada: Catching the next wave. In C. Dunn (Ed.), *The handbook of Canadian public administration* (pp. 36–52). Toronto, ON: Oxford University Press.

Auditor General of Canada. (1999). *Report of the Auditor General of Canada.* Chapter 23: Involving others in governing: Accountability at risk. Ottawa.

Auditor General of Canada. (2005). *Report of the Auditor General of Canada.* Chapter 4: Managing horizontal initiatives. Retrieved from

http://www.oag-bvg.gc.ca/internet/English/parl_oag_200511_e_894
.html

Bardach, E. (1977). *The implementation game: What happens after a bill becomes a law.* Cambridge, MA: MIT Press.

Borins, S. (2002). Transformation of the public sector: Canada in comparative perspective. In C. Dunn (Ed.), *The handbook of Canadian public administration* (pp. 3–17). Toronto, ON: Oxford University Press.

Borins, S. (2007). Conceptual framework. In S. Borins et al., *Digital state at the leading edge.* (pp. 14–36). Toronto, ON: IPAC and the University of Toronto Press.

Borins, S. (2008). Introduction. In S. Borins (Ed.), *Innovations in government: Research, recognition, and replication* (pp. 1–12). Boston and Washington: Ash Institute for Democratic Governance and Innovation, and Brookings Institution Press.

Boston, J., Martin, J., Pallot, J., & Walsh, P. (1996). *Public management: The New Zealand model.* Auckland, NZ: Oxford University Press.

Bourgon, J. (2007). Responsive, responsible and respected government: Towards a new public administration theory. *International Review of Administrative Sciences, 73*(1), 7–26.

Bourgon, J. (2011). *A new synthesis of public administration: Serving in the 21st century.* Montréal and Kingston: Queen's School of Policy Studies and McGill-Queen's University Press.

Bovens, M., & t'Hart, P. (1996). *Understanding policy fiascoes.* New Brunswick, NJ: Transaction.

Cheung, A. (1997). Understanding public sector reforms: Global trends and diverse agendas. *International Review of Administrative Science, 63*(4), 435–457.

Christensen, T., & Laegreid, P. (Eds.). (2002). *New public management: The transformation of ideas and practice.* Aldershot, UK: Ashgate.

Christensen, T., & Laegreid, P. (Eds.). (2011). *The Ashgate research companion to new public management.* Burlington, VT.: Ashgate.

Denhardt, R. B., & Denhardt, J. V. (2000). The new public service: Serving rather than steering. *Public Administration Review, 60*(6), 549–559.

Denhardt, R. B., & Denhardt, J. V. (2003). *The new public service: Serving, not steering.* Armonk, NY: M.E. Sharpe.

Department of Finance (Canada). (1995). *Budget speech.*

Department of Finance (Canada). (2012). *Budget plan.* Retrieved from http://www.budget.gc.ca/2012/plan/toc-tdm-eng.html

Drache, D. (Ed.). (2001). *The market or the public domain: Global governance and the asymmetry of power.* London, UK: Routledge.

Dunleavy, P., et al. (2005). New public management is dead—Long live digital-era governance. *Journal of Public Administration Research and Theory, 16,* 467–494.

Edwards, G. C., III. (1984). Introduction. In G. C. Edwards III (Ed.), *Public policy implementation* (pp. ix–xv). Greenwich, CT: JAI Press.

Eggers, W., & O'Leary, J. (2009). *If we can put a man on the moon … Getting big things done in government.* Boston, MA: Harvard Business Press.

Elmore, R. F. (1982). Backward mapping: Implementation research and policy decisions. In W. Williams (Ed.), *Studying implementation: Methodological and administrative issues* (pp. 18–35). Chatham, NJ: Chatham House.

Fafard, P., Rocher, F., & Côté, C. (2009). Clients, citizens and federalism: A critical appraisal of integrated service delivery in Canada. *Canadian Public Administration, 52*(4), 549–568.

Fancy, H. (2007a). *Development goals for the New Zealand State Services— Draft milestones for 2015.* Retrieved from http://www.ssc.govt.nz/ display/document.asp?docid=6331&PageType=toc&displaytype=pf

Fancy, H. (2007b). *Refresh the Development Goals Milestones project* (Discussion paper). Retrieved from http://www.ssc.govt.nz/display/ document.asp?docid=6343&PageType=toc&displaytype=pf

Federal Accountability Act. (2006). Retrieved from http://www.faa-lfi .gc.ca/faa-lfi/faa-lfi00_e.asp

Flumian, M., Coe, A., & Kernaghan, K. (2007). Transforming service to Canadians: The Service Canada Model. *International Review of Administrative Sciences, 73*(4), 557–568.

Fountain, J. E. (2001). *Building the virtual state: Information technology and institutional change.* Washington, DC: Brookings Institution Press.

Goggin, M. L., Bowman, A., Lester, J., and O'Toole, L. (1990). *Implementation theory and practice: Toward a third generation.* Glenview, IL: Scott, Foresman/Little, Brown Higher Education.

Good, D. A. (2003). *The politics of public management: The HRDC audit of grants and contributions.* Toronto, ON: University of Toronto Press.

Government of Canada. (2003). *Values and ethics code for the public service.* Retrieved from http://www.tbs-sct.gc.ca/pubs_pol/hrpubs/ tb_851/vec-cve-eng.asp

Gow, J. I. (2004). *A Canadian model of public administration?* Ottawa, ON: Canada School of Public Service.

Gregory, R. (2002). Transforming governmental culture: A sceptical view of new public management. In T. Christensen & P. Laegreid (Eds.), *New public management: The transformation of ideas and practice* (pp. 231–258). Aldershot, UK: Ashgate.

Halligan, J., with Wills, J. (2008). *The Centrelink experiment: Innovation in service delivery.* Canberra, AU: The Australia National University E Press and the Australia and New Zealand School of Government.

Heintzman, R. (2007a, May). *Toward a new moral contract: Reclaiming trust in public service.* The Vanier Lecture, Regina, SK. Retrieved from http://www.ipac.ca/saskatchewan/files/Heintzman_final.pdf

Heintzman, R. (2007b). Public-service values and ethics: Dead end or strong foundation? *Canadian Public Administration, 50*(4), 573–602.

Hill, M., & Hupe, P. (2009). *Implementing public policy: An introduction to the study of operational governance* (2nd ed.). Thousand Oaks, CA: Sage.

Hogwood, B. W., & Gunn, L. A. (1984). *Policy analysis for the real world.* Oxford: Oxford University Press.

Hood, C., & Peters, B. G. (2004). The middle aging of new public management: Into the age of paradox? *Journal of Public Administration Research and Theory, 14*(3), 267–282.

Howard, C. (2010). Are we being served? A critical perspective on Canada's *Citizens First* satisfaction surveys. *International Review of Administrative Sciences, 76*(1), 65–83.

Institute for Citizen-Centred Service. (2012). *Citizen's First: Top 8 highlights.* Retrieved from http://www.iccs-isac.org/en/cf/cfdocs/Top%208%20Highlights%20CF5.pdf

IPAC [Institute of Public Administration of Canada]. (2012). *IPAC award for innovative management 2011: The leading edge.* Retrieved from http://www.ipac.ca/IM-Home

John F. Kennedy School of Government. (2012). *Government innovators network, a portal for democratic governance and innovation.* Retrieved from http://www.innovations.harvard.edu/

Jørgensen, T. B., & Andersen, L. B. (2011). An aftermath of NPM: Regained relevance of public values and public service motivation. In T. Christensen & P. Laegreid (Eds.), *The Ashgate research companion to new public management* (pp. 335–347). Burlington, VT: Ashgate.

Kernaghan, K. (2007). Beyond bubble gum and good will: Integrating service delivery. In S. Borins et al., *Digital state at the leading edge* (pp. 102–136). Toronto, ON: IPAC and the University of Toronto Press.

Kettl, D. F. (2005). *The global public management revolution* (2nd ed.). Washington, DC: Brookings Institution Press.

Langford, J., & Tupper, A. (2006). How Ottawa does business: Ethics as a government program. In G. B. Doern (Ed.), *How Ottawa spends, 2006–2007: In from the cold: The Tory rise and the Liberal demise* (pp. 116–137). Montréal, QC: McGill-Queen's University Press.

Linder, S. H., & Peters, B. G. (1990). Research perspectives on the design of public policy: Implementation, formulation, and design. In D. J. Palumbo & D. J. Calista (Eds.), *Implementation and the policy process: Opening up the black box* (pp. 51–66). New York, NY: Greenwood Press.

Majone, G., & Wildavsky, A. (1984). Implementation as evolution. In J. L. Pressman & A. Wildavsky (Eds.), *Implementation: How great expectations in Washington are dashed in Oakland: Or, why it's amazing that federal programs work at all, this being a saga of the economic development administration as told by two sympathetic observers who seek to build morals on a foundation of ruined hopes* (3rd ed.). (pp. 163–180). Berkeley, CA: University of California Press.

OECD [Organisation for Economic Co-operation and Development]. (2004). *Enhancing the effectiveness of public spending: Experience in OECD countries.* Retrieved from http://ideas.repec.org/p/oec/ecoaaa/380-en.html

OECD. (2005). *Modernising government: The way forward.* Paris: OECD.

Osborne, D., & Gaebler, T. (1993). *Reinventing government: How the entrepreneurial spirit is transforming the public sector.* New York, NY: Penguin.

Pal, L. A., & Weaver, K. W. (Eds.). (2003). *The government taketh away: The politics of pain in the United States and Canada.* Washington, DC: Georgetown University Press.

Peters, T., & Waterman, R. H. (1982). *In search of excellence.* New York, NY: Harper.

Pollitt, C. (2007). 'Towards a new public administration theory': Some comments on Jocelyne Bourgon's 5th Briabant lecture. *International Review of Administrative Sciences, 73*(1), 37–41.

Pressman, J. L., & Wildavsky, A. (1984). *Implementation: How great expectations in Washington are dashed in Oakland: Or, why it's amazing that federal programs work at all, this being a saga of the economic development administration as told by two sympathetic observers who seek to build morals on a foundation of ruined hopes* (3rd ed.). Berkeley, CA: University of California Press.

Privy Council Office (Canada). (2000). *Fonctionnaires sans frontières: Operating at the speed of the public interest* [Notes for an Address by Mel Cappe]. Ottawa.

Privy Council Office (Canada). (2007). *Fourteenth annual report to the Prime Minister on the public service of Canada.* Retrieved from http://www.clerk.gc.ca/eng/feature.asp?featureid=19&pageid=77

Privy Council Office (Canada). (2008). *Fifteenth annual report to the Prime Minister on the public service of Canada.* Retrieved from http://www.clerk.gc.ca/eng/feature.asp?featureid=19&pageid=77

Privy Council Office (Canada). (2011a). *Eighteenth annual report to the Prime Minister on the public service of Canada.* Retrieved from http://www.clerk.gc.ca/local_grfx/docs/18rpt-eng.pdf

Privy Council Office (Canada). (2011b). *2010–2011 public service renewal action plan.* Retrieved from http://www.clerk.gc.ca/local_grfx/docs/2010-11_PS_Renewal_Action_Plan.pdf

Roy, J. (2006). *E-government in Canada: Transformation for the digital age.* Ottawa, ON: University of Ottawa Press.

Sabatier, P. A., & Mazmanian, D. A. (1981). The implementation of public policy: A framework of analysis. In D. A. Mazmanian & P.A. Sabatier (Eds.), *Effective policy implementation* (pp. 3–35). Lexington, MA: Lexington Books.

Savoie, D. J. (1994). *Thatcher, Reagan, Mulroney: In search of a new bureaucracy.* Toronto, ON: University of Toronto Press.

Savoie, D. J. (2004). Searching for accountability in a government without boundaries. *Canadian Public Administration, 47,* 1–26.

State Services Commission (New Zealand). (2005). *Development Goals for the State Services.* Retrieved from http://www.ssc.govt.nz/node/4091

State Services Commission (New Zealand). (2007). *Transforming the State Services: State of the Development Goals Report 2007.* Retrieved from http://www.ssc.govt.nz/upload/downloadable_files/Transforming-the-State-Services-SoDG-Report07.pdf

Statistics Canada. (2004). *Employment and average weekly earnings (including overtime), public administration and all industries.* Ottawa, ON: Statistics Canada.

Statistics Canada. (2008). *Federal government employment, wages and salaries, by census metropolitan area.* Retrieved from http://www40.statcan.ca/l01/cst01/govt58a.htm

Tapscott, D., & Williams, A. D. (2006). *Wikinomics: How mass collaboration changes everything.* New York, NY: Portfolio.

Task Force on Public Service Values and Ethics. (2000). *A strong foundation: Report of the task force on public service values and ethics* (Tait Report). Ottawa, ON: Canadian Centre for Management Development.

Tellier, P. M. (1990, Summer). Public Service 2000: The renewal of the public service. *Canadian Public Administration, 33*, 123–132.

Treasury Board of Canada. (1996, September 30). *Getting government right: A progress report.* Retrieved from http://www.tbs-sct.gc.ca/report/govrev/Gfce.asp

Treasury Board of Canada. (2000a). *Business plan: 1999–2000 to 2001–2002.* Ottawa.

Treasury Board of Canada. (2000b). *Results for Canadians: A management framework for the government of Canada.* Retrieved from http://www.tbs-sct.gc.ca/report/res_can/rc_1_e.asp#pre

Treasury Board of Canada. (2011). *Values and ethics code for the public sector* [future version]. Retrieved from http://www.tbs-sct.gc.ca/pol/doc-eng.aspx?id=25049&section=text

Winter, S. (1990). Integrating implementation research. In D. J. Palumbo & D. J. Calista (Eds.), *Implementation and the policy process: Opening up the black box* (pp. 19–38). New York, NY: Greenwood Press.

CHAPTER

Policy Communities and Networks

C hapter 1 outlined the foundations of traditional policy analysis
and the major critiques of those foundations. It pointed out that,
nonetheless, there is a resurgence of interest in making good
policy but with a sensitivity to the limitations of the traditional approach
and the challenges of contemporary governance. Chapter 2 explored
those challenges and their broad consequences for how governments
today, in Canada and throughout the world, are changing the way in
which they organize their policy thinking, their policy processes, their
organizations, and their partners. We developed a detailed understanding
of these changes in Chapters 3 to 5. What kind of conceptual lens can
we use to understand the more complicated range of players and institutions involved in making policy, and how those players and institutions
might change depending on circumstances and the policy issue at hand?
In recent years the policy literature has placed great emphasis on policy
communities and **policy networks**, two concepts that try to capture the
degree to which any policy field or sector is populated by a host of government agencies, interest groups, associations, **social movements**, and
other stakeholders, both domestically and globally. It has been argued
that the nature of these policy communities and networks is crucial both
to policy development and to implementation, especially in a globalized
world. On the development side, governments need information that
nongovernmental actors possess. On the implementation side, the more
coherent the interests and organizations in a sector, the easier it is to
implement a decision through partnerships, or the harder it is if stakeholders resist and oppose. In both cases, **global public policy networks**
are becoming increasingly important. This chapter reviews the literature
on networks and then shows how contemporary policymaking practice is
coming to grips with issues of consultation, citizen engagement, opposition, and partnerships.

Politics without interests is an oxymoron, but for many years key strands of the policy literature were prepared to think about policymaking as a rational and largely technical enterprise consisting of priority-setting, options analysis, and careful consideration of costs and benefits. Interests did not enter the picture or, if they did, it was more as a complicating and confusing factor than as a constituent component of the process (Nagel, 1988). As we noted in Chapter 1, the origins of policy analysis in the "policy sciences" were steeped in a sense that policy and politics would be immeasurably improved if the messy interplay of political interests could be tamed (if not completely supplanted) by the rational application of technical and expert knowledge: "Insofar as possible, science and factual information should replace the politics of bargaining and negotiating that characterize pluralist democracy" (Schneider & Ingram, 1997, p. 30).

Chapter 2 described a different world in the making, one where the state is a central but not dominant player in policy processes, where citizens and **interest groups** demand more access to policy development and implementation, and consequently where there is a broader tableau of players and actors. Of course, the financial crisis since 2008 has spawned broad movements on both the left and the right that want to change the fundamentals of the policymaking process (e.g., Occupy Wall Street and the Tea Party). The contemporary study and practice of public policy-making acknowledges this changed reality, and "policy networks" and "policy communities" have emerged as master concepts for conceptualizing new patterns of players and institutions. These are by no means the only frameworks, but they, and a small subset of others, will be examined here in some detail. A sampling of the larger universe of ideas about interests in the policy process is provided in Box 6.1.

Twenty years ago, the idea of policy networks was considered a "new key term" (Marin & Mayntz, 1991, p. 11), one that, when joined to policy communities, constituted "two of the most important conceptual innovations to emerge" in recent studies of the policy process (Atkinson & Coleman, 1992, p. 158; see Thatcher, 1998, for a detailed intellectual history). Even now policy network theory is "a major approach to the study of public policy making in Canada and elsewhere" (Howlett, 2002, p. 235). For some, the concepts are at best "metaphors" (Dowding, 1995), and for others, the overlap and confusion of the complementary network concepts (see Box 6.1) lead to little more than a "debate over terminology" (Lindquist, 1996, p. 219; for more debates over the utility of the concept, see Dowding, 2001; Klijn & Skelcher, 2007; Marsh & Smith, 2000, 2001; Raab, 2001; and Rhodes, 2007). While the terms **"policy community"** and "policy network" are often used interchangeably, the former refers to a wider set of actors who understand the ideas and terminology that define a policy area and

BOX 6.1   CONCEPTUALIZING INTERESTS IN POLICYMAKING: A GLOSSARY

Concept	Definition	Key Source
Advocacy coalitions	• A wide range of actors, including government from all levels, officials, interest organizations, research groups, journalists, and even other countries, who share a belief system about a policy area and over time demonstrate some degree of coordinated activity • An important feature is the idea that policy fields are marked by competing advocacy coalitions.	• Sabatier & Jenkins-Smith, 1993
Discourse coalitions	• A range of policy actors united by broad ideas about the policy field: ideas that include assumptions, images, rhetoric, and linguistic turns • Appears similar to advocacy coalitions but has a stronger emphasis on language and meaning	• Fischer & Forester, 1993
Epistemic community	• Originally developed in the field of international relations, this concept tries to capture the influence of international groups of scientific experts on policymaking, for example, in the environmental field. • Emphasis on the power of ideas and expertise, as expressed through professional organizations or individuals	• Haas, 1992

(continued)

BOX 6.1 (continued)

Concept	Definition	Key Source
Global public policy network	• Quasi-official constellations of state actors, international organizations, and nongovernmental organizations that do more than advocate, but develop and sometimes even implement policies and assist in global coordination	• Reinicke, 1999/2000 • Slaughter, 2004 • Stone, 2004
Iron triangle	• The stable and cozy relationships among U.S. congressional committees, executive agencies (primarily regulatory), and economic interest groups • Implies long-term, stable interactions among a few actors, insulated from the rest of the policy process	• Carter, 1964 • Ripley & Franklin, 1984
Issue network	• Offered as a critique of the "iron triangle" concept in that most policy subsystems were quite fluid and changing, with actors coalescing as necessary around issues, not policy sectors.	• Heclo & Wildavsky, 1974
Policy community	• The wide set of actors interested in and informed about a policy issue, who share at least some common language, but who may be opponents on the issue • Differs from the advocacy coalition approach in that policy communities are presumed to include everyone active in a field	• Coleman & Skogstad, 1990 • Wright, 1988

Term	Description	References
Policy network	• A subset of actors in the policy community who have a consistently higher level of interest in the policy issue, and interact regularly • The most important feature is the discerning of patterns of relations that have consequences for the development and delivery of policy.	• Atkinson & Coleman, 1992 • Van Waarden, 1992
Public interest groups	• Interest groups that advocate on behalf of the public good rather than the direct self-interest of their members • Emphasis is on advocacy for "causes" and the public interest rather than on economic lobbying.	• Berry, 1977 • Pal, 1993 • Phillips, 1993
Social movement organizations	• Interest groups rooted in social transformations of the 1960s that led to new values, new class structures, and new social coalitions (e.g., environmentalism, feminism) • Key feature is the link between organizations and their social foundations, as well as the new dynamics of participation that arise with these organizations.	• Klandermans & Tarrow, 1988 • Melucci, 1989 • Offe, 1987 • Zald, 1987
Subgovernment	• A generic concept that expresses the idea that policy does not get made in a single "system" but in subsystems that consist of microcosms of all the relevant political and institutional actors • This concept was developed in the 1950s as part of pluralist analyses of policymaking.	• Jordan, 1990 • Pross, 1992 • Truman, 1951

have some level of interest in that area, while the latter refers to a subset of those actors whose level of interest is consistently higher and who interact with each other, often due to interdependencies (Compston, 2009; Sørensen & Torfing, 2007). The concerns we will raise in this chapter tap into another issue as well: the degree to which the network concept goes far enough in capturing the realities and contradictions of contemporary policymaking. There has been tremendous pressure in Canada and elsewhere to broaden the policy development process to include more actors such as interest associations, experts, and citizens. Governments today favour alternative modes of program delivery, many of which stress partnerships. **Consultation** and partnering are the order of the day, but managing those relationships is challenging. It becomes even more challenging when we step back and look at networks not simply as domestic players but as internationally and globally engaged. By 2012 the fight against Canada's oil sands, for example, was being led and funded by an international consortium of Canadian and American environmental groups, which the Harper government labelled "special interests" (McCarthy, 2012). These groups were also active in trying to block the Northern Gateway project (a pipeline from Alberta to the British Columbia coast that would ship resources to Asia)—the National Energy Board would hear from some 4000 intervenors (McLean, 2012).

The next section provides background on the communities and networks literature and then proceeds to analyze the ways in which the realities of policy communities and networks are intruding on the consciousness of policymakers and being addressed through consultation, engagement schemes, and partnership models of implementing public programs, but also conflict and opposition. The conclusion returns to the tensions implied by these new pressures. Are our traditional forms of governance up to the challenge?

Communities and Networks: Conceptual Frameworks

APPROACHES AND CONCEPTS

While there has been a harmonic convergence around the ideas of policy networks and communities, that convergence has come from several different directions. Each of the origins suggests a different aspect of the policy process that was inadequately grasped by older theoretical frameworks. The broad backdrop to the various origins of network analyses is a concern with understanding the relationship between state and society and, in particular, the organization of interests in society. The early postwar history of political science and public policy wrestled with the best way of theorizing the connections. The Marxist literature focused on class, while the non-Marxist literature eventually settled on the notion of **interest group pluralism** as its master concept (for a broad survey of the literature, see Baumgartner & Leech, 1998). Truman (1951) and others in that tradition conceptualized society as consisting of an almost limitless array of interests that could mobilize around an almost equally limitless range of issues. If people shared interests, they would likely form groups and lobby government. While pluralism did not use the contemporary terms of **interest intermediation** and **associational system,** it drew a distinctive portrait of each. Interest intermediation, or the way in which societal interests interact with state institutions, was sketched as a highly variable, unpredictable, unstable process that depended on the organization of interests and government institutions in each policy sector or **subgovernment.** The associational system—the patterns of groups and organizations—was also depicted as a rather confusing constellation of small, medium, and large groups, competing and cooperating as they felt necessary.

We can identify at least four major sources of inspiration for the broad concept of networks as it has been applied in a variety of different forms. One of the first breaks with pluralism was over its portrait of the associational system and patterns of policymaking. Empirical case studies showed that patterns were much more stable, and relationships far more closed, than pluralists had suggested. Policymaking took place not in the legislature or the executive but in **iron triangles** that truly were subgovernments in the sense that they might all be operating according to different principles, with different rhythms and often conflicting outcomes. By the mid-1970s the notion of iron triangles seemed like a caricature too and was challenged by the idea of **issue networks** (Heclo, 1978), which were fluid, permeable, and often relying on technical experts and researchers. A second important source of work on networks came from comparative research on industrial performance and economic policy (Katzenstein, 1978a, 1978b, 1978c), which were seen to be dependent on the mix of state structures and associational systems. This work helped feed a debate about the nature of the state and its autonomy from social interests (Nordlinger, 1981; Skocpol, 1986), as well as a subsequent interest in political institutions (Weaver & Rockman, 1993), and the structuring effect of state institutions on associational systems (e.g., Baumgartner, 1996; Coleman, 1994).

A third source of inspiration for network analysis was the growing work on "new social movements" and **public interest groups.** These broad groups were motivated to challenge policy and the state through collective identity and shared values—the classic examples are the civil rights, women's, and gay/lesbian rights movements in the last decades. Another is the environmental movement that has gathered strength around concerns about climate change. The movements are very broad and spawn a large number of organizations that tackle different aspects of the issues—but they can cooperate as networks as necessary. A final source of inspiration for the network concept has been the changing nature of political reality, some elements of which are reflected in the sources described above and some of which were addressed in Chapter 2. Kenis and Schneider (1991, pp. 34–36) captured these changes almost two decades ago, but they resonate well with the current sense of what has changed on the governance landscape. The key changes they highlighted were increasingly crowded policy domains (more actors and stakeholders), decentralization and fragmentation of the state, blurring boundaries between the public and private sectors, the globalization of domestic politics, and the impact of information technologies. They concluded, "Policy networks should therefore be understood as those webs of relatively stable and ongoing relationships which mobilize dispersed resources so that collective (or parallel) action can be orchestrated toward the solution of a common policy problem" (Kenis & Schneider, 1991, p. 36).

We will return to the question of how these new realities affect the policy process and generate network dynamics. At this point, it should be clear why the network/community concept is as important as it is: it has filtered through both policy studies and the broader study of government and politics because it reflects some important shifts in our forms of governance. The increasing complexity of both society and government; the importance of information and its associated technologies; the reliance of government on nongovernmental actors to both formulate and implement policy; shifts in class structure, values, and social groups; better and more coordinated global opposition to certain policies: these are some of the forces that underpin an interest in networks and communities. All of these changes continue to exercise an important influence on modern policymaking, but they have been supplemented and reinforced by the broader factors described in Chapter 2.

In all the variants of network analysis, the central questions are, first, how to conceptualize the relationships between civil society and the state, and second, what difference certain patterns of relations make to policy outcomes. A third question of more relevance to the practitioner is rarely raised in this scholarly work but will be discussed in the second half of this chapter: how to manage and nurture relations between government agencies and their policy constituencies, and how to deal with networked resistance to policy implementation. But first, we will briefly examine the state of the art in conceptualizing policy networks.

Policy Network/Community Analysis

It is one thing to say that policy networks and communities are important; it is another thing to conceptualize those networks. Paul Pross (1995) offered an early definition as well as a diagrammatic portrait of policy communities. Policy communities are "groupings of government agencies, pressure groups, media people, and individuals, including academics, who, for various reasons, have an interest in a particular policy field and attempt to influence it" (p. 265). Figure 6.1 displays what Pross called his "bubble diagram" of policy communities. Note that it divides the policy community in any given policy field into the "subgovernment" and the **attentive public**. Decisionmaking takes place in the subgovernment, which is dominated by large institutions, groups, and core government agencies. Players in the subgovernment, Pross argued, work to limit participation from outsiders. The attentive public are the outsiders whose main influence on the process is to generate ideas and discussion through conferences, publications, and occasional lobbying. In Pross's view, the policy community is actually an insulating device to keep a grip on the process; indeed, he argued that most of the inside players in a policy community try to keep debate within the realm of the technical and routine. Figure 6.1 shows a policy community in which the federal government is dominant, but the basic structure of core agencies in the subgovernment surrounded by other groups and agencies is generic.

There are several limitations to this way of thinking about policy communities. For one thing, it is largely static (though Pross was careful to argue that, in fact, policy communities are constantly in flux). For another, it does not travel well across policy fields. Some areas are dominated by government agencies and largely insulated from outside pressures—fiscal policy comes to mind. But many others are increasingly open to pressures from the attentive public, and that public is not prepared to be polite and keep policymaking at the level of routine. In social and educational policy, for example, fundamental assumptions about the role of governments and funding levels and service delivery are constantly being posed. Another problem is that in this model, foreign governments and foreign pressure groups are relegated to the margins. This metaphor is increasingly obsolete in a globalized world. Finally, the model does not capture varying relations among the actors. The bubbles are large or small, but the figure as a whole gives no idea of the connections (or lack thereof) among the players.

Some of these limitations have been addressed in more refined models of policy networks (to which Pross's work is an important contribution). In a tradition that descends directly from Katzenstein's framework, this approach focuses on two variables: the nature of centralization in the

Figure 6.1   Policy Community "Bubble Diagram"

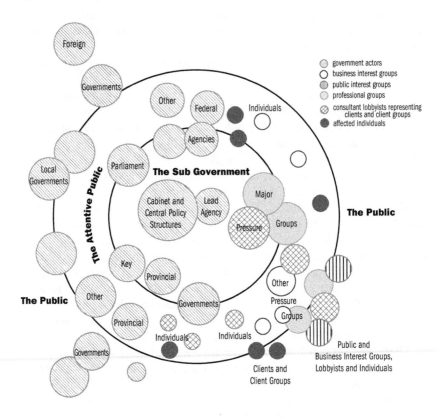

Source: © A.P. Pross October 14, 2011. Contact: 220 Indian Path Rd., R.R. 2, Lunenburg, NS B0J 2C0, Canada. From *Group Politics and Public Policy* (Oxford, 1992) by A. Paul Pross. Reprinted by permission of the author.

state and the centralization or organization of the associational system. This is often termed a "structural approach" to network analysis because it focuses on patterns of relations among actors, patterns that can be mapped and are, to some degree, distinct from the beliefs or ideas that the actors carry in the policy process. If we take a simple dichotomy of high organization/low organization, then we have a straightforward group of four categories to start with. In his early survey of the policy network literature, Lindquist (1992) drew on work by Atkinson and Coleman (1989a, 1989b) and Coleman and Skogstad (1990) to neatly summarize the network types. The degree of organization here means things such as analytic capacity, access to important data and information, ability to act unilaterally, coordination, focus on long-term or short-term issues, and a reactive or anticipatory policy stance (Lindquist, 1992, p. 134). For example, when both the associational system and the government's organization are "low," we can expect a pluralistic, disaggregated system. When government is highly organized and the associational system is not, we can expect a state-dominated policymaking system.

This approach to policy network types has the advantage of variety. It is clear that there will be variation in policy networks across policy fields (though why that is, and if there are any underlying patterns to network organization in a specific political system, is a tougher question). Governments, or more precisely, the core agencies in the subgovernment, can be either well organized, strong, and policy capable or weakly organized without much policy capacity. Atkinson and Coleman (1989a, pp. 80–81) identify four conditions for what they call "state autonomy at the sectoral level": the bureau should have (1) a clear conception of its role and a value system that supports its mandate, as well as support from the minister, (2) a professional ethos distinct from that of its clients, (3) a body of law and regulation that it firmly administers, and (4) the capacity to generate its own information related to its mandate. In addition, the authors argue that state agencies are distinguished by their degree of concentration, by which they mean strong, informal alliances between the political executive and officials. By the same token, associational systems can be weak or strong. Atkinson and Coleman (1989a, pp. 82–83) identify six conditions for a "highly mobilized sector." Business groups (their focus) should have (1) separate associations representing different products and producers, without overlap or competition, (2) only one association that speaks for the sector as a whole, (3) a high proportion of firms represented in the sector's associations, (4) large firms that demonstrate leadership in the sector, (5) in-house capacity to generate information among firms and associations, and (6) associations that can strike deals with government and make them stick with members.

The Atkinson and Coleman schema yields eight categories of networks. The more criteria one adds, of course, the more types of networks one can generate. Van Waarden (1992), for example, argued that the major dimensions of policy networks are "(1) actors, (2) function, (3) structure, (4) institutionalization, (5) rules of conduct, (6) power relations, and (7) actor strategies" (p. 32). He further subdivided each of these dimensions to arrive at a list of 38 criteria defining 13 different types of policy networks! Recognizing that this was unmanageable, Van Waarden recommended concentrating on three criteria: the number and type of societal actors involved, the major functions of networks (e.g., negotiation, consultation, coordination, cooperation in policy formation, or implementation), and the balance of power between state and societal interests.

What do policy networks tell us about policymaking? Most of this network literature has been applied to economic policy fields and assumes that concentration plus organization equals policy-capable systems. While this assumption makes some intuitive sense, it needs to be treated cautiously. For one thing, it has a vaguely undemocratic flavour. The more hierarchical, coordinated, and tidy the policy sector, the fewer opportunities there will be for the "attentive public" to get into the act. Current policy thinking is that the wider the networks and the more competition among players, the better policy outcomes will be. For another, as policy sectors get more complex and more globalized, the demands for information from all sectors and connections among the players rise exponentially. The tightly coordinated policy networks recommended in this literature may not be adequate to the new dynamics of modern policy process. Howlett (2002) zeroes in on this issue by attempting to correlate the nature of policy change with the nature of the policy networks associated with the policy field. He hypothesized that the more closed the subsystem of actors to new ideas and to new actors, the more difficult it would be to make radical changes in policy. His empirical findings demonstrated that "subsystem structure is important because when the same core sets of policy actors are involved in defining policy options ..., the common understanding of a policy problem and the solutions they develop from shared experiences, combined with the durability of subsystem members' interests, promotes 'incremental' change" (p. 259).

In addition to the structure of networks, some approaches argue that the tactics and skills of actors in those networks are an important factor in explaining outcomes (Marsh & Smith, 2000). This view is essentially an attempt to make the concept more dynamic and to understand policy networks as both structures and processes. At any given point, a network can be mapped or visualized in terms of its characteristics (Raab, 2002) or the actual processes, over time, that give rise to those characteristics and that have feedback loops from outcomes that, in turn, affect the network and its behaviour. For example, it's one thing to know that a soccer team is "structurally" weak because of the quality of its players and how they interact on the field. It's quite another thing to observe the same team in action, watching the flow of play, how they react to each other and their opponents. This latter, more dynamic way of viewing networks allows us to bring in both communication/interaction and learning or reacting to the results of that interaction (Pemberton, 2000).

ADVOCACY COALITIONS

The **advocacy coalition** framework (ACF) shares many of the insights of the policy community/subgovernment literature but approaches networks completely differently from the work discussed above. As Paul Sabatier (1993) describes it,

> The advocacy coalition framework (ACF) has at least four basic premises: (1) that understanding the process of policy change—and the role of policy-oriented learning therein—requires a time perspective of a decade or more; (2) that the most useful way to think about policy change over such a time span is through a focus on "policy subsystems," that is, the interaction of actors from different institutions who follow and seek to influence governmental decisions in a policy area; (3) that those subsystems must include an intergovernmental dimension, that is, they must involve all levels of government (at least for domestic policy); and, (4) that public policies (or programs) can be conceptualized in the same manner as belief systems, that is, as sets of value priorities and causal assumptions about how to realize them. (p. 16)*

A distinctive feature of the advocacy coalition framework is its emphasis on the role of ideas and values in the policy process. The framework assumes that both policy actors and policies can be understood in terms of the structure of their belief systems. These systems have three key elements. The first is the deep or normative core, which consists of fundamental axioms about human nature, justice, and priorities among values such as security, health, and life. These ideas are very difficult to change through policy arguments. The second set of ideas is the near (policy) core, and it comprises notions about the proper scope of government activity, distributions of power and authority, orientations on substantive policy conflicts, and basic choices about policy instruments. These are difficult to change but can be altered if experience seriously differs from theory. The final set contains secondary aspects and consists of instrumental decisions needed to implement the policy core, such as decisions about administrative rules, budgetary allocations, and statutory interpretation. These are comparatively easy to shift or change and constitute the bulk of technical policy argumentation.

Figure 6.2 illustrates the main elements of the advocacy coalition framework. Note that it has both a strong dynamic quality as well as a contextual dimension that places policy subsystems into the larger socio-economic and political situation of the polity. The relatively stable parameters are system variables that change only slowly over time but set the stage in terms of institutions as well as resources for policy actors. The external events embrace both unpredictable shocks to the subsystem as well as the interaction effects with other subsystems.

---

*Copyright © 1993 Paul A. Sabatier, Hank C. Jenkins-Smith. Reprinted by permission of Westview Press, a member of the Perseus Books Group.

Figure 6.2   The Advocacy Coalition Framework

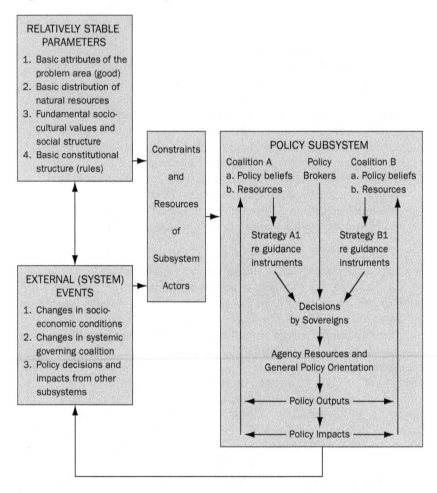

Source: Sabatier, P. A. (1993). Policy change over a decade or more. In P. A. Sabatier & H. Jenkins-Smith (Eds.), *Policy change and learning: An advocacy coalition approach* (p. 18). Boulder, CO: Westview. See also Sabatier and Jenkins-Smith (1999).

Together, these provide constraints, resources, and opportunities for the policy subsystem, which, in the framework, is dominated by a number of advocacy coalitions "composed of people from various governmental and private organizations who share a set of normative and causal beliefs and who often act in concert" (Sabatier, 1993, p. 18). These coalitions pursue competing strategies to achieve their policy objectives, a conflict that is usually mediated by policy brokers interested in compromise. At any given time, the policy sector will be dominated by a winning coalition.

The framework is interested in what it calls "policy oriented learning" or "relatively enduring alterations of thought or behavioral intentions that result from experience and are concerned with the attainment (or revision) of policy objectives" (Sabatier, 1993, p. 19). Most change in policy subsystems occurs because of external shocks, but instrumental learning is important, especially if the goal is better public policy.

The advocacy coalition framework also has several distinct hypotheses about how policy subsystems operate. Among them are: (1) in any subsystem, the lineup of allies and opponents is stable over periods of a decade or so, (2) there is more consensus within coalitions on core beliefs than on secondary ones, (3) government policies rarely change if the original sponsoring coalition is still in power, (4) policies for which there are quantitative data are more amenable to policy learning than areas distinguished by qualitative data, and (5) policy learning across belief systems is more likely when there exists a prestigious forum that forces professionals from all sides to participate.

The advocacy coalition framework is a useful framework for mapping out, in a dynamic fashion, the players, issues, and debates in a policy subsystem. Its incorporation of ideas and values, as well as the impact (usually limited) of expertise and scientific professionals, is welcome. Also, the idea of a coalition gets around the more rigid and insular conceptualization in the network literature that divides subsystems into decisionmakers and attentive, but impotent, publics. Unlike the structural approach to policy networks, however, it does not provide any *a priori* typologies. Indeed, it is relatively weak in describing patterns of relationships either among the coalitions or among brokers.

Policy Communities, Networks, and Policy Management

The various approaches to policy networks discussed above give us the ability to map actors, understand their relationships, and possibly make some predictions about policy processes characterized by different types of networks or coalitions. But do these theories go far enough in capturing the contemporary complexities of the policy process? As we argued, the network idea can be seen as a response to changing political realities. If the realities continue to change, should the concept of networks be refined as well?

THE CONTEMPORARY IMPORTANCE OF POLICY NETWORKS

It is no coincidence that the concepts related to policy communities and networks began to multiply and develop just around the time that associational systems were becoming more complex. Both Canada and the

United States saw a surge in the growth of various social movements and public interest groups in the 1970s (Baumgartner& Mahoney, 2005; Paltiel, 1982; Walker, 1991). While there are no reliable data on broad trends in the last decade, there is no doubt that groups continue to multiply across most sectors, though not likely at the same pace that marked the 1970s and early 1980s. The complexity, intensity, and importance of the associational system and policy networks or communities for policymaking continue to be affected by the various factors outlined in Chapter 2, along with several other factors that define the new mode of governance that is emerging in Canada and elsewhere.

Globalization and increasingly sophisticated forms of communications also continue to change the nature of policy networks. With the early exception of the notion of **epistemic communities** (see Box 6.1)—which draws explicitly on international connections among experts—much of the communities/networks and associational literature still presumes a national or domestic framework. As policy issues increasingly get driven upward to the international level, and as government officials and NGOs increasingly respond by connecting to counterparts everywhere around the globe, the idea that policy networks are primarily domestic is being rethought. Domestic human rights groups, for example, now are routinely connected to international networks (Keck & Sikkink, 1998; Khagram, Riker, & Sikkink, 2002), as are groups organized around population issues, economic development, and the environment. Chapter 1 pointed to the emergence of a "global civil society," something that has been anticipated as an aspect of a new world order for some time (Falk, 1987; Walker, 1988; for a more recent snapshot, see Glasius, Kaldor, & Anheier, 2003; Messner, 2002; and Scholte, 2004). Statistics Canada estimated that, in 2003 (the latest numbers), there were more than 161 000 nonprofit and voluntary organizations in Canada, drawing on 19 million Canadian volunteers (Statistics Canada, 2005). Leading domestic organizations have complex and wide-ranging contacts with counterparts around the world, particularly if they have mandates that encourage cross-border collaboration, such as in environment, trade, or human rights (North-South Institute, 2009). As we noted in Chapter 2, this emergence, while not entirely new (think of the global Anti-Slavery Society of the 1800s), has benefited greatly from modern information and communications technologies. Technology makes it easier for both domestic and international networks to mobilize. While technology is important, conscious choices also have been made to bring nongovernmental actors into the global policy process. International agencies such as the United Nations (UN), for example, particularly in the 1990s, "accelerated the global associational revolution by affirming the right of nongovernmental actors to participate in shaping national and global policies on the environment, population, human rights, economic development, and women" (Batliwala, 2002,

p. 394). International UN conferences on the environment (Rio in 1992), human rights (Vienna in 1993), population (Cairo in 1994), social policy (Copenhagen in 1995), women (Beijing in 1995), and housing and cities (Istanbul in 1996) became platforms for the development of international networks of activists. The Organisation for Economic Co-operation and Development (OECD), as well, has broadened its consultations with "civil society organizations," principally because they have become so numerous and vocal in recent years.

Globalization of policy networks and the impact of technology continue apace in the 2000s. Stone (2008, p. 22) vividly describes what she calls the "global agora" of policy making.

> In the Athenian agora, the mint, shrines and statuary, shops and law courts, the market hall and the council house, and the Assembly were all in physical proximity even if women, slaves, or resident foreigners had little participation in these forums. In the global agora, the international institutions are dispersed between Washington, DC, the Hague, Geneva, and Paris. The nodes of global finance are found in exclusive venues in New York, London, Tokyo, and a few other global cities such as Basle or Davos.... policy networks and self-regulation privatize decision making. Consequently, the institutional locations are dispersed and the boundaries of the global agora are indeterminate and opaque. Policy activity is as likely to take place inside private associations and among nonstate actors as in intergovernmental conferences.

The range of global policy actors is increasing exponentially. The most obvious and visible are international governmental organizations such as the UN, the OECD, and the World Trade Organization (WTO). As we mentioned in previous chapters, this tier has now been supplemented with disaggregated global coordination among state officials, dealing with specific policy sectors such as finance, criminal activity, and corruption. Yet another layer consists of NGOs active on the global level, but connected to domestic concerns (e.g., the environment, human rights). The result is a diffuse system of transnational networks of loosely coordinated governance and, of course, networks of protest and opposition to that governance. These global social movements of protest are organized in ways that do not necessarily reflect common identity or even common interest—they articulate "experiences of displacement" (McDonald, 2006, p. 18).

Technology makes these networks possible—the technology of travel, of communications, of the transfer and circulation of information. A little more than 20 years ago, NGO activists attending UN conferences would have had to queue at the phones to make long-distance calls to their colleagues at home. Cellphones, laptops, PDAs (personal digital assistants), Google, Facebook, Twitter, and email were unknown. That has all obviously changed, and the next wave will build on these platforms and create even more empowered network capabilities. The explosion of social networking technologies in the mid-2000s shows the potential. These technologies were at the heart of the Occupy Wall Street movement in 2011–12 (see Box 6.2).

BOX 6.2   **OCCUPY WALL STREET AND SOCIAL NETWORKING**

Occupy Wall Street (OWS) started in July 2011, as a single blog post that was inspired by the Arab Spring. The blog was started by the anticonsumerism magazine *Adbusters*, based in Vancouver, British Columbia. The movement claimed to have no central leadership or hierarchy. It protested against the "99 per cent," the financial crisis, bailouts, and capitalism in general. Both its strength and weakness were its reliance on networked politics.

July 13, 2011: *Adbusters* publishes a blog post calling for "a shift in revolutionary tactics" and urging tens of thousands of people to converge on lower Manhattan. The plan was to "set up tents, kitchens, peaceful barricades and occupy Wall Street for a few months. Once there, we shall incessantly repeat one simple demand in a plurality of voices." http://www.adbusters.org/blogs/adbusters-blog/occupywallstreet.html

July 23, 2011: The activist hacking group Anonymous extends support to Occupy Wall Street and uses its Twitter feed to promote the demonstration.

September 17, 2011: A rally takes place in Manhattan's Zuccotti Park. Clashes with police are a daily occurrence, and as expected, the Internet savvy OWS movement is quick to post this on YouTube.

September 24, 2011: New York police arrest more than 80 protesters as they spread north to Union Square, further igniting the situation and increasing public awareness. Zuccotti Park (a private park) is now set up as a permanent base for Occupy Wall Street. http://cityroom.blogs.nytimes.com/2011/09/24/80-arrested-as-financial-district-protest-moves-north/

October 1, 2011: More than 700 people are arrested as they march across Brooklyn Bridge. http://www.npr.org/2011/10/01/140983353/about-500-arrested-after-protest-on-brooklyn-bridge

---

October 5, 2011: A poll reports that Occupy Wall Street enjoys a higher approval rating (33 percent) than does the U.S. Congress (14 percent). http://www.npr.org/blogs/thetwo-way/2011/10/05/141089001/ occupy-wall-street-gets-union-backing-approval-rating-tops-congress

October 6, 2011: Protests spread to other U.S. cities.

October 12, 2011: Owners of Zuccotti Park try to clear it, but politicians fear the political backlash, and back off.

October 15, 2011: Worldwide protests take place in 951 cities in 82 countries, as well as at more than 100 colleges across the United States. http://www.npr.org/2011/10/15/141382468/occupy-wall-street-inspires-worldwide-protests

October 16, 2011: President Obama lends his support to Occupy Wall Street.

October 25, 2011: Police fire rubber bullets at protesters in Oakland, California, followed by almost one hundred arrests.

November 5, 2011: An estimated 600 000 people close their bank accounts and open accounts with local credit unions.

November 14, 2011: A New York State judge rules that sleeping bags and tents are unacceptable in public parks. As a result, police begin late-night evictions all over the country, as evidenced by a more emboldened police force.

Occupy Wall Street—and its inspiration in the Arab Spring—would have been impossible without networking and networked technology. As *Wired* put it: "Social media helped pull together protesters around the globe in 2010 and 2011. Egyptian dictator Hosni Mubarak so feared Twitter and Facebook that he shut down Egypt's internet service. A YouTube video posted in the name of Anonymous propelled Occupy Wall Street from an insider memo to national news. And top-trending Twitter hashtags turned Occupy from a ho-hum rally on Sept. 17 into a national and even international movement." http://www.wired.com/threatlevel/2011/12/occupy-facebook/all/1

Another aspect of communities and networks that is changing in the current policy climate is their alignment with levels of government. Two interesting dynamics are involved. The first is the more obvious one of the last few years: as governments devolve more of their policy responsibilities to jurisdictions that are closer to the people or closer to the policy problem (even as they shift some responsibilities upward), policy communities change to reflect the new "core" in the subgovernment. Municipal restructuring in Ontario, for example, compelled amalgamation in cities such as Toronto and Ottawa. Services that were once dispersed are now part of single regional or consolidated governments in both cases, and local policy communities that previously would have been fragmented in terms of different communities now have to re-organize and focus their efforts on a new "core" government. The other dynamic reflects some of the forces cited in Chapter 2, wherein the lines between policy fields get increasingly blurred, thereby encouraging governments to "migrate" into new areas to meet their policy objectives. A good example is the federal government's gas tax transfers to municipalities, which was made permanent in the 2008 budget and provides about $2 billion per year (the program was initially launched by the Liberals in 2004). The rising importance of cities for social and political reasons as key concentrations of the population means that the federal government began to liaise with municipalities and various groups and networks representing them, even though the constitution does not give Ottawa any jurisdiction per se in this field (Hilton & Stoney, 2009).

Finally, governments are increasingly attracted to the ideas of partnerships and **framework policies** (setting parameters, providing funding, but letting others deliver programs). Partly this is due to resource constraints, and shifting responsibilities onto third parties is a way of offloading expenses. However, the still enduring view of the limitations of governments, and the virtues of setting frameworks within which private actors can pursue their interests, places greater emphasis on partnerships between the public and private/nonprofit sectors. Policy communities and networks are important today not only because they represent interests that have to be integrated into the policy process, or information that is crucial to analysis, or even important loci of opposition, but because they are important sinews for implementation and delivery. The concept of working partnerships for the development and delivery of services implies a very different set of relationships than is typically envisaged in the communities/networks literature. That literature focuses more on the political dynamics of interest representation, whereas the challenges of partnerships focus more on the management logistics of joint action to achieve common goals.

The preceding suggests a somewhat confusing array of forces that serve to make policy communities and networks—domestic and global— even more important than they have been in the past, but also perhaps more challenging to integrate into the policy process. The associational system shows no signs of shrinking, and some elements of it, such as those involved in the delivery of public services, may face considerable pressures to expand. Information technologies make possible even wider, global connections of interests and communities, and better organized opposition to government policy. Some movements such as human rights, the environment, and women's issues are truly global in scope. At the same time, some policy issues get driven further down, and so some networks that would have had their centre of gravity at the national level now become truly local or regional.

We can conclude then that contemporary importance of policy networks and communities has not diminished; indeed, it has grown. However, the realities of the policy process continue to change the nature and dynamic of those communities, posing substantial challenges for policymakers. Lindquist (1992, 1996) offered the concept of "stewardship" to capture what these challenges entail. More recently, the same theme has been taken up by Goldsmith and Eggers (2004) with their notion of networked government: "The hierarchical model of government persists, but its influence is steadily waning ... government by network bears less resemblance to a traditional organizational chart than it does to a more dynamic web of computer networks that can organize or reorganize, expand or contract, depending on the problem at hand" (Goldsmith & Eggers, 2004, p. 8). Assuming that policy communities and networks are crucial components in the development and implementation of public policy, a core responsibility for any public manager is the improvement of learning and adaptive capacities, leading to higher levels of policy debate and relevant policy expertise. What this entails in practice depends on the type of policy community or network in question and its specific needs. Capacity-building for intellectual communities may mean enhancing informational resources and communication abilities. For communities involved in policy delivery, it may mean development of organizational capacity through training. The governance dynamics of small, dense networks will be different from networks with larger numbers of members, and so the way in which government interacts with those networks will differ as well (Provan & Kenis, 2008). Whatever it means, thinking about the policy networks and communities relevant to one's policy mandate is a key responsibility for the public manager in 2012 and beyond (Klijn, Edelenbos, & Steijn, 2010; Turrini, Cristofoli, Frosini, & Nasi, 2009).

CONSULTING, ENGAGING, AND PARTNERING

The two big trends in policy community relations or management have been public consultations/citizen engagement and partnerships. Both of these can be viewed cynically. Consultations and citizen engagement can be seen as empty theatrics where interest groups rant predictably while decisionmakers watch the clock, waiting for it all to be over so that they can then go and make the decisions they were going to make anyway. Both also keep everyone busy in a ritualistic way, ultimately validating what decisionmakers wanted to do in the first place (Cooke & Kothari, 2001). Partnerships can be viewed as an attempt to get out of key areas of government responsibility by shifting delivery (but not adequate financial or logistical support) over to the private/nonprofit sector. More subtly, civil society associations can be roped into monitoring performance and results, apparently playing an important role in the policy process, but more or less watching the horse's back end, and not contributing to what goes into the front (Laforest & Phillips, 2007). There is a strong element of truth in these critiques, but they capture, at best, only half of the reality. Policymakers realize the limitations of these strategies (and sometimes manipulate those limitations to their own ends), but they also genuinely believe that consultation in policy design and partnership in policy delivery are important aspects of their jobs. They may not always like it, but they will undertake it, often willingly but also because some form of consultation with the public is increasingly mandated as an aspect of public policy development. There are real puzzles in this engagement, however—challenges that have to be recognized and addressed if governance is to evolve in the next decade. With consultations, the challenge is balancing public demands with the realities of hard decisions. With partnerships, the challenge is balancing accountability with autonomy. With both, the challenge is keeping the public onside in an era of cutbacks and program reductions. We discussed the Occupy Wall Street movement earlier, but it was just a particularly vivid example of other civil society resistance: environmental groups around climate change, seniors against reductions to the Old Age Security, human rights groups opposing crime legislation, health professionals demanding more resources ... The list is endless.

The dictionary definition of consultation is simply to ask for advice or opinion, or a type of communication between two or more parties. Any government that purports to be democratic, one would think, is intrinsically a government that consults. The recent emphasis on consultation therefore seems a bit puzzling from this perspective. If governments have not been consulting when making and implementing policy, then what have they been doing? In fact, there is a more specific meaning to consultation in the current context, one that reflects the forces described in Chapter 2. Almost any form of communication can be seen as a consultation, if by that term we mean only the exchange of information or views. Government polling, for example, might be seen as a form of consultation since it probes for the views of citizens on a wide variety of subjects. The same might be true of task forces, royal commissions, parliamentary committees, referenda, and even elections, all of which are often described as consultations with the public. Using the term this broadly, however, wrings out almost any of its usefulness.

Consultation is different. First, it is usually focused on the operational and programmatic level, as opposed to broad values or directions for policy development. One can still consult about broad values, but these should be clearly connected to specific issues and programs. The interlocutors, therefore, are the agencies responsible for program design and delivery, and the direct clients or stakeholders in the relevant policy community or network. This characteristic distinguishes consultation as a policy management activity from broader forms of political representation, such as parliamentary committee hearings on a piece of legislation, for example. The objective is ongoing development and management of the policy or program in question, not the establishment of parameters for political discussion and debate.

The emphasis on consultation with stakeholders at the federal level goes back to the early 1990s, for example, with the report of the PS2000 Task Force on Service to the Public, which argued that consultation should become a routine aspect of public policymaking (Privy Council Office, 1993). Consultation practices vary quite widely across departments, depending on the issues and the preferences of ministers and senior officials. Ever since 1992, federal departments and agencies have been formally urged to consider public consultation a key part of the development of policy. The 2003 federal *Guide to Making Federal Acts and Regulations* noted that consultation in instrument choice is "essential" to making good choices and includes public consultation under the rubric of "good governance guidelines" (Privy Council Office, 2003). The 2010 federal guide to drafting a **Memorandum to Cabinet**, the policy document outlining the rationale for any proposed bill, requires a statement of a consultation strategy (Privy Council Office, 2010). The rules of strict confidentiality of draft legislation have also been relaxed somewhat, so that consultations can now be undertaken around proposed legislation. The only federal policy area in which consultations are mandated is in the creation of new regulations. The *Cabinet Directive on Streamlining Regulation* states, "Departments and agencies are responsible for identifying interested and affected parties, and for providing them with opportunities to take part in open, meaningful, and balanced consultations at all stages of the regulatory process" (Government of Canada, 2007). The guidelines go on to say:

When undertaking consultations, departments and agencies are to:

- inform and engage Canadians on the nature and implications of the public policy issue based on available evidence, science, or knowledge;
- include Canadians in developing policy objectives;
- set out the process and timelines in a clear manner so that affected parties can organize and provide input; and
- provide timely feedback to Canadians and affected parties on the outcome of the consultations and on the priorities considered in decision making.*

Cabinet directive on streamlining regulation, URL: http://www.tbs-sct.gc.ca/ri-qr/directive/directive01-eng.asp, Department of Treasury Board of Canada Secretariat, 2006. Reproduced with the permission of the Minister of Public Works and Government Services Canada, 2012.

As we noted above, and as these guidelines make clear, the focus of consultations is largely programmatic and practical—it is intended to improve policy development, design, and implementation processes. It is not usually understood to entail a broad discussion and exchange of values that underpin policy proposals. The term for this sort of communication is "citizen engagement."

The shift to "engagement" from "consultation" seems to have occurred, in part, because of the continued lack of trust that citizens have toward government and dissatisfaction with the connotations of consultation—a process that suggests a fairly passive communication of views from stakeholders to government officials who will ultimately make the key decisions. With a decline in trust has come a decline in citizen participation in politics and public deliberation. Voter turnout in the 2004 and 2006 elections was 60.9 percent and 64.7 percent respectively, declining to 59.1 percent in the October 2008 election, but rising in 2011 to 61.1 percent (Elections Canada, 2012). There has been much discussion in recent years of declining public trust in the public service and the public sector, fed by sensationalism around reputed scandals and ongoing exposures such as the Gomery Inquiry. Rebuilding that trust requires better engagement between the public sector and the public (Green & Côté, 2007). One can trace the earliest emergence of the idea of public participation in Canada at the level of local government in the 1970s, linked, in part, to trying to get citizens involved in increasingly complex land-use planning issues (Graham & Phillips, 1998, p. 5) but also because of civil activism and municipal reform movements (Thomas, 1995). But the concern is now part of the wider policy movement discussed in Chapter 1. The OECD, for example, as early as 1999, launched the survey Strengthening Government–Citizen Connections with the participation of 21 member countries and the European Commission: "OECD countries clearly view the issue of government–citizen relations with growing concern. Several countries cited low or declining confidence in public institutions as one motivation for recent initiatives to strengthen government–citizen connections (OECD, 2000, p. 1; also see OECD, 2001). This survey was followed up with a study in 2003 that argued that "active participation is the new frontier" of governance (OECD, 2003), and in 2008 by the Global Forum on Governance, which concluded, "Citizen-centricism, citizen engagement, and the need to incorporate the public's perspective in policy thinking were central in each session" (OECD, 2008). A 2010 ministerial meeting of the OECD's Public Governance Committee was organized around the theme of "open government" (OECD, 2010).

The concern to engage citizens is also, in part, a reflection of a deeper concern about the eroding democratic foundation of contemporary politics and policymaking, particularly in an era of financial crisis. Citizen engagement thus has both an instrumental dimension—trying to tap into the knowledge and perspectives of citizens, unfiltered by media or interest groups—and a legitimating dimension—trying to shore up the public's support for policy initiatives—often unpleasant ones—by bringing the public more actively into the process. Building open government has become a major project for OECD members. Almost all to date have Freedom of Information Acts and an Ombudsman's office (OECD, 2010). In line with the argument we made in Chapter 5 about new trends in public management, the emphasis on consultation and engagement has deepened into a new concept of "social accountability." The range of efforts is wide, and includes binding legal strictures on information exposure, support for specific target groups, the use of information and communication technologies (ICTs), and engagement with media or advocacy groups (Caddy, Peixoto, & McNeil, 2006). The European Union maintains the website "Your Voice in Europe," a one-stop shop for all EU-wide consultations on all policy issues. Citizens can participate in Internet-based consultations by accessing discussion papers and other documents on the website through a knowledge base, and then answer questionnaires. Live chat with policymakers is also available (European Commission, 2012).

The key challenge in citizen engagement is developing techniques to engage citizens. Consultations, as we described them above, can naturally be assumed to attract stakeholders and interest groups, but even in that context it is a challenge to go beyond simple tabling of inflexible views and to move to a more deliberative process. Seasoned policymakers wince at the idea of consultation that simply collects together "the usual suspects" who have a particular axe to grind. Citizen engagement is exactly what it says—somehow getting ordinary citizens to come forward and thoughtfully engage on a policy question. Various innovative techniques have been suggested to genuinely bring citizens into an informed dialogue and exchange with government. Some, like **study circles**, are designed to facilitate decisionmaking at the community level. Study circles are championed by Everyday Democracy in Connecticut and the model entails bringing people from all over a neighbourhood, town, or city together in groups of eight to 12 who work through the same issue for a period of time and then all come together to share ideas and develop plans. The technique has been used in hundreds of communities in the United States to address citizens' concerns about schools, youth, racial equity, and other issues (Everyday Democracy, 2012).

Another technique is **citizens' juries** or panels, originally developed by the Jefferson Center for New Democratic Processes in Minnesota. A randomly selected jury of about 18 individuals hears from a variety of expert witnesses and deliberates together on a given issue. The jury then presents its recommendations to the public. The technique has been used in the United States to address issues such as national healthcare reform, budget priorities, environmental issues, and elections, as well as by organizations in Great Britain, Germany, Denmark, Spain, Australia, and other countries. It still is used in some instances, but the Center itself was not able to generate enough "repeat business" to keep itself growing (Jefferson Center, 2012). This small-scale consultation stands in contrast to **deliberative polling,** a technique pioneered by the American social scientist James Fishkin (1991, 2009; Fishkin & Laslett, 2003). It involves between 250 and 600 people who form a representative sample of the community and who are polled for their preliminary views on an issue. They then engage in small-group discussions and pose questions to experts and politicians, and are once again polled at the end of the process once they have had the opportunity to reflect and deliberate. Similar techniques include standing panels, community issue groups, and consensus conferences. Fishkin has even suggested a national version—"deliberation day"—to be held every presidential election day (Ackerman & Fishkin, 2004).

It is easier to list principles and techniques than to put them into practice, particularly by governments; most of the techniques cited above were pioneered and are used by nonprofit organizations. Whereas consultation and engagement at all levels of government have become a sort of rhetorical policy mantra, the realities and challenges are more complex. For one thing, consultations are only one stream of information and advice into the policy process, but those who are consulted naturally want to see their efforts reflected in policy outputs. As well, the openness demanded by consultation can run against the organizational grain of government, which sometimes requires a high degree of confidentiality (e.g., sensitive information about third parties) or strong executive action (e.g., responding to an emergency). The financial crisis has also created some contradictory dynamics around state–citizen relations. On the one hand, public disaffection has risen dramatically across Europe (riots in Greece, Spain, and Ireland) and in the United States (the Tea Party and Occupy Wall Street movements). On the other hand, the strong medicine needed to deal with the crisis led to the appointment of "governments of technocrats" (unelected "experts") in Greece and Italy. To the extent that governments at all levels feel the need to introduce unpopular policies, particularly cuts to services and social protection, they will avoid "citizen engagement" since they know perfectly well what the outcome will be— howls of pain and outrage.

PARTNERSHIPS AND HORIZONTAL MANAGEMENT

There is some overlap between the concept of consultation and of partnership. Indeed, Kernaghan's (1993) seminal classification of partnerships has consultation as one end of a continuum of power sharing over decisions and implementation: (1) consultative partnerships: exchanging advice and information, (2) contributory partnerships: money or other forms of support for projects managed by a third party, (3) operational partnerships: sharing work in achieving goals, but the main decisions are still made by one partner, usually government, and (4) collaborative partnerships: sharing both work and decisionmaking (pp. 62–65). While it seems puzzling that public officials would willingly relinquish some of their autonomy, there has been a rising interest in collaborative partnerships, both with private sector entities and nonprofit, noncommercial organizations such as those in the social services sector. And partnerships can also involve different government departments, either at the same level or across jurisdictions. The reasons for partnering reflect our earlier arguments in this chapter. Governments want to save money, and partnerships with firms or nonprofit organizations can be a way (possibly) of offloading services. But governments also recognize some of their own limitations in directly delivering services, and so partnerships can be a means of improving service delivery, getting better feedback, and encouraging civic engagement.

There are many forms of partnerships (Rosenau, 2000), but as a general mode of implementation (and of policymaking), partnership is seen as a major departure as well as a major challenge. The reason is that traditional governance is hierarchical and sees government authorities as having the core responsibility for delivering services. True partnerships imply a degree of equality and shared responsibility (Auditor General of Canada, 2005). From a management perspective, that means that new skills of collaboration and coordination will be required as partnerships become more pervasive. This type of management is called "horizontal" management and has attracted a great deal of attention recently:

> Horizontal management can be defined as the coordination and management of a set of activities between two or more organizational units, where the units in question do not have hierarchical control over each other and where the aim is to generate outcomes that cannot be achieved by units working in isolation. (Bakvis & Juillet, 2004, p. 9)

Governments around the world are increasingly concerned with policy coherence and developing "horizontality." In a sense, any government is itself an example of horizontal management; cabinets are, for example, mechanisms to develop collective decisionmaking across portfolios. Central agencies such as the Privy Council Office or the Treasury Board are also mechanisms of coordination. What is new is that this interest in horizontality is extending to all levels of government bureaucracy, with the growing expectation that government departments will work more closely and collaboratively with each other to solve problems that cut across bureaucratic jurisdictions, that they will work more closely and collaboratively with other departments in other jurisdictions, and that they will increasingly partner with nongovernmental actors. While horizontal management is not necessarily the best way to approach every policy issue, at the federal level there is a sense that it is a reality that is here to stay. In fact, in 2010, the Treasury Board issued guidelines on developing "results-based management and accountability frameworks" (RMAFs) for horizontal initiatives (Treasury Board of Canada, 2010).

It is best to think of horizontal management as a continuum running from a minimalist to a maximalist level of coordination (Peters, 1998). The minimal level entails nothing more than mutual recognition of activities and an effort not to duplicate or interfere. At the maximalist end of the continuum, one will find partnerships based on formal agreements about objectives, resource sharing, and coordinating procedures. Partnering arrangements can be of various types: consultative (sharing information), operational (sharing work), or truly collaborative (sharing decisionmaking). Over 10 years ago, the Auditor General of Canada issued a report on best practices in horizontal management, highlighting the importance of coordinating structures, common objectives, performance measurement, results orientation, and reporting. Around the same time, the Canada School of Public Service issued a report arguing that the key dimensions of horizontal management are mobilizing teams and networks, developing shared frameworks, building supportive structures, and maintaining momentum (Hopkins, Couture, & Moore, 2001). As with the best practices above, these call for different skill sets from public managers. They also pose important organizational challenges. Perhaps the preeminent one is accountability. When governments enter into partnerships, by necessity they relinquish power and control. In cases of substantial loss of control, however, the government agency is still in some measure responsible for the expenditure of public funds and for outcomes, yet those expenditures and outcomes may be determined more by the partner than by the government agency. Government organizations are used to operating in a hierarchical, top-down fashion, but partnering implies spheres of autonomy as well as coordination for the different partners. How should they combine that autonomy, the prime contribution of the partnership agreement, with accountability for performance and results? As Langford put it: "As part of this move, contemporary managers must develop the relationship-building, negotiating, contract management, risk assessment, and performance measurement skills required to work effectively in a partnership world" (Langford, 1999, p. 108).

A good example of the challenge is Canada's Asia-Pacific Gateway and Corridor Initiative. Launched in 2005, it aims to make Canada and the West Coast the main conduit for goods, services, and cultural exchanges between Asia and North America. Since it means moving goods from

Asia through British Columbia, and then through rail and highway transport to Ontario and the United States, several provinces are involved, as are municipalities and private companies and, of course, Asian governments such as China, Hong Kong, and Singapore. The initiative refers to partnerships as a component of "21st century governance":

> Since various issues directly impacting Gateway and Corridor effectiveness and exploitation interact with each other in important ways, they are best addressed in an integrated fashion rather than in isolation. Partnership is essential. The Gateway approach offers a coherent framework for joint leadership and focused collaboration among the different public and private sector actors who control or influence the key issues.

> New approaches· to governance, reflecting an outward-looking perspective on global commerce, are necessary to ensure maximum efficiency of existing assets. For the Government of Canada, there is an internal dimension as well. Various federal departments have responsibilities that directly impact the Gateway. The immediate measures identified under this Initiative include activities led by Transport Canada, the Department of Foreign Affairs and International Trade, Western Economic Diversification Canada, the Canada Border Services Agency, Parks Canada and Human Resources and Social Development Canada. An ongoing element of the Initiative will be a policy renewal agenda that aims in part to work across the "silos" to advance the long-term development and exploitation of the Gateway and Corridor. (Government of Canada, 2012)*

A specific variant of the more generic notion of partnering is **public–private partnerships** (P3s or PPPs). The Canadian Council for Public-Private Partnerships defines such partnerships in this way: "A cooperative venture between the public and private sectors, built on the expertise of each partner, that best meets clearly defined public needs through the appropriate allocation of resources, risks and rewards" (2012). There are various models of public–private partnerships that combine risk and resources in different ways:

> **Design-Build (DB):** The private sector designs and builds infrastructure to meet public sector performance specifications, often for a fixed price, so the risk of cost overruns is transferred to the private sector. (Many do not consider DB's to be within the spectrum of PPP's).

Finance Only: A private entity, usually a financial services company, funds a project directly or uses various mechanisms such as a long-term lease or bond issue.

Operation & Maintenance Contract (O & M): A private operator, under contract, operates a publicly owned asset for a specified term. Ownership of the asset remains with the public entity.

Build-Finance: The private sector constructs an asset and finances the capital cost only during the construction period.

Design-Build-Finance-Maintain (DBFM): The private sector designs, builds, and finances an asset and provides hard facility management (hard fm) or maintenance services under a long-term agreement.

Design-Build-Finance-Maintain-Operate (DBFMO): The private sector designs, builds, and finances an asset, provides hard and/or soft facility management services as well as operations under a long-term agreement.

Build-Own-Operate (BOO): The private sector finances, builds, owns, and operates a facility or service in perpetuity. The public constraints are stated in the original agreement and through ongoing regulatory authority.

Concession: A private sector concessionaire undertakes investments and operates the facility for a fixed period of time after which the ownership reverts back to the public sector.
(Canadian Council for Public-Private Partnerships, 2012)

As of February 2012, there were 162 public–private partnerships across Canada, prominent examples being Confederation Bridge, Highway 407 Electronic Toll Route, Moncton Water Treatment Plant, St. Lawrence Seaway Commercialization, Kelowna Skyreach Place, and the Bruce Nuclear Power Plant lease. As well, there were more than 50 P3 hospitals in operation or development. One measure of the seriousness with which all levels of government now take such partnerships is Ottawa's pledge to create a $1.2 billion Public-Private Partnerships Fund to increase opportunities for infrastructure development. The fund, announced in the 2007 federal budget, is now managed by PPP Canada, a Crown corporation with an independent board of directors. Nonetheless, as a collaborative strategy, public–private partnerships are still opposed by some as "hybrids" of incompatible private-sector and public sector logics, and moreover, not as beneficial and efficient as is touted by its proponents (Loxley & Loxley, 2010). The ingredients of success seem to be clear communication and buy-in from all partners, credible evaluations, fair sharing of risks, strong management, effective and continuous external evaluation, and good dispute resolution mechanisms (Hubbard & Paquet, 2007).

Conclusion

This chapter has examined the two sides of policy communities and networks: (1) the academic side with its emphasis on the explanation and description of patterns of associational–state linkages in policy domains, and (2) the public management approach to consultation and partnerships. The two overlap in important ways but are also distinct. They share the insight that contemporary governance entails a substantial degree of private, nonprofit, and public cooperation and interaction at every phase of the policy process, and that the quality of policy outcomes often depends on the nature of these interactions. However, the emphasis in the policy communities and networks literature has been on describing the actors and evaluating the implications of the broad character of their relationships in terms of associational and organizational cohesion. The work on consultation/engagement and partnerships has had a more microscopic and management orientation: how do we get these things to work at the level of a specific program or policy issue?

In keeping with the theme of this book, both streams converge on the same idea: modern policymaking cannot be directed by government and simply supplemented by representations from the public or interest groups (Goldsmith & Eggers, 2004). That model died years ago, as analysts and practitioners realized the importance of new social movements, public interest groups, more complex national and global associational systems, and the strategic value of information. As we argued in this chapter, at one level networks are, if anything, more important now than before, even as their fundamental characteristics have changed in light of globalization and other forces. Government has a more sober assessment of its own capacities. It cannot monopolize information anymore, and, in many policy areas, is heavily dependent on the specialized expertise or experience of its partners. Even with the resurgence of the role of government after 2008, it will still be as much a maestro as a master. The key point about networks is that they are systems of mutual interdependence where no one actor—including government—can dominate the rest. The government's policy role remains crucial, but it shifts its focus to network management strategies. "Network management provides a way for actors to cooperate without solutions being forcibly imposed or cooperation becoming redundant as a result of decentralization or privatization" (Kickert & Koppenjan, 1997, p. 43).

Does that mean that government is necessarily weaker? In some ways, yes. In other ways, however, network management suggests a broadening and deepening of government influence through its leverage in policy networks and partnerships. The crucial question is the degree to which government remains a leader in these networks and partnerships. Also, we sometimes forget the other powers and instruments that governments have at their disposal to encourage private–public partnerships, what some analysts have referred to as "**strategic governance**" (de Bruijn & ten Heuvelhof, 1995; Rethemeyer, 2005). Policy networks, for example, are characterized by the interdependency of actors, the complexity of coalitions and organizational players, the reluctance to cooperate because of uncertainties about real interests and ultimate outcomes, and instability in that players shift constantly. Government can facilitate the effectiveness of networks by addressing these characteristics; for example, by distributing information, by helping organizations and interests coalesce and participate, and by developing novel proposals for exchange and cooperation.

If policy communities and networks are as important to the policy process as we suspect, then policy analysis and policy management have to change considerably. Analysis has to come to terms with the fact that policy outcomes depend crucially on the actors in the community and the nature of the network. Policy management has to shift its attention to new organizational forms of public sector and private sector cooperation and interaction.

As we noted earlier, there is a host of challenges that come with this new importance of networks. One such challenge is the ability to balance the more traditional forms of governance (which do not go away entirely) with network practices. Another one is ensuring that the participation of citizens is real, is influential, and reinforces and supports democratic practice (Klijn & Skelcher, 2007; Laforest & Phillips, 2007).

Yet another—perhaps today the deepest challenge of the three—is dealing with networked opposition and resistance. Our brief discussion of the Occupy Wall Street movement showed that it was highly disaggregated and disorganized, but grew through networked connections and replicants. Today's policymaking has to take on complex problems— from global warming to recession to aging populations—problems that demand networked governance that connects societal stakeholders and government players to work together. Big problems create big wins and big losses, and consequently, networks of defence and resistance. This network management issue has barely been addressed in the literature, but it stares policymakers in the face every day.

One tool that policymakers have is to show the evidence of what works and what doesn't. Doing that requires evidence and evaluation. The next chapter explores that tool, both its blunt and sharp edges.

KEY TERMS

advocacy coalition—a wide range of actors, including government from all levels, officials, interest organizations, research groups, journalists, and even other countries, who share a belief system about a policy area and over time demonstrate some degree of coordinated activities

associational system—constellation of small, medium, and large groups, competing and cooperating as they feel necessary

attentive public—the outsiders whose main influence on the process is to generate ideas and discussion through conferences, publications, and occasional lobbying

citizens' jury—a randomly selected jury of about 18 individuals that hears from a variety of expert witnesses and deliberates together on a given issue

consultation—process whereby government gauges the views and opinions of nongovernmental organizations, citizen groups, and associations

deliberative polling—a technique that usually involves between 250 and 600 people who form a representative sample of the community and who are first polled on their views on an issue, informed in some depth on that issue, and then polled again

epistemic community—originally developed in the field of international relations, this concept tries to capture the influence of international groups of scientific experts on policymaking; for example, in the environmental field

framework policies—a technique whereby government sets the broad parameters for policy outcomes but lets others deliver programs

global public policy networks—quasi-official constellations of state actors, international organizations, and nongovernmental organizations that do more than advocate, but develop and sometimes even implement policies and assist in global coordination

interest group—a voluntary, membership-based organization that lobbies governments on issues of concern to its members

interest group pluralism—a system in which a wide variety of interests succeed in getting themselves heard throughout government

interest intermediation—the process whereby societal interests interact with state institutions

iron triangle—the stable and cozy relationships among congressional committees, executive agencies (primarily regulatory), and economic interest groups

issue network—offered as a critique of the "iron triangle" concept in that most policy subsystems were quite fluid and changing, with actors coalescing as necessary around issues, not policy sectors

Memorandum to Cabinet—the policy document outlining the rationale for any proposed bill, which now must state what consultations the cabinet minister has undertaken or plans to undertake

policy community—the actors in a policy network, presumably those who share at least some common language and conceptual reference points but who may be opponents on the issue

policy network—the patterns of relations among members of the policy community

public interest group—interest groups whose emphasis is on advocacy for "causes" and the public interest rather than economic lobbying

public–private partnership—a cooperative venture between the public and private sectors, built on the expertise of each partner, that meets well-defined public needs through the appropriate allocation of resources, risks, and rewards

social movement—an informal network of organizations and individuals who, on the basis of a collective identity and shared values, engage in political and/or cultural struggle intended to break or expand the boundaries of the existing system, and undertake collective action designed to affect both state and society

strategic governance—the use of the powers and instruments that governments have at their disposal to encourage private–public partnerships, networks, framework agreements, and broad direction for the policy system as a whole

study circles—a consultation technique designed to facilitate broadly based, grassroots decisionmaking at the community level

subgovernment—a generic concept that expresses the idea that policy does not get made in a single "system" but in subsystems that consist of microcosms of all the relevant political and institutional actors

FURTHER READINGS

Caddy, J., Peixoto, T., & McNeil, M. (2007). *Beyond public scrutiny: Stocktaking of social accountability in OECD countries* (World Bank Institute Working Paper). Retrieved from http://www.oecd.org/dataoecd/43/3/38983242.pdf

Fishkin, J. S. (2009). *When the people speak: Deliberative democracy and public consultation.* Oxford: Oxford University Press.

Goldsmith, S., & Eggers, W. (2004). *Governing by network: The new shape of the public sector.* Washington, DC: Brookings Institution Press.

Keck, M. E., & Sikkink, K. (1998). *Activists beyond borders: Advocacy networks in international politics.* Ithaca, NY: Cornell University Press.

Kickert, W. J. M., Klijn, E.-H., & Koppenjan, J. F. M. (Eds.). (1997). *Managing complex networks: Strategies for the public sector.* London, UK: Sage.

Klijn, E.-H., Steijn, B., & Edelenbos, J. (2010). The impact of network management on outcomes in governance networks. *Public Administration, 88*(4), 1063–1082.

Sabatier, P. A., & Jenkins-Smith, H. (Eds.). (1993). *Policy change and learning: An advocacy coalition approach.* Boulder, CO: Westview.

REFERENCES

Ackerman, B., & Fishkin, J. S. (2004). *Deliberation day.* New Haven, CT: Yale University Press.

Atkinson, M. M., & Coleman, W. D. (1989a). *The state, business, and industrial change in Canada.* Toronto, ON: University of Toronto Press.

Atkinson, M. M., & Coleman, W. D. (1989b). Strong states and weak states: Sectoral policy networks in advanced capitalist economies. *British Journal of Political Science, 19,* 47–67.

Atkinson, M. M., & Coleman, W. D. (1992, April). Policy networks, policy communities and the problems of governance. *Governance, 5,* 154–180.

Auditor General of Canada. (2005). *Report of the Auditor General of Canada to the House of Commons.* Chapter 4: Managing horizontal initiatives. Retrieved from http://www.oag-bvg.gc.ca/internet/docs/20051104ce.pdf

Bakvis, H., & Juillet, L. (2004). *The horizontal challenge: Line departments, central agencies, and leadership.* Ottawa, ON: Canada School of Public Service.

Batliwala, S. (2002, December). Grassroots movements as transnational actors: Implications for global civil society. *Voluntas: International Journal of Voluntary and Nonprofit Organizations, 13,* 393–408.

Baumgartner, F. R. (1996, January). Public interest groups in France and the United States. *Governance, 9,* 1–22.

Baumgartner, F. R., & Leech, B. L. (1998). *Basic interests: The importance of groups in politics and in political science*. Princeton, NJ: Princeton University Press.

Baumgartner, F. R., & Mahoney, C. (2005). Social movements, the rise of new issues, and the public agenda. In D. S. Meyer, V. Jenness, & H. Ingram (Eds.), *Routing the opposition: Social movements, public policy, and democracy* (pp. 65–86). Minneapolis, MN: University of Minnesota Press.

Berry, J. M. (1977). *Lobbying for the people: The political behavior of public interest groups*. Princeton, NJ: Princeton University Press.

Caddy, J., Peixoto, T., & McNeil, M. (2007). *Beyond public scrutiny: Stocktaking of social accountability in OECD countries* (World Bank Institute Working Paper). Retrieved from http://www.oecd.org/dataoecd/43/3/38983242.pdf

Canadian Council for Public-Private Partnerships. (2012). Definitions. Retrieved from http://www.pppcouncil.ca/resources/about-ppp/definitions.html

Carter, D. (1964). *Power in Washington: A critical look at today's struggle in the nation's capital*. New York, NY: Random House.

Coleman, W. D. (1994, July). Banking, interest intermediation and political power. *European Journal of Political Research, 26*, 31–58.

Coleman, W. D., & Skogstad, G. (1990). Policy communities and policy networks: A structural approach. In W. D. Coleman & G. Skogstad (Eds.), *Organized interests and public policy* (pp. 14–33). Toronto, ON: Copp-Clark.

Compston, H. (2009). *Policy networks and policy change: Putting policy network theory to the test*. Houndmills, UK: Palgrave Macmillan.

Cooke, B., & Kothari, U. (Eds.). (2001). *Participation: The new tyranny*. London, UK: Zed Books.

de Bruijn, J. A., & ten Heuvelhof, E. F. (1995). Policy networks and governance. In D. Weimer (Ed.), *Institutional design* (pp. 161–179). Boston, MA: Kluwer Academic Publishers.

Dowding, K. (1995). Model or metaphor? A critical review of the policy network approach. *Political Studies, 43*, 136–158.

Dowding, K. (2001, March). There must be end to confusion: Policy networks, intellectual fatigue, and the need for political science methods courses in British universities. *Political Studies, 49*, 89–105.

Elections Canada. (2012). Voter turnout at federal elections and referendums. Retrieved from http://www.elections.ca/content.aspx?section=ele&dir=turn&document=index&lang=e

European Commission. (2012). Your voice in Europe. Retrieved from http://ec.europa.eu/yourvoice/index%5Fen.htm

Everyday Democracy. (2012). *Ideas and tools for community change.* Retrieved from http://www.everyday-democracy.org/en/Index.aspx

Falk, R. (1987). The global promise of social movements: Explorations at the edge of time. *Alternatives, 7,* 173–196.

Fischer, F., & Forester, J. (Eds.). (1993). *The argumentative turn in policy analysis and planning.* Durham, NC: Duke University Press.

Fishkin, J. S. (1991). *Democracy and deliberation: New directions for democratic reform.* New Haven, CT: Yale University Press.

Fishkin, J. S. (2009). *When the people speak: Deliberative democracy and public consultation.* Oxford, UK: Oxford University Press.

Fishkin, J. S., & Laslett, P. (Eds.). (2003). *Debating deliberative democracy.* Malden, MA: Blackwell.

Fitzpatrick, T. (2000). *Horizontal management: Trends in governance and accountability.* Action-Research Roundtable on the Management of Horizontal Issues. Ottawa, ON: Canada School of Public Service. Retrieved from http://www.csps-efpc.gc.ca/pbp/pub/pdfs/W2_e.pdf

Geist, M. (2008). Fair copyright for Canada. Retrieved from http://www.facebook.com/group.php?gid=6315846683

Glasius, M., Kaldor, M., & Anheier, H. (2003). *Global civil society 2002.* Oxford, UK: Oxford University Press.

Goldsmith, S., & Eggers, W. D. (2004). *Governing by network: The new shape of the public sector.* Washington, DC: Brookings Institution Press.

Government of Canada. (2007). *Cabinet directive on streamlining regulation.* Retrieved from http://www.tbs-sct.gc.ca/ri-qr/directive/directive01-eng.asp

Government of Canada. (2012). Canada's Pacific Gateway: 21st century governance. Retrieved from http://www.pacificgateway.gc.ca/launchbooklet4d.html

Graham, K. A., & Phillips, S. D. (1998). Making public participation more effective: Issues for local government. In K. A. Graham & S. D. Phillips (Eds.), *Citizen engagement: Lessons in participation from local government* (pp. 1–24). Toronto, ON: Institute of Public Administration of Canada.

Green, I., & Côté, A. (2007). *Leading by example.* Ottawa, ON: Public Policy Forum.

Haas, P. M. (1992, Winter). Introduction: Epistemic communities and international policy coordination. *International Organization, 46,* 1–35.

Heclo, H. (1978). Issue networks and the executive establishment. In A. King (Ed.), *The new American political system* (pp. 87–124). Washington, DC: American Enterprise Institute for Public Policy Research.

Heclo, H., & Wildavsky, A. (1974). *The private government of public money*. London, UK: Macmillan.

Hilton, R., & Stoney, C. (2009). Federal gas tax transfers: Politics and perverse policy. In A. M. Maslove (Ed.), *How Ottawa spends, 2009–2010: Economic upheaval and political dysfunction* (pp. 175–193). Montréal and Kingston: McGill-Queen's University Press.

Hopkins, M., Couture, C., & Moore, E. (2001). *Moving from the heroic to the everyday: Lessons learned from leading horizontal projects*. Roundtable on the Management of Horizontal Initiatives. Ottawa, ON: Canada School of Public Service. Retrieved from http://www.csps-efpc.gc.ca/pbp/pub/pdfs/P99_e.pdf

Howlett, M. (2002, June). Do networks matter? Linking policy network structure to policy outcomes: Evidence from four Canadian policy sectors 1990–2000. *Canadian Journal of Political Science, 35*, 235–267.

Hubbard, R., & Paquet, G. (2007). Public–private partnerships: P3 and the "porcupine problem." In G. B. Doern (Ed.), *How Ottawa spends, 2007–2008: The Harper Conservatives—Climate of change* (pp. 254–272). Montréal and Kingston: McGill-Queen's University Press.

Jefferson Center. (2012). Home page. Retrieved from http://www.jefferson-center.org

Jordan, G. (1990). Subgovernments, policy communities and networks: Refilling the old bottles? *Journal of Theoretical Politics, 2*, 319–338.

Katzenstein, P. J. (1978a). *Between power and plenty: Foreign economic policies of advanced industrial states*. Madison, WI: University of Wisconsin Press.

Katzenstein, P. J. (1978b). Introduction: Domestic and international forces and strategies of foreign economic policy. In P. J. Katzenstein (Ed.), *Between power and plenty: Foreign economic policies of advanced industrial states* (pp. 3–22). Madison, WI: University of Wisconsin Press.

Katzenstein, P. J. (1978c). Conclusion: Domestic structures and strategies of foreign economic policy. In P. J. Katzenstein (Ed.), *Between power and plenty: Foreign economic policies of advanced industrial states* (pp. 295–336). Madison, WI: University of Wisconsin Press.

Keck, M. E., & Sikkink, K. (1998). *Activists beyond borders: Advocacy networks in international politics*. Ithaca, NY: Cornell University Press.

Kenis, P., & Schneider, V. (1991). Policy networks and policy analysis: Scrutinizing a new analytical toolbox. In B. Marin & R. Mayntz (Eds.), *Policy networks: Empirical evidence and theoretical considerations* (pp. 25–59). Boulder, CO: Westview.

Kernaghan, K. (1993, Spring). Partnership and public administration: Conceptual and practical considerations. *Canadian Public Administration, 36,* 57–76.

Khagram, S., Riker, J. V., & Sikkink, K. (Eds.). (2002). *Restructuring world politics: Transnational social movements, networks, and norms.* Minneapolis, MN: University of Minnesota Press.

Kickert, W. J. M., & Koppenjan, J. F. M. (1997). Public management and network management: An overview. In W. J. M. Kickert, E.-H. Klijn, & J. F. M. Koppenjan (Eds.), *Managing complex networks: Strategies for the public sector* (pp. 35–61). London, UK: Sage.

Klandermans, B., & Tarrow, S. (1988). Mobilization into social movements: Synthesizing European and American approaches. *International Social Movement Research, 1,* 1–38.

Klijn, E.-H., & Skelcher, C. (2007). Democracy and governance networks: Compatible or not? *Public Administration, 85*(3), 587–608.

Klijn, E.-H., Edelenbos, J., & Steijn, B. (2010). The impact of network management on outcomes in governance networks. *Public Administration, 88*(4), 1063–1082.

Laforest, R., & Phillips, S. (2007). Citizen engagement: Rewiring the policy process. In M. Orsini & M. Smith (Eds.), *Critical policy studies* (pp. 67–90). Vancouver, BC: UBC Press.

Langford, J. (1999). Governance challenges of public-private partnerships. In S. Delacourt & D. G. Lenihan (Eds.), *Collaborative government: Is there a Canadian way?* (pp. 105–111). Toronto, ON: Institute of Public Administration of Canada.

Lindquist, E. A. (1992, Summer). Public managers and policy communities: Learning to meet new challenges. *Canadian Public Administration, 35,* 127–159.

Lindquist, E. A. (1996). New agendas for research on policy communities: Policy analysis, administration, and governance. In L. Dobuzinskis, M. Howlett, & D. Laycock (Eds.), *Policy studies in Canada: The state of the art* (pp. 219–241). Toronto, ON: University of Toronto Press.

Loxley, J., & Loxley, S. (2010). *Public service, private profits: The political economy of public/private partnerships in Canada.* Black Point, NS: Fernwood Publishing.

McCarthy, S. (2012, January 21). The day the oil-sands battle went global. *The Globe and Mail.* Retrieved from http://license.icopyright.net/user/viewFreeUse.act?fuid=MTUzODUzNTU%3D

McDonald, K. (2006). *Global movements: Action and culture.* Oxford, UK: Blackwell.

McLean, T. (2012, February 1). Officials mum on cost of Gateway hearings. *Toronto Sun*. Retrieved from http://m.torontosun.com/2012/02/01/officials-mum-on-cost-of-gateway-hearings

Marin, B., & Mayntz, R. (1991). Introduction: Studying policy networks. In B. Marin & R. Mayntz (Eds.), *Policy networks: Empirical evidence and theoretical considerations* (pp. 11–23). Boulder, CO: Westview Press.

Marsh, D., & Smith, M. (2000, March). Understanding policy networks: Towards a dialectical approach. *Political Studies, 48*, 4–21.

Marsh, D., & Smith, M. J. (2001, August). There is more than one way to do political science: On different ways to study policy networks. *Political Studies, 49*, 528–541.

Melucci, A. (1989). *Nomads of the present: Social movements and individual needs in contemporary society*. Philadelphia, PA: Temple University Press.

Messner, D. (2002). World society—structures and trends. In P. Kennedy, D. Messner, & F. Nuscheler (Eds.), *Global trends and global governance* (pp. 22–64). London, UK: Pluto Press.

Nagel, S. (1988). *Policy studies: Integration and evaluation*. New York, NY: Praeger.

Nordlinger, E. A. (1981). *On the autonomy of the democratic state*. Cambridge, MA: Harvard University Press.

North-South Institute. (2009). *The Canadian Development Report 2009—Financing development in times of global crisis*. Ottawa, ON: North-South Institute.

OECD [Organisation for Economic Co-operation and Development]. (2000, December–February). *Focus: Public Management Newsletter*, no. 15.

OECD. (2001). *Engaging citizens in policy-making: Information, consultation and public participation* (PUMA Policy Brief No. 10). Retrieved from http://www.oecd.org/dataoecd/24/34/2384040.pdf

OECD. (2003). *Open Government: Fostering dialogue with civil society*. Paris: OECD.

OECD. (2008). *Summary of global forum on governance: Modernising government—Strategies and tools for change*. Paris: OECD.

OECD. (2010, November 15). *Towards recovery and partnership with citizens: The call for innovative and open government*. Retrieved from http://www.oecd.org/dataoecd/48/56/46342001.pdf

Offe, C. (1987). Challenging the boundaries of institutional politics. In C. S. Maier (Ed.), *Changing boundaries of the political: Essays on the* evolving balance between the state and society, public and private in Europe (pp. 63–105). Cambridge, UK: Cambridge University Press.

Pal, L. A. (1993). *Interests of state: The politics of language, multiculturalism and feminism in Canada*. Montréal: McGill-Queen's University Press.

Paltiel, K. Z. (1982). The changing environment and role of special interest groups. *Canadian Public Administration, 25*, 198–210.

Pemberton, H. (2000, December). Policy networks and policy learning: UK economic policy in the 1960s and 1970s. *Public Administration, 78*, 771–792.

Peters, B. G. (1998). *Managing horizontal government: The politics of coordination* (Research Paper No. 21). Ottawa, ON: Canadian Centre for Management Development.

Phillips, S. D. (1993, Winter). Of public interest groups and sceptics: A realist's reply to Privy Council Office (Canada). (1993). *Task force report: Service to the public*. Ottawa, ON: Minister of Supply and Services.

Privy Council Office (Canada). (2003). *Guide to making federal acts and regulations* (2nd ed.). Retrieved from http://www.pco-bcp.gc.ca/docs/information/publications/legislation/pdf-eng.pdf

Privy Council Office (Canada). (2010). *Memorandum to Cabinet*. Retrieved from http://www.pco-bcp.gc.ca/index.asp?lang=eng&page=information&sub=publications&doc=mc/mc-eng.htm

Pross, A. P. (1992). *Group politics and public policy* (2nd ed.). Toronto, ON: Oxford University Press.

Pross, A. P. (1995). Pressure groups: Talking chameleons. In M. S. Whittington & G. Williams (Eds.), *Canadian politics in the 1990s* (pp. 252–275). Toronto, ON: Nelson Canada.

Provan, K. G., & Kenis, P. (2008). Modes of networked governance: Structure, management, and effectiveness. *Journal of Public Administration Research and Theory, 18*(2), 229–252.

Raab, C. (2001, August). Understanding policy networks: A comment on Marsh and Smith. *Political Studies, 49*, 551–556.

Raab, C. (2002, October). Where do policy networks come from? *Journal of Public Administration Research and Theory, 12*, 581–622.

Reinicke, W. H. (1999/2000). The other world wide web: Global public policy networks. *Foreign Policy, 117*, 44–57.

Rethemeyer, R. K. (2005). Conceptualizing and measuring complex networks. *Public Administration Review, 65*(1), 117–121.

Rhodes, R. A. W. (2007). Understanding governance: Ten years on. *Organization Studies, 28*(8), 1243–1264.

Ripley, R. B., & Franklin, G. A. (1984). *Congress, the bureaucracy and public policy* (2nd ed.). Homewood, IL: Dorsey.

Rosenau, P. V. (Ed.). (2000). *Public-private policy partnerships*. Cambridge, MA: MIT Press.

Sabatier, P. A. (1993). Policy change over a decade or more. In P. A. Sabatier & H. Jenkins-Smith (Eds.), *Policy change and learning: An advocacy coalition approach* (pp. 13–39). Boulder, CO: Westview.

Sabatier, P. A., & Jenkins-Smith, H. (Eds.). (1993). *Policy change and learning: An advocacy coalition approach*. Boulder, CO: Westview.

Sabatier, P. A., & Jenkins-Smith, H. (1999). The advocacy coalition framework: An assessment. In P. A. Sabatier (Ed.), *Theories of the policy process* (pp. 117–166). Boulder, CO: Westview.

Schneider, A. L., & Ingram, H. (1997). *Policy design for democracy*. Lawrence, KS: University Press of Kansas.

Scholte, J. A. (2004). Civil society and democratically accountable global governance. *Government and Opposition, 39*, 211–233.

Skocpol, T. (1986). Rediscovering the state: Strategies of analysis in current research. In P. B. Evans, D. Reuschemeyer, & T. Skocpol (Eds.), *Bringing the state back in* (pp. 3–37). Cambridge, UK: Cambridge University Press.

Slaughter, A.-M. (2004). *A new world order*. Princeton, NJ: Princeton University Press.

Sørensen, E., & Torfing, J. (Eds.). (2007). *Theories of democratic network governance*. Houndmills, UK: Palgrave Macmillan.

Statistics Canada. (2005). *Cornerstones of community: Highlights of the national survey of nonprofit and voluntary organizations—2003 revised* (Catalogue No. 61-533-XPE). Retrieved from http://www.statcan.gc.ca/access_acces/alternative_alternatif.action?l=eng&loc=http://www.statcan.gc.ca/pub/61-533-x/61-533-x2004001-eng.pdf&t=Cornerstones%20of%20Community:%20Highlights%20from%20the%20National%20Survey%20of%20Nonprofit%20and%20Voluntary%20Organizations

Stone, D. (2004). Transfer agents and global networks in the "transnationalization" of policy. *Journal of European Public Policy, 11*(3), 545–566.

Stone, D. (2008). Global public policy, transnational policy communities, and their networks. *Policy Studies Journal, 36*(1), 19–38.

Thatcher, M. (1998, October). The development of policy network analyses: From modest origins to overarching frameworks. *Journal of Theoretical Politics, 10*, 389–416.

Thomas, T. (1995). When "they" is "we": Movements, municipal parties, and participatory politics. In J. Lightbody (Ed.), *Canadian metropolitics: Governing our cities* (pp. 115–136). Toronto, ON: Copp Clark.

Treasury Board of Canada. (2010). *Companion guide: The development of results-based management and accountability frameworks for horizontal initiatives.* Retrieved from http://www.statcan.gc.ca/access_acces/alternative_alternatif.action?l=eng&loc=http://www.statcan.gc.ca/pub/61-533-x/61-533-x2004001-eng.pdf&t=Cornerstones%20of%20Community:%20Highlights%20from%20the%20National%20Survey%20of%20Nonprofit%20and%20Voluntary%20Organizations

Truman, D. (1951). *The governmental process: Political interests and public opinion.* New York, NY: Alfred A. Knopf.

Turrini, A., Cristofoli, D., Frosini, F., & Nasi, G. (2009). Networking literature about determinants of network effectiveness. *Public Administration, 88*(2), 528–550.

Van Waarden, F. (1992). Dimensions and types of policy networks. *European Journal of Political Research, 21,* 29–52.

Walker, J. (1991). *Mobilizing interest groups in America: Patrons, professions and social movements.* Ann Arbor, MI: University of Michigan Press.

Walker, R. B. J. (1988). *One world, many worlds: Struggles for a just world peace.* Boulder, CO: Lynne Rienner.

Weaver, R. K., & Rockman, B. A. (1993). Assessing the effects of institutions. In R. K. Weaver & B. A. Rockman (Eds.), *Do institutions matter? Government capabilities in the United States and abroad* (pp. 1–41). Washington, DC: Brookings Institution Press.

Wright, M. (1988). Policy community, policy network, and comparative industrial policies. *Political Studies, 36,* 593–614.

Zald, M. N. (1987). *Social movements in an organizational society: Collected essays.* New Brunswick, NJ: Transaction.

CHAPTER

Evaluation

Consult any text on policy analysis and you will find passages extolling the indispensability of policy and program evaluation. It could hardly be otherwise, given that program evaluation is primarily about trying to figure out how successful a policy has been, whether it met its objectives, how far it fell short, and what might be done to improve its impact. The same passages that extol evaluation, however, are usually complemented by ones that say it is expensive, difficult, rarely conclusive, and politically unpopular. Precisely because evaluation is so potentially crucial to the fortunes of a policy or program, opponents and supporters work hard to get the evaluation results they need to strengthen their case—that is, if evaluation takes place at all. Not only is it politically sensitive (who wants to hear bad news?), it can seem secondary to the really important job of designing and implementing solutions to public problems. Policy evaluation therefore has enjoyed more theoretical than practical popularity, and in Canada at least, has not been enthusiastically supported either as a government or as a third-party (foundation or think-tank) activity. This situation is changing. The renewed emphasis on results, accountability, and performance, coupled with a shift to public–private partnerships and networks of collaboration, increases the need for evaluation because it places new pressures on governments to demonstrate value for money. Not only does evaluation have a higher profile, but also different forms of evaluation (such as client satisfaction and overall program performance) are becoming increasingly important. Thus, what is happening in this field directly reflects developments described in Chapters 3 to 6.

Policy analysis, defined as the disciplined application of intellect to public problems, encompasses everything from reading a newspaper to careful scientific research. In practice, much of what passes for professional policy

NEL   **271** analysis is called "policy evaluation." It is conducted by governments as well as private firms, assumes a mastery of certain quantitative and qualitative techniques, and is aimed at the improvement or betterment of public policies and programs. Its central questions are these: Does this program do what it is supposed to be doing? If not, why not? What should be done? Policy analysis is openly prescriptive, and serves to monitor government activities. Policies attempt to solve or manage public problems; at some point governments (and citizens) need to know whether interventions are making a difference and are worthwhile. Since most government services are on a not-for-profit basis, there are no clear market signals—profit, loss, increase or decrease in demand—to measure performance.

The improvement of programs is the core function or purpose of evaluation as it is conducted in governments, but there are other purposes as well. Rossi, Lipsey, and Freeman (2004) highlight four (pp. 34–38). The first is the one we have already mentioned and will develop further below: program improvement. Typically this means working with program managers as the program is being implemented, or what is called **formative evaluation**. Another purpose is for **accountability**—in this instance, the objective is oversight once the program is close to completion, or what is called **summative evaluation**. Evaluations can also be done to generate more general knowledge that may or may not be directly relevant to the program but that might cast light on a social issue or casual questions. Finally, evaluations can be done as a political ruse or for public relations—either to produce data to support a program or justify a decision that has already been made. In this chapter, we will concentrate on evaluation with the first objective.

Policy evaluation seems deceptively simple, but determining whether a program has its intended effect, in a world in which every effect has multiple causes and every cause a vast stream of effects, is always difficult and sometimes impossible. This challenge is the core of what is termed the **attribution problem**—what was the contribution of a given policy intervention to resolving a given issue? Information is sometimes faulty or nonexistent, people uncooperative, policies' objectives vague, or measuring instruments weak. As well, evaluation is by its nature unpopular. Who wants to be told their program is a failure? Evaluation often delivers unpleasant truths, creating great temptations to shoot, or at least ignore, the messenger. However, despite these built-in limitations and liabilities, as well as a history of, at best, tepid support from most policy managers, evaluation experienced a renewed popularity in the mid-1990s. The 1995 OECD update on public management developments in 25 countries, for example, noted: "A wide range of performance-oriented initiatives has been reported in 1994 as the shift of management focus from processes to results gains momentum. Those mentioned here cover two main aspects: a drive for better reporting of performance; and increased emphasis on setting targets for service quality levels and measuring results against them" (p. 10). A decade later the emphasis was just as strong if not stronger. *Modernising Government* observed that the clearest trend in performance across OECD members was "the introduction of performance-oriented budgeting and performance management" (Organisation for Economic Co-operation and Development [OECD], 2005, p. 58).

There are several reasons for this resurgence. First, evaluation is typically championed by the management consulting industry, since that is where a great deal of its claims to expertise lie (Saint-Martin, 2000). As governments in recent years have tried to borrow more management practices from the private sector, they have also tended to import a greater appetite for evaluation. Second, fiscal pressures from the 1990s and especially now with the financial crisis, have created a mindset—through program reviews and reallocation exercises—that, at least in principle, no program is sacred and everything should be evaluated for best results and monies redirected as necessary. A third related reason is that many of the new techniques of governance discussed in Chapters 3 to 6 on design, implementation, and policy communities demand better accountability mechanisms. That means evaluation or assessment. A fourth reason is entangled with the sense that citizens have declining levels of trust in public authorities and public policies. Rigorous evaluation of the performance of public agencies, and the communication of that evaluation to the wider public, is one means for re-establishing support for public institutions. "Today, global and domestic forces demand more effective management and higher levels of organizational performance. Leaders and managers in public and non-profit organizations face demanding constituencies, higher public expectations, and aggressive media scrutiny" (Wholey, 2003, p. 44).

This chapter has two primary objectives. The first is to introduce some of the main techniques used in evaluation research, as well as some of the benchmarks and rules of thumb for successful evaluations. This section is merely an overview of the logic of the techniques and does not pretend to be comprehensive. The second objective is to review the history of federal government evaluation efforts in the last 20 years and provide a sense of context about the state of evaluation in this country and the potential for its new and enhanced status. To date, Canadian practice has restricted evaluation to more of a management tool than a real challenge to government programs. The chapter closes with a discussion of the place of evaluation both in policy analysis and in democratic governance.

Types of Evaluation

Michael Patton (2008) states that "**program evaluation** is the systematic collection of information about the activities, characteristics, and outcomes of programs to make judgments about the program, improve program effectiveness, and/or inform decisions about future programming." Weiss defined evaluation as "the *systematic assessment* of the *operations* and/or the *outcomes* of a program or policy, compared to a set of *explicit* or *implicit standards,* as a means of contributing to the *improvement* of the program or policy" (1998, p. 4; emphasis in original). Rossi, Lipsey, and Freeman (2004) define program evaluation as "the use of social research procedures to systematically investigate the effectiveness of social intervention programs in ways that are adapted to their political and organizational environments and are designed to inform social action to improve social conditions" (p. 16).

Several features of these definitions should be noted. First, they refer to "practice" and "application" of techniques. Second, they identify "improvement" of public policy decisionmaking processes as the ultimate goal of evaluation. Third, they highlight the "systematic" character of evaluation research. Evaluation presents itself, in short, as a scientific, systematic, empirically oriented, applied discipline or set of disciplines that analyze current programs in order to generate intelligent information that can be used to improve those programs or the decision processes that produced them. The creative and intuitive aspect of evaluation should not be understated: Patton (1987) listed 100 different types of evaluation and argued persuasively that each one demands creativity (pp. 98–205). As we mentioned in Chapter 1, one of the most deceptively simple things about a policy is stating its goals. Before a program can be evaluated, its underlying problem definition and its goals must be understood, and so evaluators spend a good deal of time in what is usually termed the pre-evaluation phase, talking to program administrators and piecing together what people think they are doing. This approach is closer to cultural anthropology than regression analysis. Nonetheless, it is fair to say that of all the subfields within policy analysis, evaluation has remained closest to the traditional empiricist model. Evaluators are the accountants of the policy profession and, like balance sheets, their reports on effectiveness and impact can sometimes be received with glum resignation. Indeed, because the traditional empirical techniques used in most conventional evaluations are fairly standardized (even though they vary in their application case by case), and because evaluation results are supposed to be neutral and unbiased, there has been a greater momentum behind the professionalization of evaluation than in other fields of policy analysis. The American Evaluation Association (formed in 1986), for example, adopted the following guiding principles in 1994:

1. *Systematic Inquiry:* Evaluators conduct systematic, data-based inquiries.

2. *Competence:* Evaluators provide competent performance to stakeholders.

3. *Integrity/Honesty:* Evaluators display honesty and integrity in their own behavior, and attempt to ensure the honesty and integrity of the entire evaluation process.

4. *Respect for People:* Evaluators respect the security, dignity and self-worth of respondents, program participants, clients, and other evaluation stakeholders.

5. *Responsibilities for General and Public Welfare:* Evaluators articulate and take into account the diversity of general and public interests and values that may be related to the evaluation. (American Evaluation Society, 2012)*

The Canadian Evaluation Society has similar guidelines that emphasize competence, integrity, and accountability (Canadian Evaluation Society, 2012). Evaluators must be aware that while they are engaged in providing information to improve programs, ultimately those programs are delivered by people and for people, and moreover their assessments inevitably will be coloured to some degree by choices and values.

While these definitions appear to give evaluation a wide scope of application in policymaking, indeed to the point that it seems synonymous with policy analysis, it is worth keeping some fundamental distinctions in mind between policy analysis and evaluation (Geva-May & Pal, 1999). A careful reading shows that evaluation is almost always linked to existing programs, either through the analysis of those programs or of information relevant to them. Because of their expertise, evaluators are also often involved in generating and analyzing data that are relevant to problem definition, trend forecasting, and program design aspects such as target populations. Rossi, Lipsey, and Freeman (2004) term these **"diagnostic procedures"** that entail, for example, the use of census data, existing **social indicators** such as literacy or crime rates, and surveys to determine the nature and scope of a problem (pp. 110–111). **Needs assessment** can be even more specific—for example, the health needs of a small rural community—and would depend on specially designed surveys and reviews of existing data. This component of evaluation is certainly respectable and important, but it is not its core. Program evaluation "is the application of systematic methods to address questions about program operations and results. It may include ongoing monitoring of a program as well as one-shot studies of program processes or program impact" (Newcomer, Hatry, & Wholey, 2010, pp. 5–6). Figure 7.1 sketches these three categories with some illustrative questions.

Before program evaluation can be conducted, therefore, we normally have programs in place—evaluation typically is *ex post* analysis, or after the launch of a program. As obvious as this seems, it reminds us that the

---

*American Evaluation Society Guiding Principles for Evaluators, 2008. Retrieved March 20, 2008, from http://www.eval.org/Publications/GuidingPrinciples.asp

Figure 7.1 Core Categories of Program Evaluation

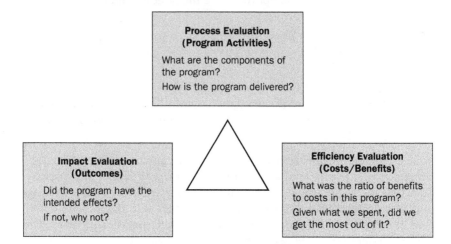

**Process Evaluation
(Program Activities)**

What are the components of
the program?
How is the program delivered?

**Impact Evaluation
(Outcomes)**

Did the program have the
intended effects?
If not, why not?

**Efficiency Evaluation
(Costs/Benefits)**

What was the ratio of benefits
to costs in this program?
Given what we spent, did we
get the most out of it?

very first step in any policy evaluation is trying to understand the policy
and its programs, primarily in terms described in Chapter 1—what is the
problem, what are the goals, and how are programs designed to address
that problem? As Weiss points out, there are many cases where programs
are quite unambiguous—changing highway speeds, increasing benefits
in some income support program, or introducing a new medical testing
program such as mammograms for a target population. However, many
other programs, and often the most interesting or controversial ones,
combine resources, people, and practices in complex ways. "In most
social programs, it takes effort to understand the content of the program,
what actually goes on. Operations often differ markedly from day to day
and from staff member to staff member" (1998, p. 49).

Before conducting an evaluation, therefore, evaluators should learn about
the program as it really is as well as what it was designed to be. They can
review previous evaluations, published literature, and program materials,
and conduct both formal and information interviews with a variety of
program and policy personnel as well as clients to put the puzzle together.
They can then develop two related models to help them map out what the
program is and how it tries to accomplish its objectives. The first guide is
program theory, or hypotheses and explanations about the "causal links that
tie program inputs to expected program outputs" (Weiss, 1998, p. 55). We
discuss this in detail below in connection with **impact evaluation,** but it is a
theory about how the program will exercise its ultimate effect or outcome.
For example, a training program for unemployed youth has a target of
increasing the numbers of youth who get jobs. The program theory might be
that the reason the youth are unemployed is because of lack of skills, and so
by providing training, the program provides the skills and makes the youth

more attractive to employers. However, it might be that the program offers young people the opportunity to widen their circle of contacts and thereby learn about more job opportunities. In both instances, the program and the outcomes are the same, but the "mechanisms" (what Weiss terms not the activities, but the responses to these activities) are different.

The second guide or map that is crucial for evaluators (especially when they conduct **process evaluations**) is the **implementation theory** that lies behind the program. This theory captures the specific activities and resources that are mobilized in connection with each of the links in the program's **causal chain** or **logic model**. To use the youth training program once again as an example, the implementation theory would detail steps such as publicizing the program among targeted youth groups and arranging the counselling and the content of the training, the rooms, and other forms of support. For program administrators, the assumption—since their job is to implement the program as it was designed in the belief that it is supposed to work—is that if all the steps in the implementation theory are fulfilled, the program will achieve its results. The relationship between program theory and implementation theory is illustrated in Figure 7.2.

Logic models, another way of mapping programs, bring together program theory and implementation theory. "A logic model is a plausible and sensible model of how the program will work under certain environmental conditions to solve identified problems" (McLaughlin & Jordan, 2010, p. 56). While usually depicted as a chart or diagram, the essence of a logic model is a narrative of what the program is targeting, how it works, and what it is trying to achieve. Figure 7.3 illustrates the key elements of a logic model, though these can be extended considerably. As an example, we could take the needle exchange program that has been in place in Ottawa since 1991 (City of Ottawa, 2012). The policy targets people at risk or infected with either or both HIV and hepatitis. These include those who use and inject drugs, have sexual partners who use drugs, or who are sex industry workers.

Figure 7.2 Program Theory and Implementation Theory (Example)

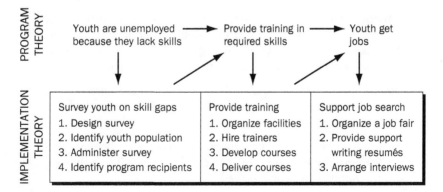

Figure 7.3   Key Elements of a Logic Model

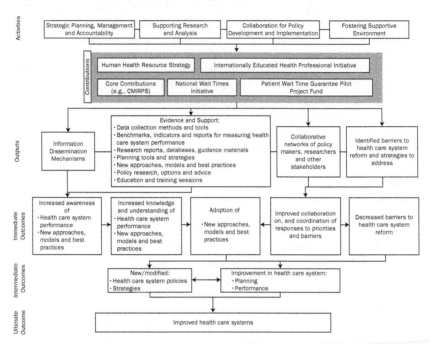

Source: Supporting Effective Evaluations: A Guide to Developing Performance Management Strategies. Fig. 1, http://www.tbs-sct.gc.ca/cee/dpms-esmr/dpms-esmr05-eng.asp#fig1, Treasury Board of Canada. Reproduced with the permission of the Minister of Public Works and Government Services Canada, 2012.

Based on Figure 7.3, what would a logic model of this program look like?

Resources: Financial, materiel, human resources that are marshalled for a program. Staff, exchange sites, needles, disposal facilities, biohazard containers, finances. It could include partners such as pharmacies that will accept used needles.

Activities: All of the actions necessary to produce the output and eventually the outcomes. Even in a small program like this one, the range is enormous, from training staff, to inspections, to site establishment, to logs of returned needles, to reporting.

Outputs: Products, goods, and services provided through the program. Needles made available for exchange, sites available for those exchanges.

Immediate Outcomes: The short-term changes or benefits that are "caused" by the program. The number of needles exchanged and the number of people served.

Intermediate Outcomes: Usually defined as behavioural changes that occur as a result of immediate outcomes. People exchanging needles instead of reusing them.

Final Outcome: The ultimate objective of the program. Reduction of harm to needle users and reduction of the incidence of the spread of HIV and hepatitis.

There are several points to note about logic models. Figure 7.3 makes it clear that the "area of control" for an organization in this chain of cause and effect is between inputs and outputs. As one moves to outcomes, and especially to final outcomes, external factors have a greater role to play and bring back the attribution issue mentioned earlier. The figure also illustrates the two dimensions of efficiency and effectiveness that will be discussed in greater detail below. Efficiency is about the allocation of resources within organizations to meet stated goals. Effectiveness is about whether that allocation meets those goals and has the desired outcomes.

IMPACT EVALUATION

A central evaluative question is whether a policy or program has an impact. Evaluating outcomes is critical to determining whether a program is successful or not in terms of its intended effects. Impact evaluation takes the program as the independent or causal variable and tries to isolate its effect from other influences in the environment. This approach assumes that goals are clear, but sometimes they are not. As we noted above, in addition to trying to understand the goals, the evaluator should also develop a map of the causal theory that underpins the program, along with mechanisms of change. Logic models help do this, since they explicitly connect resources and activities to outputs and outcomes. The arrows or connections between the elements of a logic model are the causal mechanisms. The connections not only help in determining what data to gather and which indicators to highlight, but also provides alternative causal path explanations that might be examined if the evaluation turns up ambiguous results. In the training example, if the employment rate for youth who complete the program is lower than expected, this might be because the skill enhancement occurred only for those youth who had certain background characteristics (e.g., finished secondary school, had had at least one other training program). If the needle exchange program had low take-up, it might be because of where the sites were located.

Having determined a program theory, impact evaluation goes on to look at actual causal chains by examining the program's effects. Impact evaluation tries to isolate causes and effects, but this is no easy task since any single cause or effect is (or may be seen to be) intimately bound to numerous other causes and effects. A single effect may conceivably have several causes, and the policy intervention is only one of them. Figure 7.4 provides a schematic diagram of the assumption and the problem. It helps to begin with a simple model of policy impact: here, some policy P is intended to affect some casual variable C, which will then have a desired effect on some outcome O. Note that a policy or program never has a direct influence on behaviour; it is always targeted on some factor that is assumed to influence behaviour, and by influencing that factor yields desired outcomes. Speed limits, for example, assume that accidents are in part caused by driving too quickly. Accident rates are the O, or outcome, while speeding is C. A program to either set lower limits or enforce them more rigorously is an example of interventions. But now consider the more complex model in Figure 7.4. It adds variables to the C and the O categories. Speeding itself can be regarded as a **dependent variable**, something caused by other factors. Speeding is affected by such things as weather conditions, road congestion, safety quality of cars, and so on. If an anti-speeding campaign were found to be associated with lower accident rates, would that mean that the program was successful? Not at all, since it may be that fewer speeders were about or that other conditions were responsible for the diminution of accident rates.

Figure 7.4 Causal Model of Program Impact

A. Simple Model of Program Impact

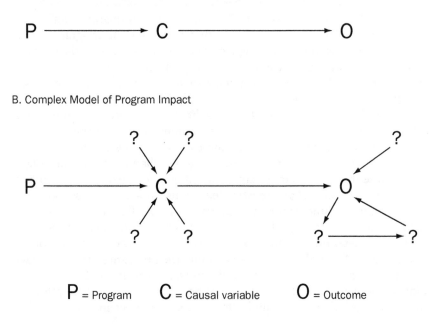

B. Complex Model of Program Impact

P = Program   C = Causal variable   O = Outcome

Various strategies have been developed to deal with this problem. They all rely on statistical techniques to a greater or lesser degree, and all strive to control or neutralize the extraneous causal variables that might have produced the effect. In cases where these preferred strategies are unavailable, too expensive, or time consuming, a technique called "meta-analysis" is sometimes used (Boruch & Petrosino, 2010). Instead of gathering new data, evaluators review the existing literature on a specific program, treating each evaluation study as a single case. This pooling of evaluations requires a fairly large set, however, sometimes in the hundreds, in order to be valid. One advantage of meta-analysis, on the other hand, is that this pooling increases the number of observations of the effects of a particular intervention in a variety of settings and thereby can increase the confidence level of any assertions about its effects. Weiss points out, for example, that meta-analysis has, in some instances, shown that many kinds of social programs that were once thought to have little effect have statistically significant cumulative outcomes (1998, p. 242).

The ideal method to try to empirically isolate cause and effect is the classic **experimental design**. In this design, people are randomly assigned to one of two groups; measures are taken of target variables before the program is introduced and again afterward. The program is applied to only one group, the **experimental group**. The second group is the **control group**. If there is a sufficiently large difference in post-program scores, then the program or intervention is deemed to have caused it. The **random assignment** of individuals to the two groups controls for alternative explanations or causes, since the odds of being in either group are the same. In aggregate, the groups are identical in every respect except for the policy intervention (Weiss, 1998, p. 215). Experimental designs are frequently used in the educational policy field, where, for example, a new reading program might be tested on two groups of students. Pre-program reading scores for the experimental group and the control group would be gathered, the program administered, and post-program scores compared to see if they are statistically different.

Despite their statistical superiority as a measure of impact, experimental designs are rarely used in policy evaluation in Canada, though more widely in the United States, especially in the education policy field (Torgerson, Torgerson, & Taylor, 2010). That is because they are costly and time consuming; decisionmakers frequently want quick answers. There are also political and ethical problems with separating people into experimental and control groups. Many public programs deliver benefits to the populace, and from a political perspective, it might be imprudent to deliberately withhold a benefit from some group simply to meet testing requirements. As Rossi, Lipsey, and Freeman (2004) point out, randomized experiments run into major ethical dilemmas, as in the controversy over withholding potentially beneficial AIDS drugs. Finally, some important policy variables cannot be disaggregated to observe differential effects on separate groups. Interest rates, the value of the dollar, and budget deficits are examples of policy variables that apply nationally or not at all. Classic experimental designs are useless in trying to determine their impact.

Nonetheless, while rare in comparison with other techniques, program evaluation based on experimental design does take place. In Canada the leading exponent is the nonprofit Social Research and Demonstration Corporation (SRDC)—modelled after the Manpower Demonstration Research Corporation launched more than 25 years ago in the United States. SRDC brings together researchers around the analysis and evaluation of social programs in multiple locales and over extended time periods to see what works and what does not. SRDC's areas of policy research include "early child development, access to post-secondary education, adult learning and literacy, labour market information, employment insurance, community-based employment, welfare-to-work, population health, programs for persons with disabilities, and crime prevention" (SRDC, 2012). Box 7.1 provides descriptions of several SRDC evaluation projects. Randomized experiments have also been used in development studies to try to determine basic answers about what works in alleviating extreme poverty (Banerjee & Duflo, 2011).

Experimental designs of the type engineered by SRDC are time consuming and expensive, as well as technically challenging. In the face of these difficulties, rigorous experimental design often gives way to other, **quasi-experimental** forms of impact evaluation. One technique is to use time-series data to establish **pre-program and post-program** comparisons. Another, weaker form of impact evaluation is the **single observation** or pre-experimental design. In this method, a program or policy is implemented and then measurements are taken of outcomes. Assume, for example, that a government job creation program allocates $300 million for employment in depressed regions. Within a year it is found that 80 percent of program participants are regularly employed. This fact says little about the real program impact, however, because the participants might have been self-selecting—that is, only motivated individuals participated—or because the economy might have improved generally. A variation of the single observation technique is the pre-program/post-program scheme, which does try to compare scores before and after an intervention, but only for a single group. Without a control group, it is impossible to tell whether any differences in the scores are due to the program intervention or some other cause. A final, widely used, but not very powerful, design for determining impact is **contrasted group design**. In this design, program recipients are compared to nonrecipients, and the differences are ascribed to the program.

BOX 7.1   SOCIAL RESEARCH AND
DEMONSTRATION CORPORATION

BC Workplace Training Project—SRDC is working in collaboration with Douglas College to design and conduct an evaluation of an Essential Skills training program designed to upgrade the transferable skills of 1,200 eligible participants working in the tourism and retail sectors throughout British Columbia. The Workplace Training Program is funded by the BC Ministry of Jobs, Tourism and Innovation. The program will be delivered by the Continuing Education and Training Association of BC (CETABC), which is a consortium of post-secondary institutions. The evaluation involves both implementation and outcomes research.

An Overview of Financial and Social Supports for Students with Dependants in Canada—This project is expected to fill knowledge gaps pertaining to existing policy and program levers in place to respond to the needs of students with dependants. The initiative entails jurisdictional policy review to identify the range of federal, provincial, and territorial social and financial programs available to students with dependants and provide an in-depth analysis of the extent to which these programs interact with each other, their degree of integration, and identification of existing program gaps that may prevent these students from undertaking and completing post-secondary education. The analysis will inform policy decision-making on the accessibility issues faced by post-secondary students with dependants.

A Multidimensional Approach to Reducing the Appeal of Sweet Beverages—The main goal of the project is to gain a better understanding of how sweet beverages are marketed to target young Canadians so that it is easier to take concrete actions in the future to make environments more conducive to healthy lifestyle habits. To accomplish this, the project incorporates three main thrusts: 1) provide a comprehensive picture of the sweet beverage market in Canada and existing marketing strategies targeting young people; 2) adapt the Gobes-tu ça? project developed by Réseau du sport étudiant du Québec for young Francophones age 13 to 17 in Alberta and, if funding is extended beyond this period, identify other potential sponsors for the Gobes-tu ça? project elsewhere in the country; and 3) disseminate and use our study of the sweet beverage market and adapt this knowledge transfer tool accordingly.

Source: Reprinted by permission of the Social Research and Demonstration Corporation (SRCD). www.srcd.org.

PROCESS/IMPLEMENTATION EVALUATION

Process or implementation evaluation monitors an existing program to assess the effort put into it (Posvac & Carey, 1980, p. 12). This is not the same as measuring success. As Patton (2002) put it, process evaluation involves looking at "how something happens rather than or in addition to examining outputs and outcomes" (p. 159). Typically, reporting systems are developed to provide agencies with information about target populations, extent of coverage, and delivery mechanisms. Process evaluation can review program guidelines, the organization of field offices, staff training, communications systems, and even staff morale to improve organizational performance. It takes the program for granted and aims at improving the process whereby goals are met. This thrust may sound routine, but is conceptually important and, in practical terms, accounts for a great deal of what passes for program evaluation.

Process evaluation is clearly linked to implementation and can be thought of as the evaluation of implementation procedures. This perspective helps clarify the importance of process evaluation to program evaluation as a whole, as well as its link to impact analysis. In Chapter 5 we pointed out that the quality of implementation is quite distinct from the quality of a program—bad programs can be well implemented, and vice versa. Process evaluation is a natural complement to impact evaluation, since we need to know whether observed outcomes are the result of the program intervention as it was planned or are due to quirks in the delivery. In other words, program theory and design (the causal links and interventions sketched in Figure 7.4) may be fine, but the execution is flawed. If we can assure ourselves that execution is as planned, then any failures will be due to program design. This idea, of course, makes it sound as though implementation and impact can be neatly severed, but they cannot. They represent different orientations in evaluative work.

The full description of **program components** is the foundation of process analysis, though the concept of **program logic** is sometimes used to sketch out the causal links for impact evaluation (Framst, 1995). Program components are all the various bits and pieces, technologies and resources, as well as intended targets and delivery modes. Mapping this out is tougher than it sounds and requires extended interviews with both program administrators and clients to see what the components are and how well they are being implemented. The next trick is to determine what good or effective implementation entails. It is not directly linked to desired outcomes, which is the realm of impact evaluation. Rather, it tries to determine what the desired outcome is and then asks what steps or mechanisms the program envisions in delivering the intervention to achieve that outcome. A training program for middle-aged unemployed workers, for example, assumes that better training will lead to jobs.

This assumption is questionable in many cases, but the process evaluator takes it as given. She then asks what program components go into the delivery of that training: classrooms, syllabus, materials, staff, and equipment. It should be possible to develop criteria that let us measure whether a training program is being delivered well or badly (e.g., run-down facilities, disorganization, unqualified instructors, broken equipment). If delivery quality varies, then assuming that the program is properly designed, the path to improvement is to work on better implementation. If the quality of implementation is generally high across a range of sites, but outcomes are still poor, then the problem would seem to be in program design.

As we will see in the next section of this chapter, the general field of process and implementation evaluation has grown dramatically in the last 20 years. Evaluation as a whole has become more important as governments are under pressure to be more results oriented and accountable. Impact evaluation, the analysis of results, is not easy or cheap, and there is a natural inclination to assume that the design is fine and that disappointing outcomes must be due to inadequate effort. At the same time, governments are looking more to consumer or client satisfaction as a key program outcome, and this often has more to do with delivery parameters than with the causal modelling underlying program design. Delivery parameters are more commonly referred to as "benchmarks" and typically focus on performance rather than process, though the two are related. Performance measures or benchmarks for concrete services are usually based on measures of workload, efficiency, effectiveness, or productivity. Finally, as more and more programs are delivered by nongovernmental organizations, and as more of their financial and organizational support comes from groups of partners (firms, government, foundations), these partners want to monitor how well things are proceeding. Monitoring tends to be more casual and less systematic than process evaluation, but they are "similar kinds of inquiry" (Weiss, 1998, p. 181). These, and other forces, have conspired in recent years to raise the profile of process and implementation analysis quite significantly.

A type of process evaluation known as performance reporting, or managing for results, has become quite important in Canada, the United States, and many other OECD countries. In fact, in the United States, as a result of the 1993 Government Performance and Results Act, all federal government agencies must submit to the Director of the Office of Management and Budget and to Congress strategic plans on performance goals and evaluation plans to measure that performance. These have to include an agency mission statement, one or more strategic goals, means to achieve those goals, the link between annual goals and long-term outcomes, identification of key factors that could affect achievement of strategic goals, and a description of program evaluations used in preparing the plan and a schedule for future evaluations (Office of Management and Budget, 2011).

Performance reporting and management depends on the distinction between inputs, outputs, outcomes, and indicators (Schacter, 1999). Inputs are the resources allocated to programs and organizations. Outputs are the activities government agencies undertake, such as the provision of services. Outcomes are the eventual results of those activities in terms of the public good. Indicators are the empirical measures of inputs, outputs, and outcomes. The thrust of performance measurement is to train attention on outcomes—what ultimately matters the most—and link them to a logical model that connects inputs (resources) with activities, outputs, and outcomes. Looked at in this way, performance measurement is about much more than simply measuring things—it entails a management regime that requires a public organization to have a clear idea of what its objectives are and a regular means of reporting on its success in achieving those objectives. Performance reporting is thus different from policy or program evaluation, which typically takes place near the end of a program's life and is more of a one-time analysis of program impacts. Performance measurement should be viewed as part of a larger management regime, which should try to link results with strategic planning and budgeting and resource allocation.

It is important to get several key factors right in order to do performance measurement properly and successfully (Holden & Zimmerman, 2009; Performance-Based Management Special Interest Group, 2001).

- *Clarity about the program.* Since performance measurement is about measuring the success of a program, it is vital to know what that program is about and what its intended objectives are. Determining this is more difficult than it seems, since different people in an organization may have different ideas about what their program is about. "Profile—a concise description of the policy, program or initiative, including a discussion of the background, need, target population, delivery approach, resources, governance structure and planned results" (Treasury Board of Canada, 2010).

- *Logic model.* As discussed above, at the heart of any process of performance reporting is a "logic model" that ties inputs to activities, to short-term, intermediate, and final or ultimate outcomes. Part of the challenge of performance measurement is coming up with indicators for these different levels of outcomes, and coming to judgments about the specific contribution of an agency and its activities to eventual outcomes. A logic model is "an illustration of the results chain or how the activities of a policy, program, or initiative are expected to lead to the achievement of the final outcomes" (Treasury Board of Canada, 2010).

- *Judgment.* The paradox of performance measurement is that while it is driven by a desire for precision and a clear assessment of the contribution of government programs to specific outcomes, the literature acknowledges that there are huge technical problems associated with disentangling the specific effect of those programs from all of the other factors that might contribute to those outcomes. This challenge means that successful performance measurement has to acknowledge that there is always an element of judgment. That judgment can be disciplined and careful, but it still is judgment. It is important to acknowledge the limits of both the indicators one chooses and the evidence for those indicators. This acknowledgment, in turn, has consequences for the presentation of the performance report. Rather than try to come up with hard, conclusive links between inputs, activities, and outcomes, evaluators are encouraged to tell a **performance story** that provides a credible portrait in narrative form of results and expectations, mentioning both anticipated as well as unanticipated outcomes.

- *Attribution.* A key challenge in performance measurement is attribution, or determining what a program's contribution has been to a specific outcome. The more difficult question is usually determining just what contribution the specific program in question made to the outcome. How much of the success (or failure) can we attribute to the program? What has been the contribution made by the program? Despite the measurement difficulty, attribution is a problem that cannot be ignored when trying to assess the performance of government programs. Without an answer to this question, little can be said about the worth of the program, nor can advice be provided about future directions (Mayne, 2001).

- *Credible indicators.* Performance can be measured only if there are indicators of both outputs and outcomes. Selecting indicators is not automatic, even if a program is explicit about what its intended outcomes are supposed to be. Successful performance measurement depends, in part, on finding credible indicators that tell you something important about a program and that can be successfully measured.

- *Linking resources to results.* Performance measurement is not an end in itself. It should contribute to the wider process of governmental resource allocation. In principle, if programs are found to be underperforming, resources should be moved out of them to other programs that are achieving deeper public benefits. Moreover, linking resources to results is a mechanism for supporting transparency in government decisions as well as stronger accountability to citizens.

- *Sustainability—part of a strategy.* Performance measurement needs to be part of a broader, ongoing strategy of performance assessment. It cannot be episodic or occasional. This feature touches quite closely on the issue of organizational culture, since it highlights the fact that proponents of performance measurement are not simply looking for a new tool of governance, but at changing the way in which governance operates. The ultimate goal is government that continually tries to do better, to be more responsive, and to assess its activities against standards and benchmarks. This focus is strategic, not simply technical.

Getting these factors right is a critical ingredient in the successful establishment of a performance measurement regime. At one level, most of these factors reflect technical considerations and methodological issues—this is clear, for example, for the design of a logic model that links inputs to ultimate outcomes, the selection of indicators, and dealing with the attribution problem. But at another level, performance measurement requires organizational change—this is clear, for example, for linking resources to results, and sustainability. But it is also implied in the more technical success factors. "Know the program" means development of consensus on program objectives. The same is true for designing a logic model. The exercise of judgment and allocation of attribution require reflection on an organization's environment—the organization has to be outward looking.

What then does performance measurement demand of organizations and the people who work in them? The literature highlights four organizational implications of performance measurement. The first is that if a true performance measurement regime is established, there is a focus on performance and outcomes rather than on process or outputs. The latter are clearly easier and safer to deal with. The second is a willingness to be evaluated at both an organizational and a personal level (at minimum through the performance of programs for which one is responsible). The third is a focus on continuous improvement; if performance measurement is to mean anything, it needs to be linked both to the development and adjustment of new programs and to resource allocation. The fourth is greater transparency and accountability; performance measurement means reporting both to the public and to senior managers and political managers.

Combined, these implications can make life in public organizations quite uncomfortable. Assuming that there are sufficient resources in place to establish an effective performance measurement regime, the critical success factor boils down to people thinking and behaving differently in their organizations.

EFFICIENCY EVALUATION

Even if a policy achieves all its objectives and impacts, this might be at an exorbitant cost. Having the desired impact means a policy is effective, but if it is achieved only at great cost, it may not be efficient. Two major techniques are typically used to address this sort of concern: **cost–benefit analysis** and **cost-effectiveness analysis**. Both techniques focus on the problem of resource allocation, since the issue of efficiency in public programs is really the issue of alternative and superior allocations of scarce resources. For a detailed overview, see Rossi, Lipsey, and Freeman (2004, Chapter 11).

Cost–Benefit Analysis

The logic of cost–benefit analysis is quite simple. The question is not only whether a policy or program has an impact, but at what cost. Policymakers want to relate costs and benefits in some way. Private businesses do this by measuring profits, though they also monitor other indicators such as productivity. Profit equals income minus expenses, both of which are calculated in monetary terms. As well, business firms measure income (or benefits) from their own perspective, not from the perspective of the consumer using a given product. Government services rarely yield revenue, and since they are services to the community, what counts as "income" is the benefit from the point of view of the community. The translation of these **social benefits** into purely monetary terms is sometimes difficult compared to a private firm, which simply bases its calculations on a market price. The challenge for government is to go beyond the bottom line (which is either impossible or inappropriate for public programs), and determine the net social benefit by calculating the difference between total benefits and total costs associated with a program. Thus, the basic steps in cost–benefit analysis are logically quite clear (these are explained in more detail below): decide on the accounting unit (whose costs and benefits are to be calculated); catalogue all costs and all benefits over time; monetize (attach a monetary value) to those costs and benefits; discount those costs and benefits over the period of time that the project or program will be operating; and determine the net social benefit.

Table 7.1 gives a simplified example of three policy choices for which costs and benefits have been calculated. Both choices A and B have higher net benefits than choice C, but each of them is less efficient in terms of the ratio of benefits to costs. In other words, each dollar of expenditure in choice C purchases $2 of benefits, while choices A and B purchase only $1.50 of benefits. The table also illustrates some of the problems of program choice. Alternative C is clearly the most efficient and would be chosen on that basis. But it also delivers the least net benefit, $1 million compared to $3 million and $2 million for alternatives A and B respectively. One technique is to try to combine net benefit and ratio measures in some way, for example, by comparing the gain in net benefits to the loss in efficiency. The proportional loss in efficiency by moving from C to A (25 percent) is outweighed by the gain in net benefits (200 percent) so that from this perspective, A might be the preferred alternative.

Table 7.1
NET BENEFIT AND COST-BENEFIT CALCULATIONS

Alternative	Benefits	Costs	Net Benefits	Benefit/Cost Ratio
A	$9 000 000	$6 000 000	$3 000 000	1.50
B	$6 000 000	$4 000 000	$2 000 000	1.50
C	$2 000 000	$1 000 000	$1 000 000	2.00

A is also preferred over B since, while the ratios of benefits to costs are the same, the net benefits of A are greater than those of B. These examples show that the selection of alternatives is not a mechanical process that follows easily once costs and benefits have been determined. While in the abstract it may seem easy to choose efficiency over net benefits, in the real world, decision criteria are less sharp.

It may appear that a cost–benefit ratio greater than 1.00 is self-evidently good, since there is some net gain for an investment of resources. But benefits and costs affect different groups of people, and thus may involve equity considerations. Cost–benefit analysis, however, is not concerned with distributional or equity issues; it relies on a social welfare criterion known as **Pareto optimality**. This criterion states that a change is worthwhile if at least one person is made better off while no one else is worse off. It is not the same as an increase in total benefits, if that increase depends on someone else's loss. For example, consider a string of 10 rural homes, nine of which have barely adequate road access and the tenth none at all. A tax levy on all 10 homes to build a new road connecting them could possibly be Pareto optimal, as long as the benefits of improved access for the nine homes equalled the levy. The tenth home would, of course, be much better off. In this example, everyone is at least as well off as before, and one person may be much better off. Few policy decisions are this clear. The limitations of the Pareto criterion led economists to develop another, more flexible one: the **Kaldor-Hicks criterion**, which identifies potential Pareto improvements as those that, assuming that net gainers could compensate losers, would leave at least one person better off without anyone else worse off. The redistribution is hypothetical, and so, in effect, the Kaldor-Hicks version of Pareto optimality is a criterion of net benefits. Potential Pareto improvements, it is argued, will increase total societal benefits (for both winners and losers) over time.

Practising evaluators normally leave these arcane matters of social welfare functions to academic economists. From a practical perspective, the tough issues in cost–benefit analysis are the determination and quantification of costs and benefits. Two such general problems are the selection of the **accounting unit** and the issue of **intangibles.** The accounting unit problem is about *whose* costs and benefits are to be measured. Three basic choices are the individual, the government, and society. Consider an employment agency decision on whether to provide counselling services to its clients. One way of assessing costs and benefits is to focus on the individual program participants: costs might include less time for leisure or job search, while benefits might be increased job skills. From the governmental or agency perspective, costs would be the budgetary ones of mounting the program, while benefits might be increased hiring rates and tax revenues as former clients get jobs. The societal perspective is the most comprehensive, weighing costs and benefits for total national income. Benefits, for instance, might include the value to the national economy of the jobs that clients get. The estimates of benefits and costs will differ depending on the accounting unit chosen.

The problem of intangibles concerns the difficulty of placing monetary values on some costs and benefits. Aesthetic considerations in town planning, the value people place on leisure, the sense of security provided by a tough criminal justice system: all are presumably important in determining costs and benefits, but are difficult to quantify. It is arguable that cost–benefit analyses of public programs tend to estimate costs (program or budget costs) more accurately than benefits, many of which are intangible. Educational policy evaluation, for example, has trouble measuring such benefits as civility and cultural breadth and tends by default to concentrate on job-related benefits. Cost–benefit calculations usually avoid quantifying intangibles, preferring instead to simply mention them as considerations. A related issue is that even if costs and benefits can be monetized, not all of them have an equal chance of occurring. Evaluations thus sometimes attach probabilities to costs and benefits.

The careful classification and treatment of different types of costs is the first step in competent cost–benefit analysis. One important category is **opportunity cost,** or the forgone benefits of doing one thing and not another. Assuming scarce resources, doing one thing always means forgoing something else. Cost–benefit analysis, insofar as it tries to facilitate comparisons across alternatives, tries to address the issue of opportunity cost. Other common distinctions are made in determining costs. External versus internal costs and benefits refer to indirect or unintended spillovers from a program. For example, polluting industries sometimes create jobs at home (internal benefit) while generating environmental costs elsewhere (external costs). Incremental versus **sunk costs** is another important distinction. Sunk costs are those incurred in the past; incremental costs are additional or future costs expended to mount or continue a program. A final distinction is between total and **marginal costs.** The total costs of a new counselling program for unwed mothers, for example, would include the proportion of total costs of the agency (e.g., clerical services, furniture, building, heat, light) accounted for by the program. But since these costs would occur anyway, the marginal cost of the program would be the additional resources devoted to it.

Costs and benefits usually do not occur immediately, and each may flow in different streams. In the case of capital projects or pensions, it may take many years before benefits are realized. This lag time raises a problem of measurement, since most people prefer their benefits to come now and their costs to come later. The element of time therefore has to be assessed in estimates of future costs and benefits. The usual procedure is to apply a **discount rate** to the present value of costs and benefits incurred in a project, to arrive at a measure of net present value (Boardman, Greenberg, Vining, & Weimer, 2011, Chapters 6, 10). The trick is in selecting an appropriate rate. The predominant method assesses the opportunity costs of capital, meaning the rate of return if program sums were invested in the private sector. If the economy were uncluttered by monopolies or by taxation regimes that alter pretax rates of return and restrictive foreign trade, then market rate of interest could be taken as the discount rate. Because rates of return are affected by these institutional features, economists make numerous and contentious adjustments to arrive at estimates of the real discount rate.

Cost–Effectiveness Analysis

Cost-effectiveness analysis is closely related to cost-benefit analysis and shares many of its concepts. It is a somewhat simpler and more limited technique, but one that acknowledges the shortcomings of cost-benefit approaches. Cost-effectiveness analysis restricts itself to comparing different program alternatives for achieving a given set of goals. It thus differs from cost-benefit analysis, which purports to compare programs with different goals in terms of a common denominator of benefits. Cost-effectiveness analysis refrains from efforts to monetize benefits. It simply takes program goals or outcomes as given, and then assesses different cost strategies for achieving those goals. It assumes that the least-cost strategy is the preferred alternative. Cost-effectiveness techniques can also be applied in reverse by assuming a fixed budget and choosing alternatives that provide the highest rate of goal achievement—the "biggest bang for the buck." So, "cost-effectiveness analysis is most appropriately used where there is already general agreement on the nature of the program outcomes and where the outcomes of the alternatives being compared are the same or very similar" (Guess & Farnham, 2000, p. 251).

Typical cost-effectiveness analysis relates the monetized costs of a program to a nonmonetized measure of effects. A fisheries department, for example, may want to increase the fish stock in a lake by 30 percent over five years, or by 10 0000 fish. It can choose between restricting fishing licences and stocking the lake. Restricting licences would require greater surveillance expenditures in the amount of $30 000 per year, while restocking the lake might incur a one-time expenditure of $100 000. Over five years, the first alternative yields a cost-effectiveness ratio of $1.50 per fish, while the second costs $1.00 per fish. It would appear that the second alternative would be more efficient or cost-effective.

Cost-effectiveness analysis poses the same problems as cost-benefit analysis. Which costs to consider? In the fisheries case, only departmental costs were counted, but the first alternative should also include forgone fishing by those excluded from licences. Defining the different types of costs and their relationship would also be necessary as would discounting for the project over the implementation period. But cost-effectiveness analysis makes no judgments of relative benefits; it passes these considerations on to decisionmakers, who apply other criteria. A cost-effectiveness analysis may help determine the cheapest way to build a fighter jet but is incapable of showing whether other uses of those funds would be of greater benefit to society.

Policy Evaluation in Canada

The tone of the first part of this chapter conveys the impression that program evaluation is an essential part of any reasonable approach to policymaking: how could we presume to make policies and programs, trying to solve policy problems, if we had no idea of impact or efficacy? As odd as it may sound, however, evaluation as it is currently understood and practised is a relatively recent development in governance. Its first golden age was in the 1970s, after which it went into slight decline, although another golden (or at least, silver) age may be dawning. This relatively late start, however, coincides with the rise of the policy analysis movement itself. Both, as Chapter 1 showed, were postwar phenomena associated with the rise of more activist government, particularly in the 1960s. Program evaluation, for example, depends on the application of social science tools that were developed only in this period. More subtly, program evaluation depends on viewing what government does in program terms. We do that now, because after a quarter century of public policy development and the assumption that governments have a wide horizon of responsibilities to deal with social problems, we simply take it for granted that government activity can be understood in terms of numerous clusters of programs, which, after all, are interventions to solve social issues. There was a time when the scope of government was considerably narrower, and its activities could be understood more simply in terms of activities like building roads or bridges, or providing relatively uncomplicated services such as basic education. If everyone gets the same basic education, and the presumption is that the content of that education should adhere to well-established guidelines (e.g., the three Rs, the literary canon), then there is not much point in talking about programs. The type of policy evaluation that goes on within this framework is typically a financial audit, to ensure that monies are spent appropriately. When, however, the different needs of different students (e.g., recent immigrants, people with disabilities, gifted children, girls, boys, adults, illiterate people) have to be addressed, and when different educational goals are targeted (e.g., occupational, academic, life skills), or linked to developing a knowledge economy, then suddenly what once passed as simply education now needs to be understood in terms of a range of specialized education *programs*. The type of evaluation that goes on in this context shifts from financial audits to program evaluation of outcomes and efficiency.

The term "program" first came into formal use in the Canadian federal government's estimates of expenditure only after 1971 (Sutherland, 1990, p. 140). Previously, a program "could be anything from the whole effort and apparatus of unemployment insurance to a regrouping of activities to realize a short-term special project" (p. 140). The change was due to the introduction and implementation of the **planning-programming-budgeting system (PPBS)**, pioneered in the United States (and ironically, abandoned the same year that the Canadian federal government succeeded in applying it across all departments and in the expenditure budget process). PPBS was foreshadowed in 1969 by the Treasury Board's release of its PPBS Guide (Government of Canada, 1969). The idea was that the system would be gradually introduced into the Canadian budgetary process, eventually encouraging all departments to state their activities in programmatic terms, that is, in terms of goals and objectives, specific costs associated with programs designed to achieve those goals, and resources devoted to each program. Ideally, this articulation would permit comparisons across all government agencies of related goals and their related programs. Moreover, the 1969 Guide presumed that once goals and associated programs and resources were identified, then the work of evaluation (principally cost-benefit) could go forward almost automatically. Again, to quote Sutherland (1990): "It was thought that both alternative ways of delivering the same program and different programs could be compared with one another in productivity terms—output per input unit. Analysts would be able to compare strategies for reaching given goals within a given program, but also to compare programs/goals with one another in terms of their expensiveness" (p. 143).

As Savoie (1990) noted, at the time, PPBS was thought by most practitioners and observers to hold "great promise, and few dissident voices were heard" (p. 57). Some provincial governments swiftly followed suit, most notably New Brunswick, which introduced PPBS in 1970. However, by the mid-1970s, the bloom was off the PPBS rose. Some of the wilting had to do with the failure of the system to help manage expenditures. In the

Canadian context, PPBS had been introduced as part of the budget system, on the assumption that rigorous analysis and comparison of objectives and programs would automatically generate information that would clarify planning as well as facilitate reallocations of resources to more efficient and effective programs. That did not happen, in part because PPBS logic was entangled with another agenda at the time to reduce central agency control over departments. Given that PPBS did not produce a lot of good analysis, the result was less overview and more spending (Savoie, 1990, pp. 60–61). The second problem was that, even with substantially new resources being devoted to analysis, evaluation, and consulting, the results of cost-benefit and performance analysis "could generate only a drop in the ocean of analysis that would be required if every identified purpose-oriented spending entity was to be tracked" (Sutherland, 1990, p. 144).

There were two responses to this. The first, from the Treasury Board, consisted of an odd blend of both extending and limiting the scope of program evaluation. In 1977 it issued Treasury Board Policy Circular 1977-47, which, for the first time, formally stated the requirement that all federal government programs periodically undergo an evaluation. The 1977 circular was followed in 1981 with a formal guide to evaluation that remained in place for a decade (Treasury Board of Canada, 1981). However, whereas the earlier PPBS framework had implicitly assumed that evaluations would take place automatically, rely principally on cost-benefit analysis, and generate comparative information across programs, the new policy left the evaluation cycle (three to five years) and the selection of programs to be reviewed up to administrators; it did not recommend any specific form of evaluation and eschewed comparison (Sutherland, 1990, pp. 144–145). Thus, with a kind of logic that would delight Lewis Carroll, program evaluation became both universally mandated for all federal government programs over time and yet was left up to the discretion of departmental managers as to targets and techniques of evaluation. The context had been set for ad hoc, politically inspired, and relatively insipid evaluation. Evaluation, as it came to be understood and institutionalized in Canada, evolved into a simple tool for management and review by departments and agencies. Program evaluation sank into the soft folds of the bureaucratic underbelly and became an information source for managers to improve programs rather than a real tool of accountability and comparison. In itself, there is nothing objectionable in the use of program evaluation for management purposes, but its almost exclusive dedication to this end falls far short of its potential.

The second response to the failure of PPBS came from the Auditor General of Canada. J. J. Macdonnell was appointed Auditor General in 1973 and began to press for the establishment of a comptroller general for the government of Canada. (A position by that name had existed previously but had been abolished in the mid-1960s.) Macdonnell, a private sector accountant, wanted to establish private-sector accounting practices in the government. He tried to persuade senior cabinet ministers of the idea, but they balked at the duplication of existing Treasury Board functions. Macdonnell then dropped a verbal bombshell in his 1976 report when he stated, "I am deeply concerned that Parliament—and indeed the Government—has lost, or is close to losing, effective control of the public purse" (Auditor General of Canada, 1976, p. 9). The media seized on this, and the government was forced to announce a Royal Commission on Financial Management and Accountability as well as negotiate with Macdonnell on the establishment of the Office of Comptroller General. The office was indeed established, with "full responsibility for the coordination of evaluation planning, for policy guidance, and for assessing the quality of evaluation findings in studies carried out by departments" (Savoie, 1990, p. 114). It was more a political sop than an indication of commitment to evaluation. Nonetheless, it happened that "program evaluation did indeed develop into a growth industry and that it grew around the Office of the Comptroller General" (Savoie, 1990, p. 114). The special link through program evaluation was thus established between the comptroller general, the Auditor General, and departments. As a result of these changes, "the scope of the 'audit' of government spending in federal Canada has undergone a more significant transformation than in any other Westminster system ... from reporting on the ledgers of expenditure to contesting ... the legitimacy of policy conceived by elected Governments" (Sutherland, 1999, p. 112).

The 1981 evaluation guide was updated and altered in 1991 as a result of a policy shift to reflect the logic of PS2000 (the federal public-sector reform effort in the late 1980s). This change and subsequent developments illustrate the degree to which evaluation is a reflection of the institutional and policy environment and not simply a bundle of techniques that can be generically applied. The key change was a new emphasis on evaluations that would focus on quality of service to the public. In *Into the 90s: Government Program Evaluation Perspectives*, the comptroller general explained that the new approach was about "reorienting the public service" (Treasury Board of Canada, 1991).

What did this new evaluation industry achieve between 1977 and the early 1990s? First, the quantity of evaluations began to rise dramatically. In 1980 there were only seven program evaluations in the government of Canada that met the definition in the guidelines. By 1984–85, 37 federal departments were conducting them and there were more than 100 studies (Savoie, 1990, p. 114). The Auditor General reported that in 1991–92 there were 80 evaluations conducted across the federal government, compared with 99 in 1987–88 (Auditor General of Canada, 1993, p. 247). The Auditor General conducted wide-ranging reviews of the evaluation function in the federal government in his annual reports in 1983 and 1986 and was generally critical of their quality. The 1993 report, based on data from 42 program evaluation units, noted that both the annual number of evaluations and the resources devoted to them were in decline (pp. 244–245). Examining a sample of these, the report noted that "in only about half of the programs did evaluation deal with program relevance and cost-effectiveness" (p. 230).

The 1996 annual report of the Auditor General, while noting that the context for evaluation in the federal government had changed quite dramatically in three years since its last review of evaluation, still found the government's efforts wanting (Auditor General of Canada, 1996, Chapter 3). In examining four departments in detail, the Auditor General found that evaluations still focused on smaller operational details of greater interest to administrators than to Parliament or the public. On balance, there had been some improvements, but the Auditor General's conclusions were still mixed: "We still see weaknesses in planning, in monitoring action in response to the findings of evaluation studies, and in implementing systematic approaches to assessing the performance of evaluation units" (Auditor General of Canada, 1996, Chapter 3).

The emphasis on the evaluation function was renewed in the late 1990s, partly as a result of the Auditor General's critique, but also, other forces. It began, as we outlined earlier, with the 1995 budget and the new framework introduced in Program Review. It brought together guidelines for program review, internal audit, and evaluation under one roof. Program Review goals set the parameters for the other functions, all of which were harnessed to "support the principles of managing by results" (Treasury Board of Canada, 1994, p. 1-1-2). Another key feature was the attempt to integrate the evaluative function more closely with management. In characteristic Canadian fashion, evaluation still remained a management tool, and the 1994 policy urged a "productive alliance between managers and review professionals that will link review more visibly to management decision-making and innovation, as well as accountability" (Treasury Board of Canada, 1994, p. 1-1-2). The 1994 policy was superseded by a new one in 2001, and that, in turn, was superseded by one in 2009. The focus in both policies was on linking evaluation to management. Supporting the new *Results for Canadians* management framework and the new evaluation policy was the development of a template for a Results-based Management and Accountability Framework (RMAF). Departments were required, in addition to the normal reporting functions (consisting of annual **departmental performance reports (DPRs)**, and **reports on plans and priorities (RPPs)**), to develop RMAFs for all policies and programs. This signalled, as we noted in Chapter 2, a new public management focus on **results orientation**. The key components of an RMAF are as follows:

1. *Profile*—a concise description of the policy, program, or initiative, including a discussion of the background, need, target population, delivery approach, resources, governance structure, and planned results.

2. *Logic model*—an illustration of the results chain or how the activities of a policy, program or initiative are expected to lead to the achievement of the final ... outcomes.

3. *Ongoing performance measurement strategy*—a plan for the ongoing measurement of performance, including the identification of indicators for the outputs and outcomes in the logic model and a measurement strategy describing how these indicators will be collected, how often and at what cost.

4. *Evaluation strategy*—a plan for the evaluation of the policy, program or initiative, including the identification of formative and summative evaluation issues and questions, the identification of associated data requirements, and a data collection strategy which will serve as the foundation for subsequent evaluation activities.

5. *Reporting strategy*—a plan to ensure the systematic reporting on the results of ongoing performance measurement as well as evaluation, to ensure that all reporting requirements are met. (Treasury Board of Canada, 2010)*

In 2003, the Treasury Board conducted an interim assessment of its evaluation policy (Treasury Board of Canada, 2003). The policy had been in existence for only 18 months, but continued funding for initiatives under the policy was contingent on an evaluation. The results were mixed. Implementation of the policy varied significantly among departments, and smaller agencies reported limited or nonexistent evaluation functions. While departments were making improvements, there was still a "capacity gap" of roughly one-third in terms of personnel needs to staff evaluation positions. More worryingly, the report noted, "Projected workloads are forecast to increase at a rate of approximately 200% over the upcoming two years while the number of evaluation staff is expected to increase by only 20–30% over the same time period." The general evaluation capacity in both large and small (but especially small) departments was considered "minimal," and it was not clear whether RMAFs were being effectively implemented.

Another factor propelling the new emphasis on evaluation was the announcement in 2003 of an Action Plan for Democratic Reform. The plan reinforced the importance of RMAFs and the expectation that there would be a strong evaluation function within departments (Treasury Board of Canada, 2005). With the adoption, in 2006, of the

---

*Guide for the development of results-based management and accountability frameworks, Section 2. Components of an RMAF, URL: http://www.tbs-sct.gc.ca/cee/tools-outils/rmaf-cgrr/guide02-eng.asp#note, Department of Treasury Board of Canada Secretariat, 2010. Reproduced with the permission of the Minister of Public Works and Government Services Canada, 2012.

requirement that each department develop and report on its Program Activity Architecture (PAA), there was an additional stress on linking activities to strategic outcomes. Finally, the Federal Accountability Act of 2006 introduced new requirements that departments evaluate the relevance and effectiveness of their grants and contributions programs each year. The result was that by that year, 97 percent of departments and large agencies had evaluation committees (Treasury Board of Canada, 2006). Problems remained, however. Most evaluations focused on program improvement, not on cost-effectiveness. This emphasis once again demonstrated the continuing bias in the federal government's evaluation function toward program management (Aucoin, 2005). Half of all evaluations were of programs that had budgets of less than $4 million, and 12 percent covered programs with budgets of less than $500 000 (Treasury Board of Canada, 2006). Some important, though small agencies had virtually no evaluative capacity at all, for example, the Office of the Commissioner of Official Languages, the Canadian Nuclear Safety Commission, and the National Energy Board. Most damning, perhaps, was that 23 percent of evaluations in 2004–05 were deemed to be of poor quality (Treasury Board of Canada, 2007).

Performance evaluation and reporting has been a perennial focus for the Canadian government since the 1970s, and clearly became even more important during the 1990s with Program Review and budget-cutting exercises. That importance has only grown with continued efforts at tighter expenditure management and new, tighter accountability regimes and a stronger emphasis on performance. But there can be no avoiding the conclusion that performance evaluation and reporting has not made as much headway in the federal government as one would think studying the policy documents. There are several possible reasons for this. First, as we noted, the Canadian approach has been to avoid strong external evaluation functions and integrate evaluation with management. There is nothing wrong with this, but it does leave the fox guarding the chicken coop. Second, it has to be recognized that performance evaluation takes place in specific institutional contexts. De Bruijn (2002) talks about the "perverse effects" of performance measurement: among other things, it can stimulate strategic behaviour where organizations focus on performance indicators only (in order to score points); it can stifle innovation if organizations decide that innovation is too risky (and hence will lose performance points); and good performance may even sometimes lead to punishment (for example, when a well-performing organization gets its budget cut because "it's doing so well it can probably do as well with less"). Introducing a performance regime without addressing these perversities means that it might become more a charade than a viable management tool.

Conclusion

Program evaluation has always enjoyed support, in principle, from policymakers. The logic of policy analysis, as described in Chapter 1, emphasizes careful definition of policy problems, consideration of options, and interventions that lead to amelioration or improvement. Policy as intervention depends on some idea of causal connections. In this sense, every policy or program is a guess, a hypothesis about social problems. Evaluation serves the vital function of providing empirical feedback on those hypotheses in action: Did they work? What impact did the intervention have, at what cost? It is for this reason that public policy theory urges the integration of policy evaluation into every stage of the policy process; since evaluation in a sense is the collective memory of what worked and what did not, integration of that information can save errors and effort.

But just as evaluation has been granted this pivotal role in theory, in practice it has been viewed skeptically and often marginalized in the policy process (Bogenschneider & Corbett, 2010). The reasons are not hard to understand. Even the strongest partisans of evaluation acknowledge the often severe methodological limitations of answering impact and efficiency questions (Radin, 2006). More art than science, it is always possible to find reasons why positive or negative evaluation results are flawed. These very limitations, as well as the sheer expense of doing thorough evaluations, have usually limited evaluation to routine monitoring or process studies. Also, as we noted, there is the paradox that while evaluation seems essential in theory, in practice it can appear to be a frill when compared to direct program responsibilities and delivery. Thus, in the past, evaluation has been the poor cousin of the policy process, often relegated to small policy analysis units divorced from direct policy management responsibilities (Hollander & Prince, 1993). Insofar as evaluation tends to be the dismal science of policy analysis—showing that impacts are weak or dubious, and often much more expensive than first anticipated—nobody really appreciates the bad news. Again, this dark view seems to have changed somewhat, with the requirement of audit and evaluation committees within departments and agencies, and the integration of evaluation into the RMAF as a key management function.

To these generic reasons for the limited impact of evaluation (noted even as recently as 2006) should be added some specific Canadian twists. First, the development of evaluation guidelines and institutions in the Canadian federal government in the early 1980s was done partly to placate the Auditor General and was implemented without much enthusiasm. The drivers for enhanced evaluation seem to continue to be external, and an evaluation culture is only gradually taking hold in the federal government. That said, it should also be noted that the institutional scaffolding supporting the evaluation function has been considerably strengthened in recent years. Second, the Canadian practice, and this is true of the provincial level of government as well, has been to use evaluation as a management tool. Evaluation units have been embedded in departments, and departmental managers have been responsible for the evaluation function, governed by loose central agency guidelines. This approach contrasts with the United States, where congressional committees aggressively sponsor evaluation of programs within their policy fields as a challenge to the executive and where independent **think tanks** and policy groups abound. The parliamentary system tends to be more closed to outside influences than the U.S. congressional system, and so the evaluation climate created by vibrant and vocal think tanks is not as rich in Canada as it is in the United States. To this must be added cultural influences (Canada seems to encourage less policy entrepreneurship) and economic influences (Canada's philanthropists have not channelled as much money into think tanks and foundations) (Abelson, 2002; Abelson & Carberry, 1998; Abelson & Lindquist, 2000). The best estimate is that there are only about 100 think tanks in Canada and, among them, fewer than 10 major nongovernmental, noncommercial policy institutes (e.g., C. D. Howe Research Institute, Canada West Foundation, Conference Board of Canada, Canadian Tax Foundation, Fraser Institute, Institute for Research on Public Policy, Canadian Institute for Economic Policy, and Canadian Energy Research Institute). Despite the high visibility of some think tanks and policy institutes in the media and at specific points in the policy cycle (Abelson, 1999), as well as the occasionally headline-grabbing report (e.g., the Fraser Institute's 2004 report on legalizing and taxing marijuana), most think tanks generate relatively bland publications.

Despite this gloomy assessment of evaluation and its potential to influence policymaking, this chapter has shown that evaluation may be enjoying a fitful renaissance of sorts. Evaluation may not only be getting marginally more important in government, but also the nature of evaluation may be changing. For example, the new emphasis on accountability and performance results means that the goals or outcomes of policy and programs are defined more broadly than ever before. A focus on results will encourage more impact-oriented evaluations; however, current policy paradigms also stress client satisfaction and a service orientation as outcomes. Having this dual emphasis means that the old division between process and impact analysis might be blurring, and increasingly the key impacts sought by policymakers are satisfaction and support of the process and program itself. The heightened importance of evaluation has generated discussions about better training for evaluators, possibly through newly created certificate programs at Canadian universities (Gussman, 2006).

There is a great deal to be skeptical about in policy and program evaluation, in performance measurement and results, but we prefer to end on an optimistic and uplifting note. Yes, in practice, evaluation studies can seem so insipid, qualified, and immersed in murky politics as to appear useless. Some critics dismiss evaluation as a policy sideshow, a carnival of dubious methodological handsprings and somersaults that rarely yields serious results (Radin, 2006). For other critics, insofar as evaluation is dominated by expert discourse, it threatens democracy by drawing debate away from ordinary citizens and entrapping it in a closed universe of language only a few can speak. This fear is surely overdrawn, particularly given the limited role that evaluation has played in Canadian policymaking and the emphasis on making performance and results measurement accessible to citizens. We make the opposite argument, though well aware that it holds certain dangers as well. The basic questions that form the foundations of program evaluation are vital to any democratic discussion of public policy—what works and at what cost? These are not the only questions that one can pose about policy, but they are important ones, which, if seriously addressed, can only benefit policy discussion. Canadian efforts should continue to emphasize the importance of broad evaluation of policy, as well as the wider exposure and dissemination of evaluation results.

KEY TERMS

accountability—the quality of being accountable to another for one's actions; entailing an obligation to respond to questions and regularly report

accounting unit—in doing cost-benefit analysis, the unit or jurisdiction in which costs and benefits will be ascribed

attribution problem—the difficulty of determining what the specific contribution of a policy or program intervention has been to outcomes, in contrast to all other possible factors that might have affected those outcomes

causal chain—the link of various causes and effects in producing outcomes in the implementation process

contrasted group design—an experimental evaluation design where recipients are compared to nonrecipients, and the differences are ascribed to the program

control group—in experimental designs, the randomly assigned group that will not be the recipient of the intervention or program and that will form the basis of comparison with the experimental group

cost–benefit analysis—evaluation of a program in terms of its total costs compared to its total benefits, expressed in monetary terms

cost-effectiveness analysis—compares different program alternatives for achieving a given set of goals; it is also applied by considering a fixed budget and choosing alternatives that provide the highest rate of goal achievement

departmental performance report (DPR)—annual report on performance of each federal department for the previous fiscal year

dependent variable—the variable that is being explained

diagnostic procedures—procedures in which the evaluators are often involved in generating and analyzing data that are relevant to problem definition, trend forecasting, and program design aspects

discount rate—the rate chosen to discount future benefits, usually assessed as the opportunity costs of capital, meaning the rate of return if program sums were invested in the private sector

experimental design—the evaluation of impact based on randomly assigned experimental and control groups

experimental group—the randomly assigned group to which the program or intervention is applied in an experimental design

formative evaluation—evaluation designed to support development and improvement of a program as it is being implemented

impact evaluation—analysis of the actual effect or impact of a program on its intended target, along with unintended consequences

implementation theory—the specific activities and resources that need to be mobilized in connection with each of the links in the program's causal chain to achieve the desired outcome

intangibles—the costs and benefits of a program for which it is difficult to place monetary values

Kaldor-Hicks criterion—identifies potential Pareto improvements as those that, assuming that net gainers could compensate losers, would leave at least one person better off without anyone else worse off

logic model—usually a graphical representation of the links between program inputs, activities, outputs, immediate outcomes, and long-term results

marginal cost—the additional cost of producing one more unit of a good or service

meta-analysis—a technique where evaluators review the existing literature on a specific program, treating each evaluation study as a single case and building statistical conclusions based on these observations

needs assessment—a review of the service and support needs of a particular agency or group

opportunity cost—the forgone benefits of doing one thing and not another

Pareto optimality—the criterion of optimization that states that a change is worthwhile if at least one person is made better off while no one else is worse off

performance story—reporting of program results in such a way as to highlight both successes and shortcomings, the challenges faced by the organization, and what it might do in the future to improve results

planning-programming-budgeting system (PPBS)—encourages departments to state their activities in programmatic terms, that is, in terms of goals and objectives, specific costs associated with programs designed to achieve those goals, and resources devoted to each program

pre-program/post-program design—an evaluation technique that uses time-series data for the period before program implementation and after to draw conclusions about the likely impact of the intervention

process evaluation—monitors an existing program to assess the effort and organizational resources put into it

program components—typically, the strategies, activities, behaviours, media products, and technologies needed to deliver the program, along with a specification of the intended recipients and delivery situations

program evaluation—an essential part of any reasonable approach to policymaking that assesses, in some sense, how well programs are doing in terms of their stated objectives

program logic—sketches out the assumed causal links that will yield specified outcomes in order to conduct impact evaluation

program theory—the hypotheses and explanations about the causal links that tie program inputs to expected program outputs

quasi-experimental design—all contrasted or comparing group designs that fall short of the demand for completely random assignment of the groups

random assignment—a method used in experimental design where the odds of being in either the experimental or the control group are the same

reports on plans and priorities (RPPs)—annual report required from each federal government department and agency about its plans and priorities for the coming fiscal year

results orientation—a management focus on new forms of review, audit, and evaluation based on results

single observation design—a method of evaluation that relies on a measure of impact only after the program is introduced

social benefits—the benefits obtained from the point of view of the community of the services provided by government

social indicators—data that represent important characteristics of society such as crime, literacy, health; contrasted to the usual economic indicators such as inflation and unemployment

summative evaluation—an evaluation undertaken at the end of a program to gauge its success

sunk cost—costs that have incurred in the past and that are not recoverable

think tanks—nongovernmental, sometimes for-profit and sometimes nonprofit, organizations dedicated to research and discussion of policy issues with the wider public and decisionmakers

FURTHER READINGS

Boardman, A. E., Greenberg, D. H., Vining, A., & Weimer, D. L. (2011). *Cost-benefit analysis: Concepts and practice* (4th ed.). Boston, MA: Prentice-Hall.

De Bruijn, H. (2002). *Managing performance in the public sector*. London, UK: Routledge.

Patton, M. Q. (2002). *Qualitative research and evaluation methods* (3rd ed.). Thousand Oaks, CA: Sage.

Rossi, P. H., Lipsey, M. W., & Freeman, H. E. (2004). *Evaluation: A systematic approach* (7th ed.). Thousand Oaks, CA: Sage.

Treasury Board of Canada. (2009). *Policy on evaluation*. Retrieved from http://www.tbs-sct.gc.ca/pol/doc-eng.aspx?id=15024&section=text#cha1

Wholey, J. S., Hatry, H. P., & Newcomer, K. E. (Eds.). (2010). *Handbook of practical program evaluation* (3rd ed.). San Francisco, CA: Jossey-Bass.

REFERENCES

Abelson, D. E. (1999). Public visibility and policy relevance: Assessing the impact and influence of Canadian policy institutes. *Canadian Public Administration, 42*(2), 240–270.

Abelson, D. E. (2002). *Do think tanks matter: Assessing the impact of public policy institutes*. Montréal, QC: McGill-Queen's University Press.

Abelson, D. E., & Carberry, C. M. (1998). Following suit or falling behind?: A comparative analysis of think tanks in Canada and the United States. *Canadian Journal of Political Science, 31*(3), 525–556.

Abelson, D. E., & Lindquist, E. A. (2000). Think tanks in North America. In J. G. McGann & R. K. Weaver (Eds.), *Think tanks and civil society: Catalysts for ideas and action* (pp. 37–66). New Brunswick, NJ: Transaction.

American Evaluation Society. (2012). *Guiding principles for evaluators.* Retrieved from http://www.eval.org/Publications/GuidingPrinciples.asp

Aucoin, P. (2005). *Decision-making in government: The role of program evaluation* (Discussion Paper). Ottawa, ON: Treasury Board of Canada. Retrieved from http://www.tbs-sct.gc.ca/cee/tools-outils/aucoin-eng.asp

Auditor General of Canada. (1976). *Annual report 1976.* Retrieved from http://www.oag-bvg.gc.ca/internet/English/parl_lp_e_933.html

Auditor General of Canada. (1993). *Annual report 1993.* Retrieved from http://www.oag-bvg.gc.ca/internet/English/parl_lp_e_933.html

Auditor General of Canada. (1996). *Annual report 1996.* Retrieved from http://www.oag-bvg.gc.ca/internet/English/parl_lp_e_933.html

Banerjee, A. V., & Duflo, E. (2011). *Poor economics: A radical rethinking of the way to fight global poverty.* New York, NY: Public Affairs.

Boardman, A. E., Greenberg, D. H., Vining, A., & Weimer, D. L. (2011). *Cost-benefit analysis: Concepts and practice* (4th ed.). Boston, MA: Prentice-Hall.

Bogenschneider, K., & Corbett, T. J. (2010). *Evidence-based policymaking: Insights from policy-minded researchers and research-minded policymakers.* New York, NY: Routledge.

Boruch, R. F., & Petrosino, A. (2010). Meta-analyses, systemic reviews, and evaluation syntheses. In J. S. Wholey, H. P. Hatry, & K. E. Newcomer (Eds.), *Handbook of practical program evaluation* (3rd ed.). (pp. 531–553). San Francisco, CA: Jossey-Bass.

Canadian Evaluation Society. (2012). *CES guidelines for ethical conduct.* Retrieved from http://www.evaluationcanada.ca/site.cgi?s=5&ss=4&_lang=an

City of Ottawa. (2012). *Clean needle syringe program.* Retrieved from http://ottawa.ca/en/health_safety/living/dat/drug/needles/

De Bruijn, H. (2002). *Managing performance in the public sector.* London, UK: Routledge.

Framst, G. (1995, October/November). Application of program logic model to agricultural technology transfer programs. *Canadian Journal of Program Evaluation, 10*, 123–132.

Geva-May, I., & Pal, L. A. (1999). Good fences make good neighbours: Policy evaluation and policy analysis—exploring the differences. *Evaluation, 5*(3), 259–277.

Government of Canada. (1969). *Planning, programming and budgeting guide.* Ottawa, ON: Information Canada.

Guess, G. M., & Farnham, P. G. (2000). *Cases in public policy analysis.* Washington, DC: Georgetown University Press.

Gussman, T. (2006). Improving the profession of evaluation. *Canadian Evaluation Society.* Retrieved from http://www.evaluationcanada.ca/site.cgi?s=1&ss=1&_lang=en&num=00627

Holden, D. J., & Zimmerman, M. A. (Eds.) (2009). *A practical guide to program evaluation planning.* Los Angeles, CA: Sage.

Hollander, M. J., & Prince, M. J. (1993, Summer). Analytical units in federal and provincial governments: Origins, functions and suggestions for effectiveness. *Canadian Public Administration, 36,* 190–224.

Mayne, J. (2001, Spring). Addressing attribution through contribution analysis: Using performance measures sensibly. *The Canadian Journal of Program Evaluation, 16,* 1–24.

McLaughlin, J. A., & Jordan, G. B. (2010). Using logic models. In J. S. Wholey, H. P. Hatry, & K. E. Newcomer (Eds.), *Handbook of practical program evaluation* (3rd ed.). (pp. 55–80). San Francisco, CA: Jossey-Bass.

Newcomer, K. E., Hatry, H. P., & Wholey, J. S. (2010). Planning and designing useful evaluations. In J. S. Wholey, H. P. Hatry, & K. E. Newcomer (Eds.), *Handbook of practical program evaluation* (3rd ed.). (pp. 5–29). San Francisco, CA: Jossey-Bass.

OECD [Organisation for Economic Co-operation and Development]. (1995). *Public management developments: Update 1995.* Paris: OECD.

OECD. (2005). *Modernising government: The way forward.* Paris: OECD.

Office of Management and Budget (United States). (2011). *Circular no. A-11: Preparation, submission and execution of the budget.* Retrieved from http://www.whitehouse.gov/omb/circulars_a11_current_year_a11_toc/

Patton, M. Q. (1987). *Creative evaluation* (2nd ed.). Newbury Park, CA: Sage.

Patton, M. Q. (2002). *Qualitative research and evaluation methods* (3rd ed.). Thousand Oaks, CA: Sage.

Patton, M. Q. (2008). *Utilization-focused evaluation: The new century text* (4th ed.). Thousand Oaks, CA: Sage.

Performance-Based Management Special Interest Group. (2001). *The performance-based management handbook: A six-volume compilation of techniques and tools for implementing the Government Performance and Results Act of 1993.* Washington, DC: Training Resources and Data Exchange, Performance-Based Management Special Interest Group for the Office of Strategic Planning and Program Evaluation. Retrieved from http://www.orau.gov/pbm/pbmhandbook/pbmhandbook.html

Posvac, E. J., & Carey, R. G. (1980). *Program evaluation: Methods and case studies.* Englewood Cliffs, NJ: Prentice-Hall.

Radin, B. A. (2006). *Challenging the performance movement: Accountability, complexity, and democratic values.* Washington, DC: Georgetown University Press.

Rossi, P. H., Lipsey, M. W., & Freeman, H. E. (2004). *Evaluation: A systematic approach* (7th ed.). Thousand Oaks, CA: Sage.

Saint-Martin, D. (2000). *Building the new managerialist state: Consultants and the politics of public sector reform in comparative perspective.* Oxford: Oxford University Press.

Savoie, D. J. (1990). *The politics of public spending in Canada.* Toronto, ON: University of Toronto Press.

Schacter, M. (1999). *Means ... ends ... indicators: Performance measurement in the public sector.* Ottawa, ON: Institute on Governance.

SRDC [Social Research and Demonstration Corporation]. (2012). *What we do.* Retrieved from http://www.srdc.org/en_what_we_do.asp

Sutherland, S. L. (1990, Summer). The evolution of program budget ideas in Canada: Does Parliament benefit from estimates reform? *Canadian Public Administration, 33,* 133–164.

Sutherland, S. L. (1999). Bossing democracy: The value-for-money audit and the electorate's loss of political power to the auditor general. In R. M. Bird, M. J. Trebilcock, & T. A. Wilson (Eds.), *Rationality in public policy: Retrospect and prospect, a tribute to Douglas Hartle* (Canadian Tax Paper No. 104) (pp. 109–140). Toronto, ON: Canadian Tax Foundation.

Torgerson, C. J., Torgerson, D. J., & Taylor, C. A. (2010). Randomized controlled trials and nonrandomized designs. In J. S. Wholey, H. P. Hatry, & K. E. Newcomer (Eds.), *Handbook of practical program evaluation* (3rd ed.). (pp. 144–162). San Francisco, CA: Jossey-Bass.

Treasury Board of Canada. (1981). *Guide on the program evaluation function.* Ottawa, ON: Minister of Supply and Services.

Treasury Board of Canada. (1991). *Into the 90s: Government program evaluation perspectives.* Ottawa, ON: Office of the Comptroller General.

Treasury Board of Canada. (1994, July). *Treasury Board manual—Review, internal audit and evaluation* (Amendment RIE/94-1). Ottawa, ON: Treasury Board of Canada.

Treasury Board of Canada. (2000). *Results for Canadians: A management framework for the government of Canada.* Retrieved from http://www.tbs-sct.gc.ca/report/res_can/rc-eng.asp

Treasury Board of Canada. (2003). *Interim evaluation of the Treasury Board's evaluation policy.* Retrieved from http://www.tbs-sct.gc.ca/cee/pubs/int-prov-eng.asp

Treasury Board of Canada. (2005). *The health of the evaluation function in the government of Canada: Report for the fiscal year 2004–05.* Retrieved from http://www.tbs-sct.gc.ca/cee/pubs/hefgc-sfegc-eng.asp

Treasury Board of Canada. (2006). *Valuing the evaluation function: Problems and perspectives.* Originally retrieved from http://www.tbs-sct.gc.ca/eval/ppt/jun06-001/vef-vfe_e.asp [Website no longer available].

Treasury Board of Canada. (2007). *Evaluation policy renewal—overview.* Originally retrieved from http://www.tbs-sct.gc.ca/presentations/rma-dpr/overview-apercu/overview-apercu_e.pdf [Website no longer available].

Treasury Board of Canada. (2010). *Guide for the development of results-based management and accountability frameworks.* Retrieved from http://www.tbs-sct.gc.ca/cee/tools-outils/rmaf-cgrr/guide02-eng.asp#note

Weiss, C. H. (1998). *Evaluation* (2nd ed.). Upper Saddle River, NJ: Prentice Hall.

Wholey, J. S. (2003). Improving performance and accountability: Responding to emerging management challenges. In S. I. Donaldson & Michael Scriven (Eds.), *Evaluating social programs and problems* (pp. 43–61). Mahwah, NJ: Lawrence Erlbaum Associates.

Policymaking under Pressure

This book is based on the idea that the context for policymaking has changed significantly in recent years and that consequently, we need to rethink our tools and the way that we do policy analysis. One major and relatively new change seems to be the degree to which policymaking increasingly takes place under pressure, in circumstances of adversity and uncertainty, dealing with crises, disasters, and emergencies. The most obvious are terrorist threats and bombings, environmental and weather threats, epidemics, and the continuing global financial crisis. There are several reasons for this: the increasing interdependency of complex systems such as the Internet, pan-continental energy grids, or global financial markets; the rapid transmission of disease because of global markets for food products and enhanced ability of individuals to travel around the world; the possibility that environmental changes are inducing new natural disasters (e.g., flooding, climate change, erosion); the ability of modern media to both instantly magnify events and broadcast them in real time; and conflict zones that drive refugees to seek safety. Whatever the reasons, the modern reality of policymaking is marked increasingly by dealing with crisis. The problem is that most of the models of decisionmaking used in the policy literature are models predicated on the normal, the everyday, the linear, and the expected. What happens when policymakers are confronted with the abnormal, the unusual, the uncertain, and the unexpected? This chapter provides an overview of some themes in an increasingly important area of policymaking and public management: handling crisis and emergency.

Conventional policy theory and practice are strongly influenced by the rational model, described in Chapter 1. We discussed the assumptions that underpin the model, and some of the challenges. But we can go a little deeper. The model tends to assume a relatively small number of decisionmakers, perhaps even only one. It assumes, if not complete information, at least reasonably high levels of information and data to inform decisions. In order for the sequence to take place, the model assumes that there is sufficient time for that sequence to unfold. And finally, coupled to the assumption that there is sufficient information to make choices, is the notion that problems are reasonably well defined.

There are many instances of public policy in which these assumptions hold reasonably well. Routine or "normal" policy analysis therefore can be undertaken more or less within the broad framework of the rational model: problems are defined, models of causal variables developed, data gathered, options or alternatives generated, and choices made based on some set of criteria. But we also know that the real world of public policy is marked at times—and seems increasingly to be marked—by emergencies and crises. Policy decisions have to be made under pressure, and all the assumptions of the rational model are stretched if not broken. Most crises and emergencies involve multiple actors, with overlapping authorities. Instead of single decisionmakers, there are many, and they have to be coordinated. Instead of reasonably high levels of information and data, randomness and uncertainty are apparent. Time seems to be truncated, and major decisions have to be made quickly. Finally, as we noted in Chapter 3, the policy problem is often ill defined or so complex that it defies easy categorization and analysis. All of these characteristics marked the global financial crisis that began in October 2008, as well as the Fukushima nuclear disaster that occurred in 2011.

While we commonly think of crisis and emergency as the same thing, there is a distinction between them that affects the way we think about them and the way we react to them. An **emergency** is an abnormal and unexpected threat event that requires immediate action. A **crisis** is a turning point or moment of danger that threatens the survival of an entire system. A house fire, for example, would usually be considered an emergency rather than a family crisis. The latter would be some event or development that threatens the existence of the family as such (the death of a member). Something can be a crisis and an emergency at the same time, from different perspectives. A forest fire or a flood that threatens to destroy a community is evidently a crisis for that community since it threatens its very existence. From the government's perspective, it is an emergency since it does not threaten the government's existence. As well, emergencies can quickly evolve into crises. The 9/11 attack on the World Trade Center was a massive emergency, but for a short time it looked as well as if it might be a crisis for all the United States (in case this was the first phase of an attack on the country) and for the government (in case leading members of the administration were killed). There is somewhat less scope for interpretation in the cases of emergency, though naturally there can be differences in point of view. But most emergencies, by definition, are abnormalities with severe consequences occurring in a short time. We can mistake some unwanted events as emergencies (e.g., someone faints, but others think it is a heart attack), but generally emergencies are defined in terms of significant and immediate threat, usually to physical property or life. A crisis, since it is a threat event that affects the integrity of the system, is more debatable precisely because a judgment has to be made about what the system is, what its component elements are, how they work together to maintain that system, and why the threat event might undermine those elements. A "cabinet crisis" requires a judgment about whether a threat event (e.g., the resignation of a prominent minister) might bring down the government as a whole.

There is obviously a relationship between emergency and crisis, but they call forth different types of responses and different forms of public management. These will be explored later in the chapter. For the moment, it is worth trying to discern the generic elements of a substantial threat event, whether it falls into one category or another. Substantial threat events seem to be determined by four factors: randomness, severity, uniqueness, and time compression. Events that are highly random (not expected), severe in terms of consequences, unique or previously not encountered and, hence, without an information base, and compressed in time (moving rapidly; requiring rapid response) pose the greatest type of threat. Events that are low on all four dimensions pose the least threat and are the easiest to manage. The other two categories are mixed. Events such as some floods and forest fires are predictable to a degree, but still pose severe threats and need a quick response. Since they have happened before and have typical configurations, there are routines in place to deal with them. In the other category, severity is low, but the event is unexpected or difficult to predict, and largely unknown. Types of events can migrate into different categories as more is known about them. A flu virus that is unknown in one year, even while it is predictable that it will move through the population in the fall and winter, is unique. Once the strain has been determined, a vaccine can be prepared the next year.

The challenge for contemporary policymakers is that crisis and emergency threat events that promise severe and widespread impacts seem to be increasingly common. By definition, crises and emergencies are events that strain a policymaking system and perhaps even cause it to collapse. Too many emergencies—indeed, sometimes only one—that are not handled well can pose a crisis for the system. The question is what techniques of analysis and of management can be drawn upon to deal with these types of challenges. The rest of the chapter begins by reviewing some of the theoretical foundations of crisis management and policymaking under pressure, and then moves to risk assessment, emergency preparedness, and crisis management.

Modelling Chaos

Some of the ingredients of policymaking under pressure have been mentioned above, but are there more precise ways of conceptualizing those elements? One of the first attempts in the policy literature to come to grips with this problem was Ira Sharkansky's (1986) notion of "policymaking under adversity": "Shifts and time-compressed turns in the nature of issues make traditional policy paradigms, policy assumptions, policy habits, policy 'grammars,' and grand policies increasingly doubtful" (Sharkansky, 1986, p. 23). Crises involve discontinuities and jumps that create challenges. As we noted above, if normal policymaking may be seen as incremental, with each step more or less predictably or controllably emanating from the last, then what is nonincremental, unpredictable, and not immediately controllable has the potential to create crisis. On August 14, 2003, for example, parts of the northeastern United States and Ontario experienced a power blackout. It lasted for four days in some parts of the United States, and Ontario saw rolling blackouts for more than a week before power was restored (U.S.–Canada Power System Outage Taskforce, 2004). The outage was estimated to have cost the United States upward of US$10 billion, and as much as $2.3 billion in lost manufacturing shipments from Ontario. This was a shift and jump with vengeance. The linear continuity of power at a flip of a switch is taken for granted by citizens, and while there are peaks and surges in demand, these can normally be managed. Ironically, that day was considered normal, without unusually heavy power demands in and around Ohio, where the first system collapse occurred. Due to a combination of human and software error, failures in that region's power grid were not noticed in time, and because of the integration of the North American power grid system, a failure in Ohio rippled through and hit Ontario and several other U.S. states. We will discuss the nature of causation in chaotic events in a moment, but the point here is the shifts and jumps that Sharkansky mentions.

Shifts and jumps indicate a break from a linear routine. Every threat event contains a large element of surprise that makes it different from normal. People who live in earthquake zones, for example, know that there is likely to be an earthquake sometime, but not exactly when. In some instances, like H1N1 flu epidemic in 2009, the event is a total surprise since it has never happened before (this strain of influenza had never been seen before). Beyond the element of surprise, however, crises or emergencies as nonlinear *policy* problems are collective action problems. Comfort (1999), for example, looks at what she calls "shared risk" problems—crises or emergencies that affect large communities—as **nonlinear policy problems**. Her 1999 classic study reviewed examples of earthquakes and emergency response to them, and concluded that they were characterized by small, unpredictable shifts and ripple effects, where the methods to address them "differ from those used in traditional policy analysis" (Comfort, 1999, p. 4).

The idea of nonlinearity in policy problems of emergency situations poses more than an incidental challenge to policy analysis. As we noted in Chapter 1, the conventional discipline is based on a rational model, which, in turn, has deeply embedded assumptions of what constitutes knowledge and the techniques to generate knowledge, as well as how that knowledge is used—essentially as information through communication. "Breakdowns" occur through communication or informational failures. Comfort (2007) argues that in a case like Hurricane Katrina (2005), information about the impending storm and its communication were remarkably accurate; the underlying problem was "cognition," or developing a shared picture of the likely threat among a very heterogeneous group of actors (multiple jurisdictions at multiple levels, with private sector and nonprofit organizations as well). The rational model of decisionmaking assumes linearity—reasoning from information to decisions. In emergencies, whether floods or fires, that process is too slow. "Emergency managers using cognition do not review the entire set of rules of operation for the system but rather scan the margins for discrepancies or malfunctions. It is the discrepancy between what they view as normal performance and the change in status of key indicators that alerts them to potential danger" (Comfort, 2007, p. 193). Klein, for example, shows that actors involved in providing emergency services (e.g., firefighters, crisis ward nurses) rely on "recognition-primed decisionmaking" that draws rapidly and almost intuitively on analogies of previous experiences (Klein, 1998).

Another strand in this critique of linear reasoning is based on the challenge of recent scientific theories that break with Newtonian mechanics and deterministic science. These theories include quantum mechanics, complexity theory, chaos theory, and cognitive science (Morçöl, 2002). The difference is between seeing the world as a clock or as a cloud. A clock has deterministic mechanisms, the system works on the basis of clear causality and connections, and the clock, as a whole, is stably configured as a clock and nothing else. Imagine a cloud, either of vapour or of thousands of tiny insects. Its boundary is constantly shifting and changing, its shape elongates and contracts, and yet it is still recognizably a cloud. The mechanisms of interaction are much more challenging to explain—there are no pulleys or gears, only what appear to be random interactions of particles or insects that constantly ripple through the system. And yet the system, with all of its disparate elements, manages to maintain an equilibrium, and is self-correcting and adaptive.

As Comfort (2006) notes, the "effective mobilization of response to extreme events on a large scale is one of the least understood problems in public management. This process requires the rapid search, exchange and absorption of valid information regarding sudden, damaging events transmitted through a network of organizations that crosses disciplinary, organizational and jurisdictional boundaries" (p. 312). Normal policy-making and normal responses can be organized hierarchically, but in emergencies with high stress, high uncertainty, and multiple actors, hierarchy breaks down quickly. What are needed instead are dynamic, complex, nonlinear systems of adaptive self-organization. Comfort (1999, pp. 8–9) provides an example, drawing eight key concepts from the scientific literature on complexity and chaos that describes elements of these types of systems. First, the evolution and dynamics of these communities, like all complex systems, depend greatly on initial conditions and characteristics of the system. Even small differences among systems in these initial conditions can have far-reaching consequences. Second, random events occurring outside the system can have great effects on the system itself and take it into unpredicted directions. Third, these random events are irreversible within the system in the sense that whatever impacts they have become part of the system itself—Comfort's example is how an unexpected earthquake led to revisions in building codes that significantly altered construction in seismic zones in California. Fourth, feedback loops of communication and coordination lead to adaptation by mutual adjustment (our cloud example above, or a school of fish). Fifth, because multiple actors create constraints for action through the need for coordination, centres of energy and influence crop up in these systems (leaders or "strange attractors") that move the system forward. Sixth, this forward motion in a complex system can involve a transition to a new equilibrium of a substantially changed system. Seventh, the behaviour of the system often yields unpredictable results, and, finally, these systems can develop recurring patterns of behaviour in different contexts to achieve similar system-wide goals. Later in this chapter we will examine the implications for policy and, in particular, for emergency preparedness and response from these ideas.

A final illustration of thinking differently about complex systems and change that casts light on shifts and jumps is the idea of the **tipping point**. Gladwell (2000) argues that the world is full of instances—from fashion to crime rates to drug use—of often abrupt, dramatic, and inexplicable changes. Certain books and clothing styles appear out of nowhere and become social phenomena. Inner-city crime can suddenly leap up or decline precipitously. These phenomena are equivalent to systems that undergo a sudden transition. Gladwell is focusing on social systems and rapid transitions, and argues that these tipping points are analogous to epidemics and function with similar mechanisms. "Epidemics are a function of the people who transmit infectious agents, the infectious agent itself, and the environment in which the infectious agent is operating. And when an epidemic tips, when it is jolted out of equilibrium, it tips because something has happened, some change has occurred in one (or two or three) of those areas" (pp. 18–19). He somewhat dramatically calls these three agents of change the Law of the Few, the Stickiness Factor, and the Power of Context.

The Law of the Few builds on the simple insight that epidemics typically are spread by just a tiny subset of everyone who gets infected. The most jarring example is of Gaetan Dugas, the Canadian flight attendant who claimed to have had 2500 sexual partners all over North America and who was linked to 40 of the earliest AIDS cases in New York and California. In social dynamics, the idea is that a small number of unique individuals spread the word. Not just any individual, however. Gladwell identifies three types of individuals whose unique gifts make a large difference in the social distribution of information: connectors, mavens (a Yiddish word that means collectors of knowledge), and salespeople. Connectors are those types of persons with lots of social connections, and moreover, social connections to the right people—others who themselves are influential in their circle. Connectors are people who span various social worlds and who can effectively "market" an idea or a product. Mavens, on the other hand, are basically information brokers who know a great amount of detail about something and pass that information along to connectors, who, in turn, distribute it more widely. Salespeople are another select group of people "with the skills to persuade us when we are unconvinced of what we are hearing" (Gladwell, 2000, p. 70).

If social epidemics depend on the nature of the messenger, they also depend on the nature of the message, or what Gladwell calls the stickiness factor, or how memorable something is, which, in turn, depends on small cues and small aspects of the message that appeal to people.

Finally, the power of context is analogous to the conditions in which a medical epidemic takes place—the same communicable disease in a context of poverty and crowding versus sanitation and space. Gladwell cites the well-known "broken windows" theory of crime contagion (Kelling & Coles, 1996). The idea is that broken windows in a community signal to passersby that no one cares about that community, and soon more windows get broken. All sorts of small disorders—graffiti, for example—encourage an epidemic of crime because criminals are encouraged to believe that no one cares enough to challenge their behaviour. The classic illustration of this was the condition of the New York subway system in the mid-1980s—inefficient and overrun by petty crime. A consultant at the time encouraged the city to focus on the lurid graffiti that graced almost every subway car, because it was a visible symbol of the system's decay. The city established cleaning stations and ensured that any car with graffiti was cleaned immediately. At the same time, in the face of serious crimes on the subway, the authorities bore down on fare cheating, on the same principle that a small expression of disorder (it was estimated that 170 000 people a day were using the system without paying) sent a clear message that any other criminal act was fine.

Tipping points, chaos theory, complexity theory—all seem far removed from practical policymaking. But, in fact, they are conceptual schemes and approaches that try, in some measure, to capture reality in ways superior to a more linear, rationalist, positivist model. What are some of the practical implications of these types of more dynamic models for the way we think about public policy? For one thing, initial conditions make a difference in how systems evolve. Coupled with this is an emphasis on a system of interactions, not on a single problem (Perrow, 1984). Conventional policy analysis, as explained in Chapter 3, begins with problem structuring. Even though we alluded to the fact that problems are complex and that they come in clusters, it is still largely an analysis that focuses on one vector of issues or challenges. And it presumes that one can make an intervention along that vector and change causal relations and thus change outcomes. An example might be an inner-city community-based program to counsel teenagers on sexuality and drugs. A conventional approach would see the "problem" in terms of negative outcomes from unsafe sexual practices and dependency on drugs. Obviously, the analysis would highlight the role of schools and families, but it would target youth as "clients" of the program and seek interventions. A complex systems approach would look at teenagers within the community context and at "systems" embedded in teenage groups (peer pressure, social bonding, what is considered "cool") and take that as a point of departure. It might also be sensitive to the fact that the same program might have very different results depending on what community and what groups of youths were being supported—the initial conditions of each system would make a big difference in outcomes. A real-world example is Canada's program on fetal alcohol spectrum disorder (FASD): "Call them root causes, life conditions and experiences or determinants of health ... they are the factors that set the stage for women's use of alcohol during pregnancy.... Clearly, women have an important role in preventing FASD. What is equally important, and not as clear to many, is that family, community, governments and society have a vital role in understanding and dealing with the root causes of women's use of alcohol during pregnancy" (Public Health Agency of Canada, 2005).

A second implication is the importance and, indeed, the inevitability of small, random events that can shock a system and change its trajectory dramatically. "Planning for the unexpected" is, of course, difficult to do, but this mindset encourages a mentality of monitoring the environment as well as internal processes regularly. It might also encourage deliberate redundancy in systems that are fragile or whose failure will have far-reaching consequences. A third implication is that large changes can come from small interventions. This insight is embedded in the idea of tipping points, but it is a feature, as well, of other complex systems theories. From a policy point of view, it implies that significant change can be generated from small, focused interventions that take system characteristics seriously. Fourth, in line with the notion that complex systems have internal mechanisms of modest equilibrium, there is an emphasis on feedback loops of communication and information. When a school of fish is observed in motion, it seems almost like a single organism, even while it is made up of hundreds of actors mutually adjusting to the myriad of each other's actions. Complex social systems—from loose coalitions to formal organizations—also require inordinate amounts of communication and information exchange to work. This lesson comes from the implementation literature, of course, but it takes on a new angle in the context of complex systems theory. In traditional implementation thinking, the problem is communication from above down the line, to ensure that the original policy idea unfolds as planned and that everyone is more or less operating in the same framework. From a complex systems perspective, the communication has to be 360 degrees in three dimensions. It is about information moving up as well as sideways and from top to down. It is about information and communication as the loose glue that ties the system together, but also makes it possible to adapt and adjust.

The final implication is about adaptation. The conventional approach to policy analysis and implementation sees it as a linear unfolding. But bring in randomness, unpredictability, and the impact of small events, and it is likely that at any given point, the system (an organization, a political party) will need to respond to shocks and either regroup or transform itself in the light of that external shock. This need means adaptation as well as learning that maintains the integrity of the system in some fashion. There needs to be a capacity to build on experiences, incorporate them into practice, and embed them into some sort of collective memory. Conventional theory also presumes a fairly flat organization. Learning does not happen as well in systems that are grounded in command-and-control frameworks. Interestingly, Sharkansky assumed that policymaking under adversity would require "power concentration" (Sharkansky, 1986, p. 123). More contemporary complex systems theory argues that what is required for resilience is distributed and shared responsibility so that lessons can be learned quickly and moved through the system.

Having looked through some theoretical lenses on the issues of emergency and crisis, we can now turn to real-world examples. The next sections address three important areas that fall under the rubric of policymaking under pressure: risk assessment, emergency management, and crisis management.

Risk Assessment

From a policy perspective, **risk** is increasingly an important component about thinking through policy issues and managing policy organizations. Risk is associated with threats to government assets and personnel, and can arise from cataclysmic terrorist acts or simple accidents in the field. Another factor is the rise in insurance costs, which makes risk management more than a matter of taking out a policy; it becomes a matter of actively mitigating or avoiding risks. Finally, the public is less tolerant of even small errors made by private and public organizations, and is more ready to litigate in a climate where courts are prepared to hand out increasingly punitive damages.

The federal government has had a **risk management** policy in place since 2001, which was revised in 2010. It notes that in "a dynamic and complex public sector context, risk management plays a significant role in strengthening government capacity to recognize, understand, accommodate and capitalize on new challenges and opportunities" (Treasury Board of Canada, 2010). It outlines basic concepts that underpin the policy framework:

> Integrated risk management: Is a continuous, proactive and systematic process to understand, manage and communicate risk from an organization-wide perspective. It is about supporting strategic decision-making that contributes to the achievement of an organization's overall objectives.
>
> Risk: Refers to the effect of uncertainty on objectives. It is the expression of the likelihood and impact of an event with the potential to affect the achievement of an organization's objectives.
>
> Risk management: Is a systematic approach to setting the best course of action under uncertainty by identifying, assessing, understanding, making decisions on and communicating risk issues.

Risk, of course, is, to some large extent, a subjective assessment at both the individual and the cultural level. Some people see no risks in activities that make others quail. Societies define risk differently as well. For example, there is a case to be made that contemporary industrial societies have elevated "safety" to almost a religious level (Beck, 1992, 1999; Furedi, 2002). On almost any conceivable measure, from life expectancy to the likelihood of suffering accidents, people generally today (in developed countries, to be sure) are safer than ever before. Paradoxically, that very condition of relative safety may inflate people's expectations about how safe things should be and, hence, lower their tolerance to risk. Nonetheless, there are internationally recognized definitions of risk. The International Organization for Standards defines risk as a "combination of the probability of an event and its consequences." This definition highlights two key points about risk: chance or probability, and severity of consequences. This is exactly the logic behind auto insurance. Companies calibrate their insurance premiums to age, sex, type of car, driving environment, and use. These are all measures of probability. Young male drivers of sports cars in urban centres who will use their cars a lot are a greater risk—that is, the probability of a car accident is higher—than middle-aged, rural drivers who go out only to church on Sunday in the family sedan. The other dimension is the severity of the consequence. If the consequence, usually defined in negative terms (but not always, as in "take a chance on love") is slight, even if the probability is high, then the risk factor would be considered negligible. However, a low probability of a severe consequence (a nuclear plant explosion) can give one pause, simply because the result might be so awful. In normal language, the concept of risk is associated with probabilities that negatively valued events or outcomes will occur. We don't think it a "risk" to possibly encounter an old dear friend on the street; it is more of a chance or an opportunity. However, it makes perfect sense to view meeting up with someone you dislike as a "risk." The other common language feature of risk is that it should be a probability of not just something severe happening, but something severe that is relevant to the core mission of the risk-assessing organization. From a policy point of view, this feature means assessing risks that would impede program development and delivery, and risks that would challenge the organizational mission as a whole.

What does risk management entail? Clearly, it requires the assessment of risk in the first instance and developing strategies to deal with the risk. Assessing risk is part and parcel of developing a risk management system for the organization (Treasury Board of Canada, 2011a). The first step in that process is conducting an internal and external **environmental scan**. The internal risk factors typically are organizational: personnel, resources, information technology, and so on. A standard way of assessing the external environment is in terms of the PEST schema (also known as the STEP schema): political (federal–provincial relations, turf wars with other agencies, other governments, international bodies, international and domestic social movements, and stakeholders that may take adverse positions to policy); economic (local and national markets, price fluctuations, currency fluctuations, labour force movements, competition in one's target markets); social (demographic trends, current social debates and fashions); and technological (new technologies on the horizon and how they will be integrated into operations, scientific discoveries, new uses for old technologies, adequacy of internal technologies in the face of changing external technological environment). The next step is the consideration of the types and nature of risk facing the organization. The Treasury Board of Canada (2011b) provides the following categorization of risks:

Business processes: Threats and opportunities associated with business process design or implementation.

Capital infrastructure: Threats and opportunities associated with an organization's capital infrastructure including hard assets (e.g., buildings, vessels, scientific equipment, fleet), but excluding IT.

Communications: Threats and opportunities associated with an organization's approach and culture of communication, consultation, transparency and information-sharing, both within and outside the organization.

Conflict of interest: Threats and opportunities associated with perceived or potential conflicts between private and public interests.

Financial management: Threats and opportunities associated with the structures and processes of an organization to ensure sound management of financial resources and its compliance with financial management policies and standards.

Governance and strategic direction: Threats and opportunities associated with an organization's approach to leadership, decision-making and management capacity.

Human resources management: Threats and opportunities associated with staff/management turnover; employment/work culture; recruitment, retention and staffing processes and practices; succession planning and talent management; and employee development, training and capacity building.

Information management: Threats and opportunities associated with an organization's capacity and sustainability of information management procedures and practices.

Information technology: Threats and opportunities associated with an organization's capacity and sustainability of information technology, both the infrastructure and utilization of technological applications.

Knowledge management: Threats and opportunities associated with an organization's collection and management of knowledge, including intellectual property, organizational or operational information and records, and scientific data.

Legal: Threats and opportunities associated with an organization's management of its legislative, advisory and litigation activities, including the development and renewal of, and compliance with, laws, regulations, international treaties/agreements and policies.

Organizational transformation and change management: Threats and opportunities associated with significant structural or behavioural change within an organization related to mandate, operating context, leadership and strategic direction.

Policy development and implementation: Threats and opportunities associated with an organization's design, implementation and compliance with the government-wide policy suite as well as its own internal policies and procedures.

Privacy/Information stewardship: Threats and opportunities associated with an organization's protection of intellectual property and personal information.

Program design and delivery: Threats and opportunities associated with an organization's design and delivery of specific programs, which may impact the organization's overall objectives.

Project management: Threats and opportunities associated with an organization's process and practice of developing and managing major projects in support of its overall mandate, as well as risks associated with specific projects that may require ongoing management.

Political: Threats and opportunities associated with the political climate and operating context of an organization.

Reputational: Threats and opportunities associated with an organization's reputation and credibility with its partners, stakeholders and the Canadian public.

Resource management: Threats and opportunities associated with the availability and level of resources of an organization to deliver on its mandate, as well as the organization's management of these resources.

Stakeholders and partnerships: Threats and opportunities associated with an organization's partners and stakeholder demographics, characteristics and activities.

Values and ethics: Threats and opportunities associated with an organization's culture and capacity to adhere to the spirit and intent of the Values and Ethics Code for the Public Service.*

Guide to risk taxonomie, URL: http://www.tbs-sct.gc.ca/tbs-sct/rm-gr/guides/grt-gtr01-eng. asp#toc2, Department of Treasury Board of Canada Secretariat, 2011. Reproduced with the permission of the Minister of Public Works and Government Services Canada, 2012.

As we noted earlier, risk is, to some extent, in the eye of the beholder. It is linked to the notion of probability, but distinct from it nonetheless. For example, it might be possible to mathematically calculate the probability of some accident at 80 percent. Some would see that figure and consider it too high. Others—less "risk averse"—would look at it and consider the 20 percent probability of it not occurring as being quite comforting. Security and stock markets work in exactly the same way, offering products with different risks attached that appeal to different segments of the market. This distinction underlines the point that an organization's risk profile is only the classification of the types and probabilities of risks it faces. It is not an assessment of how seriously to take those risks. Doing that is a more difficult process, one that ultimately depends on the judgment of management, based, in turn, on the risk aversion (or organizational culture) of key stakeholders. For private firms this is a matter of checking with stakeholders; for public organizations it is trickier since the potential stakeholder base is quite large, and in any event, the organization is supposed to be motivated by the public interest (Pal & Maxwell, 2004).

Public organizations face a special problem in developing risk profiles because of the risk aversion of most clients. Many public services are monopoly services not provided in the same degree in the private sector—education, health, and the myriad of social services are prime examples. With few or no alternatives, clients of these services demonstrate a strong negativity bias—the risk of any change or withdrawal of benefit is considered very serious. This point of view is a standard problem that all democratic governments face when they inflict pain or losses on their citizens (Pal & Weaver, 2003). On the other hand, risk analysis can become a smokescreen for bad policy. If there is a "risk," for example, that the media will learn about a badly performing program and that risk is "managed"—the net effect in terms of democracy is probably negative. A risk that truth will be told, that abuses will be exposed, that malfeasance might see the light of day—these are indeed risks, but "managing" them so they do not cause problems is the antithesis of good public service. Managing risk always has to be put in the broader context of ethical government behaviour. A risk, by definition, is the probability of bad news—but what counts as bad has to be measured against the yardstick of ethics.

Emergency Management

Managing emergencies might, at first blush, appear to be a contradiction. In times of emergency or disaster, public and private authorities are put to the ultimate test. The public interest always appears abstract and distant when discussed in terms of broad policy or hypotheticals. However, when a bridge collapses, when forest fires rage, when terrorists strike, or when financial markets implode, there is a clear and present imperative for governments to act. They need to show that in some way they were prepared, that they can deal with the emergency, and that they will manage the aftermath.

Emergency management has been defined as the "process of developing and implementing policies and programs to avoid and cope with the risks to people and property from natural and man-made hazards" (Cigler, 1988, p. 5). Obviously, there has been a response function in government as long as government has been around—to fires, medical services, disaster relief, and crime. But the field of emergency management has emerged only in the last 20 years as a distinct area of public administration. It has taken on even greater importance since 9/11 and subsequent terrorist attacks in Madrid and London, as well as natural disasters such as floods and earthquakes. The possibility of deliberate and calamitous damage to life and property has increased exponentially in the last few years. Emergency and crisis are now much more closely aligned—something that, at one time, might have been a mere emergency, if the result of a terrorist attack—could become a crisis that challenges the entire political and economic system. Yet the issues are similar to those discussed above—shared risk, uncertainty, and response under conditions of incomplete knowledge with severe time pressures. An emergency, by definition, is something that happens unexpectedly and requires immediate response. The question is how to frame that response, and how to prepare.

There have been several challenges to emergency management in the past. One is that most emergencies conventionally occur "on the ground"—that is, they require a response from local governments and communities. This expectation places a huge burden on levels of government that are not usually well endowed with funds and personnel. The second traditional problem is that many emergencies are low-probability events. In the normal course of things, people try to avoid the hazards that lead to emergencies. However, while the probability is low, the consequences can be severe. So there is a compulsion on the part of governments to prepare for possible emergencies, but not much of a public constituency pushing for that response or lobbying for it. There is also a psychological bias to underestimate broadly based risk and a commensurate reluctance to pay the taxes required to deal with it. This bias has changed completely since 9/11. There is a much heightened sense of the possibilities of deliberate danger, and the pummelling that Canada and other countries have received through emergencies such as mad cow, SARS, H1N1, and natural disasters has driven home the importance of preparation and the importance of having the capacity to deal with threats.

The standard framework for emergency management has four phases or elements (see Figure 8.1). The first is **mitigation**, which includes some of the steps discussed above under the heading "Risk Assessment."

Figure 8.1 Categorizing Threat Events

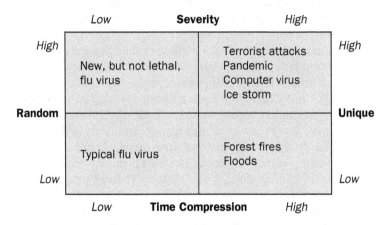

Source: *Crisis and emergency*, URL: http://www.csps-efpc.gc.ca/pbp/pub/pdfs/P117_e.pdf, Department of Canadian Centre for Management Development, 2003. Reproduced with the permission of the Minister of Public Works and Government Services Canada, 2012.

A government agency has to scan its internal procedures and its external environment, assess the probabilities of disaster, and take steps to mitigate or reduce those probabilities. The reason this is part of a management framework is that risk assessment and mitigation is an ongoing process that should be woven into daily organizational practices. The second step or phase is preparedness. Whereas mitigation involves the active effort to prevent or avoid disasters, preparedness is about being ready for the inevitable but unpredictable accidents that will occur. Readyness requires planning and, indeed, the establishment of some sort of emergency response plan that outlines who is in charge, what kind of coordination will take place, and the distribution of resources and responses. Part of being prepared is simulating an actual emergency and going through the steps. Doing this can sometimes seem silly to the public at large, but trained emergency professionals know that an effective response to disaster depends on calm threat assessment and reaction. It helps if people have gone through something similar before. The third step or phase is response—what one does when the emergency occurs. In part, responding involves following the plans made during the preparation phase, but every situation is unique. Moreover, there has to be an element of innovation and creativity in responding to a particular situation, so plans need to be supple enough that they provide guidance without tying people to the specifics. The final phase is recovery—reviewing what happened, how well the response went, and what lessons there are to be learned for the next event. Box 8.1 describes how the very success of the program monitoring the safety of Canadian cattle turned into a liability for the industry.

BOX 8.1   MAD COW IN CANADA

In August 2006, the Canadian Food Inspection Agency, the federal regulator responsible for monitoring the safety of Canadian cattle, confirmed a case of mad cow disease in an older cow in Alberta. It was the fifth case in 2006 and the eighth since 2003. The agency said locating the cow shows the success of its monitoring program. Brad Wildeman, vice-president of the Canadian Cattlemen's Association, took the same line, saying that more infected animals have been found because of the extent of the testing. "We probably have the most aggressive, safest beef supply of any country in the world," he said.

For years, Canada had been virtually free of mad cow disease. But in May 2003, veterinary officials in Alberta confirmed that a sick cow sent to a slaughterhouse in January of that year had been inspected, found to be substandard, and removed so that it would not end up as food for humans or other animals. The carcass was, however, sent to a processing plant for rendering into oils. Its head was kept for testing. Samples were sent to the world testing laboratories in the United Kingdom, which confirmed the case of mad cow.

"What is important is that the system worked," said Shirley McClellan, Alberta's agriculture minister at the time. "We have a very thorough and respected inspection system." She was insistent to remind the public that the disease is not contagious within a herd.

But McClellan's assurances didn't stop the United States, Japan, South Korea, Australia, and other countries from imposing temporary import bans of Canadian beef.

Several ranches in Alberta, British Columbia, and Saskatchewan were quarantined as a precaution, including the infected cow's home ranch.

In an investigation into the source of the infection, 1400 cows were slaughtered and tested for the disease. No other cows were found to have mad cow disease, or BSE as it is more formally known, until late December 2004.

Western premiers demanded $360 million compensation from the federal government for losses to the beef industry because of the mad cow scare. Ottawa would later offer $190 million.

Over the summer of 2003, cattle ranchers held barbeques across Canada to help promote Canadian beef.

In August, the United States reopened its borders to some Canadian beef, but the border was still closed to live cattle. By this time, a cow that would have normally sold for $1300 was selling for $15. Canadian beef producers asked Ottawa to approve a mass slaughter of 620 000 cattle to reduce the size of the herd and prevent further damage to the industry.

(continued)

BOX 8.1 (continued)

In October, CBC News reported that the border would reopen to live cattle in December 2003. But on December 23, 2003, the United States announced that it had discovered its first apparent case of BSE in a cow in Washington state.

Several countries banned beef from the United States soon after the announcement, but Canada restricted imports only on some products made from cattle and other ruminants. It still allowed the import of cattle destined for immediate slaughter, boneless beef from cattle under 30 months of age and dairy products.

DNA evidence later revealed that the cow was born in Canada, and the United States kept its border shut to live Canadian cattle.

It took a little more than a year for the United States to announce that it would reopen its border to live Canadian cattle younger than 30 months.

On December 29, 2004, the U.S. Department of Agriculture announced that it recognized Canada as a "minimal-risk region" for BSE and imports of young Canadian cattle would resume March 7, 2005.

The new classification means that the United States will not again close its borders to Canadian beef unless there are two or more cases of BSE per one million cattle older than 24 months of age in each of four consecutive years. Simply put, Canada can have up to 11 cases of BSE and still be considered a safe country for cattle exports.

The move came less than a month after U.S. President George W. Bush made his first official visit to Canada and said the process for reopening the border was under way.

Five days before the ban was to be lifted, however, a U.S. judge granted a temporary injunction to stop the reopening of the border. The ban came at the request of a group of American ranchers called R-CALF, who filed a lawsuit saying reopening the border would cause irreparable damage to the U.S. beef market.

In June 2005, the U.S. Department of Agriculture confirmed the country's second known case of BSE, in a Texas-born cow.

And on July 14, 2005, a three-judge panel of the U.S. Ninth Circuit Court of Appeals overturned a temporary injunction that banned importation of Canadian cattle. U.S. Agriculture Secretary Mike Johanns announced that day that the U.S. border was "immediately" open to live Canadian cattle.

Source: CBC News (August 24, 2006). Mad Cow in Canada: The science and the story. Retrieved March 29, 2008, from http://www.cbc.ca/news/background/mad-cow/. Reprinted with permission.

There is a temptation to think of emergency response in terms of elaborate plans and clear command and control organization. Obviously, plans are important, as are drills and preparation. Some central authority and clear lines of responsibility are important as well. But the nature of disaster and emergency ultimately requires supple responses by interacting systems: local governments, communities, provinces, national authorities, and sometimes even international actors. As discussed in the theoretical section of this chapter, disaster and emergency response needs to be thought of in terms of complex systems made up of multiple actors who, in the end, do not have ultimate authority over anyone else. Mobilizing a complex system to respond to disaster involves an enormous amount of information processing and communication. Comfort, in discussing different models of these types of networks, notes that

> ... the objective is to critique actual performance against a prior model of organizational structure in order to improve performance in a continuous process of collective learning. The decision makers use their experience to identify gaps in the organizational system model in order to correct performance for the next event. The logic of these approaches is to identify what the organization does not know in changing environments or new situations and to devise better means of coping with unknown conditions. Acknowledgment of error is not a negative action but rather serves as the basis for learning and contributes to improved future performance. The major resource in each of these models is the capacity of individuals to learn and to transmit that knowledge to other participants in the system. Each approach acknowledges the need to design organizational structures and processes that facilitate individual and organizational learning as well as to identify and correct potential errors on a timely basis. (Comfort, 2005, p. 347)

Since 9/11, organizing for emergency response to security threats has become a priority for both Canada and the United States. Shortly after the terrorist attacks, President Bush re-organized his administration by forming the Department of Homeland Security (DHS) to coordinate a host of functions that previously were scattered through the federal government. The DHS is massive; it employs 240 000 people throughout the country from 22 former government agencies such as the Immigration and Naturalization Service, the Federal Emergency Management Agency (FEMA), the Secret Service, and the Coast Guard. The DHS is organized into three directorates, four offices, and a host of agencies. The DHS is responsible for a bewildering array of security initiatives, of which the following is just a sample:

- Operation Community Shield, a nationwide initiative that targets violent transnational street gangs, by partnering with U.S. and foreign law enforcement agencies at all levels, and making use of its authority to deport criminal aliens
- Airline Security Screening, with security officers operating at over 700 security checkpoints and nearly 7000 baggage screening areas each day
- U.S. Immigration and Customs Enforcement which, as of 2011, was investigating 479 773 fugitive alien cases
- Urban Search and Rescue, with teams spread out across the country for rapid response for emergencies involving victims in confined spaces
- A National Cyber Security Division, to protect both public and private sectors from cyber attacks (Department of Homeland Security, 2011)

These are only a few examples, but they illustrate the scope and depth of U.S. concerns about terror. They also demonstrate the point that emergency response, in most instances, happens on the ground where the emergency is first declared. The federal government can do a lot of coordination and interoperability of communications equipment, but ultimately, the first line of response to any emergency is at the community level and among businesses and firms. This understanding means that the DHS is interacting with and coordinating a vast network of governmental and nongovernmental actors to effectively deal with terrorist and other threats. The sad irony is that the protection of liberty and democratic government requires a highly centralized and, some would say, intrusive agency.

Canada has been compelled to match U.S. efforts in emergency preparedness and security. The constant flow of trade and travel between the two countries made it imperative that Canada demonstrate to the United States that it too would take terrorist threats seriously, even though the likelihood of a terrorist attack in Canada is remote. In December 2003 a new department was created to integrate all aspects of emergency preparedness and wider threats, Public Safety and Emergency Preparedness, headed then by the deputy prime minister to highlight its importance. Now named Public Safety Canada, it is responsible for emergency management (which includes critical infrastructure protection, cyber security, disaster mitigation, and emergency preparedness), national security, crime prevention, law enforcement, and corrections policy. While Public Safety Canada is the lead department for public safety, it works closely with five agencies: Canada Border Services Agency; Canadian Security Intelligence Service; Correctional Service of Canada; National Parole Board; and Royal Canadian Mounted Police) and three review bodies (Commission for Public Complaints against the RCMP; Office of the Correctional Investigator; and RCMP External Review Committee). They are united in a single portfolio and report to the same minister (Public Safety Canada, 2012a).

As well, in May 2004, the federal government issued its first comprehensive statement on national security, *Securing an Open Society*, still in effect in 2012. The document is revealing in several ways. First, the fact that it represented Canada's first comprehensive policy statement on security suggests both the new priority that security issues have and the heightened threat environment in which Canada finds itself. Second, threats that, at one time, were parcelled out among different departments and agencies are now coordinated under one umbrella—security or safety. This new classification includes natural disasters and emergencies, transportation, intelligence, public health, and border security. The policy promised to put more money into security and intelligence gathering, and proposed to create a new parliamentary committee on national security as well as a government operations centre to coordinate key national players in the event of national emergencies. It also created a national Public Health Agency and a Chief Public Health Officer for Canada. Finally, it created an external advisory body on national security (Public Safety Canada, 2012b)

Canada's counterterrorism activities are governed by the National Counter-Terrorism policy, which was significantly updated in 2001 with the passage of the Anti-terrorism Act in the wake of the 9/11 attacks (the act was passed December 2001). That policy was updated in 2011 with *Building Resilience against Terrorism* (Government of Canada, 2011). The legislation contained amendments to the Criminal Code, the Official Secrets Act, the Canada Evidence Act, and the Proceeds of Crime (Money Laundering) Act, all intended to deal with terrorist acts as well as activities, namely, raising money, in support of terrorism. With the act, it became a criminal offence to knowingly collect or provide funds to carry out terrorist activities, be a member of a terrorist group or facilitate its activities, or knowingly harbour or conceal a terrorist. It also increased police investigatory powers. A key element of the legislation, of course, is the definition of a terrorist group or entity. The law allows the authorities to maintain a public "list of entities" (a person, group, trust, partnership or fund, or an unincorporated association or organization) if there are reasonable grounds that that entity "has knowingly carried out, attempted to carry out, participated in or facilitated a terrorist activity; or is knowingly acting on behalf of, at the direction of or in association with an entity that has knowingly carried out, attempted to carry out, participated in or facilitated a terrorist activity." The listing is a public statement that the government believes that entity to be involved in terrorist activities, and it also freezes the entity's assets. As of March 2012, the list consisted of 44 entities. Five on the list are described in Box 8.2.

Emergency preparedness and counterterrorism are now part of a single continuum of policy responses, since, of course, the great fear now is that terrorist groups will induce emergencies as part of their campaigns. The Madrid subway bombings in March 2004, for instance, were likely an Al-Qaeda attack that resulted in 201 dead and 1500 injured. A year later, the London Tube bombings occurred, killing 55 people and injuring 700. The 2003 blackout in Ontario and the northeastern United States could just as easily have been caused by a terrorist attack, and would have had the same effect of paralyzing a good part of the continent. Natural disasters still occur, of course, and there are routine ways of preparing and responding to them. The new and alarming connection between emergency preparedness and security concerns is forcing a radical rethinking across a range of policy areas that, at one time, would have been in separate organizational silos. The visible organizational evidence of this is the creation of agencies such as Homeland Security in the United States and Public Safety Canada. Legislation on terrorism, charitable donations, security and intelligence gathering, customs and border control—all have changed since 2008 and become much more closely connected to each other.

There are several significant policy challenges that flow from these changes. The first and most obvious is the threat to civil liberties. This threat has been a mounting concern in all countries where security measures have been strengthened. Intelligence services have been given strengthened mandates and new powers; new border security measures are considerably more invasive than in the past, and there have been reported instances of racial profiling. Finding the right balance between the protection of civil liberties and public safety will be an ongoing test of public authorities. A second challenge is less philosophical than it is organizational—the challenge of coordination and implementation. As we discussed in Chapter 5, all public policy faces the problem of implementation. That challenge is more acute in the emergency and security area than in most others. The sheer size of the organizations being created—as noted above, Homeland Security employs 240 000 people—means that there will be problems in internal coordination and communication. But it is in the nature of emergencies to require widely dispersed response, which is inherently difficult to manage. In the ice storm of 1998, for example, more than four million people in Ontario, Quebec, and New Brunswick lost power, and 600 000 had to evacuate their homes. A disaster of this magnitude cannot be responded to simply by government alone, even though Ottawa, the provinces, and local municipalities all had to work together. Nongovernmental organizations, charities, international agencies, and volunteers have to come together to respond, and all somehow have to be coordinated in a system of "shared governance" (May & Williams, 1986). And, of course, the context of an emergency means that, by definition, time pressures are high, as are the

BOX 8.2   LISTED ENTITIES UNDER CANADA'S ANTI-TERRORISM ACT (A SELECTION)

1. AL QAIDA

Founded in 1988 by Usama bin Laden, Al Qaida serves as the strategic hub and driver for the global Islamist terrorist movement. The group's goals include uniting Muslims to fight the United States and its allies, overthrowing regimes it deems "non-Islamic" and expelling Westerners and non-Muslims from Muslim countries. Al Qaida activities include, but are not limited to, suicide attacks, simultaneous bombings, kidnappings, and hijackings. Al Qaida has forged ties and strategic control over other like-minded Islamist terrorist groups and provides encouragement and inspiration to other affiliated and aligned groups around the world. The Al Qaida network has been directly or indirectly associated with the 1998 bombings of two United States embassies, as well as the 2000 bombing of the *USS Cole*. It was directly involved in the World Trade Center and Pentagon attacks of September 11, 2001, and in a foiled plot to bomb the New York subway system in 2009.

2. AUM SHINRIKYO

Formed in Japan in 1987, Aum Shinrikyo (Aum) is a religious organization with a belief system that mixes various religions—primarily Buddhism—with science fiction and the prophecies of Nostradamus. Aum aimed to control Japan, then the world, and subsequently create a global utopian society. Originally peaceful in nature, the group became increasingly dangerous and violent, seeking to actively bring about Armageddon. In 1994 Aum committed its first sarin attack against Japanese civilians by releasing the nerve agent in Matsumoto, killing seven people and wounding more than a hundred others. In its most infamous attack, Aum released sarin in the Tokyo subway system in 1995, killing a dozen people and wounding thousands more.

3. EJÉRCITO DE LIBERACIÓN NACIONAL (ELN)

Founded in 1964, the Ejército de Liberación Nacional (ELN) is the second-largest leftist rebel group in Colombia after the Revolutionary Armed Forces of Colombia (FARC). The ELN's principal aim is to "seize power for the people" and establish a revolutionary government. The group believes foreign involvement in Colombia's

(continued)

BOX 8.2 (continued)

oil industry violates the country's sovereignty and foreign companies are unfairly exploiting Colombia's natural resources. ELN activities include kidnapping, hijacking, bombing, extortion, and guerrilla warfare. In its attacks, the ELN primarily targets the Colombian oil industry, political events, and political figures.

4. HIZBALLAH

One of the most technically capable terrorist groups in the world, Hizballah is a radical Shia group ideologically inspired by the Iranian revolution. Its goals are the liberation of Jerusalem, the destruction of Israel, and, ultimately, the establishment of a revolutionary Shia Islamic state in Lebanon, modelled after Iran. Formed in 1982 in response to Israel's invasion of Lebanon, Hizballah carried out some of the most infamous terror attacks of the Lebanese civil war, such as the suicide bombings of the barracks of United States Marines and French paratroopers in Beirut, as well as the hijacking of TWA Flight 847. While all other Lebanese militias disarmed at the end of Lebanon's civil war in 1990, Hizballah continued to fight, waging a guerrilla war against Israeli troops stationed in southern Lebanon. Following Israel's withdrawal from Lebanon in 2000, Hizballah attacks against Israeli forces continued, concentrated on the disputed Shebaa Farms area. In 2006, Hizballah provoked Israel's invasion of Lebanon by kidnapping two Israeli soldiers and killing eight others.

5. KAHANE CHAI

Kahane Chai (Kach) is a marginal, extremist Jewish entity whose goal is the restoration of the biblical state of Israel. Kahane Chai (Kach) advocates expelling Arabs from Israel, expanding Israel's boundaries to include the occupied territories and parts of Jordan, and the strict implementation of Jewish law in Israel. Kahane Chai (Kach) has openly espoused violence against Arabs and the Israeli government as a viable method for establishing a religiously homogenous state. Its activities have included threats to government officials and infrastructure, grenade attacks, armed violence, and bombings.

Source: Currently Listed Entities, http://www.publicsafety.gc.ca/prg/ns/le/cle-eng .aspx, Public Safety Canada, 2011. Reproduced with the permission of the Minister of Public Works and Government Services, 2012.

stakes in terms of human life and property. Since most emergencies are new in some sense, relying exclusively on prepared plans can introduce inflexibilities in response. An extreme example of this comes from the initial responses by U.S. aviation and defence authorities in the 9/11 events—they relied on protocols developed in the 1970s for airplane hijackings. For all these reasons, Comfort emphasizes the importance of adaptive systems of response that rely on self-organization: "Sustaining the process of self-organization in a continuing way requires access to communication for all the participants to support the exchange of information, stored memory for actions taken that allow reflection and redesign, and evaluation and feedback from the other participants in the group" (Comfort, 1999, p. 271). This approach places the emphasis on the *system* of response, including the wide availability and exchange of information among members of that response community.

Crisis Management

We distinguished earlier between crisis and emergency. Emergencies are typically physical events that threaten human life and property. From a "system" perspective—the political system, the economic system, even the social system—an emergency is a threat event, but not one so severe that it will cause the system to collapse. A crisis is usually considered to fall in that category; we might think of it as an emergency that is so extreme that it threatens system integrity. Also, as we noted, an emergency can evolve into a crisis if it is handled badly and people lose faith in the authorities or managers. The tainted blood scandal, one of Canada's worst health crises, arose first as an emergency around the safety of Canadian blood products, but became an organizational crisis for the Red Cross, which eventually had to close its doors in Canada (see Box 8.3, page 338).

Distinguishing crisis from emergency is more than just semantics. When we are looking at crises, we are looking at specific types of events that require specific management and policy responses that are different from the responses and preparation for emergencies. And while it is difficult to find conclusive evidence on this, it seems that crisis (a threat to organizational integrity) is becoming a more important and, indeed, routine part of the context for developing and implementing public policy. There are several reasons this might be true.

First, information about what governments are doing is much more widely available than ever before thanks to the Internet (think WikiLeaks) and access-to-information legislation. And information flows more rapidly and easily because of a 24/7 media environment and communications technology. For example, when SARS broke out on the Chinese mainland

Chapter 8 Policymaking under Pressure **335**

in 2002, the authorities initially forbade any public discussion of the disease. Despite this, almost half the urban population in Guangzhou received news of it through unofficial means, principally text messaging over mobile phones (Huang, 2003, p. 12). The same was true of initial reports on the Arab Spring in 2011—they came from Twitter feeds and cellphone photos taken on the streets.

Second, in a news and media-saturated policy environment, it is easily possible for "master narratives" to be formed by the press that then feed on themselves and are very difficult to revise or rebut (we discuss this in the next chapter). David Good, for example, highlights the role the media played in the 1999 HRDC scandal. Initial reports were that $1 billion in HRDC grants and contributions had gone missing, a "billion-dollar boondoggle." Once that impression was made in the public mind, it was almost impossible to shake:

> After the immediate release of the HRDC grants and contributions audit on 19 January, and for the rest of the week, the media used a simple and dramatic storyline: "One billion dollars lost." The expression, however distorted, was dramatic and the image vivid. A seemingly dull internal administrative audit was "recontextualized" into a newsworthy sound-bite and a catchy headline. In fact, no money was lost. After months of individually reviewing 17,000 grants and contributions files across all programs in the department, representing some $1.6 billion, HRDC officials concluded that the amount of outstanding debts owing to the government was $85,000.... [T]he media developed a preformed storyline that the grants were used for political purposes and, as a consequence, corruption was inevitable. (Good, 2003, p. 64)

Third, as we have noted in previous chapters, there is a pervasive mood of cynicism and distrust of government. Bad news—any type of bad news—can very easily and quickly be framed in that mental context and seen as evidence of rank incompetence, malfeasance, or corruption. A crisis can grow out of a simple error if that error gets magnified to the point where it becomes emblematic of systemic problems. The HRDC scandal—such as it was—did, in the end, lead to the demotion of a minister who, at the time, had been widely touted as a possible future prime minister, and to the splitting of the department into two.

From a policy and management perspective, the key thing about crisis is responding to it and managing it as effectively as possible. Indeed the response itself—if badly coordinated—can become the crisis once the initial triggering event is over. In the case of HRDC, the triggering event was the release of an audit of grants and contributions that appeared to suggest that the monies were badly handled. Once the media framed the story in those terms, the actual crisis was a crisis of not being able to effectively respond and get the facts of the case on the public record. A crisis gets resolved when it is managed well and overcome. Of course, the problem is that crises are typically unexpected, take place under strong time constraints and uncertainty, and usually have enough new elements that one cannot rely exclusively on prepared plans. Nonetheless, in reviewing experiences in dealing with crises and emergencies, it is possible to distill some useful lessons (Canadian Centre for Management Development, 2003).

Perhaps the most obvious first step is to be mentally prepared to acknowledge the existence of a possible crisis. Managers should assume that crises will occur and that they can arise from almost any possible event, however innocuous. As David Good states of his own response to the HRDC stories in the press, "I believed that the matter would 'blow over.' In retrospect, I should have read the media reports in a more pessimistic manner to prepare myself, and my staff, for what lay ahead" (Good, 2003, p. 211). He goes on to say that public servants should be accustomed to expecting the unexpected and to be "overly prepared for the expected"—in this case, paying close attention to the external environment and how it might respond to information about grants and contributions.

A second step involves ensuring the ability to respond quickly and accurately to the crisis and, most important, to the way the media handles the crisis. "Once the crisis has been confirmed, it is important to immediately establish a management team to oversee the response. The designated members of the response team and spokespersons must suspend their normal activities and devote themselves fully to the crisis. It is essential to ensure that team members are prepared to assume the responsibilities assigned to them" (Canadian Centre for Management Development, 2003, p. 26).

A third step is ensuring that those who are tasked with dealing with the crisis know their respective roles and the lines of accountability and leadership. This recognition is important for a number of reasons. In government, there are usually several departments and agencies that can plausibly take a lead role, and not coordinating them can be disastrous— conflicting messages and contradictory communications are sure to make a bad situation worse. Another dimension is that in crisis situations it is often necessary to make difficult decisions, and without clear lines of accountability those necessary decisions may be delayed or confused. However, as discussed earlier, coordination should not be confused with hierarchy. To some extent there must be vertical command and control systems, but they have to be matched with adaptive horizontal networks (Farazmand, 2007, p. 156).

A fourth key step, possibly the most important of the list, is developing a good communications strategy, something that has several elements.

BOX 8.3   THE TAINTED BLOOD CRISIS (1998)

BACKGROUND

The Red Cross has a history in Canada almost as old as the country itself. It can be traced back to 1885, to the battlefield of Louis Riel's North-West Rebellion, where a surgeon general made a Red Cross flag out of white cloth and two torn strips of red artillery cotton so he could distinguish a horse-drawn wagon being used to transport the wounded. Eleven years after the rebellion, Dr. George Sterling Ryerson, the same man who flew the makeshift flag, won approval from Britain to form a Canadian branch of the Red Cross in Toronto. The organization grew quickly, and in 1909, the federal government passed the Canadian Red Cross Society Act. In 1927, the International Committee of the Red Cross recognized the society as an autonomous group. It went on to become the preeminent not-for-profit organization in the country.

On February 3, 1947, the Canadian Red Cross opened its first civilian blood donor clinic in Vancouver with the goal of providing free blood to anyone who needed it. Before that, patients had to pay for or replace the blood they were given in hospitals.

In the late 1970s and early 1980s, Canada's blood system infected approximately 1200 people with the HIV virus and it has been estimated that another 12 000 people were infected with hepatitis C. Many of the victims were hemophiliacs and people who had received blood during routine operations. At that time we had less knowledge than we do now about these viruses. Many of those who had been infected did not know they had received contaminated blood. Some people unknowingly passed on the viruses to their spouses and family members. As a result by the 1990s, it was estimated that the number of infected people had increased substantially and exponentially. The staggering number of victims illustrated that the blood system had failed the very people it was supposed to protect. In response, many people began calling for a judicial inquiry into Canada's blood system.

In 1993 Justice Horace Krever was appointed to head a Commission of Inquiry with the mandate to investigate the management and operation and contamination of the blood system in Canada. After nearly four years of a public judicial inquiry, Justice Krever issued his much-awaited final report on November 26, 1997.

Krever's report stopped short of finding the Canadian government liable for the contaminated blood or singling out individuals for blame. But he criticized federal and local authorities for their roles in distributing the tainted blood. The report also criticized the Canadian Red Cross for failing to put into place an adequate screening program for high-risk blood donors. After the report was issued the Red Cross apologized: "While we cannot know your suffering, we will weep with you. While we cannot feel your loss we grieve with you. We are very sorry."

Krever also recommended that the thousands of people infected with hepatitis C should be entitled to automatic compensation. He did not set an amount. Those infected with HIV through tainted blood products had already been compensated by the federal government. Further, the Red Cross and its insurers, together with the provinces, contributed to a second compensation program for HIV victims—the Multi-Provincial/Territorial Assistance Program. There had been no requirement for court proceedings or legal negotiations in an overwhelming number of these cases.

But federal and provincial health ministers decided not to compensate hepatitis C victims, leaving the Red Cross with billions of dollars in claims. This decision led to massive complications. By the time the issue had been sorted out, the Canadian Red Cross had been forced to seek bankruptcy protection under the Companies' Creditors Arrangement Act. It shook the organization to its foundation and nearly brought it down.

The right spokespersons should be designated early in the crisis, properly briefed, and properly trained to deal with media. It is often the case that the first messages that get out to the public as a crisis is developing set the frame for much of what follows, and are difficult to change or shift. Information has to be circulated within the organization responsible for dealing with the crisis, in order to facilitate learning and organizational coordination. To the extent possible, responses to the media and other external audiences should be complete and honest, and if information is missing or unavailable, it should be produced as quickly as is feasible. We discuss policy communication issues in the next chapter.

The fifth step, once the crisis has been resolved, is to draw lessons from the event and try to prevent a similar thing from happening in the future. Mitigation and prevention strategies have their limits, of course, like generals always fighting the last war. But they are essential for organizational development and for at least having a chance of dealing with the next potential crisis that comes along, as one inevitably will.

We have defined crisis as a threat event that can undermine the integrity of a system. This system can mean a government, a department, or even a policy or program. For this reason crises eventually have to be addressed by leaders who have key responsibilities for those organizations or programs. Crisis management is not normal, routine management, and coordinating the response to a crisis may be the single most important thing that organizational managers do. That is why crisis management, while it requires collective and coordinated response, is a severe test for those at the top of the organization. While decisive action is often required, that has to be balanced against communications, information-sharing, and teamwork.

Conclusion

Emergency, crisis, and pressure have attracted more attention as themes in the private sector management literature than in the public sector, until recently. Corporations face competitors, and so something like a product recall or losing a top executive can threaten the viability of a corporation. Public sector organizations, at least traditionally, enjoyed some insulation from these types of pressures, but, of course, political crises arise all the time. They do not, however, typically pose the same kind of threat to the entire viability of a program or the existence of a public sector agency.

The ground has shifted in many ways, and public policymaking under pressure is an increasingly important feature of doing policy work. The intensification of international terrorism in recent years is one obvious example, but is not the whole story. Dealing with natural disasters such as floods and forest fires has always been part of the government's responsibility, but it may be that, as a result of climate change, the incidence of these events is increasing (Briceno, 2004; James, 2007). And the scale can be devastating, as when Hurricane Katrina flattened New Orleans (Brinkley, 2006). The combination of interdependencies in things like trade (mad cow) and technology (Internet) means that emergencies and threat events can spread rapidly and paralyze whole populations, if not industries and economic processes, as the financial crisis and continuing economic crisis show. Pandemics and public health risks appear to be on the rise; the listeriosis crisis in late 2008 almost destroyed Maple Leaf Foods. And finally, the public mood, while perhaps more supportive of governments that are addressing emergencies or attacks, is still suspicious. Coupled with a media bias toward "gotcha journalism," this can make for a volatile environment in which to deal with emergencies. If things are badly handled, even to a modest degree, there is a new potential for escalation into full-blown crisis:

The modern crisis is the product of several modernization processes—globalization, deregulation, information and communication technology, developments and technological advances, to name but a few. These advances promote a close-knit world that is nonetheless susceptible to infestation by a single crisis. Comparatively slight mishaps within these massive and intricate infrastructures can rapidly escalate in unforeseen ways. A prime example can be found in the European food and agriculture sector. One animal was diagnosed with foot and mouth disease in a remote English farm and, within days, the disease had affected all of Europe. Farmers, slaughterhouses, distributors, butcheries, consumers, inspection agencies, policy makers, and politicians endured enormous economic and social-psychological costs. (Boin & t'Hart, 2003, p. 546)

It is important to remember the actual, political context of crisis and policymaking under pressure. Crises and emergencies are difficult to handle at the best of times, but if they are becoming both more frequent and with wider-reaching consequences, we should not be surprised that crisis management as a real process will sometimes look different than what we might hope from a "lessons learned" approach that does not take into account the real dynamics to which decisionmakers are exposed. Boin and t'Hart's (2003) review of the literature points out six broad public expectations about crisis that are not borne out by research.

To begin with, there is a public expectation that leaders should put public safety first. In reality, policy leaders always have to balance the costs and benefits of mitigation and prevention. It is simply too costly to have absolute, 100 percent safety; rather, it is a question of how much risk can be reasonably tolerated. The public is somewhat schizophrenic on risk and safety issues. On the one hand, it often complains about excessive regulation that stifles individual choice (e.g., pharmaceutical regulations that prevent access to experimental drugs), but on the other, it expects that drugs available on the market have been tested to be safe. Mitigation and prevention of non-events do not attract political credit. There is little political incentive to invest heavily in safety.

A second public expectation is that leaders should prepare themselves for worst-case scenarios, a recommendation that we made earlier. In fact, the evidence from both private and public sector organizations seems to be that, unless one has experienced crisis in the past, or is operating in a community with similar experiences, the organizational and leadership reflex is to place a low priority on continual crisis preparation. In part this is due to a rational calculation that there may be zero benefit from investing time in preparation for an event that may never occur. As well, less rationally, organizational leaders may be reluctant to confront weaknesses in their organizations.

A third expectation is that leaders should heed warnings about future crises. The reality is that many crises take time to build, and, in practice, all kinds of warning signals are misinterpreted or ignored, usually because the crisis, by definition, is a "new" event and does not fit the frame of reference of authorities. In June 2004 the National Commission on Terrorist Attacks upon the United States concluded that there had been several intelligence failures in the run-up to the 9/11 attacks. The CIA, in particular, missed clues that suggested the crisis was looming:

> The problems that prevent leaders from heeding warnings are manifold and fundamental. Leaders are routinely engulfed in oceans of information and advice. Moreover, they face ambiguous and contradictory signals. Warnings do not come with flashing lights; they are hidden in expert reports, advisory memos, or a colleague's casual remark. The warnings have to be distilled from a series of seemingly minor and insignificant indications. An additional problem is that information passageways to leaders often are obscured. Bad news, in particular, faces formidable obstacles on its way to the top of the organization, especially in bureaucratic organizations. These barriers are fundamentally social. Nobody wants to alarm his boss unnecessarily, and nobody wants to acquire the reputation of a troublemaker. In the absence of these signals, leaders run a big risk of becoming the victim of "silences" in the organizational communication pattern. (Boin & t'Hart, 2003, p. 547)

A fourth expectation is that during a crisis, leaders take charge and directly oversee the crisis management activities. In reality, crises are much more fluid and dynamic events than this would allow, and, in practice, systems or networks of responses from many agencies, NGOs, and other actors deal with the multiple facets of a crisis. As we noted earlier, coordination is definitely required in crisis response, but it is important to have realistic expectations of how tightly that can be managed and directed from above.

A fifth public expectation is that leaders show tangible sympathy for victims of a crisis or emergency. Doing this extends from making public expressions of grief and support to providing financial compensation and assistance. The problem is that, in the heat of the moment, leaders can make promises that they subsequently cannot keep or raise expectations so high that they inevitably disappoint. (This was a factor in the early responses to the global financial crisis in October 2008.)

The final public expectation that Boin and t'Hart identify is that leaders strive to learn the lessons of the crisis. Again, the political context in the aftermath of a crisis almost actively militates against that. A normal reaction after a crisis has been dealt with is to find its causes, something that rapidly degenerates (especially with the media) into a blame game. Leaders know that they are targets, and so instead of dispassionately "learning lessons," they focus on spin control and plausible deniability.

Chaos, risk, emergency, and crisis: these take us to the outer limits of the "normal" policy process, and yet they are becoming normal aspects and challenges of doing policy work. They signify the turbulence mentioned in the subtitle to this book: effective public management requires the skills and capacities to manage policy processes in conditions of great and perhaps even increasing turbulence. One key aspect of this type of management—though it pervades every other aspect of policymaking—is communication. Somewhat surprisingly, given its importance in the real world, it is largely ignored in academic analyses. The next chapter aims to address this deficit.

KEY TERMS

crisis—a turning point or moment of danger that threatens the integrity of an entire system

emergency—an abnormal and unexpected threat event that requires immediate action

emergency management—the process of developing and implementing policies and programs to avoid and cope with the risks to people and property from natural and man-made hazards

environmental scan—an assessment of both internal and external risks, usually in terms of strengths and weaknesses, and threats and opportunities

mitigation—actions taken based on a risk assessment to lower those risks and prevent them from happening

nonlinear policy problems—problems where small changes in initial conditions can have large consequences, where uncertainty is high, and where there are discontinuities in normal events and shared responsibilities for action

risk—probability of an event with negative consequences, key dimensions being level of probability and severity of risk

risk management—a management framework that encourages the identification and assessment of risk, and its mitigation or prevention as part of a medium to long-term strategy

tipping point—dramatic moment in an epidemic when everything can change; a sudden, unexpected change in what to that point has been a stable system

FURTHER READINGS

Boin, A., & t'Hart, P. (2003, September–October). Public leadership in times of crisis: "Mission Impossible"? *Public Administration Review, 63*, 544–552.

Canadian Centre for Management Development [CCMD]. (2003). *The federal experience: Case studies on crisis and emergency management.* [CCMD is now called the Canada School of Public Service.] Retrieved from http://www.csps-efpc.gc.ca/Research/publications/pdfs/crisis_case_e.pdf

Comfort, L. K. (1999). *Shared risk: Complex systems in seismic response.* Amsterdam, Netherlands: Pergamon.

Geyer, R., & Rihani, S. (2010). *Complexity and public policy.* London, UK: Routledge.

Gladwell, M. (2000). *The tipping point: How little things can make a big difference.* Boston, MA: Little, Brown.

Klein, G. A. (1998). *Sources of power: How people make decisions.* Cambridge, MA: MIT Press.

REFERENCES

Beck, U. (1992). *The risk society: Towards a new modernity.* Newbury Park, CA: Sage.

Beck, W. (1999). *World risk society.* London, UK: Polity Press.

Boin, A., & t'Hart, P. (2003, September–October). Public leadership in times of crisis: "Mission Impossible"? *Public Administration Review, 63*, 544–552.

Briceno, S. (2004, March). Global challenges in disaster reduction. *The Australian Journal of Emergency Management, 19*, 3–5.

Brinkley, D. (2006). *The great deluge: Hurricane Katrina, New Orleans, and the Mississippi Gold Coast.* New York, NY: Morrow.

Canadian Centre for Management Development. (2003). *Crisis and emergency management: A guide for managers.* Ottawa, ON: Canadian Centre for Management Development [now known as the Canada School of Public Service]. Retrieved from http://www.csps-efpc.gc.ca/pbp/pub/pdfs/P117_e.pdf

Cigler, B. A. (1988). Emergency management and public administration. In M. T. Charles & J. C. K. Kim (Eds.), *Crisis management: A casebook* (pp. 5–19). Springfield, IL: Charles C. Thomas.

Comfort, L. K. (1999). *Shared risk: Complex systems in seismic response.* Amsterdam, Netherlands: Pergamon.

Comfort, L. K. (2005). Risk, security, and disaster management. *Annual Review of Political Science, 8,* 335–356.

Comfort, L. K. (2006). Inter-organizational coordination in extreme events: The World Trade Center attacks, September 11, 2001. *Natural Hazards, 39*(2), 309–327.

Comfort, L. K. (2007). Crisis management in hindsight: Cognition, communication, coordination, and control. *Public Administration Review, 67*(Issue supplement s.1), 189–197.

Department of Homeland Security (United States). (2011). *Home page.* Retrieved from http://www.dhs.gov/index.shtm

Farazmand, A. (2007). Learning from the Katrina crisis: A global and international perspective with implications for future crisis management. *Public Administration Review, 67*(1), 149–159.

Furedi, F. (2002). *Culture of fear: Risk-taking and the morality of low expectation* (2nd ed.). London, UK: Continuum International Publishing.

Gladwell, M. (2000). *The tipping point: How little things can make a big difference.* Boston, MA: Little, Brown.

Good, D. A. (2003). *The politics of public management: The HRDC audit of grants and contributions.* Toronto, ON: University of Toronto Press.

Government of Canada. (2011). *Building resilience against terrorism: Canada's counter-terrorism strategy.* Retrieved from http://www.publicsafety.gc.ca/prg/ns/_fl/2012-cts-eng.pdf

Huang, Y. (2003, Fall). The politics of China's SARS crisis. *Harvard Asia Quarterly, 7,* 9–16.

James, M. (2007). The permanent-emergency compensation state: A "postsocialist" tale of political dystopia. In M. Orsini & M. Smith (Eds.), *Critical policy studies* (pp. 321–346). Vancouver, BC: UBC Press.

Kelling, G. L., & Coles, C. M. (1996). *Fixing broken windows.* New York, NY: Touchstone.

Klein, G. A. (1998). *Sources of power: How people make decisions.* Cambridge, MA: MIT Press.

May, P. J., & Williams, W. (1986). *Disaster policy implementation: Managing programs under shared governance.* New York, NY: Plenum Press.

Morçöl, G. (2002). *A new mind for policy analysis: Towards a post Newtonian and postpositivist epistemology and methodology.* Westport, CT: Praeger.

Pal, L. A., & Maxwell, J. (2004). *Assessing the public interest in the 21st century: A framework.* Background study for the External Advisory Committee on Smart Regulation. Retrieved from http://www.cprn.org/doc.cfm?doc=508&l=en

Pal, L. A., & Weaver, R. K. (Eds.). (2003). *The government taketh away: The politics of pain in the United States and Canada.* Washington, DC: Georgetown University Press.

Perrow, C. (1984). *Normal accidents: Living with high-risk technologies.* New York, NY: Basic Books.

Privy Council Office (Canada). (2004). *Securing an open society: Canada's national security policy.* Retrieved from http://www.bcp-pco.gc.ca/docs/information/Publications/natsec-secnat/natsec-secnat_e.pdf

Public Health Agency of Canada. (2005). *Fetal alcohol spectrum disorder (FASD).* Retrieved from http://www.phac-aspc.gc.ca/publicat/fasd-fw-etcaf-ca/pdf/fasd-fw_e.pdf

Public Safety Canada. (2012a). *About us.* Retrieved from http://www.publicsafety.gc.ca/abt/index-eng.aspx

Public Safety Canada. (2012b). *Securing and open society: Canada's national security policy.* Retrieved from http://www.publicsafety.gc.ca/pol/ns/secpol04-eng.aspx

Sharkansky, I. (1986). *Policymaking under adversity.* New Brunswick, NJ: Transaction Books.

Treasury Board of Canada. (2010). *Framework for the management of risk.* Retrieved from http://www.tbs-sct.gc.ca/pol/doc-eng.aspx?id=19422&section=text

Treasury Board of Canada. (2011a). *Guide to integrated risk management.* Retrieved from http://www.tbs-sct.gc.ca/tbs-sct/rm-gr/guides/girm-ggirtb-eng.asp

Treasury Board of Canada. (2011b). *Guide to risk taxonomies.* Retrieved from http://www.tbs-sct.gc.ca/tbs-sct/rm-gr/guides/grt-gtr01-eng.asp#toc2

U.S.–Canada Power System Outage Taskforce. (2004). *Final report on the August 14, 2003 blackout in the United States and Canada: Causes and recommendations.* Retrieved from https://reports.energy.gov/BlackoutFinal-Web.pdf

Policy Communication

T he policy cycle is one of the most ubiquitous models of the policymaking process, but most versions pay no attention to policy communication. We know, however, that, apart from moments of solitary reflection, policy analysis and policymaking are all about talk in all its guises: speech, text, image, gesture, posture, persuasion, rebuttal, response, the occasional pleading, and even expressions of guilt. Policy is inseparable from communication, which is the lubricant for every phase of the cycle. Why so little attention to communication in policy? Most likely, it reflects a division of labour: communication specialists study communication and principally media; policy specialists study the mechanics of making policy in terms of problems and solutions. There are notable exceptions, but they are relatively rare. And yet, even though communication has always been important to policy, it is clearly even more important today. Problems are more complex, there are more players with their wares on offer, and there is more noise and cacophony, as well as competition and uncertainty, to deal with. Digital media have also been a game changer: even as late as the 1980s, analysts could craft careful policy memos and feel that they had the corner on the research and ear of the audience. Today, information roils around 24/7 in endless pools, eddies, and currents. In this environment, the effective communicator is queen. This chapter reviews the academic literature and its various approaches to policy communication, looks at some guides and tips on communicating effectively, and examines some of the forces behind the changing policy communications landscape.

Public policy is not only made; it is sold, and sold to a large number of disparate and different audiences. Internal to government, political leaders have to "sell" their ideas and agendas to their officials. Policy analysts have to "sell" their diagnoses and their proposed solutions to their political masters as well as colleagues (and enemies) within the bureaucracy. Ultimately, policies have to be "sold" to the legislature (if legal frameworks are required, but at a minimum to explain the government's agenda). They also have to be "sold" to the voting public and to stakeholders. Each of these transactions involves communication of one sort or another, oral and written, and increasingly visual (websites, presentations, YouTube videos). The importance of communication has been highlighted throughout the earlier chapters in this book. In problem definition, for example, we saw the role that **policy images** play in providing a sort of snapshot of policy issues and their content, especially if they are complex. Environmental issues, such as climate change and global warming, are enormously complicated, and only a handful of scientists truly understand the issues in all of their dimensions. For the public, environmental problems get summarized by images of collapsing icebergs, forest fires, and floods, and policy solutions get conveyed by the prefix "green" or "sustainable." We also noted the importance of the structure of **policy arguments** (Dunn, 2004) and the use of arguments to persuade others about the inevitably conjectural quality of a problem definition. Complementing the logic of arguments is the art of **issue framing**, a deliberate technique for depicting a policy issue in understandable terms. It makes a great deal of practical policy difference, for example, on how the financial crisis is framed: as a result of "greedy" bankers versus "inadequate regulation" versus "wasteful" governments.

We also saw the importance of communication in other stages in the policy process. Information is a key—and increasingly important—policy instrument. How that information is structured and conveyed to have maximum impact is a major preoccupation of policymakers. For example, Michelle Obama was directly engaged in publicizing the new U.S. food guide, called "MyPlate" (see Figure 9.1). This guide replaced the confusing "pyramid" graphic by conveying information about the five food groups in a familiar format—a dinner-plate setting. In our discussion of this policy instrument in Chapter 4, we also noted uses of information that are less benign than a simple graphic, for example, anti-smoking and antidrug campaigns, as well as messaging that is deliberately designed to elicit strong emotions and attitudes that will then structure public behaviour and compliance (e.g., warnings about terrorist threats).

We also briefly discussed the role of communications in other aspects of policymaking. Implementation (Chapter 5) can be seen as a communications process, where original policy intents are progressively specified and embedded in programs. Policy communities (Chapter 6) are principally organized around ideas and policy discourses, while policy networks are in an important sense conduits for information exchanges. Evaluation (Chapter 7) is more technical than other aspects of policy

Figure 9.1 MyPlate

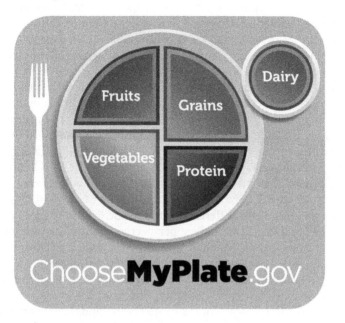

Source: Reproduced with permission from http://www.choosemyplate.gov/food-groups/
downloads/MyPlate/MyPlateGraphicsStandards.pdf.

analysis, but still has to be communicated, particularly when evaluation results are negative and unwelcome. Finally, any discussion about
crisis and emergency management emphasizes the importance of clear
and effective communication and coordination between authorities and
people or communities that are threatened.

The centrality of communication both as a skill and as a feature of
every stage in the policy process warrants a separate and detailed discussion. This chapter (new to this edition) provides that discussion, focusing
on what we will call **policy communication**. The chapter will first
examine how communication is viewed in the policy literature, revisiting
some sources we have mentioned in previous chapters, but in more detail.
This work tends to approach policy communication as an explanation of
policy outcomes. It then moves to a discussion of the practice of policy
communication, focusing on recent Canadian federal policies on government communication, as well as key tips that come from various guides
on writing and presenting policy information. This approach is less
about explanation than it is about prescription, about how policymaking
should be conducted. We conclude with some reflections on the current
communications environment and its implications for how governments
and citizens understand policy and policymaking.

It should be noted that we are looking specifically at policy communication, and not communication for purposes of lobbying or political campaigning. **Lobbying** activity is less about communication than it is about a direct effort to influence decision within government, which is a key dynamic in the policy process, but distinct even while it clearly has a strong communications dimension. **Advocacy** is closely related to lobbying, but is typically defined or perceived as a broader effort that reaches beyond decisionmakers to the wider public and aims to change the context of discussion and debate, problem definitions, or the configuration and coalition of stakeholder interests. **Political campaigning** is also about communications, but is more nakedly partisan and aimed at re-election and grasping power rather than policy objectives per se. Obviously, as we have discussed in previous chapters, policy and politics can never be completely separated. Governments with different ideological dispositions will see policy problems differently and will demand different species of solutions. They will articulate these perspectives and solutions in platform documents (sometimes a pamphlet and sometimes a more elaborate "campaign book" of promises and costing), and so a political campaign, though its ultimate objective is to win power, consists of a blend of partisan manoeuvring and policy prescriptions. For example, more conservative parties (e.g., the Republicans in the United States and the Conservatives in Canada) tend to favour tax reductions over stimulus spending in dealing with economic downturns, though there are many examples where so-called right wing governments have been quite happy to drive up deficits through higher spending, which has the benefit of giving the electorate various goodies (Pal, 2011). Good examples are the Harper Conservatives since 2006 and the Alberta Progressive Conservatives in the last decade.

Ideas and values often structure policy responses and put some options on the table while others are off. Nonetheless, once these choices have been made and the broad policy orientations indicated, the hard work of design, implementation, and evaluation normally proceeds on a professional level. And this work includes effective communication inside government and between government and citizens. Partisan and advocacy communication are important in their own right, but this chapter focuses on policy communication, that is, communication that supports the development and the eventual successful implementation of policies and their accompanying programs.

Approaches to Policy Communication

Communication is addressed in almost every discussion of policymaking and public policy analysis, but in different ways. This section provides an overview of six of these approaches, categorized as follows. Some, more rationalistically oriented approaches to policy see communication as a *supplementary component* to doing good analytical work. Most of that work is technically informed, but there is an obvious reality that even the best technical analysis needs to make a persuasive case to policymakers and to the public. A second approach does not emphasize communication as much as it does the *role of ideas* in forming policy positions. Ideas can be defined as **policy paradigms** (e.g., Keynesian or monetarist economic theory), or values (e.g., a strong belief in gender equality), or simpler beliefs (e.g., vouchers are a good way of delivering services). Of course, these ideas (however defined) end up shaping problem definition and options and recommendations, which themselves have to be communicated in opposition to other ideas and policy prescriptions on offer. The advocacy coalition model discussed in Chapter 6 is a good example of this approach. Yet another approach in the literature has been designated as **post-positivist policy analysis,** or *constructivist* policy analysis. Here, ideas and discourse are the prime elements—indeed, almost the only elements—in policymaking and policy analysis. Developing policy positions is less about technical analysis and much more about discourses and ideas that shape the way that people think about and discuss issues. Rational, technical analysis is inevitably hobbled by our inability to disassociate ourselves from our biases and mental frameworks. The policy process is thus less about analysis than it is about argument, and understanding policy (and, it is hoped, sometimes coming to "solutions"—that is, things people can agree upon) is a function of understanding the ideational frameworks through which they are communicated. A fourth approach is related to the preceding ones, in that it looks more closely and systematically at exactly what *rhetorical and discursive strategies* are used in policy debates and policy communication. In Chapter 3, for example, we briefly mentioned the use of labels and metaphors as ways of tilting perceptions of complicated policy issues. A fifth area of examination has been the *effects of the media* on policymaking. The jury is still out on whether the media drive policy agendas through the way they select and frame issues, or whether policymakers (especially politicians) use the media for their own ends to convey messages or "spin." Finally, the recent surge of interest in *behavioural economics* (discussed briefly in Chapter 4) has trained attention on certain limits or biases in human cognition or how people receive and process information. Overcoming these biases to ensure effective implementation and compliance has led to work on policy design and communication that either gets around cognitive limitations or uses them as leverage. Chapter 4 discussed the example of "nudges," some of which involve the communication of specific signals to policy targets (e.g., signs that display a motorist's speed as a way of "nudging" him to slow down).

We discuss each approach in turn.

COMMUNICATION AS A SUPPLEMENTARY COMPONENT TO ANALYSIS

In the early days of the development of the discipline of public policy analysis, there were many advocates of a purely rationalistic paradigm— policy analysis could be a "science," informed by systems design, cybernetics, large amounts of good data, and the impartial application of social sciences, primarily economics. Almost no one seriously believes this anymore, but there still is a strong tradition of policy analysis that emphasizes the usefulness of hard skills. At this end of the spectrum, the emphasis is on the technical skills, but there is a nod (sometimes a strong nod) to the importance of communication.

Weimer and Vining (2011) provide a good example. They have chapters on rationales for public policy such as market failures and distributional goals, benefit–cost analysis, and statistical methods. However, they also have a short section on communicating the results of a policy analysis, providing some tips on structuring a report, as well as a discussion of rhetorical strategies such as metaphors to better get a policy message across (pp. 283–285). Nonetheless, the bulk of the book is devoted to a rationalist model of policy analysis (which we discussed in Chapter 1). Carol Weiss's key text on evaluation (Weiss, 1998) is a technical review of modelling programs, planning evaluations, developing measures, and collecting data, using randomized experiments as well as qualitative data. At the same time, though, she devotes a full chapter to "writing the report and disseminating results." She provides a generic outline for an evaluation report (pp. 296–297), with practical advice such as this: "The report should be clear. It should be written in language that speaks to program and policy people. Save the abstruse statistics and sociological theory and references to Foucault for the academic paper published in professional journals" (p. 300). As well, she discusses strategies for the dissemination of results to different, influential audiences through different communication techniques.

William Dunn's influential text on policy analysis has a strong emphasis on the range of techniques available for everything from problem definition to recommendations (including cost-benefit analysis), time series analysis, and the structure of policy arguments (discussed here in Chapter 3). But like Weiss, he also has a separate chapter on "communicating policy analysis" as well as four appendices on different communication vehicles (the policy issue paper, the executive summary, the policy memorandum, and oral briefings). Dunn (2004) argues that the communication of policy-relevant knowledge is a four-stage process consisting of policy analysis, materials development, interaction, and knowledge utilization, with the policy analyst at the centre of the cycle and supporting each stage, though only indirectly when it comes to **knowledge utilization** (pp. 430–431):

- Policy analysis: Policy problems, policy futures, policy actions, policy outcomes, and policy performance.
- Materials development: Policy memoranda, policy issue papers, executive summaries, appendices, news releases. [Today we would include blogs, tweets, and Web pages.]
- Interactive communication: conversations, conferences, meetings, briefings, hearings. [Today we would include interactive Web chats, email, and SMS.]
- Knowledge utilization: Agenda-setting, policy formulation, policy adoption, policy implementation, policy assessment.*

Dunn also makes a useful distinction between **policy issue papers, policy memoranda,** and **executive summaries.** Other terms are sometimes used for the same products—for example, policy paper instead of policy issue paper—but the logic of the distinctions is virtually universal. Policy issue papers are longer, more detailed, and technical analyses of a policy problem, with consideration of options and recommendations (see Box 9.1). Whatever they may be called, policy memoranda are shorter pieces (rarely more than 3000 words), often in response to a specific request for background information, and designed for "quick and efficient reading" (p. 440). Executive summaries can be stand-alone documents (e.g., a two-page summary of a 100-page report), or the first section of a policy issue paper. They are challenging to write, since they must simultaneously be short and comprehensive.

Whatever their length and level of detail, all three of these forms of policy communication are written and are part of an older form of communication. Modern decisionmaking relies less and less on straight textual communication, and more and more on visualizations of information and data. We discuss this below, but the majority of policy communication from analysts to decisionmakers is in the form of some sort of presentation software, most likely PowerPoint.

This approach of "communication as supplementary" to rational analysis is characteristic of a good deal of the literature. Other examples would include the popular title *A Practical Guide for Policy Analysis: The Eightfold Path to More Effective Problem Solving* (Bardach, 2000), which features short sections on "telling your story" and "semantic tips." Another would be Amitai Etzioni's argument that the unique methodology of policy research is defined, in part, by the element of communication: "policy researchers often recognize the need to mobilize public support for the policies that their findings favour and hence they tend to help policy makers to mobilize such support by communicating with the

---

*DUNN, WILLIAM N., PUBLIC POLICY ANALYSIS: AN INTRODUCTION, 3rd Edition, © 2004. Reprinted by permission of Pearson Education, Inc. Upper Saddle River, N.J.

- In what ways can the policy problem be formulated?
- What is the scope and severity of the problem?
- To what extent does [the problem] require public action?
- If no action is taken, how is the problem likely to change in coming months or years?
- Have other units of government addressed the problem, and if so, what were the consequences?
- What goals and objectives should be pursued in solving the problem?
- What major policy alternatives are available to achieve these goals and objectives?
- What criteria should be employed to evaluate the performance of these alternatives?
- What alternative(s) should be adopted and implemented?
- What agency should have the responsibility for policy implementation?
- How will the policy be monitored and evaluated?

Source: DUNN, WILLIAM N., PUBLIC POLICY ANALYSIS: AN INTRODUCTION, 3rd Edition, © 2004. Reprinted by permission of Pearson Education , Inc. Upper Saddle River, N.J.

public.... Hence, basic researchers are more likely to use technical terms (which may sound like jargon to outsiders), mathematical notations, extensive footnotes, and other such scientific features. On the other hand, policy researchers are more likely to express themselves in the vernacular and avoid technical terms" (Etzioni, 2006, p. 840).

A somewhat more determined version of this approach is Majone's (1989) classic analysis of the role of argument and persuasion in the policy process. He calls the rational model of analysis "decisionism" and finds it wanting, but he still refers to its "limitations" rather than dismissing it entirely. Instead, the book rests on the assumption that the

> policy analyst is a producer of arguments, more similar to a lawyer—a specialist in legal arguments—than to an engineer or a scientist. His basic skills are not algorithmical but argumentative: the ability to probe assumptions critically, to produce and evaluate evidence, to keep many threads in hand, to draw for an argument from many disparate sources, to communicate effectively. (pp. 21–22)

The Role of Ideas

Majone's emphasis on argument and communication, of course, implies something that will be argued and communicated, and this is likely to include ideas as well as rhetorical devices (see below). But it can just as well include data, research results (coupled with specific interpretations), and other "facts." The stream of work in the policy sciences that emphasizes the role of ideas takes a slightly different epistemological approach. While it does not claim that there are no such things as "facts" or "reality" (see post-positivism below), it does assume that our appreciation of facts and reality is heavily filtered and mediated by ideas. These ideas are not merely individual biases, but collective ideational frameworks that help policy analysts, decisionmakers, and other actors make sense of the world. Depending on how deep these ideas are buried, and how fundamental they are for our interpretation of the world, they may not even be noticed—they are simply taken as "given." Since they are taken as given only by subsets of the population, however, and opposing ideas might animate others, inevitably the policy process becomes one of a clash of these ideas or frameworks, and so they do not remain unarticulated or unconscious for long. A good example is the model of the family that underpinned both labour and social policies a generation ago. That model was premised on a single (male) breadwinner, with a stay-at-home spouse (female), and 2.5 children. It assumed that the breadwinner would have a single career or occupation throughout his life and that the marriage (a formal marriage) would be generally stable. Even as the reality began to change as women entered the permanent labour force in the 1970s, as family patterns changed, as labour markets evolved, the traditional model continued to inform public policy.

The two best examples of this approach are advocacy coalitions and policy paradigms. The advocacy coalition approach was discussed in some detail in Chapter 6, so we need only highlight the fourth of its four key elements: public policies as belief systems.

> The fourth important premise is that public policies and programs incorporate implicit theories about how to achieve their objectives ... and thus can be conceptualized in much the same way as belief systems. They involve value priorities, perceptions of important causal relationships, perceptions of world states (including the magnitude of the problem), perceptions of the efficacy of policy instruments, and so on. This ability to map beliefs and policies on the same "canvas" provides a vehicle for assessing the influence of various actors over time, particularly the role of technical information (beliefs) on policy change. (Sabatier, 1993, p. 17)

For Sabatier (the originator of the approach), policy subsystems (e.g., health or immigration) can be analyzed in terms of actors (governmental and nongovernmental) who are aggregated into coalitions that are defined by shared normative and causal beliefs. These beliefs are the "glue" that bind coalitions. However, actors are not forever trapped in their ideational universes—reality in the form of external shocks (e.g., an economic crisis) or simply learning through experience and research (e.g., smoking is harmful) can change some of these beliefs. The approach distinguishes among three levels of ideas or beliefs that define a coalition: "a deep core of fundamental normative and ontological axioms that define a person's underlying personal philosophy, a near (policy) core of basic strategies and policy positions for achieving deep core beliefs in the policy area or subsystem in question, and a set of secondary aspects comprising a multitude of instrumental decisions and information searches necessary to implement the policy core in the specific policy area" (Sabatier, 1993, p. 30). The **deep core beliefs** are the most impervious to change and argument: Sabatier's examples include the nature of human beings as either inherently good or evil, and the relative priority of such ultimate values as freedom, security, health, and love. **Near (policy) beliefs** are difficult to change as well, but change might happen in the face of serious anomalies. Examples include basic choice of policy instruments between coercive and inducement, or the identification of social groups most in need. **Secondary aspects** deal with organizational rules, implementation techniques, and the like, and can change quite easily. Different coalitions are in conflict in policy subsystems, seeking different goals and outcomes, and part of that conflict involves the effective communication of their belief systems across all three levels.

A similar approach to understanding the impact of ideas is through policy paradigms, first proposed in a seminal article by Peter Hall (1993). Challenging the notion that governments are motivated only by power and interests, Hall argued for a social learning model in which governments face puzzles, uncertainties, and anomalies and strive to find solutions through the development of consistent ideational frameworks. Somewhat like Sabatier, Hall also discerned three kinds of changes in policy (his case study was British macroeconomic policy between 1970 and 1989). The first order of change was the levels or settings of basic macroeconomic policy instruments such as minimum lending rates—they could be increased or decreased, but the instrument remained the same. These happened frequently, even as the broader goals and objectives of policy remained the same. Second-order change occurred less frequently and involved the choice of new basic techniques or instruments, based on dissatisfaction with previous experience. Hall's example was the introduction of a new monetary control system in 1971. Finally, third-order change involves "simultaneous changes in all three components of policy:

the instrument settings, the instruments themselves, and the hierarchy of goals behind policy" (Hall, 1993, p. 279). This kind of change qualified as a "paradigm shift," in this case, from Keynesian to monetarist macroeconomic policy. Hall defined a policy paradigm as "a framework of ideas and standards that specifies not only the goals of policy and the kind of instruments that can be used to attain them, but also the very nature of the problems they are meant to be addressing.... this framework is embedded in the very terminology through which policymakers communicate about their work, and it is influential precisely because so much of it is taken for granted and unamenable to scrutiny as a whole" (Hall, 1993, p. 279). Hall was at pains to emphasize that the paradigm shift from Keynesianism to monetarism was, in large part, a function of a wider political debate during the 1979 British election as well as policy arguments led by influential journalists.

POST-POSITIVIST OR CONSTRUCTIVIST ANALYSIS

Both of the approaches described above acknowledge that while argument, persuasion, and ideas are key components of the policy process, and while deep norms and values change very slowly, there is nonetheless an external reality that can impose itself on our consciousness and induce us to change our minds and learn from mistakes. The approach known as "post-positivist" or "constructivist" (sometimes "postmodern" or "interpretivist") takes a more radical approach. It argues that while there is indeed a reality external to ourselves, we can never perceive it unfiltered. Our ideas, our beliefs, our norms, even our language, structure perception so deeply that we can perceive only "social facts," not facts themselves. The shorthand term often used for this structure of ideas and perceptions is **discourse**, which itself gestures to the dialogical nature of argument and persuasion.

The main target in this approach is, once again, the rational model or what Majone termed "decisionism," both for its claims about reason and science, and for its elevation of "experts" in rational analysis to a privileged place in the policy process. For post-positivists, embracing the rational model means elevating experts, which, in turn, means choking democracy or the meaningful participation of non-expert, ordinary citizens. The alternative approach emphasizes both the uncertainty in our perceptions and ideas (because we cannot come to a definitive assessment of reality or truth), and the crucial role of argument and debate as we collectively search for answers. For example, in an early contribution, Hawkesworth noted that while we do deliberate about policy choices, we do so against multiple criteria, and "however exhaustive the arguments advanced in support of one position, considered judgements concerning the best theory will remain contentious and tentative ..." (Hawkesworth, 1988, p. 87).

Stone (2012) makes a similar post-positivist critique to Hawkesworth's, though less in terms of methodology and science than in terms of the implications of the traditional, rationalist approach for our understanding of politics and the policymaking process. Stone notes that what she calls the "rationality project" necessarily holds out science, facts, and reason as the means for arriving at policy choices. But policymaking takes place in the political community—the polis:

> [T]he categories of thought behind reasoned analysis are themselves constructed in political struggle, and nonviolent political conflict is conducted primarily through reasoned analysis. It is not simply, therefore, a matter that sometimes analysis is used in partisan fashion or for political purposes. *Reasoned analysis is necessarily political*. Reason doesn't start with a clean slate on which our brains record their pure observations. Reason proceeds from choices to notice some things but not others, to include some things and exclude others, and to view the world in a particular way when other visions are possible. Policy analysis is political argument, and vice versa. (Stone, 2012, p. 380; emphasis in original)

In the early 1990s, Frank Fischer and John Forester, two leading lights in this approach, termed this emphasis the "argumentative turn" in policy analysis and planning (Fischer & Forester, 1993). For them, policymaking is a "struggle over the criteria of social classification, the boundaries of problem categories, the intersubjective interpretation of common experiences, the conceptual framing of problems, and the definitions of ideas that guide the ways people create the shared meanings which motivate them to act" (p. 2). The argumentative turn entails, among other things, the critical study of the structure of argument in policy analysis (Fischer, 1980), the role of values (Fischer & Forester, 1987), the deep impact of rationalism through its associated logic of technocratic mastery (Fischer, 1990), and the search for some sort of "deliberative democracy" that builds on the communicative competence of social actors as they honestly, and without domination or constraint, search for solutions together through dialogue (Dryzek, 1990; Dryzek & Niemeyer, 2010).

The last point about **deliberative democracy** is important to understanding post-positivist or interpretivist policy analysis as a practice rather than simply as a philosophy or an epistemology. If technocratic or rationalist policy analysis is undemocratic, and if people inevitably "frame" reality in terms of discourse and ideas and orient their actions in terms of these discourses and ideas, the only democratic way forward is exchange, discussion, and deliberation. Policy analysts thus become less interested in finding solutions than in exploring discourses, understanding their structure and (sometimes unconscious) effects, and facilitating exchange and open deliberation among citizens and stakeholders as interpretive mediators (Fischer, 2009; Hajer & Wagenaar, 2003). It should also be noted that not all discourses are created equal. Post-positivists pay serious attention to the link between discourse and power and, indeed, in the way that discourse and communication can become the foundation for governmental power and public policy. As Dryzek and Dunleavy (2009) argue:

> a discourse can be thought of in terms of shared concepts, categories and ideas that yield a way of comprehending situations. A discourse will therefore contain and be defined by particular judgments, assumptions, capabilities, dispositions and intentions. The individuals subject to a particular discourse will weave fragments of information they receive into "storylines" that are meaningful to others who share the discourse in question.... Particular discourses serve some interests and marginalize others. (pp. 298–299)

Consider how the discourse on the "War on Terror" became the "frame" for the securitization of North American and European states, as well as wars in Iraq and Afghanistan.

Whereas the two previous approaches discussed above essentially heighten the emphasis on communication without completely abandoning the rational model, the post-positivist approach rejects the rational model in its entirety and tries to develop a new methodology based on discourse analysis and interpretive mediation. It has made important contributions to policy analysis, but has also been criticized for indulging in relativism. It recognizes power and dominant discourses, but typically lays out competing discourses—for example, different theories about the causes and hence solutions to crime—on a level playing field. It resists making prescriptions about "best" or "good" policy, other than urging as broad and open a participatory process as possible.

RHETORICAL AND DISCURSIVE STRATEGIES

Almost everyone has had the experience of listening to a particularly powerful speaker, or reading a moving and persuasive piece of prose. We expect works of literature to be marked by narrative skill and grace, and expect that works of social science and public policy will be dry and demanding. But if we accept that policy analysis and recommendations have to be communicated, understood, accepted, and implemented, we can appreciate the importance of crafting the message. As we have noted above, most students of public policy acknowledge the importance of effective communication, and at least a few have tried to examine the specific rhetorical and discursive strategies behind those communications.

They can draw on ancient reflections such as Aristotle's *Rhetoric* as well as more contemporary ones (Riker, 1986, 1996). The key is that policy communication is not only about analysis, but about persuasion through language and rhetorical strategies, whether deliberate or through unconscious art and instinct.

Stone, for example, notes that we "talk of policy problems in words" (Stone, 1988, p. 108). She highlights four modes of symbolic representation: narrative stories, synechdoches, metaphors, and ambiguity. Narratives are stories that draw on the tropes of deep human experience: decline, loss, survival, triumph. Synechdoche is the representation of the whole by a part or by a single instance. Disability, which has many dimensions, is usually represented by an image of a person in a wheelchair. The entire logic behind "spokespersons" for different causes or issues relies on synechdoche. How you see the issue depends on how you see its apparent representation. **Metaphors** are subtle, sometimes invisible, denotations of one thing in terms of another: *a* is like *b*. Ambiguity is the quality of symbols to simultaneously mean more than one thing, and from Stone's perspective, to provide policymakers with a tool to bring together disparate groups under one banner. Her focus is on the political advantages of ambiguity less than its role in policy advice, so we will leave this out of our discussion.

Analytical policy statements are often less important than the structural elements of language that stimulate almost unconscious reactions to the argument. Let's consider narratives. We are all familiar with certain archetypal storylines, and a policy argument that can tap into one of these draws on the power of the narrative structure itself. Arguments about social policy and the deficit, for example, can be seen as "redemption stories." In the past, goodwill and good intentions built a welfare state to meet important needs, but then temptation led us astray and we indulged in excesses and financial debauchery. Our problems got worse, but we ignored them and continued our profligate ways. Now the only option is a complete renunciation of our past sins, and with much pain and suffering, we will be redeemed. No wonder some finance ministers have sounded like preachers in recent years. Their narrative line has been about weakness, temptation, and eventual, if painful, redemption. The narrative line makes sense of the dense budget documents and arcane statistics. Challengers to this narrative write their own stories. The Occupy movement presented a narrative of greed, privilege, excess, and exploitation—the 99 percent screwed the 1 percent, and now they should pay.

Policy analysts have to do the heavy lifting of problem definition and the search for options and recommendations, but they cannot avoid the imperative of packaging their work in some sort of narrative, a story that compels attention, if not agreement. As Borins argues: "if narratives so pervade the public sector, skill at engaging with, creating, and communicating compelling stories must be considered essential for both persuasive and public servants" (Borins, 2011, p. 3). He calls this "narrative competence," drawing attention to various "fables" about the public sphere that help us grapple with complex public issues—fables about heroes, sacrifice, tragedy, and satire.

Synechdoche is an awkward term for something we see all the time—the representation of the whole through a part. We mentioned the representation of disability, but think about the importance of representation in making arguments and in persuading. Advertisers and marketers know this: a simple picture of one starving child represents all of Africa's dying children. An image of a single missile represents an arsenal. A swastika is Nazi Germany. A condom is sex. In policy communication, this rhetorical device is often expressed as "the average ... X." Here, the average is supposed to mean the normal, the typical, the representative of the group. In making policy presentations with PowerPoint, well-chosen, single images can convey dense and more complex messages. An upward tilting arrow means the stock market is rising. A handshake means an international treaty has been signed. These are parts representing a whole. The parts matter. In a policy analysis of Aboriginal poverty in Canada, what part would you choose to represent the whole? A destitute and doomed family, or one just as poor but with some hope?

Metaphors and labels are used to tilt meaning and stimulate reactions. **Labels** are dense words or phrases that convey subtle but powerful meanings: "axis of evil" versus "enemies," "gay" versus "homosexual," "homeless" versus "vagrant," "user fee" versus "tax," "sex-worker" versus "prostitute," "pro-life" versus "anti-abortion," "smart regulation" versus "deregulation." Intense policy battles are often fought over labels, because labels are often the first way in which the public is acquainted with a policy issue. Box 9.2 presents some labels that are politically charged but also frequently used in the communication of policy advice.

Metaphors are another weapon in the linguistic arsenal. Consider some of the most famous: Cold War, Iron Curtain, Third World, pork barrel, social safety net, spaceship Earth, global village, and, of course, war metaphors such as the War on Poverty, line in the sand, and so on—and these do not even include the ubiquitous sports metaphors! If people accept that spanking "is *like* child abuse," or whether marijuana is "*like* alcohol" or "*like* cocaine," a good deal of the policy argument has been won. Medical analogies also can sway thinking: for example, consider the terms "epidemic," "quarantine," "virus," "infection," and "healthy." Governments prefer to have "healthy" surpluses. If something has gone "viral," that means that it has spread quickly and is probably not good. A particularly powerful use of metaphor is the identification of opponents with socially unsavoury groups—in effect, opponents are said to be "like" those groups. For example, while defending the Protecting

BOX 9.2   POLICY COMMUNICATION THROUGH LABELS

PEOPLE/GROUP LABELS	ISSUE LABELS
Average/Typical/Elite/Middle class	Innovative/Innovation
Main street/Bay Street/Wall Street	Green
Diverse	Smart
Struggling	Crisis
Extremist/Right wing/Left wing	Emerging
Marginalized	Pressing
Discriminated/Privileged	Latent
Powerful/Weak/Vulnerable	Popular
Boss/Czar/Factory floor	Forgotten/Ignored
Hardworking/Entrepreneurial/	Commonsense/Complex
Passive	Competitiveness/Well-being
Citizens/Taxpayers	

Children from Internet Predators bill in the House of Commons, federal Safety Minister Vic Toews said: "He [a member of Parliament opposing the bill] can either stand with us or with the child pornographers" ("Online Surveillance Bill Critics," 2012).

The use of rhetorical strategies at best may seem like little more than spin and at worst something unsavoury that politicians do to sell policies. But the alternatives are not between sober, flat analysis and sexy slogan-eering. No matter how solid the analysis, if it is presented awkwardly and is indigestible or unclear, it will fail. At minimum, it should have clarity of structure and message. At best, it can be both clear and engaging. Even titles matter. Which would you read first—*Losing Ground, Losing Faith: Growing Inequality and Secularism in Canada*, or *An Analysis of Income Differentials and Their Statistical Correlation with Declines in Religiosity*?

EFFECT OF THE MEDIA

Public policy is shaped and fashioned by a host of actors—ordinary citizens, politicians, public officials, think tanks, academic institutions, government relations experts, nongovernmental organizations, and third-party panels such as task forces and ad hoc panels. However, debates over policy rarely take place directly, and most citizens get exposed to these debates through the media, typically television news, magazines, newspapers, and so on. The question is whether these media simply and faithfully channel those debates to the public, or whether they have their own biases and agendas, and consequently an independent effect by shaping how people think about policy issues. Moreover, this question about the role and impact of the media can be posed in different ways. For example, one way to think about media bias is to look for deliberate "spin" that intentionally is designed to influence readers/viewers in a particular direction. The *New York Times*, for example, is generally conceded to be both the newspaper of record in the United States, as well as generally on the "liberal" side of the political spectrum. In editorials and in its decisions about what to cover, the paper can be relied on to give Democratic approaches to public policy favourable coverage. Conservatives and Republicans typically come in for more scrutiny and critique. In Canada, the *Globe and Mail* is broadly considered to be the national newspaper of record, and its editorial approach and columnists tend to be slightly right of centre.

This notion of deliberate bias in the media is a regular theme of more conservatively oriented policy advocates. For example, in discussing his "ten commandments" for successful conservative political campaigns, Flanagan argues that the "media can be savage with any party that lacks discipline, but they are particularly suspicious of conservatives. There is no point complaining about it; the situation is the same everywhere in the democratic world. But it means that conservative parties must put special emphasis on self-discipline if they expect to win elections" (Flanagan, 2009, p. 284). Kheiriddin and Daifallah use even stronger language: "Conservatives can never forget a basic fact: most of the media are out to get them," and they single out the Canadian Broadcasting Corporation (CBC) for having an animus against Tories because only the Tories have ever seriously called for funding cuts to the national broadcaster (Kheiriddin & Daifallah, 2005, p. 84). Content analysis of news stories has purported to demonstrate a hidden, "liberal" agenda in the media, especially the CBC (Cooper, 1994), and a "postmaterialist" culture among journalists that makes them considerably different from the majority of citizens (Miljan & Cooper, 2003). Ironically, these complaints from the right that the media are too liberal are matched by complaints on the left that media reflect the biases of a capitalist system and its concentrations of power among the elite, as well as a set of economic and political assumptions—that they constantly reinforce—about the system itself (Hackett & Carroll, 2006; Hackett & Gruneau, 1999). In fact, both positions could be simultaneously correct. The mainstream media could be supporting the capitalist system in a broad sense, even while preferring a less conservative version of public policy and politics. Of course, if media ownership is considered, then another type of bias filters in, that of owners and proprietors. Because of media competition for public attention, the media tend to cling to the middle ground, but there are examples of when an owner's ideas and political ideology can affect a media organ's political and policy position. Conrad Black, for example, started the *National Post* newspaper specifically to counteract what he thought was a "liberal" consensus in news media (Siklos, 1995). An even more vivid example is Rupert Murdoch, owner of the News Corp media empire and of the former *News of the World*, often described as the most influential paper in Britain (see Box 9.3). Conservative news channels such as Fox News in the United States, and the Sun News Network and Quebecor in Canada, have recently gained prominence.

Another kind of bias in the media has also attracted attention: the structural bias of the way in which the media are organized and how they function. This is not a specific or even deliberate political or policy bias. Altheide and Snow (1991) first introduced the idea of "media logics" to capture this structural feature. "Thus, television as a medium, for instance, is visual and exists in time; the press is a textual medium that takes up space. They have different communicative forms and time frames of production. Hence political actors using these media will have to use different approaches. Also, within any given medium there are important genre differences: A local radio talk show is not the same as a national news broadcast, and a popular television magazine operates differently from a highbrow debate program" (Dahlgren, 2009, p. 53). The usual concern that is expressed is that modern media, especially television, operate on a logic that is rapidly "dumbing down" the citizenry and eroding public trust and civic engagement. Television thrives on "infotainment" and visuals, driving out hard journalism in favour of slick images that titillate and mesmerize. Modern media have been accused of creating an artificial environment of fear since that sells advertising (Altheide, 2002), of reducing citizens to passive spectators in election campaigns, and of contributing to more inequality and marginalization, which gets reflected in lower and lower voter turnouts (Stanyer, 2007). Other analysts are not so pessimistic, pointing to the emergence of digital media and the almost limitless amount of information available to citizens if they choose to access it (Norris, 2000), thereby enhancing participation and engagement rather than reducing it.

These two approaches to media bias (the personal/cultural and the structural) raise an important question we touched on in Chapter 3: agenda-setting. How do the media contribute to setting the societal policy agenda? Do decisionmakers and politicians take their cues from media stories (e.g., developing an anti-crime policy agenda simply because crime news sells, and so the public demands that "something be done")? The more pessimistic analyses of the impact of the media assume that they do perform an agenda-setting role, or at the very least provide an important set of filters for people to make judgments about policy issues and what is considered important on the political agenda. For example, the workday for any political adviser begins with a scan of the media "clippings" (increasingly, electronic stories, blogs, and tweets) to anticipate and prepare for the issues that will intrude on the day ahead. This review sets the agenda for Question Period (for both government and opposition sides) and can also overtake the agendas of political and bureaucratic officials who must drop their normal to-do list to develop media lines to respond to a reporter's inquiry or prepare a cabinet minister for the first media scrum on the heels of a story relevant to his or her portfolio.

At their best, the media inform and enlighten, but they may also train attention in a distorting way. Part of the problem is attribution—we might see an overemphasis on crime in relation to actual statistics (which show that it is gradually decreasing over time), but does that mean that the media influenced the federal Omnibus Crime Bill introduced by the Conservative government in early 2012? Even the complaints we cited earlier about liberal bias in the media generally agree that, with enough discipline, the media can be partially managed (e.g., "killing" a potentially damaging story through rapid response with text messages, tweets, and blogs, or feeding the media's insatiable appetite for material by releasing mountains of prewritten press releases and other "stories"). Which way do the causal arrows point? Recent research suggests that the agenda-setting power of the media has been somewhat exaggerated.

Soroka conducted an exhaustive analysis of eight public policy issues on the assumption that different issues with different characteristics will have different agenda dynamics: AIDS, crime, debt/deficit, environment, inflation, national unity, taxes, and unemployment (Soroka, 2002). Previous work on issue types had arrived at several key characteristics: obtrusiveness, duration, abstractness, and drama. Massaging these slightly, he arrived at a fresh typology of three types of issues: prominent, sensational, and governmental. Prominent issues are obtrusive and concrete, and affect people directly, and so there is little scope for either media or policy impact on public opinion. Sensational issues lack a direct impact on most people, but are unobtrusive and concrete and so have the greatest potential to be media driven. Governmental issues, again, do not affect most people directly, but are usually not chosen by the media since they lack exciting or dramatic features. In these cases, the policy agenda, not the media, drives the issue. By tracking media reports, public opinion polls, and government/policy activities (e.g., budget speech, committee reports), Soroka found reasonably strong evidence for the salience of different types of issues: "… inflation and unemployment display exactly what the prominent issue type leads us to expect. These issues are real-world driven, with little room for other dynamics. Environment, on the other hand, demonstrates considerable media impact…."

Chapter 9 Policy Communication **365**

Debt/deficit appears to be a good illustration of governmental issue dynamics: media content, sparked by the 1989 Throne Speech, led public attention"(Soroka, 2002, p. 97). Similar findings have been reported in the United States: "The path from media to policymaking activity is not significant, while the path from policymaking to media is" (Jones & Wolfe, 2010, p. 27). Clearly, these studies still support the contribution of media to agenda-setting, but in a more subtle way, and by highlighting the continued power of politicians and legislatures to set national policy agendas, at least for some specific types of issues. But it remains a complicated and shifting picture, particularly with the advent of social media such as Twitter, Facebook, and news aggregators, notably Google News and the Huffington Post. Politicians and officials struggle to keep up and participate—and frankly, to control the policy narratives as best as they can—but doing so is far more difficult than in the days when there were only a handful of broadcast and print media outlets.

BEHAVIOURAL ECONOMICS

We touched earlier in Chapter 4 on the influence of behavioural economics on thinking about policy instruments. Possibly the most famous, popular treatise is the one we cited in the chapter, *Nudge* by Richard H. Thaler and Cass R. Sunstein (2008). Work influenced by behavioural economics takes a good deal of modern psychology into account to help understand human decisionmaking. New findings on human cognitive systems are generally agreeing that there are at least two systems: Thaler and Sunstein use the terms "automatic system" and "reflective system," similar to the distinctions made by Kahneman (2011) and Haidt (2012). The automatic system is quick and feels instinctive, whereas the reflective system is more self-conscious and calculating. One is about gut feelings and the other, about conscious thought. Sometimes we make important decisions based on our gut feelings, and sometimes we labour through careful calculations.

What psychology has revealed is that human beings make systematic errors as they reason. For example, we tend to be biased toward the status quo, the present over the future, and we often anchor our perceptions and, hence, decisions on arbitrary facts. This is where the tool of policy communication comes in: Thaler and Sunstein and other "choice architects" often recommend using communications mechanisms that will reduce some of these biases and allow people to make more effective decisions. For example, if people are given the choice of donating when the amounts on offer are $100, $200, and $300, they will tend to donate more than if the choice is $50, $75, or $100. Advertising (as an informational policy tool) is, of course, everywhere, from antidrinking and driving campaigns to the instructions on how to fill out a tax form.

BOX 9.3   RUPERT MURDOCH AND MEDIA INFLUENCE IN THE UNITED KINGDOM

In 2011 there were dramatic allegations that *News of the World*, owned by Rupert Murdoch, had routinely hacked cellphones and eavesdropped on conversations. The Leveson Inquiry was established, calling witnesses, including Murdoch and his son. The probe was to examine press and media ethics, but rapidly turned into an investigation of the close relations between Murdoch, his papers, and British politicians, including prime ministers Cameron, Blair, and Brown. These relations were based on fears of the influence of Murdoch's media holdings, amounting to about one-third of the British media, and which Murdoch had wanted to expand through a controversial $13 billion buy-out of British Sky Broadcasting, which would have given him a stranglehold on the news market. Endorsements by Murdoch's papers and TV stations allegedly—since they were the most popular in Britain—could make or break a government.

The following is an excerpt of Rupert Murdoch's testimony to the Inquiry on April 25, 2012 (*A* stands for Murdoch's answers).

A. I think that's part of the democratic process. They—all politicians of all sides—like to have their views known by the editors of newspapers or publishers, hoping that they will be put across, hoping that they will be, that they will succeed in impressing people. That's the game.

Q. Yes, but doesn't the game go somewhat further than that—that it's not just providing the politician with a large megaphone, it is also powerful institutions like *The Sun* endorsing the politician and therefore, so the argument might run, the votes of British people might be affected? Do you see that?

A. Of course. I think they certainly would like us to carry their views in a favourable way. I think that's totally normal. And that goes for both parties or all parties. And, you know, we're very lucky in this country that we have ten vibrant national newspapers to keep the national debate going. I mean, I don't—Mr Cameron might, of course, think stopping in Santorini would impress me. I don't know. But I certainly didn't—

Q. But perhaps he, like you, Mr Murdoch—

A. I didn't— I don't have any fealty to the Tory Party or to the Labour Party. Unlike Mr Barclay I don't get invited to dinner at 10 Downing Street.

(continued)

BOX 9.3 (continued)

Q. It's the importance of the face-to-face meeting, isn't it, Mr Murdoch, importance which you appreciated when you invited yourself to Chequers on 4 January 1981? He was seeking that access to you, wasn't he?
A. Let me be quite honest, Mr Jay. I enjoy meeting—let's call them our leaders. Some impress me more than others. And I meet them around the world. And I could tell you one or two who particularly impressed me.
Q. I mean, you mentioned the—
A. If one looks at their personalities, their knowledge, their policies, their principles, or, one hopes, their principles.
Q. Can I bring you back to the issue of the democratic process? Do you feel that there's any validity at least in the perception that there is an implied trade-off here? People think, and have been thinking over 30 years, that the support you give to politicians, through the endorsements in *The Sun* in particular, is met with a quid pro quo after they attain power—
A. No, I—
Q. Just wait for the end of this, Mr Murdoch.
A. Sorry, I beg your pardon.
Q. If that is right, then the democratic process is distorted. I'm not really interested, because we understand your evidence, that there's no empirical [sic] to this, you say, but do you see at least the perception of that?
A. Oh, the perception certainly irritates me, because I think it's a myth. And everything I do every day, I think, proves it to be such. Have a look at—well, it's not relevant, but how I treat Mayor Bloomberg in New York. Sends him crazy. But we support him every time he runs for re-election.
Q. Shortly after the Coalition government was set up, you went for tea at Number 10 on 18 May 2010.
A. Yes.
Q. On that occasion and possibly other occasions you go in through the back door; is that right?
A. That—yes. There are reasons for that. They always seem to—don't want me to be photographed going out the front door or I don't want to be, but it also happens to be a shortcut to my apartment, so it's quite okay.

Source: Murdoch, R. (2012, April 25). Interview [Transcript]. *Leveson Inquiry: Culture, Practice, and Ethics of the Press.* Retrieved from http://www.levesoninquiry .org.uk/evidence/?witness=rupert-murdoch.

What Thaler and Sunstein and others have encouraged is thinking about the right design of messages based on psychological principles. As they put it: "If you indirectly influence the choices other people make, you are a choice architect. And since the choices you are influencing are going to be made by Humans, you will want your architecture to reflect a good understanding of how humans behave. In particular, you will want to ensure that the Automatic System doesn't get all confused" (Thaler & Sunstein, 2008, p. 83). One simple point that they make is that since human beings make errors, there should be feedback mechanisms to let them know something is going wrong (one example is how laptops automatically tell their owners when the battery is low). Other examples are the use of default options (e.g., automatic enrolment in a savings plan, with an option to withdraw), peer pressure (e.g., reducing energy consumption by giving households information about community usage rates), and provision of comparable information (e.g., different types of bank accounts, their features and costs). These are all "nudges" in Thaler and Sunstein's scheme, but they are communication nudges.

The Practice of Policy Communication

The previous sections of this chapter have discussed how policy communication is perceived in the academic literature as part of the policy process. But there is also a stream of work that provides advice on how to craft policy communication, principally in vehicles termed policy papers or policy memos. We noted that some textbooks on policymaking have sections that provide examples and even some tips on drafting policy recommendations (e.g., Dunn), but most simply mention the importance of effective communication and leave it at that. There is a genre of work, however, that explicitly provides advice on writing techniques, style, structure, tone, and technical accompaniments such as appendices and citation of sources.

For the purposes of this chapter, policy communication will be defined to include written policy papers, briefs and memos, blogs, websites, and even emails; however, it should be noted that verbal briefings are also increasingly important and a separate art form (these will not be addressed here). As a specific form of communication, policy communication makes certain demands on those who produce it, largely in terms of those who will consume it—decisionmakers and the public. As we have discussed in previous chapters, policy analysis draws on the social and natural sciences—academic research—for data and research and, in many cases, applies the tools of the social sciences for original research on a policy problem and recommendations. But while there is an overlap between the two types of research, they are still distinct enterprises in at least six key ways, outlined in Table 9.1. These distinctions are not hard and fast, and there are always exceptions (as we will see below), but it helps, as a general rule, to distinguish the genres.

There is a world of difference, for example, between the lengthy analysis of current science undertaken by the Intergovernmental Panel on Climate Change and work that is intentionally directed to make a sharp and clear contribution to policy debates over climate change. The latter would include something like the research paper *Climate Leadership, Economic Prosperity* (Bramley, Sadik, & Marshall, 2009). That paper

Table 9.1
COMPARISON OF ACADEMIC AND POLICY RESEARCH

	Academic Research	*Public Policy Research*
Objective	Exploration of theoretical issues; answering a question from a particular literature; solving a conceptual or empirical puzzle. Usually curiosity driven.	Addressing a real-world problem; understanding the empirical characteristics of that problem; finding solutions that work.
	Most important: Making a contribution to knowledge.	*Most important:* Making a practical contribution to solving a problem and serving the public interest.
Time frame	Often takes many months if not years. Exploratory: It takes as long as it takes to get the answer.	Often conducted with short time horizons. Papers have to be produced in response to immediate crises and be responsive to decisionmakers' needs. Instrumental: What can we do in X time to get what we need?
Length	Variable, but the typical product is a book (hence, the long time horizons) or a series of articles in a variety of journals.	Usually short. Briefing notes are only a few pages, while even policy papers might not be much more than 20 to 30 pages.

Table 9.1 (continued)

Audience	Other academics, experts, and specialists in the field.	If analysis is conducted inside government, then to decisionmakers, who can be senior appointed or elected officials. If analysis is conducted outside of government (e.g., think tank or NGO), decisionmakers as well as the broad, interested public.
Institutional location	Typically universities, though some foundations or think tanks will support more in-depth research.	Varied—in government, and outside in think tanks, NGOs, private sector organizations, newspaper columns, and international organizations.
Style	Because the audience is principally other experts, the language and style can afford to be technical to the point that it would be unintelligible to the non-expert.	Because the audience is harried decisionmakers with little time, or a broad, interested but non-expert public, language and style have to be clear, simple without being simplistic, and sufficiently evocative to keep interest.

was produced by two think tanks (the Pembina Institute and the David Suzuki Foundation) with a clear agenda on environmental issues. The report was all of 16 pages long, but it dealt with a fiendishly difficult policy issue: what federal and provincial policies would be required to reduce Canada's greenhouse gas (GHG) emissions by 25 percent below what they had been in 1990 by 2020, what would the overall cost be, and what would the distributional consequences across the country be? To provide an answer, the report drew on sophisticated modelling techniques, but those models were not presented in the paper (a full technical report was available separately). The core recommendation was a carbon tax, starting at $50/tonne and rising to $200/tonne by 2020. The revenues raised through this carbon tax would be used, in part, to compensate (through reductions in personal income tax) for higher energy costs, particularly for Alberta, which would see a net economic contraction due to reductions in the oil and gas industries. In a short table that spanned two pages, the report provided a list of the different policies modelled in the analysis as well as their rationales (e.g., carbon price, vehicle emissions standards, building codes, and appliance efficiency standards). Moreover, the report modelled the effects of its preferred levels of GHG reductions, as well as the government at the time (its targets were lower). The paper drew on science, but was packaged in such a way as to be accessible to media, decisionmakers, and the public. So, newspapers across the country reported on it, and it drew mostly criticism from the federal government and the western provinces.

Too stark a distinction between these two styles or approaches is inadvisable. There are many examples of longer, more complex, academically oriented work that have "crossed the divide" and made significant contributions to policy debate. Two early ones were Michael Harrington's *The Other America* (1962), which trained national attention in the United States on poverty, and Rachel Carson's *Silent Spring* (1962), which virtually launched the environmental movement. More recent ones would include Robert Putnam's work on social capital, which introduced the term and the concept to broader policy discussions on economic development and social protection (Putnam, 2000; Putnam, Leonardi, et al., 1993), and David Foot's work on the policy implications of an aging population (Foot & Stoffman, 1998). An excellent example closer to home is the 2011 release of a study of Ontario's postsecondary system (Clark, Van Loon, et al. 2011). Its title signals a work that is clearly intended to address a specific policy problem, that of the quality of undergraduate education in Ontario: *Academic Reform: Policy Options for Improving the Quality and Cost-Effectiveness of Undergraduate Education in Ontario*. Box 9.4 provides an excerpt from the book's introduction, which is a model of succinct expression of the policy problem, constraints, anticipated objections, and the proposed solutions. As the authors point out in the second paragraph of the introduction: "Our study is intended to be useful to policy makers." And yet, it is a book more than 300 pages long, published by a university press, with chapters on funding of Ontario's universities, lessons from other systems (Germany, Denmark, Finland, Sweden, England, Australia, Alberta, British Columbia, Nova Scotia, and the United States), and a range of options. The authors presented their findings at universities across the province, met with ministers and editorial boards, all in the effort to *do* something, to *stimulate policy reform*, not simply produce a study.

All the examples to this point suggest a combination of generic intent—affecting the policy process, making a practical contribution—and creative exposition. Creativity is certainly important, but there are some generic features of most policy documents, precisely because they need to deal with the core analytical elements presented in Chapters 4 to 7. Policy

BOX 9.4

REFORMING ONTARIO'S UNDERGRADUATE PROGRAMS

OUR ARGUMENT

The argument we will put forward may be summarized as follows.

- By several measures, Ontario currently has a good higher education system.

- It depends on a binary model, increasingly rare in the world, with quite separate components, the universities and the colleges of applied arts and technology.

- Its largest component, the university sector, is entirely characterized by the highest cost model for undergraduate education, the research university model.

- Monies ostensibly intended to support undergraduate education are used to subsidize the research enterprise.

- Ontario universities do not spend much effort evaluating the actual learning of undergraduates, but we do know that the university model used in Ontario is one that does not maximize the factors that lead to the best learning outcomes for students.

- The costs of the core activities of universities have been increasing at a rate substantially faster than GDP but government grants per student are not increasing at the same pace. In addition to tuition increases, universities are forced to cope by using more and more part-time staff and further increasing class sizes. Even so, many universities are now operating in deficit positions.

- The fiscal situation of Ontario combined with other demands on the treasury will sharply constrain additional public money available to higher education in the province.

- Enrolment growth between 50,000 and 104,000 additional baccalaureate spaces will have to be accommodated in the next 14 years, mostly in the Greater Toronto Area (GTA).

- The combination of government grants and tuition increases cannot be expected to enable existing and similar institutions to cope with these increasing enrolment numbers nor to improve the current state of undergraduate instruction.

- Current GTA institutions will not be able to expand sufficiently to accommodate the influx of students. Expansion of institutions outside the GTA will not cover the demand nor could it be afforded if all expansion is in the current universities operating on a research university model.

(continued)

- To deal with the situation we need new-to-Ontario types of institutions, new-to-Ontario ways of accommodating undergraduate students in existing institutions, and new-to-Ontario ways of evaluating how those students are doing.
- The new institutions should be devoted to undergraduate instruction and to research on ways to improve this instruction.
- The existing institutions on both sides of the binary divide must cooperate better and develop new pathways and credentials to allow students to move between them.
- There are well-working examples of everything we recommend in other good higher education systems in societies like ours. We draw our recommendations from them.
- Our approach, which outlines the shape of new institutions and pathways and suggests how to improve undergraduate education in existing institutions, is affordable and will not harm the solid research capacity built up in Ontario universities.
- These reforms must be led by clear and consistent actions by the government of Ontario in concert with the current institutions of higher education in the province.

Source: I. D. Clark, R. J. Van Loon, et al. (2011). *Academic Reform: Policy Options for Improving the Quality and Cost-Effectiveness of Undergraduate Education in Ontario*. Montreal and Kingston, School of Policy Studies, McGill-Queen's University Press, pp. 13–14.

is about problems, so some discussion and definition of the problem are necessary. Decisionmakers like to have options, not for their own sake but because most policy issues involve a balance of interests and values, and having a spectrum of options that strike the balance in different ways is useful. Recommendations help. Guidance on implementation and some sort of evaluation strategy do as well. These analytical requirements are much like the colour wheel: artists can be as creative as they like, but certain core relationships among primary and secondary colours cannot be entirely ignored.

We can offer several illustrations. Smith (2010, pp. 26–28), for example, provides a "general method of communicating in a public process." As she says, "If your writing experience has been mainly in the classroom, you may be surprised by the method's questions. They represent real world writing conditions." What follows is a summary of Smith's approach.

Step 1: Prepare (ask questions about the policy process).

- Policy
  Existing policy?
- Problem
  What is the problem?
  Other definitions?
- Actors
  Who are significant actors and roles?
  Interests?
  Most influential?
- Politics
  Major conflicts?
  Major agreements?

Step 2: Plan.

- Purpose
  What is objective of the communication?
- Message
  Message?
  Other messages out there?
  Arguments in support of message?
- Response
  What will recipients know and do after reading the document?
- Setting and Situation
  Time frame for completing and delivering?
  When and where presented?
- Form and Medium
  What is appropriate medium: written document, presentation, telephone call, e-mail?
  What combination of media and how will they support each other?
- Contents
  Best arrangements of contents (e.g., executive summaries, appendices)?
  Design for maximum effect?

Step 3: Produce.

Smith advocates three main phases of writing:

- Write a draft.
- Review it (either by yourself or with others—if possible, showing it to others is usually very helpful).
- Revise.

Expect the second and third phases to iterate several times as the communication is improved.

This checklist, or ones like it, is useful as a guide to a range of policy communications. (Smith lists position papers, petitions and proposals, briefing memos, testimony at public hearings, and public comments.) There are also guides more specifically geared to policy papers. For example, *Writing Effective Public Policy Papers* (Young & Quinn, 2002) was originally designed to build policy capacity in Central and Eastern Europe, but draws from the global policy literature. Young and Quinn's generic outline for a policy paper consists of title, table of contents, abstract/executive summary, introduction, problem description, policy options, conclusion and recommendations, appendices, bibliography, and endnotes. Along the way, they have useful tidbits of advice that reflect the collective wisdom of both the study and practice of policy analysis. "The importance of writing effective titles for papers is often underestimated, but it is significant that the title is more than likely the first part of a paper readers see and it begins the process of communicating the message contained in the policy paper" (p. 24). "The abstract briefly overviews the paper, while the executive summary provides a detailed synopsis of the whole paper" (p. 34). On problem definition: "This part of the introduction represents the move from more contextual information to the specific issue which is the focus of the policy paper. This feature is crucial in convincing your reader to share your viewpoint that an urgent problem exists and that your paper is worth reading because it will offer possible solutions to the problem. It is also important that this feature clearly communicates your position on the problem so that readers can understand the policy alternatives and recommendations you will propose later in the paper" (pp. 38–39). Similar to Smith, they also provide a list of questions to ask as you work on a problem definition (see Box 9.5).

To this point we have been discussing policy communication as written communication, and a great deal of the flow of information both inside government and between government and the public takes place in that form. In most democratic states, however, the written text has been complemented if not supplanted by other media of communication. In some cases it is simply a matter of a different vehicle —tweets are still text, as are most blogs, and most Web pages still are heavy with text. Indeed,

BOX 9.5

WRITING CHECKLIST FOR
PROBLEM DEFINITION

WRITING CHECKLIST

To help you plan and write your problem description, consider the following questions:

BUILDING YOUR PROBLEM DESCRIPTION

Background of the problem

- When and how did the problem arise?
- What were its causes?
- What has been the historical, legal, political, social and economic context of the problem?
- How did the problem come to public attention?
- Who has been affected by the problem?
- What past policies have been implemented to try to address the problem?
- What were the outcomes of these policies?

Problem within its current policy environment

- What are the current legal, social, economic, political contexts and impacts of the problem?
- What is the current extent of the problem?
- What current policy is being implemented to try to address the problem?
- What are the differing opinions on the problem and the current approach?
- In what ways is the current policy succeeding/failing?
- What is wrong with the current approach?

ORGANIZING YOUR PROBLEM DESCRIPTION

- What aspects of the problem do you need to include in your problem description section in order to present a comprehensive and convincing picture?
- How are you going to organize the section to make it as understandable and readable as possible?

Source: Open Society Foundations

the great advantage of the Web is that almost all government documents are available online, so it is not a matter of digital technology replacing text, but simply making it much easier and cheaper to access it. In other cases, the form of the communication has itself changed. Most briefings to senior officials these days—indeed, it would seem most presentations of any sort—are done with presentation software such as PowerPoint or Keynote. This is more than a matter of taking text out of a document and pasting it into a slide—actually, the kiss of death for any competent or interesting presentation. Graphics, bullet points, animations, movies, and photographs—almost any type of information can be mobilized for a presentation. The grammar of visual slide presentations is thus different from textual ones, and mastering it is its own skill.

One pioneer of the visualization of data, Edward Tufte (1990, 2001), published a short but stinging attack on presentation software, *The Cognitive Style of PowerPoint* (Tufte, 2003). Tufte had several critiques that still hold today. PowerPoint (PP) is presenter oriented, not content oriented or audience oriented. It has what Tufte called "low resolution" (not much space per slide) that induces overgeneralizations, imprecision, or mere slogans. Presentations, because of low resolution, rely on bullets, which are imprecise and linear, leaving out or obscuring important causal relationships. As well, bulleted hierarchies can make the information all but indecipherable. He illustrated his argument with a deconstruction of a single slide used in a presentation on the space shuttle *Columbia* disaster in 2003, as well as a mock PP presentation of the Gettysburg Address (in six slides). Tufte is no friend of PowerPoint, but he did offer some tips on how to use it to balance some of its inherent weaknesses (also see Godin, 2001). He admitted that PowerPoint was a competent presentation tool for low-resolution materials, but "that's about it."

> Avoid elaborate hierarchies of bullets. Never read aloud from slides. Never use PP templates to format paper reports of web screens. Use PP as a projector for showing low-resolution color images, graphics, and videos that cannot be reproduced as printed handouts at a presentation. Paper handouts at a talk can effectively show text, numbers, data graphics, images. Printed materials, which should largely replace PP, bring information transfer rates in presentations up to that of everyday material in newspapers, magazines, books and internet screens.... Thoughtfully planned handouts at your talk tell the audience that you are serious and precise; that you seek to leave traces and have consequences. And that you respect your audience. (Tufte, 2003, p. 24)

This advice represents a somewhat dismal analysis of a tool that is ubiquitous. A more optimistic approach (that is not alien to Tufte's emphasis on strong visual representations of data) is the current work on "visualization." Lindquist (2011) argues that there are several reasons to be hopeful about the potential of visualizations for policy analysis and policymaking. First, the technology has improved immeasurably, is widely available, and most people these days (especially younger citizens) are quite familiar with it. Second, he notes that policy problems as well as solutions are becoming increasingly complex (see the discussion in Chapter 3 on complexity and wicked problems). He sees visualizations as an IT tool that can present complex issues in new ways, often by mashing different types of data and providing arresting and informative (what Tufte would call "high-resolution") images. Lindquist delineates the broad field of visualization into three distinct but overlapping approaches: (1) data or information visualization, whose proponents and researchers are most interested in the ability to make sense of and represent very large amounts of data, (2) graphics and information display with the objective of producing visually pleasing images, and (3) graphics recording and strategic facilitation, where the goal is to help different policy stakeholders share perspectives through visual diagrams and find ways to engage in cooperative collective action. At least for those outside of government, being able to develop visualizations of data means having access to data, and so the "visualization movement" overlaps with the "open data" movement. (For an engaged Canadian proponent, David Eaves, see www.eaves.ca.) It also requires the tools, but these are also now well developed and developing and, in some cases, free (see www.tableausoftware.com). As part of the Open Data

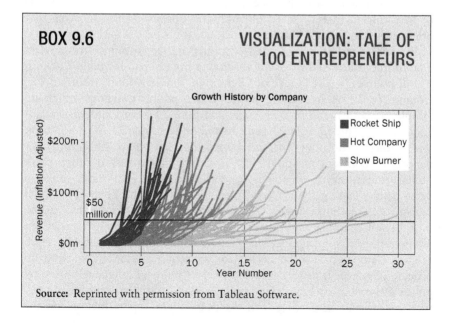

BOX 9.6

VISUALIZATION: TALE OF 100 ENTREPRENEURS

Growth History by Company

Legend:
- Rocket Ship
- Hot Company
- Slow Burner

Y-axis: Revenue (Inflation Adjusted): $0m, $100m, $200m; $50 million

X-axis: Year Number: 0, 5, 10, 15, 20, 25, 30

Source: Reprinted with permission from Tableau Software.

Chapter 9 Policy Communication **379**

Initiative, federal government departments are now required to produce machine-readable (e.g., CSV) data files to make it easier to import them into common software platforms. Statistics Canada is also now providing greater access to its CANSIM data and making online graphing tools more available. Box 9.6 contains an example of a visualization originally published in the *Wall Street Journal*, available at Tableau Public (http://www.tableausoftware.com/public/gallery/taleof100). The on-line version allows users to see growth patterns for different market segments (e.g., entertainment, security).

Conclusion

Policy communication is meant to explain and persuade, on as reasoned a basis as possible. Even while it uses rhetorical tools, its objective should be clear and effective communication that presents information with rigour and honesty. We mentioned that, in the case of media influence on public discourse, different institutional filters can distort policy communication and, hence, policy debate, well beyond reasoned limits. So there is always a tension between those filters and the model or goal of reasoned and reasonable communication. Media often distort. Partisan think tanks will often distort to make the case for what they believe in. Politics and the institutional practices of the public service can also distort. Political partisanship is inevitable in any democratic system, but can become so heated that it throws out any standard of reason in the simple desire to humiliate, attack, and win. The instinct in the public service is less one of partisanship than of self-protection and obsessive rule-following that often results in foggy officialese.

In 2009, the U.K. House of Commons, Public Administration Select Committee, addressed the issue of what it called "bad language" in official discourse ([U.K.] House of Commons, Public Administration Select Committee, 2009). Its starting point was that politics and government are "public activities, and so politicians and public servants should use language that people find clear, accurate and understandable. We undertook this inquiry because we were concerned that too often official language distorts or confuses meaning. This is damaging because it can prevent public understanding of policies and their consequences, and can also deter people from getting access to public services and benefits" ([U.K.] House of Commons, Public Administration Select Committee, 2009, p. 3). The Commons inquiry was part of a larger effort by a variety of nongovernmental groups in the United Kingdom, including the Plain English Campaign and the Local Government Association, to clean up official language. It distinguished between "political language," used by politicians to explain and defend policies, and "administrative language," used by officials in dealing with the public. The report focused on the latter and solicited public submissions of examples, as well as testimony. The examples are both hilarious and depressing.

An extract from a Departmental Report

An overarching national improvement strategy will drive up quality and performance underpinned by specific plans for strategically significant areas of activity, such as workforce and technology. The capital investment strategy will continue to renew and modernise further education establishments to create state of the art facilities. (p. 9)

A Treasury press release

A platform for generating increased Private Finance Initiative (PFI) deal flow and reducing the costs of tendering will be the outcome of new contract guidelines published by the Treasury Taskforce, Chief Secretary to the Treasury Alan Milburn said today. (p. 9)

A letter from Revenues and Customs

Thank you for your Tax Returns ended 5th April 2006 & 2007 which we received on 20th December. I will treat your Tax Return for all purposes as though you sent it in response to a notice from us which required you to deliver it to us by the day we received it. (p. 11)

Although the Commons committee focused on administrative language (communication between officials and the public), it emphasized the importance of clear and honest communication to public policy to the point that it argued that confusing language should be considered maladministration. Clumsy or deliberately foggy language also often finds its way into policy documents, even those intended only for an internal, official audience. For example, current government policies are rarely described as "failing" or having "problems." Much safer to say that they "face challenges." Programs will not experience mere "improvement" but "continued improvement." "Innovation," by definition, is a good thing, and so programs and policies are routinely described as "innovative." Even better is to string together "innovative," "green," and "smart." Then there is the routine reliance on euphemism: staff cuts and firings are described as "down-sizing" or "rationalization." Imperceptible or even non-existent economic growth is "slow growth."

Some of these communications sins might be corrected by the change in the communications environment. Government documents are much more accessible in digital form. In principle it is easier to communicate with officials directly and clear up confusions. The power that citizens have in an open data world to combine different sorts of information reduces the monopoly that government has traditionally had over its own data and documents. All of these factors might not improve the language in any single document, but they might make it less possible for those documents to dominate discourse. Perhaps the apogee of this change is WikiLeaks (Domscheit-Berg & Klopp, 2011). In 2010 it released three tranches of secret government communications: 90 000 documents on U.S. military operations in Afghanistan, almost 400 000 documents on U.S. military operations in Iraq, and finally, almost 250 000 cables between U.S. diplomatic missions and the State Department. The leaks attracted international attention and a firestorm of counteractions by U.S. commercial interests such as PayPal and Amazon that had provided services to WikiLeaks. But for enthusiasts, what WikiLeaks and Julian Assange (its founder) had accomplished was a historic reversal of the ability of governments to keep their internal information secret. That wall crumbled because of the ease of leaking documents and circulating them to a global audience. Anyone interested (and many were) could simply click on the WikiLeaks website and access what had been secret communications, often detailing (in the case of the State Department) apparent secrets of other, foreign governments.

More skeptical observers (Roberts, 2012) argue that the impact of WikiLeaks was more illusion than reality. The amount of data that was released was so huge that it was not that easy to access, even for reasonably skilled computer users. Even more telling, it was essentially a "data dump"—an unfiltered mountain of information that was meaningless unless filtered, analyzed, assessed, and then stitched together into something comprehensible. This, in part, explains the surprising lack of public outrage that followed the leaks. Without intermediation (typically by journalists and media outlets, with whom Assange deliberately made deals so that the information could be spread comprehensibly), the public in reality had no access to the data. Finally, governments were not passive observers. They fought back. As Roberts explains, transparency is an iterative game: "In one iteration of the game, activists use some new tool—perhaps a new law, or a new technology, or a new form of social mobilization—to extract and share governmental information; in the next iteration, politicians and bureaucrats respond to this new level of exposure by restricting laws or policies, changing their own use of technology, or adapting administrative procedures (perhaps to avoid recording sensitive information)" (Roberts, 2012, p. 128). The U.S. State Department, for example, assembled a dedicated team of 120 people to manage the WikiLeaks fallout. After the leaks, all U.S. federal agencies were ordered to revisit and tighten their internal procedures for managing and protecting classified data.

Transparency, open data, and policy communication are as much about content as they are about process. Policy analysts are often unwelcome messengers, surrounded by various actors with itchy trigger fingers—they should see their work in that context. For example, on May 3, 2012, the Cohen Commission (http://www.cohencommission. ca/en/), appointed by the federal government, heard testimony from a Department of Fisheries and Oceans scientist, Dr. Kristi Miller, on the decline of the sockeye salmon in the Fraser River. Miller had published a paper in the prestigious journal *Science* (Miller, Li, et al., 2011) the year before, suggesting that the collapse of the stock might be due to a virus (which she and her co-authors were not able to specify) contracted among the salmon before they make their way up the river to spawn. In her testimony, she claimed that government officials had forbidden her to talk to the press about her research (something that the press, ironically, wrote about once they failed to get access). Initially, she had thought that the gag order had come from the department, but now suspected that it might have been directed from the Privy Council (Canadian Press, 2012). Why? The government admitted the order (though Miller had been allowed to continue publishing), but claimed that it was due to her imminent appearance before a judicial inquiry. Others, including Miller herself in her testimony, speculated that it was because the possible existence of a virus—evocatively termed "fish AIDS" (Hume, 2011)—would automatically raise the suspicion that salmon farms (a powerful industry lobby in British Columbia) were responsible.

Power, politics, policy, and communication. The analyst needs to be aware of their constant entanglement, but try, nonetheless, to focus professionally on the last two and leave the first two to others.

KEY TERMS

advocacy—an effort to defend or promote a policy issue through broad strategies to change the context of discussion, problem definitions, public perceptions, or the configuration and coalition of stakeholder interests

deep core beliefs—used in the advocacy coalition approach to designate beliefs that are almost impervious to change and argument, such as human nature

deliberative democracy—a form of democracy that goes well beyond simply periodic majority voting, it emphasizes the importance of citizens, together, discussing and debating public problems, sharing perspectives, and trying to find solutions through consensus

discourse—similar to policy paradigm, but more directly connected to the frameworks of argument and thought whereby people make sense of the world around them

executive summary—usually no more than two pages, either as a stand-alone document or the summary of a much longer one, intended to provide the essence

issue framing—a way of depicting a policy issue or problem in broad, understandable if somewhat simplified terms

knowledge utilization—the acceptance by decisionmakers of policy analysis and advice, and implementation through programs

labels—dense words or phrases that convey subtle but powerful meanings

lobbying—communicating with public office-holders to influence policy, legislation, or regulations, usually (if by business) in connection with grants, contracts, or other financial benefits

metaphor—subtle denotations of one thing in terms of another, as in *a* is like *b*

near (policy) beliefs—used in the advocacy coalition approach to designate beliefs about the best policy instruments to achieve certain goals; these beliefs can change in the face of serious evidence

policy argument—an organized set of claims about a policy problem and recommended solutions that include such characteristics as causality, severity, novelty, crisis, instruments, and solutions

policy communication—any form of communication designed to convey information about policy, explain it, provide an analysis of problem and solution, and ultimately make recommendations that persuade its audience

policy images—a mixture of empirical information and emotive appeals that explain the issue and justify the public policy response

policy issue papers—longer, more detailed and technical analysis of a policy problem, with consideration of options and recommendations (sometimes referred to as "policy papers")

policy memoranda—shorter version of the policy issue paper, rarely more than 3000 words, often in response to a specific request for background information

policy paradigm—a broad framework of ideas that combines deep values, second-order preferences about policy approaches, and third-order instrumental preferences on policy instruments and their settings

political campaigning—communication and other activities designed to secure partisan benefit and ultimately election

post-positivist policy analysis—an approach that places a strong emphasis on the role of ideas and discourse over technical analysis, and is suspicious of rational techniques in that they potentially undermine democratic participation of non-expert citizens

secondary aspects—used in the advocacy coalition approach to designate beliefs about organizational rules or implementation techniques that can change quite easily

FURTHER READINGS

Orwell, G. (1946). *Politics and the English language.* Retrieved from http://www.orwell.ru/library/essays/politics/english/e_polit

Smith, C. F. (2010). *Writing public policy: A practical guide to communicating in the policy making process.* Oxford: Oxford University Press.

Taras, D., Bakardjieva, M., et al. (2007). *How Canadians communicate II: Media, globalization, and identity.* Calgary, AB: University of Calgary Press.

Tufte, E. R. (2003). *The cognitive style of PowerPoint.* Cheshire, CT: Graphics Press.

Young, E., & Quinn, L. (2002). *Writing effective public policy papers: A guide for policy advisers in Central and Eastern Europe.* Budapest: Local Government Public Service Reform Initiative. Retrieved from http://lgi.osi.hu/publications/2002/112/writing_effective_public_policy_papers___young__quinn.pdf

REFERENCES

Altheide, D. L. (2002). *Creating fear: News and the construction of crisis.* New York, NY: Aldine de Gruyter.

Altheide, D. L., & Snow, R. P. (1991). *Media worlds in the post-journalism era.* New York, NY: Aldine de Gruyter.

Bardach, E. (2000). *A practical guide for policy analysis: The eightfold path to more effective problem solving.* New York, NY: Chatham House.

Borins, S. (2011). *Governing fables: Learning from public sector narratives.* Charlotte, NC: Information Age.

Bramley, M., Sadik, P., & Marshall, D. (2009). *Climate leadership, economic prosperity: Final report on an economic study of greenhouse gas targets and policies for Canada.* Calgary and Vancouver: Pembina Institute and David Suzuki Foundation.

Canadian Press. (2012). Kristi Miller, fisheries scientist, tells inquiry her work was muzzled by feds. *The Huffington Post (Canada).* Retrieved from http://www.huffingtonpost.ca/2011/08/25/kristi-miller-fisheries-scientist_n_937247.html?view=screen

Carson, R. (1962). *Silent spring*. Boston, MA: Houghton Mifflin.

Clark, I. D., Trick, D., & Van Loon, R. J. (2011). *Academic reform: Policy options for improving the quality and cost-effectiveness of undergraduate education in Ontario*. Montréal and Kingston: School of Policy Studies, McGill-Queen's University Press.

Cooper, B. (1994). *Sins of omission: Shaping the news at CBC TV*. Toronto, ON: University of Toronto Press.

Dahlgren, P. (2009). *Media and political engagement: Citizens, communication, and democracy*. Cambridge: Cambridge University Press.

Domscheit-Berg, D., & Klopp, T. (2011). *Inside WikiLeaks: My time with Julian Assange at the world's most dangerous website*. New York, NY: Crown Publishers.

Dryzek, J. S. (1990). *Discursive democracy: Politics, policy, and political science*. Cambridge: Cambridge University Press.

Dryzek, J. S., & Dunleavy, P. (2009). *Theories of the democratic state*. New York, NY: Palgrave Macmillan.

Dryzek, J. S., & Niemeyer, S. (2010). *Foundations and frontiers of deliberative governance*. New York, NY: Oxford University Press.

Dunn, W. N. (2004). *Public policy analysis: An introduction*. Upper Saddle River, NJ: Pearson Prentice-Hall.

Etzioni, A. (2006). The unique methodology of policy research. In M. Moran, M. Rein, & R. E. Goodin (Eds.), *The Oxford handbook of public policy* (pp. 833–843). Oxford, UK: Oxford University Press.

Fischer, F. (1980). *Politics, values, and public policy: The problem of methodology*. Boulder, CO: Westview.

Fischer, F. (1990). *Technocracy and the politics of expertise*. Newbury Park, CA: Sage.

Fischer, F. (2009). *Democracy and expertise: Reorienting policy inquiry*. New York: Oxford University Press.

Fischer, F., & Forester, J. (1987). *Confronting values in policy analysis: The politics of criteria*. Newbury Park, CA: Sage.

Fischer, F., & Forester, J. (1993). *The argumentative turn in policy analysis and planning*. Durham, NC: Duke University Press.

Flanagan, T. (2009). *Harper's team: Behind the scenes in the Conservative rise to power*. Montréal and Kingston: McGill-Queen's University Press.

Foot, D., & Stoffman, D. (1998). *Boom, bust & echo 2000: Profiting from the demographic shift in the new millennium*. Toronto, ON: Macfarlane Walter & Ross.

Godin, S. (2001). *Really bad PowerPoint (and how to avoid it)*. Retrieved from http://www.sethgodin.com/freeprize/reallybad-1.pdf

Hackett, R. A., & Carroll, W. K. (2006). *Remaking media: The struggle to democratize public communication* (Communication and Society). London, UK: Routledge.

Hackett, R. A., & Gruneau, R. S. (1999). *The missing news: Filters and blind spots in Canada's media*. Ottawa, ON: Canadian Centre for Policy Alternatives.

Haidt, J. (2012). *The righteous mind: Why good people are divided by politics and religion*. New York, NY: Pantheon.

Hajer, M. A., & Wagenaar, H. (Eds.). (2003). *Deliberative policy analysis: Understanding governance in the network society* (Theories of Institutional Design). Cambridge, UK/New York, NY: Cambridge University Press.

Hall, P. A. (1993). Policy paradigms, social learning, and the state: The case of economic policymaking in Britain. *Comparative Politics 25*(3): 275–296.

Harrington, M. (1962). *The other America: Poverty in the United States*. New York, NY: Macmillan.

Hawkesworth, M. E. (1988). *Theoretical issues in policy analysis*. Albany, NY: State University of New York Press.

[U.K.] House of Commons, Public Administration Select Committee. (2009). *Bad language: The use and abuse of official language*. London, UK: The Stationery Office.

Hume, M. (2011, March 20). Researcher suggests "salmon leukemia" is to blame for decline of Fraser sockeye. [Toronto] *Globe and Mail*. Retrieved from http://thecanadian.org/hot-links/item/622-researcher-suggests-'salmon-leukemia'-is-to-blame-for-decline-of-fraser-sockeye

Jones, B. D., & Wolfe, M. (2010). Public policy and the mass media: An information processing approach. In S. Koch-Baumgarten & K. Voltmer (Eds.), *Public policy and mass media: The interplay of mass communication and political decision making* (pp. 17–43). London, UK: Routledge.

Kahneman, D. (2011). *Thinking, fast and slow*. New York, NY: Farrar, Straus, and Giroux.

Kheiriddin, T., & Daifallah, A. (2005). *Rescuing Canada's right: Blueprint for a Conservative revolution*. Mississauga, ON: John Wiley and Sons Canada.

Lindquist, E. (2011). *Grappling with complex policy challenges: Exploring the potential of visualization for analysis, advising and engagement*. Unpublished manuscript. Cited with author's permission.

Majone, G. (1989). *Evidence, argument, and persuasion in the policy process*. New Haven, CT: Yale University Press.

Miljan, L., & Cooper, B. (2003). *Hidden agendas: How journalists influence the news*. Vancouver, BC: UBC Press.

Miller, K., Li, S., et al. (2011). Genomic signatures predict migration and spawning failure in wild Canadian salmon. *Science, 331*(6014), 214–217.

Norris, P. (2000). *A virtuous circle: Political communications in postindustrial societies*. Cambridge: Cambridge University Press.

Online surveillance bill critics are iding with "child pornographers": Vic Toews. (2012, February 4). [Toronto] *National Post*. Retrieved from http://news.nationalpost.com/2012/02/14/online-surveillance-bill-critics-are-siding-with-child-pornographers-vic-toews/

Pal, L. A. (2011). Into the wild: The Politics of economic stimulus. In C. Stoney & G. B. Doern (Eds.), *How Ottawa spends, 2011–2012: Life under the knife (Again!)* (pp. 39–59). Montréal and Kingston: McGill-Queen's University Press.

Putnam, R. D. (2000). *Bowling alone: The collapse and revival of American community*. New York, NY: Simon & Schuster.

Putnam, R. D., Leonardi, R., et al. (1993). *Making democracy work: Civic traditions in modern Italy*. Princeton, NJ: Princeton University Press.

Riker, W. H. (1986). *The art of political manipulation*. New Haven, CT: Yale University Press.

Riker, W. H. (1996). *The strategy of rhetoric: Campaigning for the American Constitution*. New Haven, CT: Yale University Press.

Roberts, A. (2012). WikiLeaks: The illusion of transparency. *International Review of Administrative Sciences 78*(1), 116–133.

Sabatier, P. A. (1993). Policy change over a decade or more. In P. A. Sabatier & H. C. Jenkins-Smith (Eds.), *Policy change and learning: An advocacy coalition approach* (pp. 13–39). Boulder, CO: Westview.

Siklos, R. (1995). *Shades of Black: Conrad Black and the world's fastest growing press empire*. Toronto, ON: Reed Books.

Smith, C. F. (2010). *Writing public policy: A practical guide to communicating in the policy making process*. Oxford: Oxford University Press.

Soroka, S. N. (2002). *Agenda-setting dynamics in Canada*. Vancouver, BC: UBC Press.

Stanyer, J. (2007). *Modern political communication*. Cambridge, UK: Polity Press.

Stone, D. (1988). *Policy paradox and political reason.* New York, NY: HarperCollins.

Stone, D. (2012). *Policy paradox: The art of political decision making.* New York, NY: W. W. Norton.

Thaler, R. H., & Sunstein, C. R. (2008). *Nudge: Improving decisions about health, wealth, and happiness.* New Haven, CT: Yale University Press.

Tufte, E. R. (1990). *Envisioning information.* Cheshire, CT: Graphics Press.

Tufte, E. R. (2001). *The visual display of quantitative information.* Cheshire, CT: Graphics Press.

Tufte, E. R. (2003). *The cognitive style of PowerPoint.* Cheshire, CT: Graphics Press.

Weimer, D. L., & Vining, A. R. (2011). *Policy analysis.* Boston, MA: Longman.

Weiss, C. (1998). *Evaluation.* Upper Saddle River, NJ: Prentice-Hall.

Young, E., & Quinn, L. (2002). *Writing effective public policy papers: A guide for policy advisers in Central and Eastern Europe.* Budapest: Local Government Public Service Reform Initiative. Retrieved from http://lgi.osi.hu/publications/2002/112/writing_effective_public_policy_papers___young__quinn.pdf

CHAPTER

Conclusions

R eaders who made it this far will probably have a mixed reaction
to the arguments in this book. Some of you will be impressed at
the deep changes that governments and the policy process are
undergoing and generally supportive of a more quality-centred, client-
focused policymaking system. Others (perhaps even the same ones who
are impressed!) will be dismayed or at least uneasy with the larger portrait
drawn in this book. Governments are struggling with multiple agendas.
There still is a hangover of new public management—client-oriented
quality services, decentralization, outsourcing, and efficiency. There is the
mantra of accountability and ethics. There is the nightmare of imploding
economies and the need to use muscle and force to bail out banks and
appease bondholders. We see people rioting and marching in the most
developed and richest countries in the world, countries that, nonetheless, teeter on the edge of bankruptcy. Some of those countries are under
"technocratic governments"—experts who are unelected precisely because
they have to apply shock therapy to their seized economies. Fundamental
questions are being asked about economic and political and policy systems, questions that we have tried to illuminate if not answer in the
previous chapters. They raise the issue of the quality of the policy process
as well as its ultimate ends. We expect governments to be more accountable and transparent, and we also increasingly expect government to be a
key guarantor against major risks such as climate change, the collapse of
financial markets, pandemics, and terrorists. But that acknowledgment is
still tempered by a stronger sense of the limits of the state, both in terms
of its capacities and its procedures. And due to the factors discussed in
Chapter 2, we expect government not merely to be efficient but to be
"good" in some ethical sense, as well. This chapter briefly summarizes the
main arguments and findings from previous chapters, and then addresses
these deeper questions of policy and democratic governance.

Policy Analysis: Rethinking the Toolkit

Policy analysis is a relatively new discipline in the modern sense, though, of course, thinking about what governments do goes back as far as the invention of state structures and stable social organizations as early as the Mesopotamian period around 350 BC. As Chapter 1 pointed out, the modern roots of the policy analysis movement lie in the 1950s and particularly in the 1960s' expansion of American government programs in education and social assistance. Most of what passes today for professional policy analysis and evaluation has its foundations in the application of rational models and techniques drawn from the social sciences. There was great hope in the early years that these techniques would squeeze some, if not all of the politics out of decisionmaking—perhaps relegating it to higher-order value choices—and lead to improvements not only in the way that policies were made but, of course, in the results as well. Chapter 1 touched on some of the debates that grew up around implementation and evaluation in the 1970s and 1980s, and that ultimately contributed to the malaise in policy studies and analytical work.

The 1990s was a decade of ascendancy for new theories of public management and their application in the form of re-organizations of major agencies and programs, along with often deep expenditure cuts and steep increases in taxes. Canada was close to the middle of the OECD pack in this regard, with New Zealand and Britain, for example, going much further in changing the structure and practice of government. The changes at the federal level in Canada were nonetheless profound—50 000 civil servants were either let go or retired; departments such as Transport Canada were eviscerated; assets such as airports and harbours were divested to local authorities; major income support programs, such as employment insurance and major transfer programs for health and social assistance, were radically altered. Changes at the provincial level were no less profound: hospitals were closed, school boards abolished, cities and regions reorganized. The Harris and Klein governments were the vanguard in tax cuts, program reductions, and re-organizations, all of which invited massive illegal strikes by public sector workers in both provinces.

After a period of surpluses at both provincial and federal levels up to 2008, we are now seeing large deficits generated by economic downturn and by efforts to stimulate the economy. The effect of the wars against deficits lingers, however, even in a period when most governments will accumulate more debt. In some quarters, allegiance to balanced budgets is ideological—debt, by definition, is bad. But there is also the harsh reality of numbers—high debt means high interest payments and vulnerability to financial markets (bondholders). The current federal government embarked on stimulus reluctantly, and in the 2012 budget mapped a plan to get back to balance and even surplus by 2015. Provincial governments have, to varying degrees, dug themselves into fiscal holes and want to dig themselves out, but doing this is challenging given that the biggest expenditures are in key services such as health, education, and social assistance. In the United States and in Europe, the debate between right and left over austerity or stimulus is much sharper.

Nonetheless, there has been a growing understanding that governments—however much they might be downsized or reduced in scope and influence—have a tremendous impact on their societies. That impact is not merely instrumental in the sense of providing basic services or bailouts; it includes systemic effects on the economy, the environment, and social structures. While good governance does not necessarily result in strong economies and robust societies, bad governance will yield nothing but misery. This understanding has stimulated a resurgence of interest in good governance and good policymaking.

The modern policy movement, however, bears the scars and the lessons of the last decade. For one thing, there is more humility about the practice of policy analysis. We will return to this in a moment, but the key point is that the limits of the rational model and social science techniques are now widely acknowledged—after all, almost no one anticipated the financial crash in late 2008. Outside evaluation studies, which retain a strong empiricist and technical orientation, most other types of policy work recognize the inevitably value-laden character of policy choice, design, and implementation. For another thing, the new public management (NPM) movement of the 1990s left an indelible impression on thinking about the state and the public sector. Some of this has involved the transfer of business practices to the public sector, a transfer that is not always beneficial or appropriate. New public management introduced a more careful posture on the possibilities of state action, as well as a willingness to think about a variety of tools to attack policy problems. Despite appearances, this approach was not jettisoned in the global governmental response to the economic downturn in late 2008. The final major difference in the current policy revival is the sensitivity to how the world seems to be changing fundamentally and hence, altering both the nature of policy problems and their responses. Those changes are summarized in Chapter 2, but subsequent chapters demonstrated their impact across the full spectrum of the policy process. The traditional categories of problem definition, design, implementation, and evaluation certainly continue to apply and continue to be applied by policymakers to make sense of what they do. But the content of those categories has shifted in important ways in order to respond to the impact of globalization, culture shifts, and management theory.

Chapter 3 showed how the nature of problem definition has shifted in recent years. Problem definition remains central to thinking about policy, but the sources and the nature of the problems governments face have changed profoundly. We noted how globalization is now at the centre of the policy research agenda being discussed and debated around the country. The question of technology and productivity is entangled in the concept of the knowledge-based economy and pressures on innovation, both artifacts of globalization and the new phase of industrial or post-industrial development. These forces are generating new challenges in the areas of economic growth, human development, and social cohesion.

Chapter 4 carried this analysis forward to look at instrument choice and policy design. The new context, at least before the financial crisis, was that spending instruments were to be used cautiously and often in the form of "boutique" programs without major expenditure commitments; regulatory practices were redesigned and made more accountable. Governments around the world had a preference to design policies around self-regulative instruments or set framework regulations that look to results rather than micromanagement of behaviour. There was more reliance on individual responsibility. Governments continue to experiment with partnerships and the use of information technology for new forms of delivery of programs and services, especially through the Internet. At the same time, however, there are signs of a new interest in government as a social regulator and protector. Concerns about the economy, crime, video violence, and the environment are driving governments to be more, not less, robust in their interventions. The impact of globalization on jobs and communities is also forcing governments, even very conservative ones, to bridle their enthusiasm for market mechanisms in favour of economic and social policies that try to insulate their populations to some degree.

Chapters 5, 6, and 7 expressed the same themes. Implementation of public policy is changing everywhere to be less top-down and more explicitly designed around partnerships, with a clearer division between policy design and delivery. Policy communities have accordingly become more important in the policy mix. Governments depend, though in varying degrees, more on their partners both for policy advice and implementation. Modern policy cannot be directed by government or merely supplemented by other actors in respective policy communities.

Chapter 6 provided a good illustration of how this changed context alters the way in which we think about players in the policy process. Today, the emphasis is still on "governance" as opposed to government—that is, on nonhierarchical, multiple-stakeholder, diffuse systems of negotiation and compromise in which government is a player and an occasional leader but more rarely the dominant actor (Rhodes, 1997, 2007). The global financial crisis compelled a degree of centralization, as well as a combination of extreme interventions and bailouts, and even brute force through the imposition of austerity programs and cuts. Combine that reality with the rise of the security and surveillance state, and it is easy to conclude that Leviathan rises again. In part this is true, and worrisome. But other tendencies support the shift to a governance style—the delivery of services, the numbingly complex range of players involved in environmental programs, and the capacity that people and groups have to resist and rebel unless they are brought into the process somehow. It is simply a paradox that has to be acknowledged: governments are both weaker and stronger than they were a decade ago. Governments today increasingly have to work in networks to design and implement policy solutions. The financial crisis demonstrated that governments do have two important tools at their disposal—money and regulation—but any economic stimulus they offered still had to be brokered with communities, businesses, civil society, provinces, and foreign governments and financial institutions.

Chapter 7 showed how evaluation has changed, as well. Evaluation has enjoyed a renaissance of sorts as governments have emphasized results, accountability, performance, and client satisfaction. With the new focus on results and clients, however, have come new emphases in evaluative techniques, harnessing them more closely to continuous program review and the use of innovative implementation techniques.

Chapter 8 picked up on themes that were adumbrated in earlier chapters. Security threats—from terrorism to computer viruses to pandemics—are connected to globalization. Some of the natural disasters that loom may be connected to industrial development and climate change. Whereas risk assessment and emergency and crisis management were on the fringes of public policy and public administration studies two decades ago, they are increasingly central to the toolkit, especially after the economic meltdown in fall 2008.

Finally, Chapter 9 examined the communicative dimension of policymaking and policy analysis. Once again, communication has always been important, but the chapter showed how the academic literature has strong currents that argue that policymaking is almost about nothing else, that values and perceptions and frames structure the way that we think and so require explicit strategies to break through and persuade. The practice of policy communication emphasizes techniques of persuasion and "messaging." The communicative function is all the more important these days for at least two reasons: the pressure on decisionmakers to absorb information and make sometimes almost instant choices, and the complexity of contemporary public problems. To be effective and helpful, today's analyst needs to combine instrumental skills (problem definition, options, evaluation) with communicative acumen.

Normally, it is useful to be skeptical of the cult of the "new." Not everything changes radically all the time, whatever advertisers and politicians may tell us. However, in the case of policymaking and public management, it does not seem hyperbolic to talk about a substantially new context and the need for new responses. The evidence of change in society and economy is all around us, as is the evidence of change in the ways that governments behave and public servants think about the nature of governance. While some of the new thinking in policy and management may, indeed, be a response to fads, or driven by the interests of international agencies such as the Organisation for Economic Co-operation and Development (OECD) or international consultants, it is undeniable that the changes are substantial and real. Going "beyond policy analysis" has involved trying to think about the applicability of old tools to these new circumstances and problems.

There is yet another sense in which we may go "beyond policy analysis" or the traditional orientations of the discipline. As we noted in Chapter 1, the roots of policy analysis and evaluation were in a social science tradition of rationalism and instrumentalism. The latter means a problem-solving orientation that thinks in terms of a solid distinction between means and ends. Policy and the programs that flow from it are technical solutions as insulated as possible from values, ethics, and concepts of higher purpose. In practice, of course, policymaking is shot through with values, even though dealing with values raises substantial practical difficulties. As Peters notes,

> Despite these practical difficulties, it is important for citizens and policymakers to think about policy in ethical terms. Perhaps too much policymaking has been conducted without attention to anything but the political and economic consequences. Of course, such utilitarian values are important bases for evaluating a program, but they may not be the only relevant criteria. Both the policymaker and the citizen must be concerned also with matters of justice and trust in government. Indeed, it may be that justice and social trust ultimately make the best policies—and even the best politics. (Peters, 2010, p. 473)

The remainder of this chapter will go beyond an instrumental perspective on public policy and policy analysis and address three key issues: (1) the nature and purpose of modern governance, (2) the role of ethics and values in policy and public management, and (3) benchmarks for the policymaking process.

Nature and Purpose of Modern Governance

In the end, what's it all about? What is the purpose of public policy and public policy analysis? The conventional, formulaic answer, of course, is the improvement of the lives of the population, or the maximization of the public interest, or even "happiness" (Helliwell, Layard, & Sachs,

2012). These are formulaic answers because they have little content—everything depends on the definitions. Nonetheless, it seems that modern governments are being prodded in some new directions in terms of purpose and policy, purposes that are driven to a large extent by the changed circumstances we have discussed throughout this book. Before we address them, however, we need once again to emphasize that the changes in governance we have seen in the last decade do not necessarily imply smaller and weaker governments. We argued in previous chapters that characterizing these changes as smaller government was simplistic. Indeed, there are some areas (e.g., climate change, financial markets, and innovation) where demands for government activity have increased substantially, and there has also been a rethinking of the nature of what government does. The following list of issues or themes is obviously idiosyncratic but does touch on some contemporary concerns and debates about what governments, in the end, are all about and the major new challenges they face, both in Canada and throughout the world.

The State, Business, and Citizens

One interesting development that touches on the nature of government is a rethinking of the idea popular in the 1990s that governments should be more like businesses and treat citizens more like customers and clients. The backlash against this started almost at the same time as the recommendation itself, particularly in the academic community. It has gathered force over the years, however, with an increasing emphasis on the differences between governments and businesses and the importance of treating citizens as citizens and not just as customers. It was magnified in the financial crisis with the apparent collapse and inefficiency of private markets and even the biggest business firms and financial institutions.

The new public management, and a lot of the new policy thinking described in this book, is dedicated to making government more businesslike. There is nothing wrong with this, and in some instances, such as quality services and client satisfaction, it is long overdue. However, there is a difference between making government more businesslike and treating government just like another business, particularly in a post-Wall Street and General Motors bailout world where business practices have been severely criticized as not only foolish but venal and even immoral. The crisis was unprecedented, as was government action around the world, from Washington to Dublin. Capitalism was on the ropes, national economies teetered, and the only entity that could ride to the rescue of the masters of the universe was the state. As inglorious as the whole affair was and continues to be, it reinforced a sense that governments and markets were different if interconnected worlds. Of course, the best businesses recognize that they have public responsibilities, as well as governance responsibilities to their customers, competitors, and employees. But that does not make them governments. The two spheres of government and business are quite distinct, and each should function in ways that are appropriate to its sphere. Government is vital for any civilized society, not simply as an instrument to get things done but as a public space wherein we fulfill and enjoy our responsibilities and privileges as citizens.

Even during NPM's zenith, several observers pointed out that its emphasis on service–client relations, while helpful, was too limited a vision of the full range of responsibilities and rationales of the public sector. Gow (1995), for example, noted, "In considering citizens as clients of the administration, one must wonder about the nature of the relationship as it concerns those who fall under the disciplinary authority of the state, be they prisoners, people in regulated industries or dependents of the state" (p. 558). Doern (1994) made a similar case: "Bureaucracy seen abstractly as an 'it' serving the customer, 'us' or 'me,' in a new form of franchised 'McState' is not all or even *most* of what democratic governance is about" (p. 92). Mintzberg (1996) argued that we wear four hats in relation to government: customer, client, citizen, and subject. Governments do relatively few things for us as customers, that is, as consumers of goods and services that probably could just as easily be provided through the market. A larger proportion of the services we get from government, such as healthcare or education, are professional services for which we are clients. But we also relate to government as subjects, in the sense of the duties and obligations that we have to obey, and that, if we do not, will incur the discipline of state authority. Our relationship as citizens is more complex still, embracing both obligations as well as rights. Respecting the integrity of government does not mean that government should do all things and be all things. What it does mean is respecting the specific nature of government as well as its importance to the exercise of our democratic citizenship. It means preserving the dignity of the public square in the knowledge that, if we characterize government as just another form of business, we risk losing our own character as citizens. A world of customers and clients might be a paradise of consumption and service, but it would not be a democratic commonwealth.

As we mentioned earlier, the NPM movement left several important legacies that still affect governments around the world, including Canada's, even if public sector management thinking is now going in different directions (e.g., digital state, accountability, personalization of services, re-governmentalizing services and agentification). Being treated like a valued customer who might be able to take his or her business elsewhere is a marked improvement over being treated as a faceless and powerless citizen waiting in an endless and dreary queue for the next available official. Receiving basic services more efficiently and responsively is a good thing. Certainly, as we noted in Chapters 5 and 7, governments across the world are continuing to emphasize quality services, as well as citizen-centred service. In Chapter 2 we discussed the Drummond report as an example of a strong seam of NPM thinking about efficiency of government services coupled with an argument that public service is a higher calling. In other words, the emphasis on efficiency has not disappeared, and in some ways, it has been intensified because of fiscal pressures. But that emphasis has now been joined with a healthy skepticism about business and a richer appreciation that government is a different—and, in some respects, more demanding—sphere. This perception translates into a policy frame that seems to emphasize the special obligations that citizens have as citizens, and not simply as consumers of services. They have obligations to each other and to other generations, and might be called, not to consume, but to sacrifice, through higher taxes, deferred retirements, and military service. These are straws in the wind, but it would be remarkable if the upheavals since 2008 were not reflected in different relations between the state, business, and citizens.

CLIMATE CHANGE

The modern environmental movement was born in the late 1960s and over time has become a powerful policy driver around issues such as clean air and clean water, pollution, and forms of economic production and technology. In the early 2000s, a new dimension of environmental policy began to take shape—the concern with climate change and greenhouse gas emissions. Scientists were debating whether Earth's overall climate (not simply day-to-day weather patterns) was changing fundamentally and, in fact, warming rapidly by historical standards. Initially, there was a great deal of skepticism about the data, but over time, the weight of evidence seemed to support the climate change hypothesis. More important, the primary *cause* of this change in Earth's climate was human activity, specifically the emission of "greenhouse gases" (water vapour, carbon dioxide, methane, and some others) through development and economic production. Carbon dioxide (CO_2) accounts for about 80 percent of greenhouse gases, and its principal source is the burning of fossil fuels. As discussed in Chapter 2, this causal matrix puts human economic activity, and specific types of activities that emit more of these gases than others, front and centre in the policy debate. It is this connection that has led to international treaties such as the Kyoto Protocol (1997) and the Copenhagen Climate Summit (2010), the search for "sustainable production" or green technologies, and debates over cap-and-trade systems of emissions control versus carbon taxes. In little over a decade, Canadians and, indeed, other citizens around the world have focused on climate change as a key policy challenge and key worry for the future. Because the challenge is so substantial, and because the solution seems to be a reduction in emissions (especially carbon) linked to virtually every dimension of economic activity, dealing with climate change has the potential to become a key policy driver for most governments in the first half of the 21st century. The international prominence of the issue is underscored by the fact that the 2007 Nobel Peace Prize went to Al Gore, who tirelessly raised awareness over the years (and made a film *An Inconvenient Truth*, which won an Oscar), and the Intergovernmental Panel on Climate Change (IPCC), a scientific body established under the auspices of the World Meteorological Organization and the United Nations Environment Programme, that provides neutral and objective assessments of current international scientific opinion and research on the subject.

Climate change is caused by greenhouse gases that accumulate in the atmosphere and which trap heat that would otherwise radiate out into space. As the gases accumulate, the amount of trapped heat increases, and Earth's temperature rises. The IPCC's fourth report, released in 2007 (the latest), noted:

> Eleven of the last twelve years (1995–2006) rank among the twelve warmest years in the instrumental record of global surface temperature (since 1850). The 100-year linear trend (1906–2005) of 0.74 [0.56 to 0.92] °C is larger than the corresponding trend of 0.6 [0.4 to 0.8] °C (1901–2000) given in the Third Assessment Report (TAR).... The temperature increase is widespread over the globe and is greater at higher northern latitudes. Land regions have warmed faster than the oceans.... (IPCC, 2007, p. 2)

Scientific evidence on Canada's Arctic shows a 4 degree Celsius increase in temperatures in the western Arctic between 1953 and 2003 (Simpson, Jaccard, & Rivers, 2007, p. 4). At first blush, particularly for a northern country, a certain amount of warming might be welcome, and indeed, some of the effects of warming (on Canadian agriculture, for example, or our tourism industry) might be beneficial. Part of the policy narrative therefore is to show how, in the aggregate, global warming will lead to catastrophe. Al Gore's warnings, in his book and film, are particularly evocative on the range and scale of effects that will follow unless climate change is stopped and reversed. For example, rising temperatures will force glaciers to recede and ocean levels to increase. Gore (2006) argued that within a decade, there would be no snows on Mount Kilimanjaro in Tanzania; within 15 years the glaciers in Glacier National Park would be gone; and within 50 years the Himalayan glaciers, which produce drinking water for 40 percent of the world's population, would be severely compromised. Persistent and recurring heat waves. Rising ocean temperatures. Storms, hurricanes, and typhoons. Melting icecaps and tundra. Infestations of beetles that decimate North American forests. Disappearing species. The spread of diseases like West Nile virus well outside their normal range. And perhaps most apocalyptically, the melting or breakup of Greenland and its sinking into the sea. In the book, Gore ends this list of horrors with policy prescriptions (and some attacks on the then-Bush administration), and what are now considered fairly standard personal steps such as installing better insulation, using energy-saving light bulbs, and buying more fuel-efficient cars.

Despite a sea change in public opinion—partly induced by Al Gore's efforts—climate change remains a fiendishly difficult policy issue for several reasons. First, the climate is a common property resource—no one owns the air or the ozone, and pollution produced in one place can drift to others as a negative externality—in other words, the producer does not necessarily face the cost or impact of the pollution. Second, while climate change has accelerated in the past decades, and while there are dramatic examples of its impact such as Hurricane Katrina and infestations of pine beetles in British Columbia and Alberta, it still is occurring relatively slowly—or at least slowly relative to election cycles. Third, the science behind understanding climate change remains complicated, despite an international consensus reflected in the reports of the IPCC. Fourth, tackling climate change through reducing carbon emissions probably means slowing economic growth, which is difficult enough for developed countries, but particularly difficult for developing countries such as China and India. Fifth, for all these reasons, the only real solution to climate change is a global one, requiring international agreement from both developed and developing countries. Finally, in addition to requiring global efforts, dealing with climate change relies on individual efforts, from buying more energy-efficient appliances to reducing consumption, but people are often reluctant to comply in the short term, even if their long-term interests are better served through this behaviour.

Given these factors, it is not surprising that public policy on climate change has been, at best, uneven. For one thing, even if there is agreement that the key to dealing with climate change is controlling emissions, there are different mixes of policy instruments to tackle the problem: improved "green" technology, carbon taxes, regulated limits to industrial emissions, pollution trading systems, energy conservation, subsidies, or carbon capture. A second problem is that the sheer scope and impact of climate change policy inevitably gives it a highly political charge. Any realistic effort to reduce emissions will have different regional and sectoral effects, pitting Alberta's energy industry against central Canada's manufacturing sector. The potential impact on business means that industrial and resource lobbies have been active in resisting government intervention.

As well, the emblematic Kyoto targets were unrealistic to begin with. In the 1997 negotiations on the protocol, the Chrétien government decided that it needed to adopt domestic targets that were "better" than those proposed by the United States. Canada went into the negotiations with a federal–provincial agreement to reduce emissions to 1990 levels by 2008–12. This goal alone would have been challenging, since emissions had increased by 13 percent between 1990 and 1997 (Simpson, Jaccard, & Rivers, 2007, p. 35). On the eve of the negotiations, apparently with little or no analysis to gauge what the effects might be, Ottawa unilaterally announced that its new position would be to reduce emissions in 2008–12 by 3 percent *below* 1990 levels. In the heat of negotiations, when the Americans increased their targets, Canada was forced, again without much consideration of the policy implications or of implementation, to increase its target to 6 percent *below* 1990 levels. Canada finally ratified the treaty in 2002, in the teeth of provincial and business opposition, as well as the withdrawal of the United States and Australia, and the non-participation of China and India. Various climate change policies were announced in the wake of Kyoto, even while Canada's emissions in 2005 had grown to be 25 percent higher than they had been in 1990.

The federal Conservative government was never disposed toward a vigorous climate change policy. In April 2007, the government released a study showing that it would be impossible to meet Canada's Kyoto targets without incurring a severe recession, and it announced a new set of targets and policies to deal with the issue. The new target was a reduction in emissions by 2020 to 20 percent below 2006 levels, with 50 to 70 percent reductions by 2050. Since Canada had already missed its Kyoto targets by a wide margin at this point, the new targets were a dilution of the country's original, if unrealistic, goals under Kyoto. The policy instruments the government proposed were somewhat more robust than previous attempts at exhortation and subsidies: there would be regulated caps on large industrial emitters, new standards for automobiles and trucks, a cap-and-trade system for carbon, and a plan for carbon capture (Government of Canada, 2006).

The importance of dealing with climate change has assumed an almost universal consensus, and few governments can appear to ignore it. The policy battleground will not be over the nature of the problem any longer, as it was two decades ago, but on how best to realistically deal with it in a context of skyrocketing fuel costs. New (for Canada) policy tools such as cap-and-trade systems and carbon taxes are now on the table, and the issue can be expected to retain its prominence and visibility in the next few years, perhaps even rivalling healthcare as a Canadian policy preoccupation. However, while the idea of climate change has now become axiomatic, the political will to tackle it has been eroded even further due to the financial crisis. As mentioned before, Canada has come through the crisis better than almost any other industrialized country, but the backbone of its success has been energy exports, particularly oil and gas, as well as potash. Resource extraction creates wealth and jobs, but also major emissions. Current governments in Ottawa and in the western provinces have clearly made a choice to favour job creation and economic growth over environmental policies that might curb that growth.

HEALTHCARE

There is perhaps no issue more central to most Canadians than healthcare. It regularly tops the polls as a matter of public concern and is a key issue in almost every provincial and federal election. But it is an issue like no other. It has assumed a sacral quality—it allegedly defines who Canadians are (in contrast to Americans), it symbolizes a fundamental commitment to care and to equity, and is assumed (wrongly) to be one of the best systems in the world. This line of argument was first developed in the 2002 Romanow Commission on healthcare, which argued that public healthcare was not merely a service, but a distinguishing characteristic of Canada, a "sacred trust":

> In their discussions with me, Canadians have been clear that they still strongly support the core values on which our health care system is premised—equity, fairness and solidarity. These values are tied to their understanding of citizenship. Canadians consider equal and timely access to medically necessary health care services on the basis of need as a right of citizenship, not a privilege of status or wealth. Building from these values, Canadians have come to view their health care system as a national program, delivered locally but structured on intergovernmental collaboration and a mutual understanding of values. They want and expect their governments to work together to ensure that the policies and programs that define medicare remain true to these values. (Commission on the Future of Health Care in Canada, 2002, p. xvi)

Healthcare promises to be another key Canadian public policy issue for the foreseeable future, for several reasons. Perhaps the most pressing is its sheer cost. Approaching 50 percent of most provincial budgets, it has been increasing at rates of about 6 to 8 percent a year. This radical increase was the reason behind the Ontario government's 2004 decision to introduce highly unpopular health premiums—unless something was done to either generate more money for the system or contain it, there would be only one item in the provincial budget. It was also behind the same government's attempt in 2012 to freeze doctors' salaries. Healthcare has been costly for the federal government, as well.

The Health Accord signed by Prime Minister Jean Chrétien and the provincial premiers in 2003 promised to pump almost $39 billion more into the system over five years. Despite that pledge, the Martin government promised another $10 billion over two years to fix healthcare "for a generation" and deal with waiting lists. The federal Conservatives fought the 2006 election campaign on a promise of "patient wait times guarantees." In April 2007 Prime Minister Stephen Harper announced that all provinces and territories had agreed to establish the Patient Wait Times Guarantee by 2010 (Office of Prime Minister, 2007). Some $600 million would be put into a trust to help fund the initiative, which guarantees "timely access to health care in at least one of the following priority areas, either cancer care, hip and knee replacement, cardiac care, diagnostic imaging, cataract surgeries, or primary care. These areas have been selected by each province and territory based on their priorities, capacity and different starting points" (ibid.). The guarantee was driven by the Supreme Court's decision in *Chaouilli v. Quebec (Attorney General)* in June 2005, a decision that upheld private health insurance in cases where wait times for procedures were inordinately long (*Chaouilli*, 2005). In 2011 the federal government unilaterally announced that it would continue to increase its health transfers to the provinces by 6 percent a year until 2016–17, but after that, would tie transfers in a formula to growth in GDP. Ottawa wanted both predictable funding and to be left off the hook of ever increasing transfers for an area of provincial jurisdiction.

To some extent Canadians, and their leaders, have painted themselves into a corner on this policy issue by elevating its public character to almost religious significance. For example, it is no accident that a key recommendation of the Romanow Commission was a Canada Health "Covenant." Canada is virtually alone in the developed world in outlawing some version of a parallel private system of healthcare, usually covered by private insurance (*Chaouilli* applies only in Quebec). Ironically, despite the rhetoric, substantial portions of the system are "private" in the sense that they are for-profit but reimbursed or paid for by public funds. Hospitals are the most visible and completely public elements of the system (in the sense that they are run on a nonprofit basis, and services are free to patients and covered through provincial payments), but even they contract out ancillary services (e.g., laundry) to private firms. Virtually all physicians in Canada are effectively small businesses, since doctors work for themselves and not the state; their services are simply reimbursed on a fee-for-service basis. Services such as laboratory testing, X-rays, and medical imaging are increasingly performed by private firms, which are reimbursed with public funds. Most famously, abortion clinics, like those owned by Henry Morgentaler, are private, as are some MRI (magnetic resonance imaging) clinics. In short, the Canadian system is actually a blend of public and private, and there is nothing in the Canada

Health Act or the Constitution that forbids private provision, as long as it is covered by public funds.

Despite this reality, the general assumption in Canada is that the system is almost entirely public and that any element of private provision would undermine its foundations. The Romanow Commission offered 47 recommendations, most of which were geared to higher spending across the system: new services, including home care; addressing of specific needs in rural and Aboriginal communities; and better coordination, information sharing, and performance measurement. These are laudable, and if ever implemented, they would both expand the system and make it more transparent and accountable, and even more expensive. While healthcare has been the "third rail" in Canadian politics for at least a generation, it will not remain so forever. The federal government seems to have distanced itself from the policy field by agreeing simply to transfer money on a predictable basis and leaving policy to the provinces. As mentioned before, with costs continuing to accelerate by 6 to 8 percent per year, healthcare threatens to become a sinkhole that will suck in more than half of provincial budgets. This burden is unsustainable, and so big battles loom in the future, especially if the global recession continues and affects provincial bottom lines.

Ethics, Accountability, and Good Governance

We mentioned earlier that the dominant tradition in policy studies has been instrumentalist, a focus on means and ends. Interestingly, discussions have turned increasingly to considerations of values and ethics in the public sector as a means to support good governance. This direction is not entirely new, of course, with codes of ethics having been promoted by various professional associations of public servants for some years. But as we have argued throughout this book, some new pressures have concentrated attention on this field, pressures that began building as early as the early 1980s (Kernaghan, 1996) and blossomed in the last decade. One is the decreasing trust and faith in government among Canadian citizens. Only 61 percent of eligible voters cast a ballot in the 2011 federal election, and that was up from 58 percent in 2008. A way of addressing that is to ensure that public servants—either making or implementing policy—conduct themselves to the highest standards. Another pressure has been the effects of downsizing on morale. Encouraging public servants to cleave to strong values has been a way to forestall public sector workers' cynicism and bitterness. The emphasis on entrepreneurship, innovation, and flexibility in public sector organizations has meant less detailed oversight of the work done by public servants, fewer rules and minute procedures, and a greater focus on outcomes and performance. The sense that corners were being cut—to the point of inducing corruption—led directly to the Federal Accountability Act, the Harper government's signature piece of legislation in 2006 that dramatically raised the bar on ethics and probity in government. In fact, the combination of instruments used in the Accountability Act, from whistle-blowers' legislation, audit committees, accounting officers, new parliamentary watchdogs and commissioners, and a strong emphasis on codes of ethics has severely dampened enthusiasm for flexibility and innovation within the federal public service. Finally, the financial crisis cast an unflattering light on business practices, particularly on Wall Street, and fanned public resentment at the "1 percent" who seem beyond accountability and untroubled by ethics. The public is, of course, intolerant of corruption in any instance, but now seems inflamed by anything that smacks of lavishness, perks, or privileges in the public sector.

The modern focus on ethics, accountability, and good governance began in 1995, when the Clerk of the Privy Council appointed nine Deputy Minister Task Forces to deal with issues that would arise through the Program Review exercise. One of those task forces was dedicated to public sector values and ethics, reflecting the concern about ethics expressed in the Auditor General's 1995 annual report (Auditor General of Canada, 1995, Chapter 1). The task force's report, *A Strong Foundation* (Task Force on Public Service Values and Ethics, 2000), otherwise known as the Tait Report, highlighted some of the new pressures on the public service that were creating the need to refocus on values and ethics:

> Many public servants were shocked, and their faith in public service values was shaken, both by the *fact* of downsizing—that it was done at all—and by the way it was done. Many public servants believe that an implicit employment contract and the commitment to security of tenure were breached by personnel reductions, and by the way they were carried out. Explicit union contracts were overridden by legislation. Disrespect for public servants was read into many announcements or statements that seemed to make them scapegoats, implying they were unproductive, bureaucratic and a major reason for the problems of the debt and public distrust of government. (Task Force on Public Service Values and Ethics, 2000, p. 32)

The task force concluded that public service values can be clustered in four families or categories: democratic values, professional values, ethical values, and people values. The Tait Report laid the foundation for the federal government's June 2003 Values and Ethics Code; it relied on the same categorization of values and also dealt with conflict of interest issues (Office of Public Service Values and Ethics, 2003). A new federal government Values and Ethics Code came into effect on April 2, 2012

(Treasury Board of Canada Secretariat, 2012). It tried to go beyond a list of principles and included "expected behaviours." The values that are to guide public servants "in everything they do" are respect for democracy, respect for people, integrity, stewardship, and excellence. The value of excellence is particularly relevant from a policy perspective: "Excellence in the design and delivery of public sector policy, programs and services is beneficial to every aspect of Canadian public life. Engagement, collaboration, effective teamwork and professional development are all essential to a high-performing organization." Each of the values has behaviours associated with it. The behaviours associated with the value of integrity aim squarely at core ethical concerns:

Integrity

Public servants shall serve the public interest by:

3.1 Acting at all times with integrity and in a manner that will bear the closest public scrutiny, an obligation that may not be fully satisfied by simply acting within the law.

3.2 Never using their official roles to inappropriately obtain an advantage for themselves or to advantage or disadvantage others.

3.3 Taking all possible steps to prevent and resolve any real, apparent or potential conflicts of interest between their official responsibilities and their private affairs in favour of the public interest.

3.4 Acting in such a way as to maintain their employer's trust.

In addressing ethical issues related to changes in the nature of the public sector, Canada is, of course, dealing with a more general problem. The OECD flagged precisely the same set of concerns over a decade ago:

Public servants operate in a changing world. The nameless, faceless public servant is becoming a relic of the past. Greater transparency in government operations, through public access to official information, when coupled with an increasingly zealous media, and well organised interest groups, means that public servants today work in a virtual "fishbowl." Their actions are more visible and publicised as are their mistakes and misdemeanours. Moreover, they face pressures from increased public expectations about the quality of public services and their capacities to deliver them. This pressure is driven partly by governments' own attempts to publicly state standards to be achieved (through Citizen's Charters for example). If these standards are not met, the result is public dissatisfaction.

Public management reform itself has changed the internal environment in which public servants operate. In some countries individual government departments now enjoy substantial autonomy. This has led to concerns that systems of "professional socialisation," that is, the inculcation of public service values across the public sector, are breaking down as departments define their own "corporate culture," standards and ways of operating. This breakdown is compounded by more recruitment from the private sector. The old style coherent public service culture or ethos may be disappearing. In any case, traditional public service values may need to be amended as countries move away from an emphasis on strict compliance with rules and procedures, towards considerations such as "efficiency and effectiveness," "value for money," "service to the citizen," and "equal opportunities." For example, is it unethical to waste tax-payers' money or give bad service? (Organisation for Economic Co-operation and Development [OECD], 2000)

Much like the Accountability Act itself, the focus has remained on ethics but has been broadened quite considerably to deal with a wider range of issues concerning probity in the public sector. For example, the OECD moved from ethics per se to developing standards on anti-corruption, bribery, transparency around lobbying, integrity in public procurement, and conflict of interest (Pal, 2012). The Accountability Act also contains similar provisions on lobbying and procurement, values and ethics, public integrity, and transparency and disclosure. This focus is broadly consistent with the argument made in Chapter 5 that, in recent years, there has been a rediscovery of the special and demanding qualities of the public sector and the public service. Values and ethics were a key theme of the 1990s and into the early 2000s, but as private as well as public sector scandals appear to multiply, as demands continue to grow on government, and as a series of events from terrorist attacks to public safety to epidemics and safe drinking water dominate headlines, a new respect and appreciation for the public sector and good governance has begun to emerge.

Benchmarking the Policy Process

It is difficult to develop standards for good policy in terms of specific programs and instruments. As we argued earlier in the book, there is usually agreement about broad objectives such as reducing poverty or crime but often wide disagreements about the problem situation and the right way to tackle those perceived problems. But there is growing agreement on one thing: effective and responsive policies (however defined) are not likely to arise from flawed policy processes. An effective policy process is no guarantee of quality outputs and outcomes, but it helps. Rethinking and reforming the policy process has emerged in recent years as a complement to more general organizational redesign and reform in the public sector, as well as the new emphasis on good governance discussed in Chapter 1. It has several distinct aspects, however. One is the sense that if governments downsize and partner, and do fewer things directly, there will be greater emphasis on their capacity to develop policy objectives and monitor outcomes. As we noted in Chapter 1, the emphasis on policy capacity is also linked to a sense that the pressures on societies and governments today are increasing and are more intense. Rapid, as well as rational, response is increasingly important, and well-designed policy frameworks provide a filter and a foundation for concerted action. Another aspect has been the wider public sector reform project itself— in some countries such as New Zealand, as we pointed out in Chapter 5, there was a more radical separation of policy advice functions from central administration than has been characteristic of Canada, but the elevation of the policy function proceeded apace in many countries after 2000. Accordingly, there is greater need for benchmarking the policy development function to ensure that it meets recognized standards.

By policy development function, we mean the process of determining and elaborating policy issues or problems, articulating solutions, making recommendations, and calibrating that process with other important ones in government such as the wider priority-setting process and expenditure management. We do not include the process of actual decisionmaking and choice of options, which is primarily political and takes place through a host of governmental institutions, from cabinet to legislature. Nor do we include implementation or evaluation of selected options. Obviously, these are crucial phases in making public policy but entail different sets of standards and techniques. Implementation is a management function and involves administrative skill in combining resources and personnel in the right amounts at the right time to achieve the desired policy or programmatic outcome. Evaluation, by the same token, is normally undertaken within a fairly well-defined framework with relatively clear operational standards (see Chapter 7). Policy development, the "front end" of these processes, entails consultations and communications about policy issues. An effective policy process, in the largest sense of the term, will be effective at all these stages—policy development (analyzing the problem and developing options and recommendations), implementation (putting into effect the chosen option and elaborating on its programmatic elements), and evaluation (assessing efficiency and effectiveness). But implementation and evaluation take the option as given, the choice made. Our concern here is to address the first, crucial phase of policy development and ask if there are benchmarks of standards of practice that might improve the way it is conducted.

There are three immediate problems with posing the issue this way, the first being that, as this book has stressed, policy development is a mix of craft and science. A good deal of what goes into problem recognition and definition is subjective and not necessarily guided by well-known techniques (indeed, the same point applies even in apparently technical arenas such as cost-benefit evaluation). By definition, something that is craft-based is difficult to improve through better technique.

Second, of necessity, policy development touches on some highly politically sensitive issues. It involves "speaking truth to power," and in that sense, it may seem that truth will be sacrificed to power, that politics and political orientations are the most important part of developing policy advice. It is obviously true that public servants developing policy advice for a government of one political stripe will offer different advice, in some respects, to a government of a completely different political stripe. However, that is not the end of the story. Many problems are simply "there" as an empirical reality—the aging of the population or housing bubbles. From some perspectives these may not be problems, but they do encapsulate forces that no government can really ignore, however it might want to interpret those forces. As well, as we noted in Chapter 3, problem definition does rely on hard research, and this should not be ideologically driven. Finally, while governments and politicians may have strong ideological orientations, that does not mean that they can simply dream up policy options based on these orientations. A good deal of analytical work still has to go into the mix.

The third problem is that policy development is only in part a process that takes place inside government and between officials and their political masters; it also involves citizens, interest groups, the media, and a host of other actors. It has a wider political–social dimension and embraces the governance system more widely.

These are valid objections and issues, but the fact remains that a major responsibility for democratic governments is to develop policy, and this function is performed in large part in central agencies and departments staffed by professional public servants. Governments have not been blind to the importance of improving the policy development function—we saw various instances throughout the previous chapters where nationally and internationally there have been calls for improved governance and, as part of that, improved policy development and implementation. In the mid-1990s, the governments of Australia and New Zealand, for example, routinely assessed and evaluated the policy development function through "policy management reviews" (Uhr & Mackay, 1996). In April 2000, the Canadian federal government released a report on the lawmaking process that made explicit reference to improving the process of policy development and advice. The report argued that policymaking could be improved by better thinking about instrument choice, results and outcomes, and consultations. New Zealand has continued to emphasize the policy function among its operational agencies (Chapman & Duncan, 2007), and the Canadian Treasury Board has also underlined the importance of evidence-based analysis in submissions coming from departments (Treasury Board of Canada Secretariat, 2007).

As we noted in Chapter 1, these early efforts have been magnified in recent years in a growing international interest in good governance, on the assumption that governance is key to economic development and poverty reduction (Acemoglu & Robinson, 2012). An OECD study noted that in the last 15 years there has been "a veritable explosion in interest in the quality of 'governance' in the developing world," accompanied by "equally explosive growth in the use of quantitative governance *indicators* ..." (Arndt & Oman, 2006, p. 13; emphasis in original). The United Nations Development Programme (UNDP) notes: "There is an increasing demand from developing country governments, civil society organisations and donor agencies to measure different aspects of democracy, human rights and governance. This demand has resulted in a tremendous growth in indicator sources, which are used to measure the performance of governments, the quality of public institutions, as well as people's perceptions of various aspects of governance" (UNDP, n.d.). There are various drivers for this phenomenon, including the adoption of the Millennium Development Goals (MDGs), with requirements of specific indicators of recipient government performance. The MDGs are supported through *Global Monitoring Reports*, which include reviews of governance (Levy, 2007). The World Bank Institute estimated, in 2006, that there were some 140 user-accessible sets of governance indicators, in turn, made up of thousands of individual indicators. The more visible ones are well known: Transparency International's Corruption Perceptions Index (CPI), Freedom House's "Freedom in the World," the World Bank's Country Policy and Institutions Assessments (CPIAs), the International Country Risk Guide (ICRG), and the World Bank Institute's "KKZ" indicators. One of the interesting things about these indicators is that they contain strong and often quite explicit judgments about what constitutes good governance and good policymaking, and many of them even rank countries either in international league tables or at least in broad categories of "better" or "worse."

One of the most widely cited governance indicators comes from the World Bank Institute and is produced by Daniel Kaufmann, Aart Kray, and Massimo Mastruzzi (originally, the third author was Pablo Zoido-Lobatón—hence the reference to the "KKZ" indicators). It aggregates hundreds of perception-based indicators produced by more than 30 organizations into six dimensions of governance: (1) voice and accountability,

(2) political stability, (3) government effectiveness, (4) regulatory quality, (5) rule of law, and (6) control of corruption. "Government effectiveness," for example, is defined by the authors as "measuring the quality of public services, the quality of the civil service and the degree of its independence from political pressures, the quality of policy formulation and implementation, and the credibility of the government's commitment to such policies" (Kaufmann, Kray, & Mastruzzi, 2007, p. 3). Consulting dozens of data sources (primarily surveys), and selecting questions from those surveys that cast light on each dimension, KKZ then aggregates these to a single indicator. For example, government effectiveness concretely reflects questions about government stability, the quality of e-government, infrastructure, schools, and satisfaction with highways and other services. Most crucially, it also reflects measures on the "quality of bureaucracy" with questions about competence, public service vulnerability to political pressure, and excessive red tape. Levy (2007, p. 44) provides another example from a World Bank project in several countries to yield actionable and non-subjective indicators to monitor civil service reform. Note that these indicators are for objectives that are presumed to be positive and beneficial for governance (see Box 10.1).

As Levy (p. 42) notes, "In the early 1980s and early 1990s, a first generation of administrative reform focused principally on scaling back the

BOX 10.1   CIVIL SERVICE MANAGEMENT ACTIONABLE INDICATORS

OBJECTIVE	INDICATOR
Competition in recruitment and selection	Percentage of civil service (CS) vacancies filled through advertised, competitive procedures
Turnover unrelated to changes in political leadership	Quarterly CS turnover rates plotted against changes in political leadership
Effective performance evaluation practices	Percentage of CS staff for whom annual performance evaluations were completed
	Percentage of CS performance evaluations falling in each rating category

SOURCE: Levy, B. (2007). *Governance reform: Bridging monitoring and action.* Washington, DC: The World Bank. Box 2.3.

bloated apparatus of government. In the 1990s, attention shifted toward improving administrative capability. Some consensus has been generated on the characteristics of an effective public administration.... [one of which is] [w]ell-functioning mechanisms for policy coordination that ensure policy consistency across departmental boundaries and facilitate clear decisions on policy and spending priorities."

Our approach to good governance is guided by the conviction that policy development, despite its messiness, does have some identifiable stages or phases, principally moving through problem identification, analysis of issues, development of options, and finally, recommendations based both on analysis and other input in the process. As well, we have to acknowledge the balance of craft and skill that defines policy development work. A crucial issue, then, is how to enhance craft, how to build in mechanisms that will improve a process that resists easy categorization or measurement, despite recent attempts at developing more precise indicators. And finally, we need to acknowledge that policy work is part of a larger democratic conversation and that it should reflect strong democratic values as well as contribute to them. In these terms, then, we can suggest several benchmarks. While they will not guarantee good policy design, they will certainly contribute to it:

> *Training of policy development staff.* This effort should not be occasional but continuous. Policy development staff have to know what the policy process is about, the different elements of policy design and implementation and evaluation, and various techniques for both the development of policy ideas and communication. They should have a solid grounding in policy analysis and administration.
>
> *Well-organized information and research resources.* Having information, being able to access it quickly, and organizing it well comprise a basic requirement of good policy work. As we noted earlier in this book, there are huge new developments in social networking technology that are enabling much better pooling of and access to information.
>
> *A balance of scanning and service orientations.* Good policy work not only requires immediate and effective responses to demands from political masters but also demands the scanning of the political and social environment to see what is coming up in the near to medium term. Policy work needs to be tactical as well as strategic.
>
> *Horizontal coordination.* The policy function is a whole-of-government process, mapping out broad, consistent priorities and linking them to spending priorities. As policy problems

become more complex and multidimensional, there needs to be better horizontal policy coordination across departments, pooling knowledge and sharing perspectives.

Rigour and honesty. Policy development, as we noted above, is at the intersection of political necessity and analytical research. Policy analysts should keep that balance in mind and be wary of sacrificing professional standards and rigour for political purposes. The concepts of "speaking truth to power" and offering "fearless advice" capture this quality.

Transparency and consultation. Confidentiality is often unavoidable as policy problems and options are being debated and defined. To the greatest extent possible, however, policy development work should hear from all sides, consult widely both within and outside government, and put out as much information as possible for public discussion, debate, and review. This approach builds on the wisdom of crowds, the capacity of many independent and dispersed minds with diverse information resources to arrive at surprisingly good judgments.

Development of a good challenge function. Further to the previous point, the policy development process should be designed in such a way as to incorporate challenge and debate and testing—this is a key ingredient for ventilating policy ideas, avoiding group think, exposing unacknowledged errors, and working through limitations and unexpected design flaws.

Policymaking is nothing less than developing public responses, primarily through government but in close cooperation with citizens and other organizations in the private sector and civil society, to public problems. Doing it well matters for lots of reasons, not least because the quality of the responses affects our everyday lives as well as the texture of our democracy. In the end, governance matters, and effective public policy is a crucial ingredient of good governance.

FURTHER READINGS

Levy, B. (2007). *Governance reform: Bridging monitoring and action.* Washington, DC: The World Bank.

Peters, B. G. (2001). *The future of governing* (2nd. ed.). Lawrence, KS: University of Kansas.

Reports and Publications. (Privy Council Office) (Canada). Retrieved June 16, 2012, from http://www.pco-bcp.gc.ca/index.asp?lang=eng&page=information&sub=publications

REFERENCES

Acemoglu, D., & Robinson, J. A. (2012). *Why nations fail: The origins of power, prosperity, and poverty.* New York, NY: Crown Publishers.

Arndt, C., & Oman, C. (2006). *Uses and abuses of governance indicators.* Paris: OECD, Development Centre Studies.

Auditor General of Canada. (1995). *Annual report, 1995.* Retrieved from http://www.oag-bvg.gc.ca/internet/English/parl_lp_e_933.html

Chaouilli v. Quebec (Attorney General). (2005). 1 S.C.R. 791, 2005 SCC 35. Retrieved from http://scc.lexum.org/en/2005/2005scc35/2005scc35.pdf

Chapman, J., & Duncan, G. (2007). Is there now a new "New Zealand Model"? *Public Management Review, 9*(1), pp. 1–25.

Doern, G. B. (1994). *The road to better public services: Progress and constraints in five Canadian federal agencies.* Montréal, QC: Institute for Research on Public Policy.

Gore, A. (2006). *An inconvenient truth: The planetary emergency of global warming and what we can do about it.* Emmaus, PA: Rodale.

Government of Canada. (2006). *Canada's fourth national report on climate change: Actions to meet commitments under the United Nations Framework Convention on Climate Change.* Retrieved from http://unfccc.int/resource/docs/natc/cannc4.pdf

Gow, J. I. (1995, Winter). Frauds and victims: Some difficulties in applying the notion of service to the clientele in the public sector. *Canadian Public Administration, 38,* 557–577.

Helliwell, J., Layard, R., & Sachs, J. (Eds.). (2012). *World happiness report.* New York, NY: Earth Institute.

IPCC [Intergovernmental Panel on Climate Change]. (2007). *Climate change 2007: Synthesis report. Summary for policymakers.* Retrieved from http://www.ipcc.ch/pdf/assessment-report/ar4/syr/ar4_syr_spm.pdf

Kaufmann, D., Kray, A., & Mastruzzi, M. (2007). *Governance matters V: Aggregate and individual government indicators, 1996–2006* (World Bank Policy Research Working Paper No. 4280). Washington, DC: The World Bank.

Kernaghan, K. (1996). *The ethics era in Canadian public administration* (Research Paper No. 19). Ottawa, ON: Canadian Centre for Management Development.

Levy, B. (2007). *Governance reform: Bridging monitoring and action.* Washington, DC: The World Bank.

Mintzberg, H. (1996, May–June). Managing government, governing management. *Harvard Business Review,* pp. 75–83.

OECD [Organisation for Economic Co-operation and Development]. (2000). *Pressures affecting public service ethics and conduct*. Paris: OECD.

Office of the Prime Minister (Canada). (2007, April 4). *Canada's new government announces patient wait times guarantees*. Retrieved from http://pm.gc.ca/eng/media.asp?id=1611

Office of Public Service Values and Ethics (Canada). (2003). *Values and ethics code for the public service*.

Pal, L. A. (2012). *Frontiers of governance: The OECD and global public management reform*. New York, NY: Palgrave Macmillan.

Peters, B. G. (2010). *American public policy* (8th ed.). Washington, DC: CQ Press.

Rhodes, R. A. W. (1997). *Understanding governance: Policy networks, governance, reflexivity, and accountability*. Buckingham, UK: Open University Press.

Rhodes, R. A. W. (2007). Understanding governance: Ten years on. *Organization Studies, 28*(8), 1243–1264.

Romanow, Roy. (2002). *Building on values: The future of health care in Canada*. Ottawa, ON: Commission on the Future of Health Care in Canada. Retrieved from http://www.hc-sc.gc.ca/hcs-sss/hhr-rhs/strateg/romanow-eng.php

Simpson, J., Jaccard, M., & Rivers, N. (2007). *Hot air: Meeting Canada's climate change challenge*. Toronto, ON: McClelland and Stewart.

Task Force on Public Service Values and Ethics. (2000). *A strong foundation: Report of the task force on public service values and ethics* (Tait Report). Ottawa, ON: Canadian Centre for Management Development. Retrieved from http://www.csps-efpc.gc.ca/pbp/pub/pdfs/ve1_e.pdf [CCMD is now the Canada School of Public Service.]

Treasury Board of Canada Secretariat. (2007). *Management accountability framework assessment—Round V. "Policy and Programs."* Retrieved from http://www.tbs-sct.gc.ca/maf-crg/indicators-indicateurs/2007/policies-politiques/policies-politiques_e.asp

Treasury Board of Canada Secretariat. (2012). *Values and ethics code for the public sector*. Retrieved from http://www.tbs-sct.gc.ca/pol/doc-eng.aspx?id=25049

Uhr, J., & Mackay, K. (Eds.) (1996). *Evaluating policy advice learning from Commonwealth experience*. Canberra, AU: Federalism Research Centre, The Australian National University, and Commonwealth Department of Finance.

UNDP [United Nations Development Programme]. (n.d.). *Governance indicators: A user's guide* (2nd ed.). New York, NY: UNDP.

Index

Department of Foreign Affairs and International Trade, 168

Department of Homeland Security (DHS) (U.S.), 72, 202, 329–330

Department of Indian Affairs and Northern Development, 146

Dependent variables, 280, 303

Deputy Minister Task Force on Strengthening Our Policy Capacity, 27–28

Deregulation, 161, 173

Design-Build (DB) public–private partnership model, 255

Design-Build-Finance-Maintain (DBFM) public–private partnership model, 256

Design-Build-Finance-Maintain-Operate (DBFMO) public–private partnership model, 256

DHS (Department of Homeland Security) (U.S.), 72, 202, 329–330

Diagnostic procedures, 275, 303

Digital governance, 211–215

DiIulio, J. J., Jr., 71

Direct action policy instruments, 135–136, 147–150

Directorate for Public Governance and Territorial Development (GOV-OECD), 29

Disaggregation, 197, 202

Disclosure instruments, 140–141

Discount rate, 292, 303

Discourse, 357–359, 383

Discourse coalitions, 229

Discursive strategy, 359–362

Djibouti, on Globalization Index, 58–59

Dobuzinskis, L., 15

Doern, G. B., 160, 398

Downs, Anthony, 112

DPRs (departmental performance reports), 297, 303

Drummond, Don, 83, 399

Dryzek, J. S., 23, 359

Dugas, Gaetan, 317

Dunleavy, P., 202, 359

Dunn, W. N., 15–16, 97, 104, 109–110, 352

Dye, T., 5

Dynamic complexity, 5

Dziekanski, Robert, 103

E

Eaves, D., 379

Economic Action Plan, 83

Economic Development Administration (EDA) (U.S.), 190

Economic globalization, 44–55
  balance of power, 45
  culture of, 45
  five "scapes" of, 46
  four cul-de-sacs in conceptualizing, 45–46
  increased volume in global trade, 47
  question of inevitability and unidirectionality of, 53
  role of states, 51–52
  technology of, 45

Economic regulation, 147, 161–162, 356–357

Economic regulatory instruments, 158–160

EDA (Economic Development Administration) (U.S.), 190

Edwards, G. C., III, 186–187

Efficiency evaluation, 288–293
  cost–benefit analysis, 289–292
  cost–effectiveness analysis, 292–293
  overview, 288–289

Eggers, W., 194, 247

Egypt, Arab Spring, 59, 61–62

Ejército de Liberación Nacional (ELN), 333–334

Elmore, R. F., 193

Emergency, defined, 312–313, 343. *See also* Crisis and emergency situations

Emergency management, 324–335
  challenges to, 325
  defined, 325, 343
  mad cow disease, 327–328
  standard framework for, 325–326
  threat events, categorizing, 326

Emergent strategies, 6, 34

Empirical reasoning, 19, 34

Empowerment, 197, 208, 219

Environmental policy, 119–120, 399–403
  policy research, 370–372
  problem definition, 98
  standards issue, 147
  sustainable ECOnomic model, 120
  watched by NGOs, 62
  See also Climate change policy

Environmental scans, 321, 326, 343

Epistemic community, 229, 259

Equalization payments, 142

Ethics and accountability, 405–408
  data collection, 120
  new emphasis on, 207
  new public management, 80

Hofferbert, R. I., 25
Hogwood, B. W., 187, 194
H1N1 flu epidemic (2009), 314
Hong Kong
    on Globalization Index, 56–57
    SARS epidemic, 102
Hood, C., 132, 204
Hoppe, R., 15
Horizontal consistency, 13–14, 19, 34
Horizontal issues, 201, 219
Horizontal management, 252–257,
    413–414
Howlett, M., 2, 15, 112, 168
HRDC scandal (1999), 336–337
Human Resources Development Canada,
    79
Human resources management moderniza-
    tion, 198–199, 201, 203–204
Human resources management risk, 322
Human rights
    balance, 67
    defined, 85
    international standards, 11, 60–62
    national security and, 120
Hungary, new public management, 203
Hurricane Katrina, 315, 340

I

Iceland
    on Globalization Index, 56–57
    global recession and debt crisis, 54
    new public management, 203
ICTs (information and communications
    technologies), 165, 251
Ideas in good currency, 100, 110–112, 123
Ideas, role of, in policy formation, 351,
    355–357
IMF (International Monetary Fund), 47, 51
Immigration
    as component of globalization, 47
    marginalized youth, 121
    population growth from, 118
    "reasonable accommodation" of
        minorities, 65–66
    social cohesion, 68
Impact evaluation, 276, 279–284, 303
Implementation (process) evaluation,
    276–277, 284–288, 304
Implementation theory
    defined, 303
    program theory versus, 277
Income tax, personal federal, 155–156

Incremental costs, 291
Incrementalism, 22–23, 34
Independent Blue Ribbon Panel (BRP)
    on Grant and Contribution Programs,
    154–155
Indicators, 101–104, 123, 287
Indirect action policy instruments,
    135–136
Individual-level variables, 150
Individual rights versus group rights,
    64–65
Information and communications tech-
    nologies (ICTs), 165, 251
Information-based instruments, 134–136,
    139–141
Information (exhortation), 132, 135–136,
    140, 165–167, 174
Information management risk, 322
Information technology risk, 322
Inglehart, R., 63
Ingram, H., 107, 171, 228
Innovation networks, 206, 219
Innovations in American Government
    program, 206
Insite program, 10–11
Institute of Public Administration of
    Canada (IPAC), 205–207
Institutional design, 168
Instrumentalism, 396
Instrument design, 174. *See also* Policy
    instruments
Intangibles, 291, 303
Integrated risk management, 320
Integrated service delivery (ISD), 214,
    216–217
Interest group pluralism, 233, 259
Interest groups, 228
    defined, 259
    public, 231, 233–234, 260
Interest intermediation, 233, 259
Intergovernmental Panel on Climate
    Change (IPCC), 400–401
Internal consistency, 13, 19, 34
Internal costs and benefits, 291
International Covenant on Civil and Politi-
    cal Rights, 61
International Covenant on Economic,
    Social and Cultural Rights, 61
International Criminal Court, 61
Internationalism, 168
International Monetary Fund (IMF),
    47, 51

Network analysis, structural approach to, 236
Network targets, 169
New Brunswick
  ice storm (1998), 332
  planning-programming-budgeting system, 294
  taser use, 103
New civil service, 208
Newfoundland and Labrador, taser use, 103
New Media Project, CRTC, 161
New public management (NPM), 70–71, 195–205, 393
  broad themes of, 202
  in Canada, 76–83
  defined, 86
  ethics and accountability, 210–211
  innovations in, 205–207
  key principles of, 196–197
  policy implementation, 215–216
  public service and, 208–209
  re-governmentalization, 202, 204
  service–client relations, 398
  shifts in, 206–208
  sources of, 196
  in United Kingdom, 75–76
  in United States, 71–73, 75
News of the World, 364, 367–368
New Zealand
  carbon taxes, 157
  on Globalization Index, 56–57
  new public management, 196, 199–200, 203, 409
  policy management reviews, 410–411
  re-governmentalization, 202, 204
Next Steps (U.K.), 75, 86, 199
NGOs. *See* Nongovernmental organizations (NGOs)
Nicholson, Rob, 9
Nigeria, on Globalization Index, 58–59
9/11 terrorist attacks
  as crisis and emergency situation, 312
  effect on nation-state, 62
  effect on world trade, 47
  emergency management following, 329
  intelligence failures, 342
  policy inquiry following, 7
  profound changes resulting from, 7–8
  public management priorities following, 72, 202

Nodality, 132, 174
Nongovernmental organizations (NGOs)
  emergency management, 332
  global civil society, 62
  policy networks, 242–243
Normative analysis, 19, 35
Normative (deep) core, 239
North American Free Trade Agreement (NAFTA), 51, 159
Northwest Territories, exports, 48
Norway, new public management, 203
Nova Scotia
  exports, 48
  taser use, 103
NPM. *See* New public management (NPM)

O

O & M (Operation & Maintenance Contract) public–private partnership model, 256
Oakland Project (U.S.), 190–191
Obama, Barack, 72–73, 75
Obama, Michelle, 348
Obesity, 98
Occupy Wall Street (OWS) movement, 138, 244–245, 258, 360
OECD. *See* Organisation for Economic Co-operation and Development (OECD)
Old Age Security, 142, 248
O'Leary, J., 194
Omnibus Crime Bill (Safe Streets and Communities Act), 9, 365
Ontario
  Commission on the Reform of Ontario's Public Services, 83
  Conservatives, 26
  health premiums, 403
  ice storm (1998), 332
  municipal government, 33
  needle exchange program, 277
  new public management, 77
  postsecondary education, 372–374
  user fees, 156
Open Data project, 139, 166, 379–380
Open Government Directive, 72–73
Open Society Foundation, 31–32
Operation & Maintenance Contract (O & M) public–private partnership model, 256
Operational partnerships, 253–254
Opportunity cost, 291, 304

visual, 378–379
written, 369–377
Policy communities, 227–270, 394
 advocacy coalition framework,
  238–241
 approaches and concepts, 232–234
 bubble diagram of, 235–236
 defined, 228, 230, 260
 horizontal management, 252–257
 overview, 227–232
 partnerships, 247–257
 policy management and, 241–257
 public consultations and citizen
  engagement, 247–252
Policy consistency, 13–14, 35
 horizontal, 13–14, 19, 34
 internal, 13, 19, 34
 vertical, 13, 19, 36
Policy design, 130, 174, 186, 394
Policy development
 benchmarks for, 408–416
 defined, 35
 staff training, 413
Policy development and implementation
 risk, 323
Policy evaluation. *See* Evaluation
Policy feedback, 194, 219
Policy frameworks, 2, 11–12, 14, 35
Policy goals, 8–9, 11–12
 consistency, 13
 defined, 35
 evaluation, 274
Policy Horizons Canada, 27–28, 35
Policy images, 105, 111–112, 123, 348, 384
Policy implementation, 185–226, 394
 clearances, 190–191
 conceptual framework of process,
  187–189
 conclusion, 215–226
 digital governance and quality service, 211–215
 elements of successful, 188
 ethics and accountability, 210–211
 as evolution, 192–193
 interest in, 190
 new public management, 195–205
 overview, 185–187
 policy instruments versus, 130
 project management mindset, 194
 public service, 205–209
 relationship with policy design, 186
 success and failure, 186–187
 theory of, 187–195

Policy instruments, 9–12, 129–184, 394
 consistency, 13
 defined, 35
 direct action, 147–150
 as distinguished from implementation, 130
 expenditure-based instruments,
  141–144, 151–155
 income security programs, 131
 information-based instruments,
  139–141, 165–167
 institutional design, 168
 internationalism, 168
 legal restrictions, 11
 overview, 129–137
 partnerships, 167
 regulation, 144–147, 158–164
 static response, 137–139
 taxation, 155–158
 uniform tilt to toolbox of, 169–172
Policy issue papers, 353–354, 384
Policymaker, defined, 2
Policymaking, global agora of, 243
Policy memoranda, 353, 384
Policy networks, 227–270
 advocacy coalition framework,
  238–241
 approaches and concepts, 232–234
 contemporary importance of,
  241–247
 defined, 231, 260
 horizontal management, 252–257
 overview, 227–232
 partnerships, 247–257
 policy management and, 241–257
 public consultations and citizen
  engagement, 247–252
Policy on Service Standards for External
 Fees, 156
Policy paradigms, 356–357, 384
Policy problems
 "messy" policy problems, 113
 nonlinear policy problems, 314–316,
  343
 "squishy" policy problems, 113
 "super wicked" policy problems,
  114
 "wicked" policy problems, 113–114
 See also Problem definition
Policy-relevant information, 109–110
Policy research
 academic research versus, 370–372
 well-organized resources for, 413

PS2000, 197, 199, 219, 249

PSHRMAC (Public Service Human Resources Management Agency of Canada), 198

PSMA (Public Service Modernization Act), 78, 198–199, 204, 219

P3s (public–private partnerships), 150, 255, 260

Public Administration Select Committee, 380–381

Public consultations, 247–252

Public interest groups, 231, 233–234, 260

Public management
    defined, 87
    governance and, 68–83
    See also New public management (NPM)

Public policy, 1–15
    complexity, 5
    as course of action, 2
    defined, 2–3, 35
    elements of, 7–12
    inaction as, 2
    instrumental character of, 3
    public interest and, 3–4
    sources of, 7–8
    values and, 3–4
    what it isn't, 14

Public–private partnerships (P3s; PPPs), 150, 255, 260

Public Safety Canada, 330

Public sector reform, 26, 28–30, 32, 35, 80–83, 199–201, 209. *See also* New public management (NPM)

Public service
    digital governance, 213
    enhanced, 207–208
    ethics and accountability, 210–211
    overview, 205–208
    public sector versus, 209
    quality, 211–215
    rethinking value of, 208–209

Public Service Human Resources Management Agency of Canada (PSHRMAC), 198

Public Service Modernization Act (PSMA), 78, 198–199, 204, 219

Punctuated equilibrium, 112, 123

Putnam, R., 172, 372

Q

Qualifiers, 109–110

Quality management, 196, 219

Quality Services Initiative, 198, 219

Quasi-experimental design, 282, 304

Quebec
    carbon taxes, 157
    ice storm (1998), 332
    interculturalism, 65–67
    municipal government, 33
    new public management, 77

Quinn, L., 376

Quirk, B., 18

R

Race to the bottom, 51, 54, 87

Ramesh, M., 2

Random assignment, 281, 304

Rationalism, 19–22, 36

Rational model, 19–20
    challenges and criticisms, 22–24
    crisis and emergency situations, 311–312
    defined, 6, 36
    implications of, 20–22
    limits of, 22
    policy communication, 351–354, 357

Readyness, 326

Reagan, Ronald, 69

"Reasonable accommodation" of minorities, 65–67, 121

Recognition, 146, 174

Recovery, 326

Red Cross, 335, 338–339

Registered Retirement Savings Program (RRSP), 142

Re-governmentalization, 202, 219

Regulation, 144–147, 158–164
    defined, 174
    economic, 147, 161–162, 356–357
    self-regulation, 175
    smart, 163–164
    social, 147

Regulatory Impact Assessment Statement regime, 162

Reinventing Government, 70–71

Religious bias, 18

Reports on plans and priorities (RPPs), 297, 304

Reputational risk, 323

Re-regulation, 160–161, 174

Resource management risk, 323

Resource-related rationales for static response, 137–138

Results-based management and accountability frameworks (RMAFs), 254, 297–298, 300